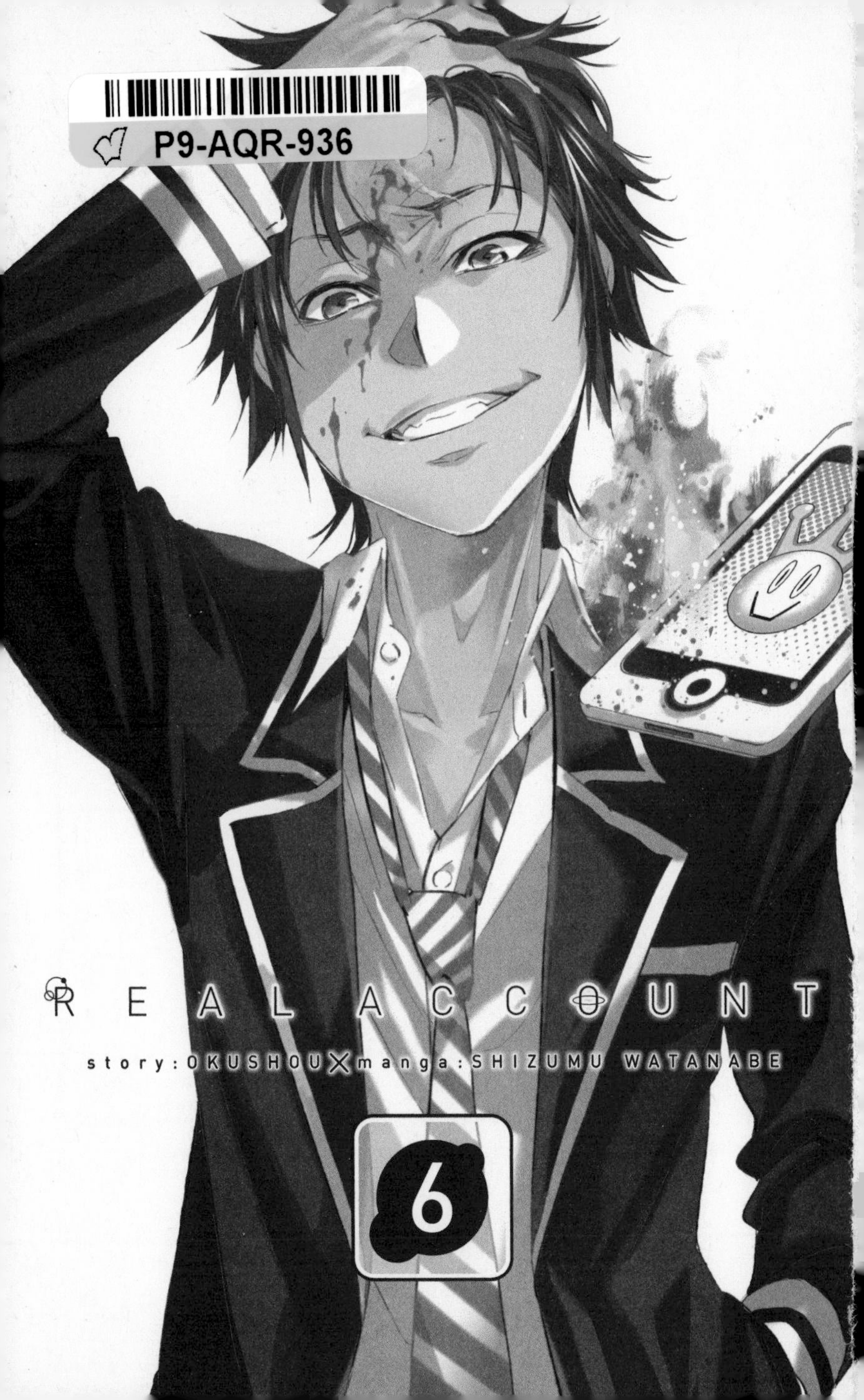
P9-AQR-936
REAL ACCOUNT
story: OKUSHOU × manga: SHIZUMU WATANABE
6

CONTENTS

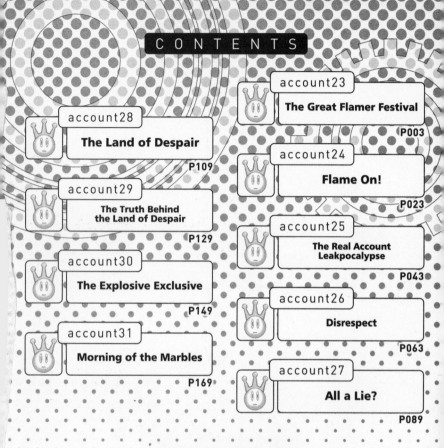

STORY

During the first game, Real Follower Diagnosis, Yuma Mukai and Ayame Kamijo were saved by their chance following of one another. In each of the ensuing contests—The Dislike Game, R.A. Live Game, and Appease the Attention Seeker—they've used a mix of wisdom, teamwork, and luck to survive to the end. In game four, Operation: Reply or Regret, the team fought off grueling fatigue to complete a full stamp collection, only to have Mizuki Kurashina interfere right at the end and dash their hopes. Undeterred, Yuma took advantage of the game's rules to kill off the Marble controlling the game, which allowed Yuma to escape death's grasp once again...

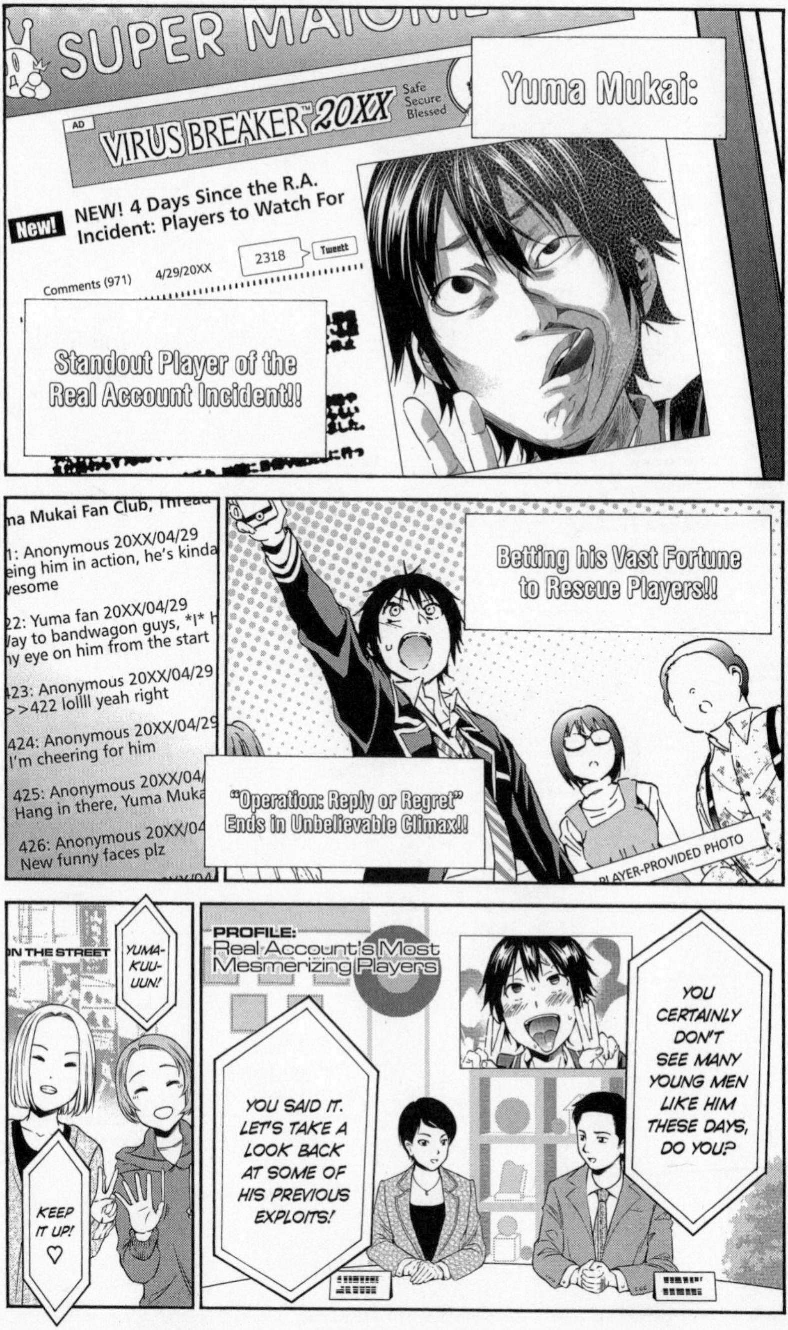
Yuma Mukai:
Safe Secure Blessed
AD
VIRUS BREAKER™ 20XX
New!
NEW! 4 Days Since the R.A. Incident: Players to Watch For
2318
Tweett
Comments (971)
4/29/20XX
Standout Player of the Real Account Incident!!
Betting his Vast Fortune to Rescue Players!!
PLAYER-PROVIDED PHOTO
“Operation: Reply or Regret” Ends in Unbelievable Climax!!
ma Mukai Fan Club, Thread
1: Anonymous 20XX/04/29
eing him in action, he's kinda
vesome
22: Yuma fan 20XX/04/29
Vay to bandwagon guys, *I* h
ny eye on him from the start
423: Anonymous 20XX/04/29
>>422 lolll yeah right
424: Anonymous 20XX/04/29
I'm cheering for him
425: Anonymous 20XX/04/
Hang in there, Yuma Muka
426: Anonymous 20XX/04
New funny faces plz
PROFILE: Real Account's Most Mesmerizing Players
YOU CERTAINLY DON'T SEE MANY YOUNG MEN LIKE HIM THESE DAYS, DO YOU?
YOU SAID IT. LET'S TAKE A LOOK BACK AT SOME OF HIS PREVIOUS EXPLOITS!
N THE STREET
YUMA-KUUUN!
KEEP IT UP! ♡

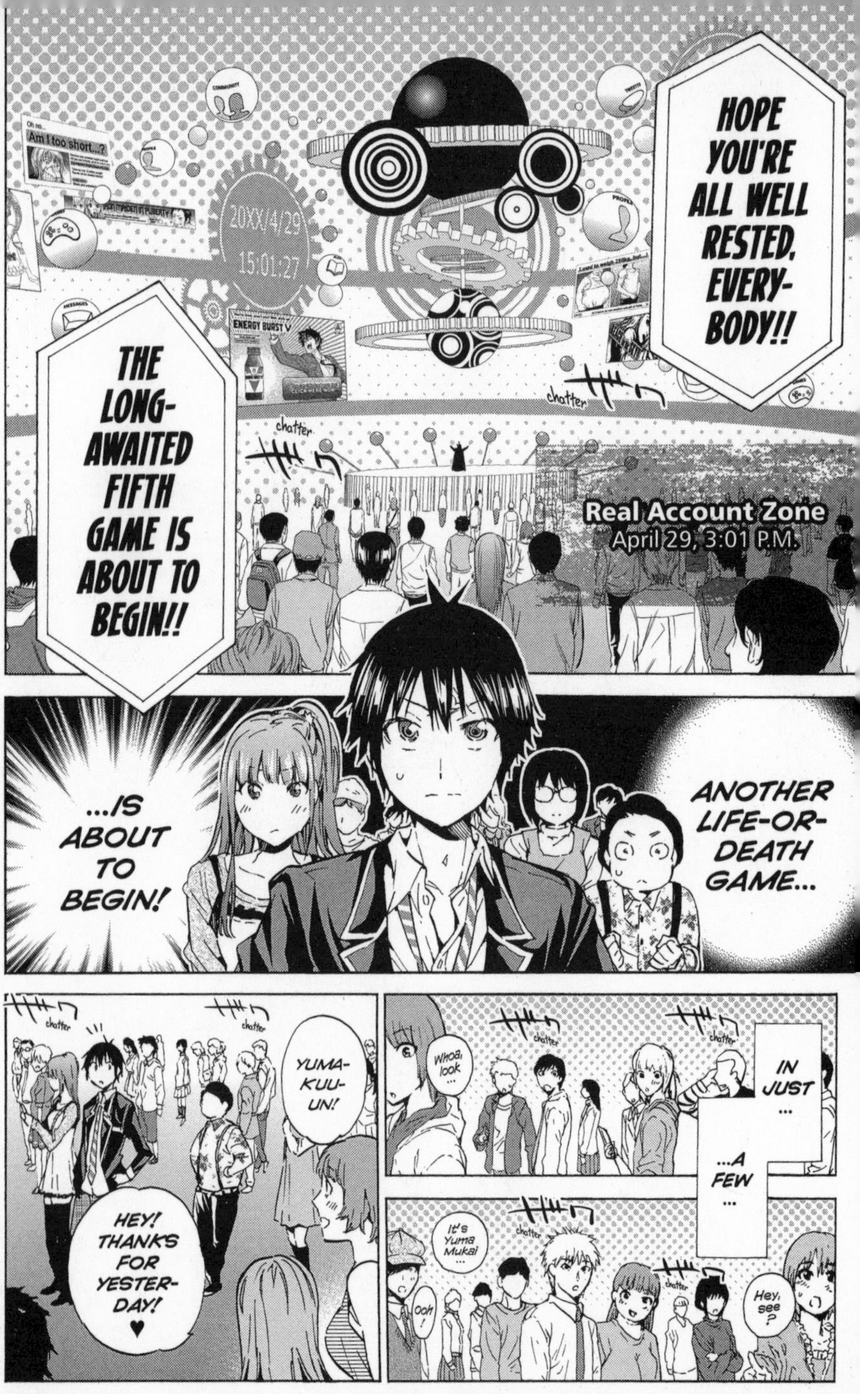
HOPE YOU'RE ALL WELL RESTED, EVERY-BODY!!
20XX/4/29
15:01:27
Am I too short...?
ENERGY BURST V
CLICK HERE NOW
chatter
chatter
THE LONG-AWAITED FIFTH GAME IS ABOUT TO BEGIN!!
Real Account Zone
April 29, 3:01 P.M.
ANOTHER LIFE-OR-DEATH GAME...
...IS ABOUT TO BEGIN!
chatter
chatter
IN JUST...
Whoa, look...
chatter
...A FEW...
Hey, see?
chatter
chatter
It's Yuma Mukai...
ooh!
chatter
chatter
YUMA-KUUU-UN!
HEY! THANKS FOR YESTER-DAY! ♥

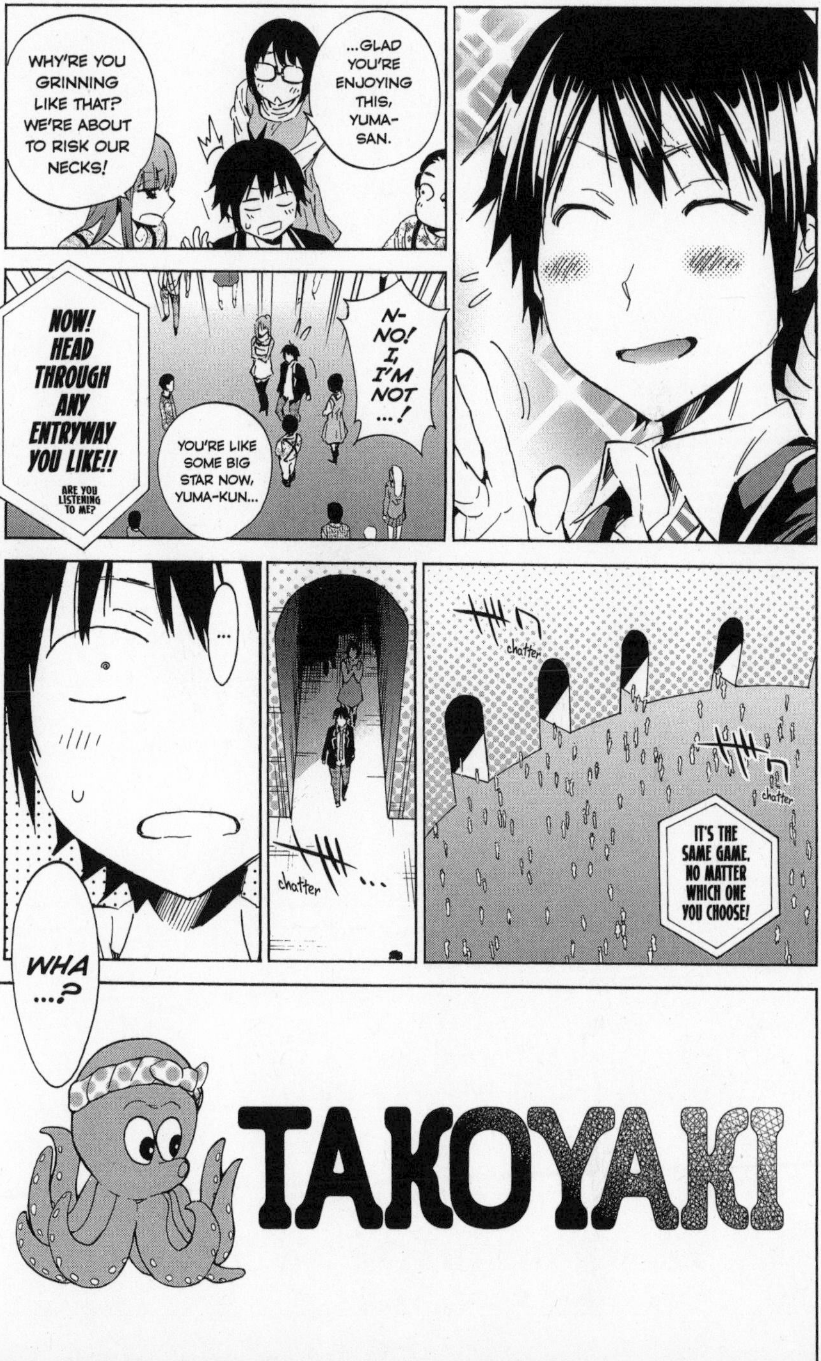
...GLAD YOU'RE ENJOYING THIS, YUMA-SAN.
WHY'RE YOU GRINNING LIKE THAT? WE'RE ABOUT TO RISK OUR NECKS!
N-NO! I, I'M NOT ...!
NOW! HEAD THROUGH ANY ENTRYWAY YOU LIKE!!
ARE YOU LISTENING TO ME?
YOU'RE LIKE SOME BIG STAR NOW, YUMA-KUN...
chatter
chatter
IT'S THE SAME GAME, NO MATTER WHICH ONE YOU CHOOSE!
chatter
...
...
WHA ...?
TAKOYAKI

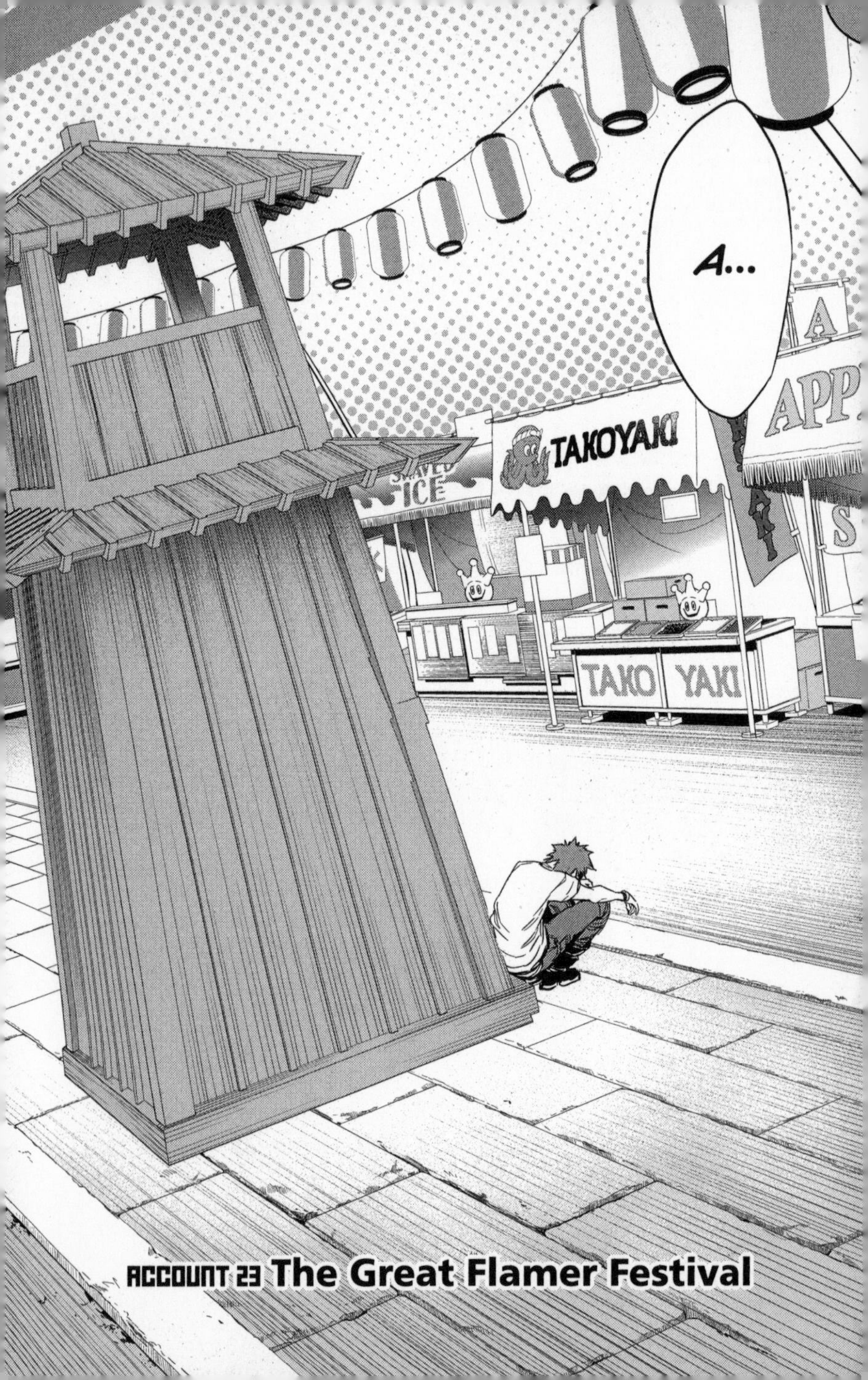
A...
TAKOYAKI
SHAVED ICE
TAKO YAKI

ACCOUNT 23 The Great Flamer Festival

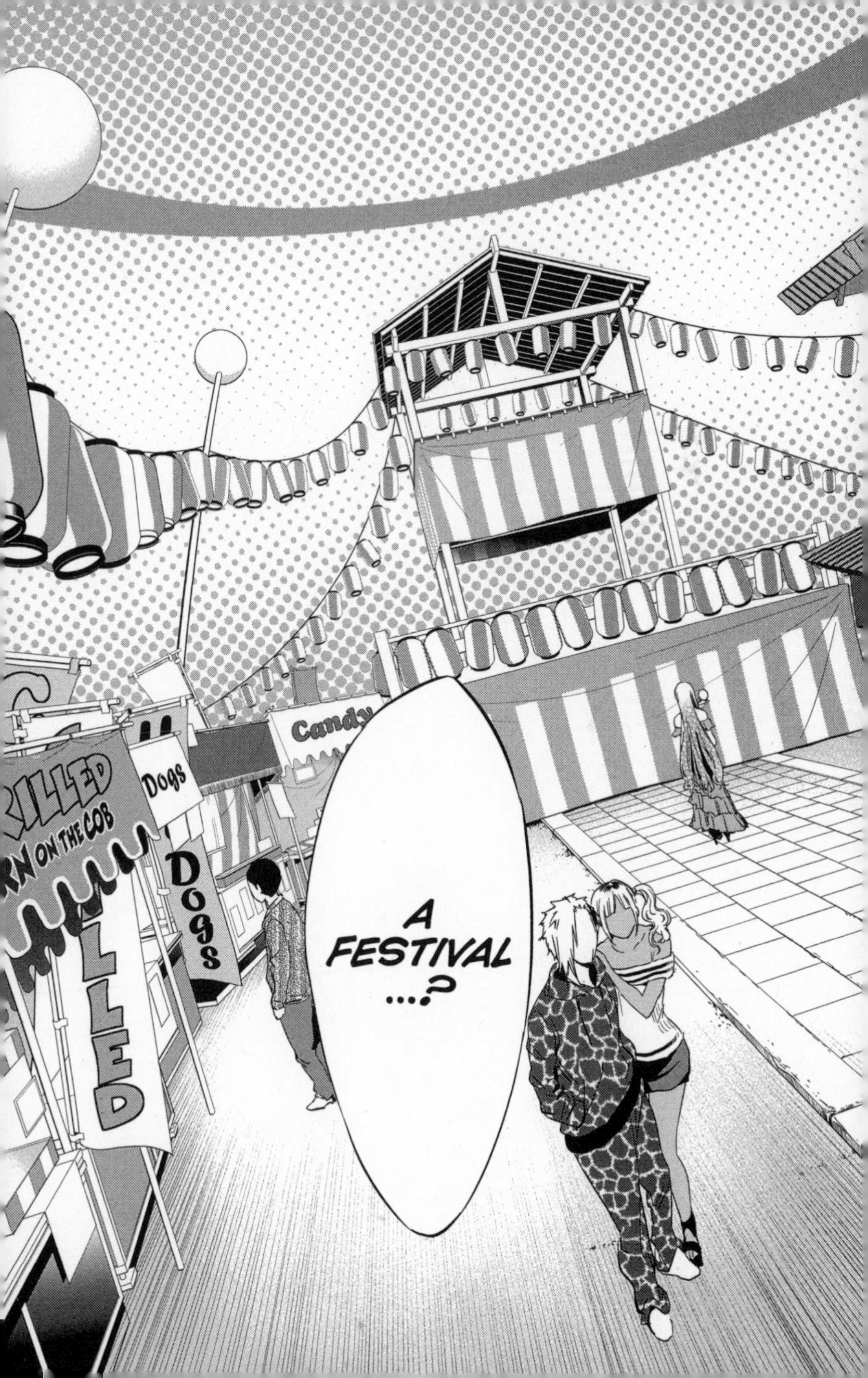
A FESTIVAL ...?
Candy
Dogs
Dogs

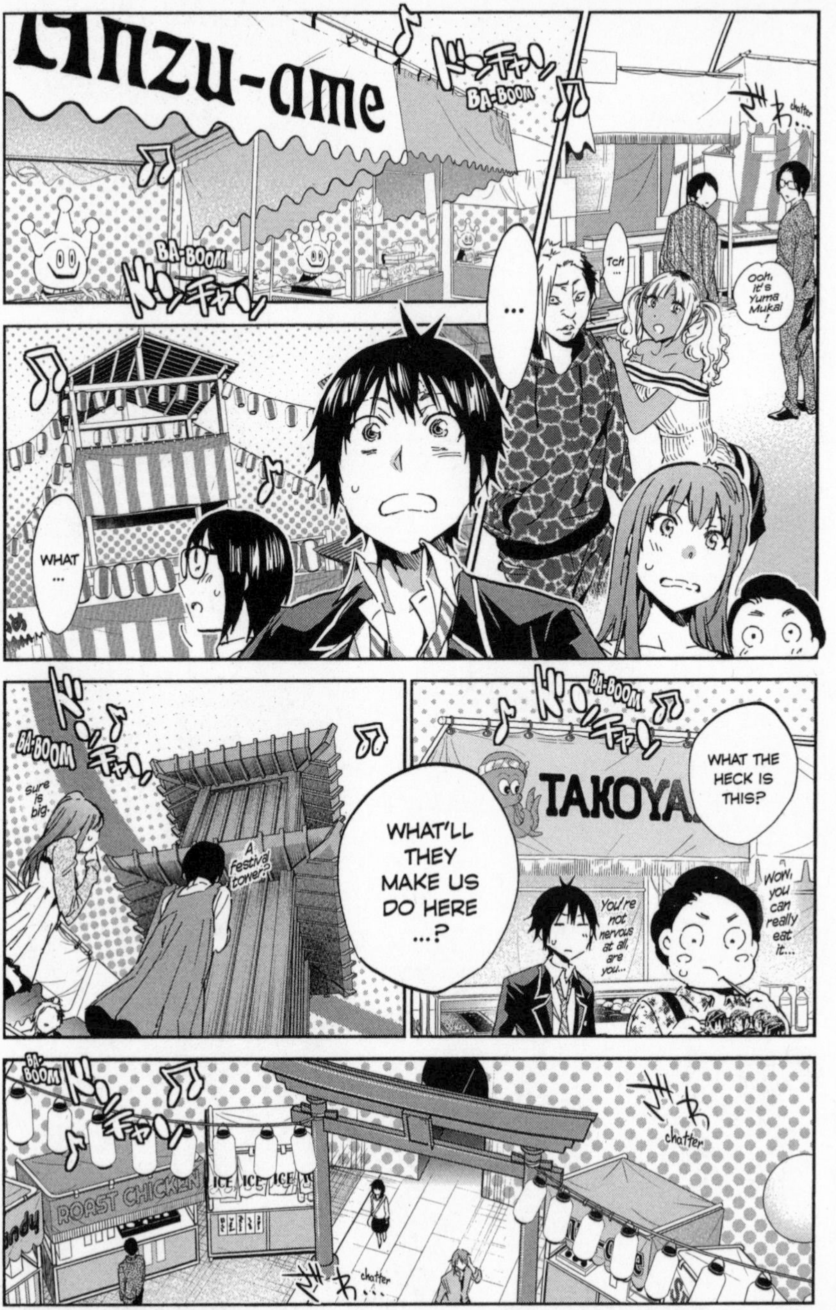
ざわ… chatter
ドンチャン BA-BOOM
Anzu-ame
BA-BOOM ドンチャン
Ooh, it's Yuma Mukai!
Tch ...
...
WHAT ...
BA-BOOM ドンチャン
WHAT THE HECK IS THIS?
TAKOYA
Wow, you can really eat it...
You're not nervous at all, are you...
WHAT'LL THEY MAKE US DO HERE ...?
ドンチャン BA-BOOM
A festival tower?
Sure is big.
ざわ chatter
BA-BOOM ドンチャン
ROAST CHICKEN
ICE ICE ICE
ざわ chatter...

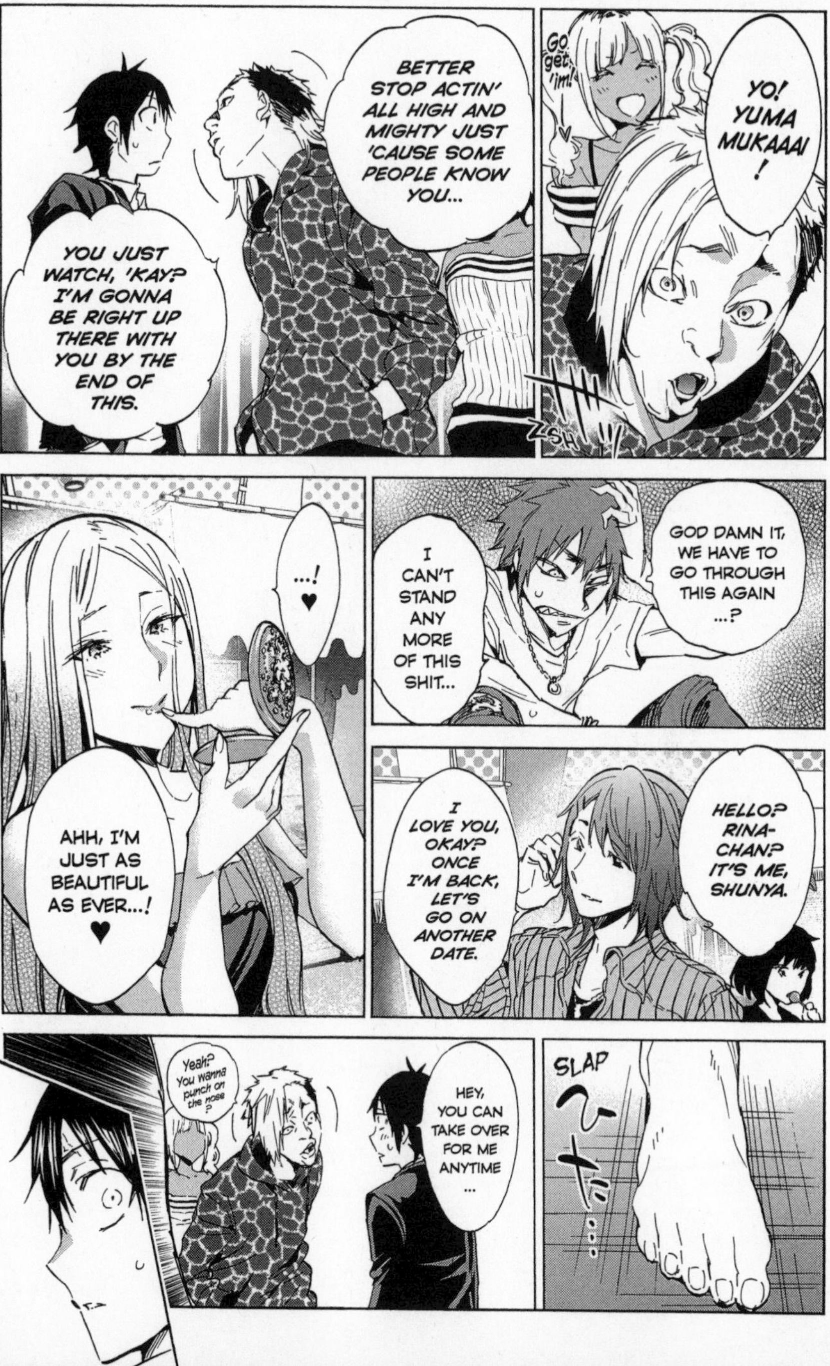
YO! YUMA MUKAAAI!
Go get 'im!
ZSH
BETTER STOP ACTIN' ALL HIGH AND MIGHTY JUST 'CAUSE SOME PEOPLE KNOW YOU...
YOU JUST WATCH, 'KAY? I'M GONNA BE RIGHT UP THERE WITH YOU BY THE END OF THIS.
GOD DAMN IT, WE HAVE TO GO THROUGH THIS AGAIN ...?
I CAN'T STAND ANY MORE OF THIS SHIT...
HELLO? RINA-CHAN? IT'S ME, SHUNYA.
I LOVE YOU, OKAY? ONCE I'M BACK, LET'S GO ON ANOTHER DATE.
...! ♥
AHH, I'M JUST AS BEAUTIFUL AS EVER...! ♥
SLAP
HEY, YOU CAN TAKE OVER FOR ME ANYTIME ...
Yeah? You wanna punch on the nose?

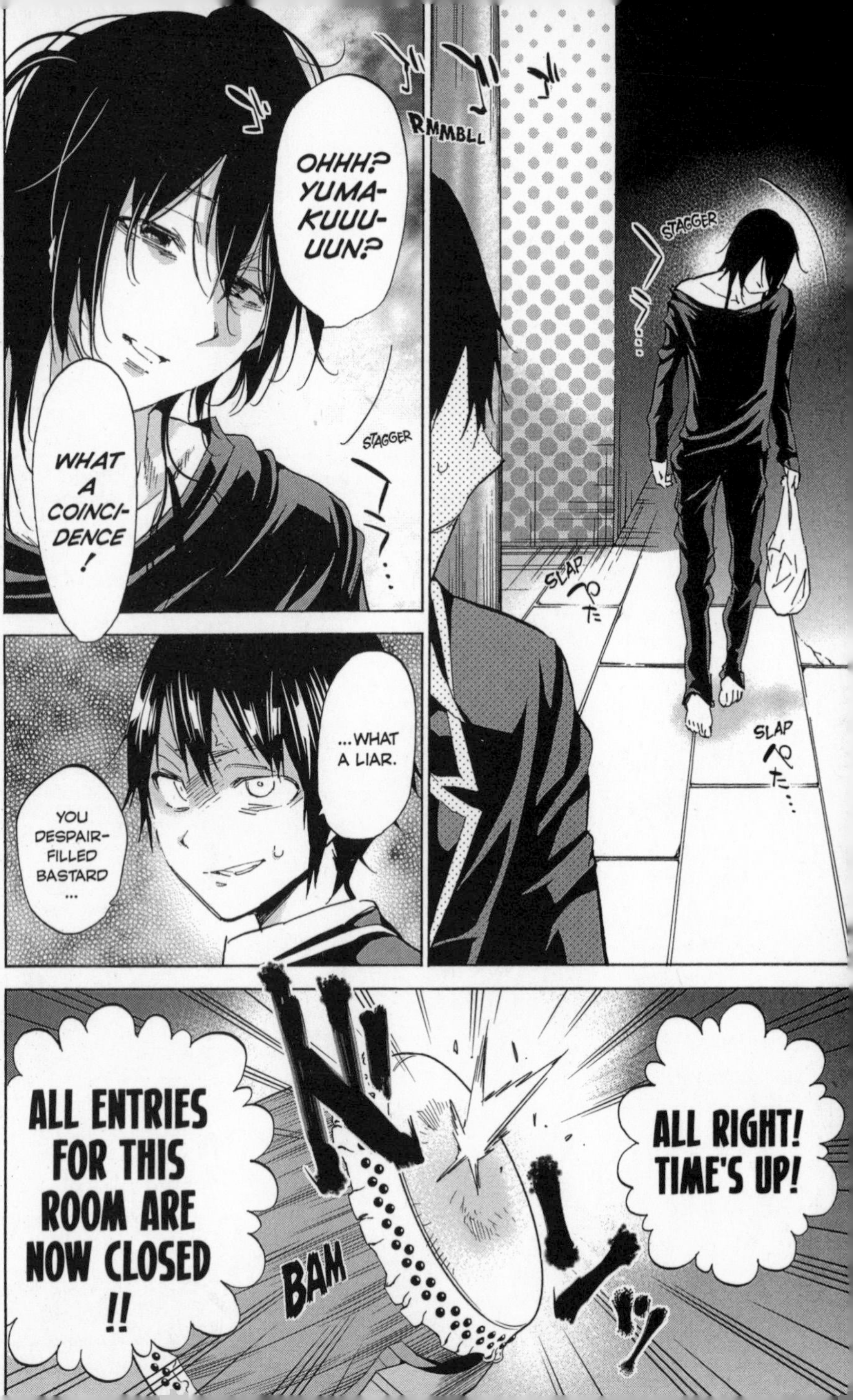
STAGGER
SLAP
SLAP
RMMBLL
STAGGER
OHHH? YUMA-KUUUU-UUN?
WHAT A COINCI-DENCE!
...WHAT A LIAR.
YOU DESPAIR-FILLED BASTARD ...
ALL RIGHT! TIME'S UP!
BAM
ALL ENTRIES FOR THIS ROOM ARE NOW CLOSED !!

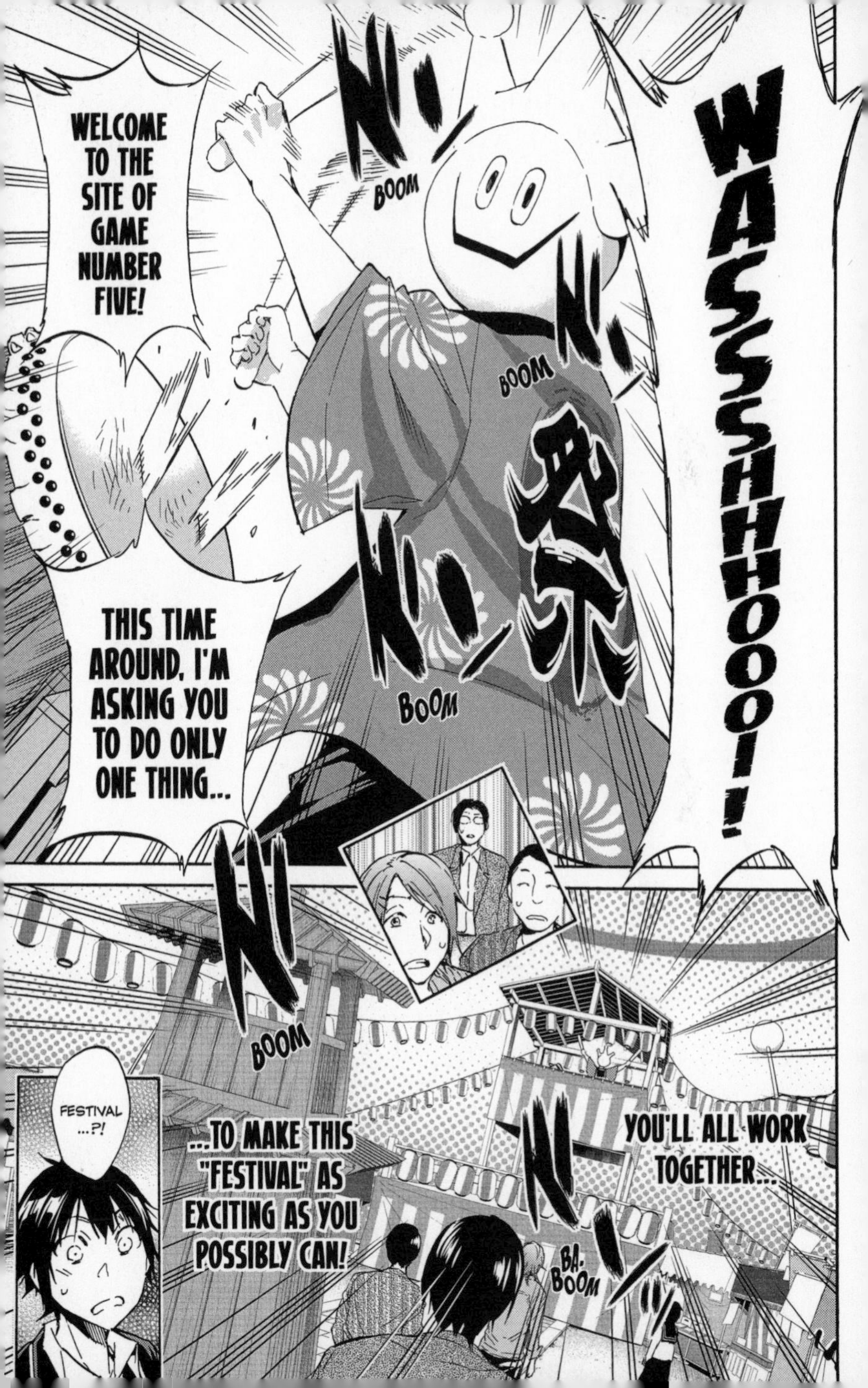
WASSHHOOOOI!!
BOOM
WELCOME TO THE SITE OF GAME NUMBER FIVE!
BOOM
BOOM
THIS TIME AROUND, I'M ASKING YOU TO DO ONLY ONE THING...
YOU'LL ALL WORK TOGETHER...
BA-BOOM
BOOM
...TO MAKE THIS "FESTIVAL" AS EXCITING AS YOU POSSIBLY CAN!
FESTIVAL ...?!

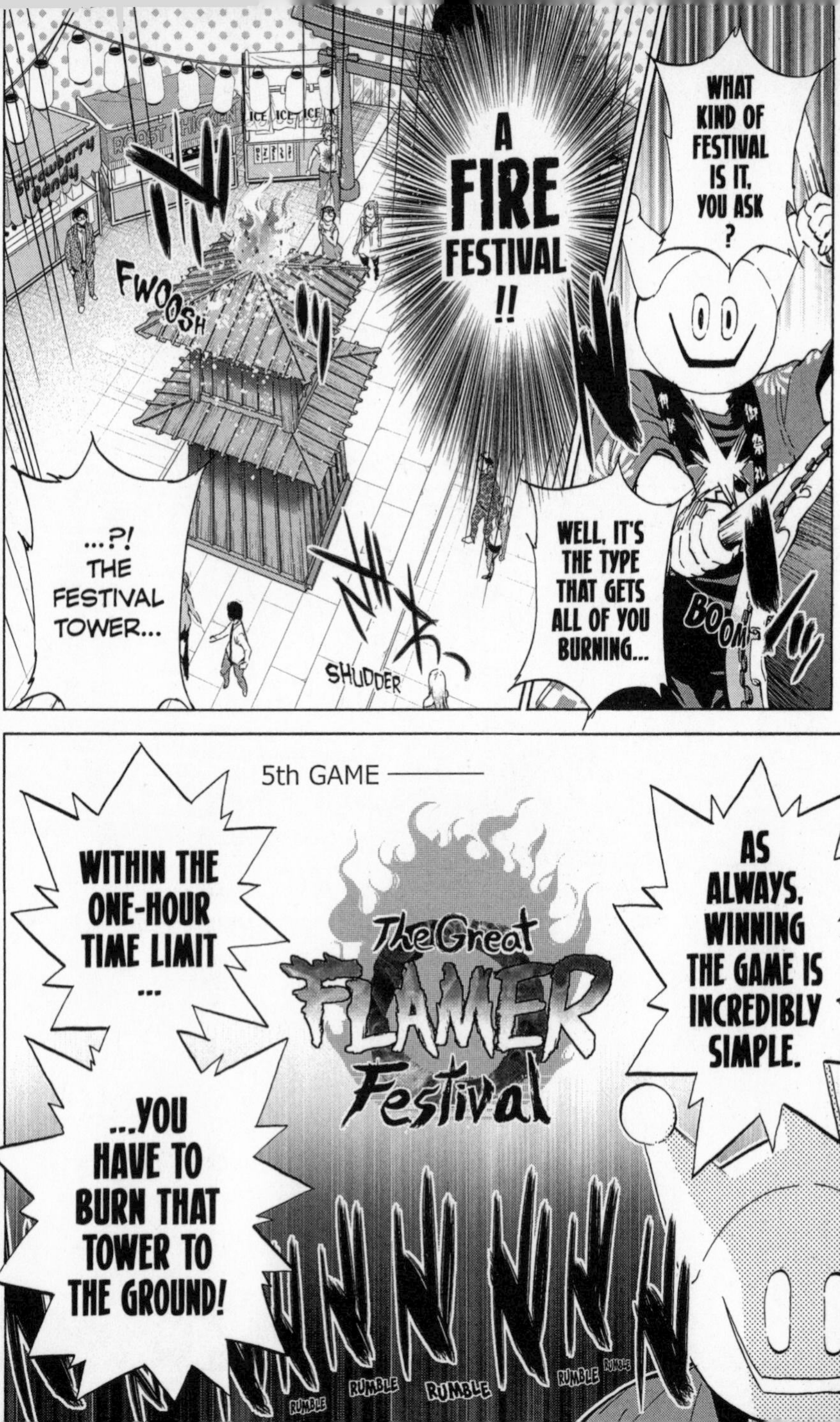
WHAT KIND OF FESTIVAL IS IT, YOU ASK?
A FIRE FESTIVAL!!
WELL, IT'S THE TYPE THAT GETS ALL OF YOU BURNING...
BOOM
Strawberry Candy
ICE ICE ICE
FWOOSH
SHUDDER
...?! THE FESTIVAL TOWER...
AS ALWAYS, WINNING THE GAME IS INCREDIBLY SIMPLE.
5th GAME
The Great FLAMER Festival
WITHIN THE ONE-HOUR TIME LIMIT...
...YOU HAVE TO BURN THAT TOWER TO THE GROUND!
RUMBLE RUMBLE RUMBLE RUMBLE RUMBLE

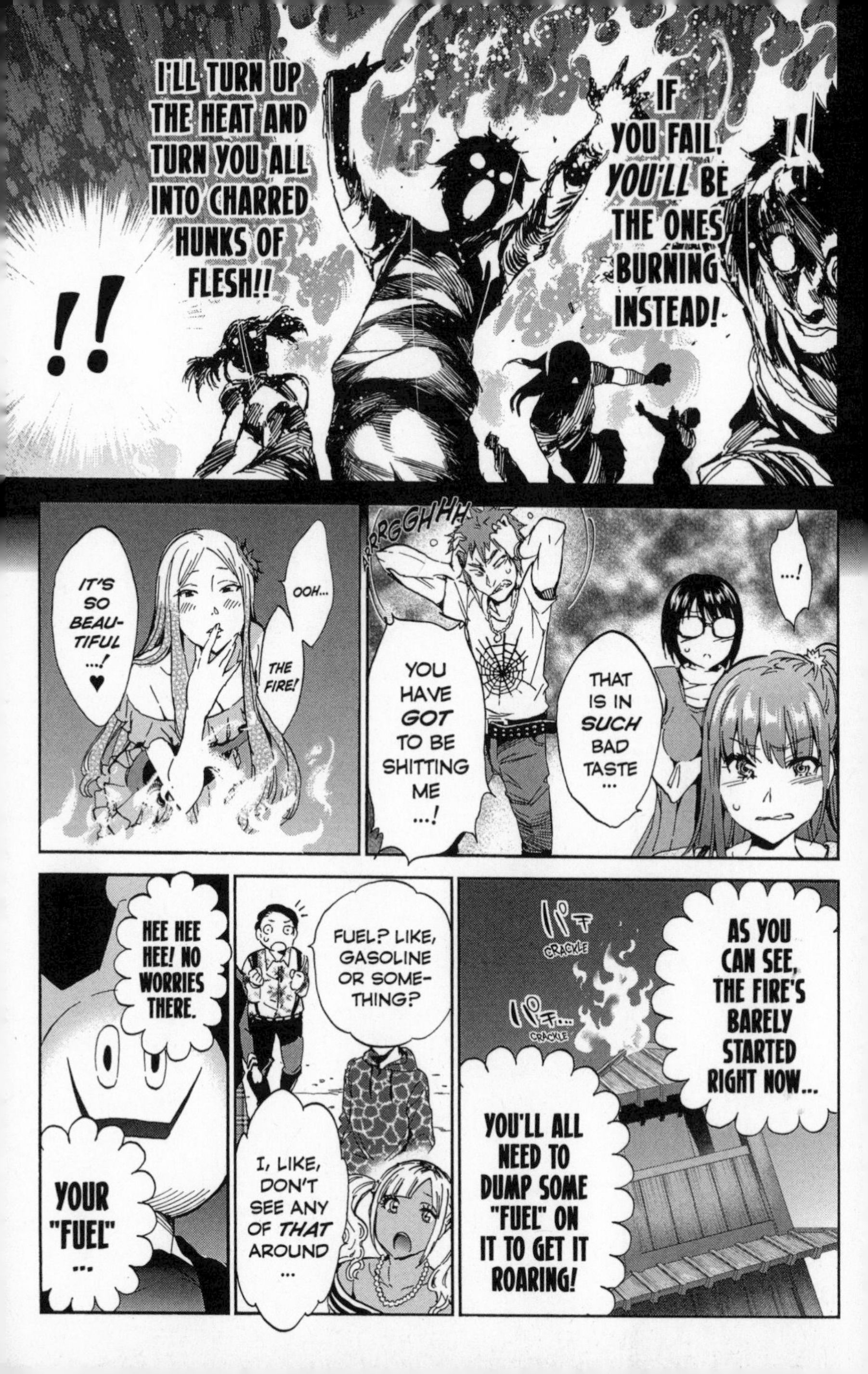
IF YOU FAIL, *YOU'LL* BE THE ONES BURNING INSTEAD!
I'LL TURN UP THE HEAT AND TURN YOU ALL INTO CHARRED HUNKS OF FLESH!!
!!
...!
ARRRGGHHH
THAT IS IN *SUCH* BAD TASTE...
YOU HAVE *GOT* TO BE SHITTING ME...!
OOH...
THE FIRE!
IT'S SO BEAUTIFUL...! ♥
AS YOU CAN SEE, THE FIRE'S BARELY STARTED RIGHT NOW...
パチ
CRACKLE
パチ...
CRACKLE
YOU'LL ALL NEED TO DUMP SOME "FUEL" ON IT TO GET IT ROARING!
FUEL? LIKE, GASOLINE OR SOME-THING?
I, LIKE, DON'T SEE ANY OF *THAT* AROUND...
HEE HEE HEE! NO WORRIES THERE.
YOUR "FUEL"...

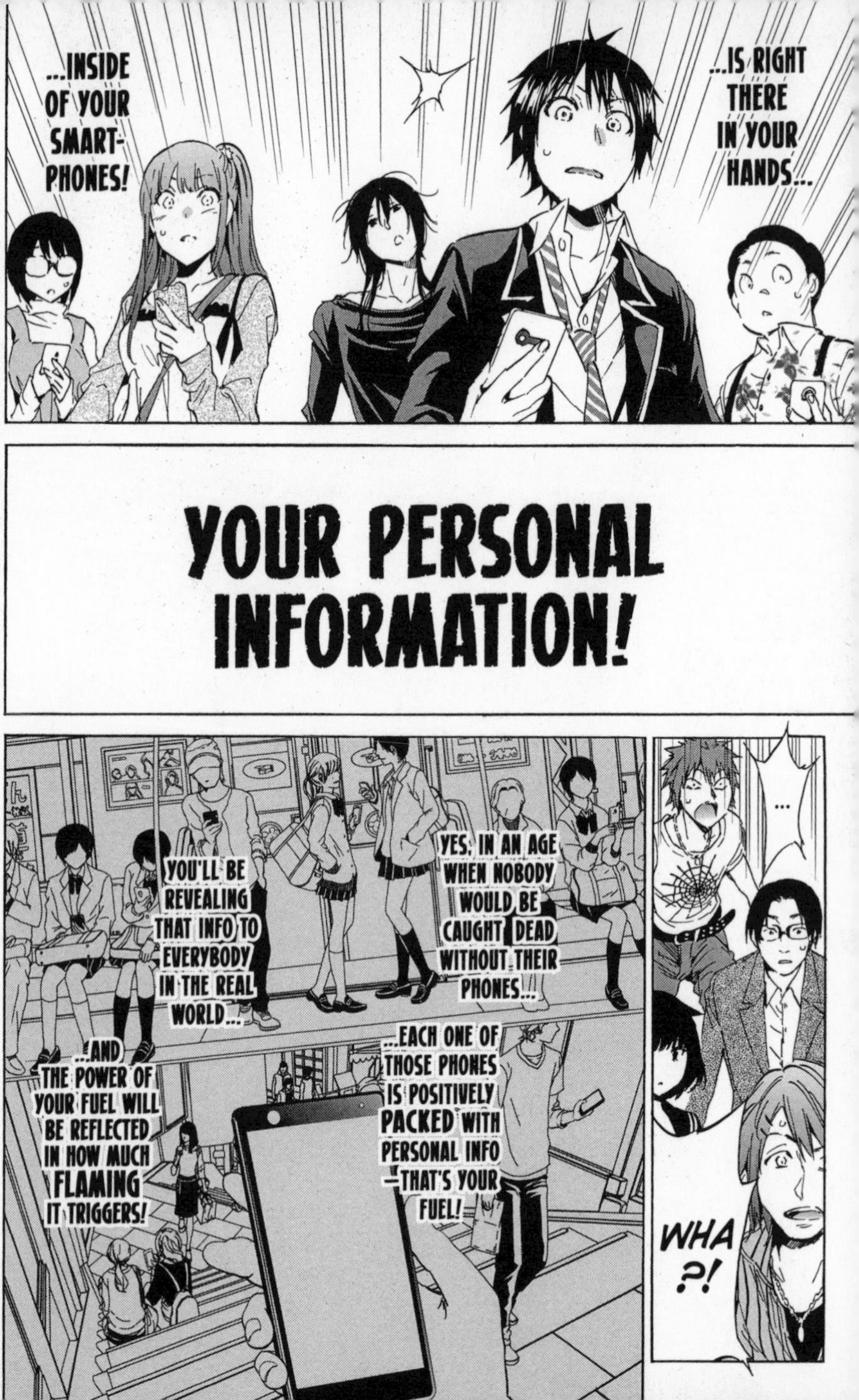
...IS RIGHT THERE IN YOUR HANDS...
...INSIDE OF YOUR SMART-PHONES!
YOUR PERSONAL INFORMATION!
...
WHA ?!
YES, IN AN AGE WHEN NOBODY WOULD BE CAUGHT DEAD WITHOUT THEIR PHONES...
...EACH ONE OF THOSE PHONES IS POSITIVELY PACKED WITH PERSONAL INFO —THAT'S YOUR FUEL!
YOU'LL BE REVEALING THAT INFO TO EVERYBODY IN THE REAL WORLD...
...AND THE POWER OF YOUR FUEL WILL BE REFLECTED IN HOW MUCH FLAMING IT TRIGGERS!

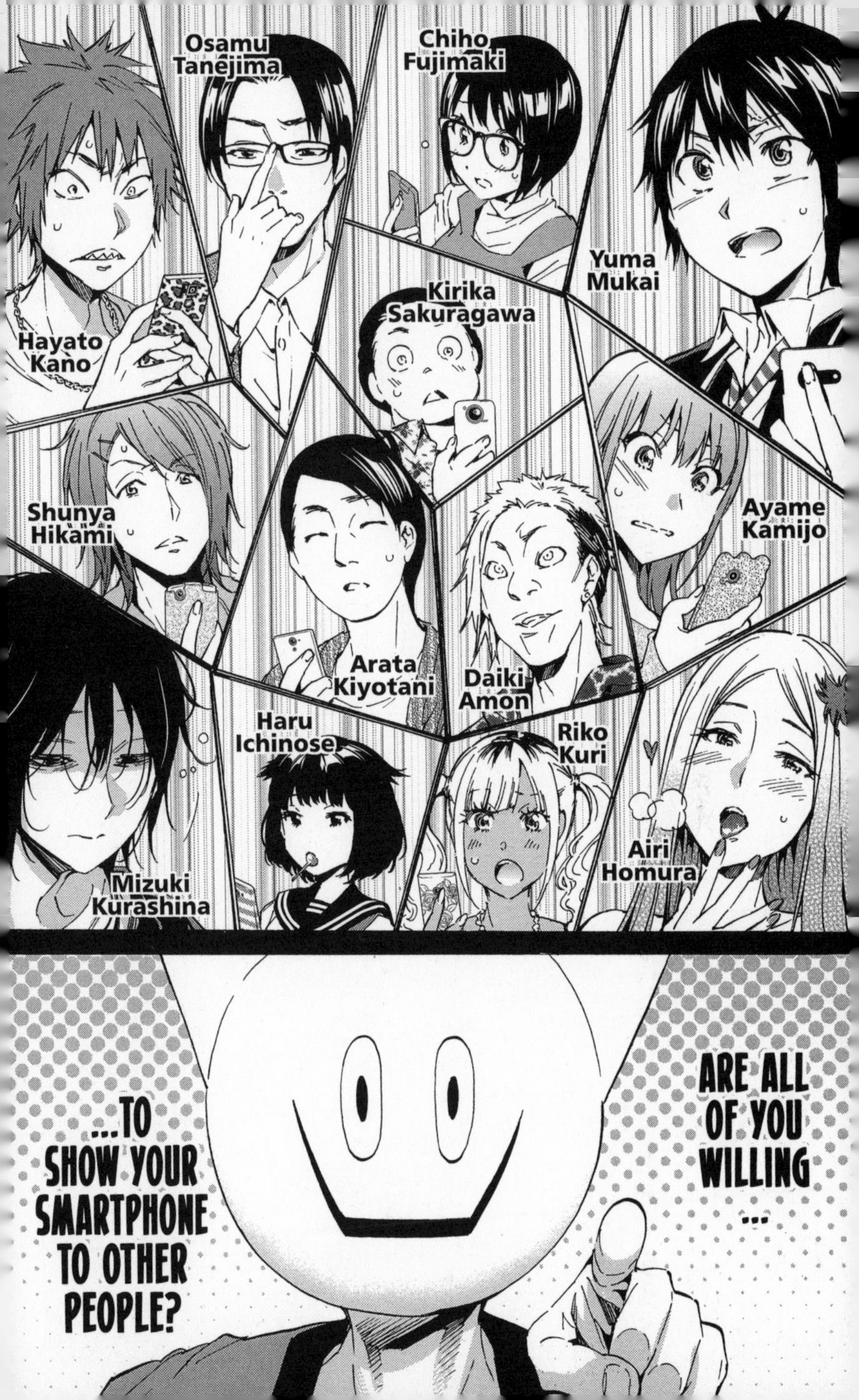
Chiho Fujimaki
Osamu Tanejima
Yuma Mukai
Kirika Sakuragawa
Hayato Kano
Ayame Kamijo
Shunya Hikami
Daiki Amon
Arata Kiyotani
Riko Kuri
Haru Ichinose
Airi Homura
Mizuki Kurashina
ARE ALL OF YOU WILLING ...
...TO SHOW YOUR SMARTPHONE TO OTHER PEOPLE?

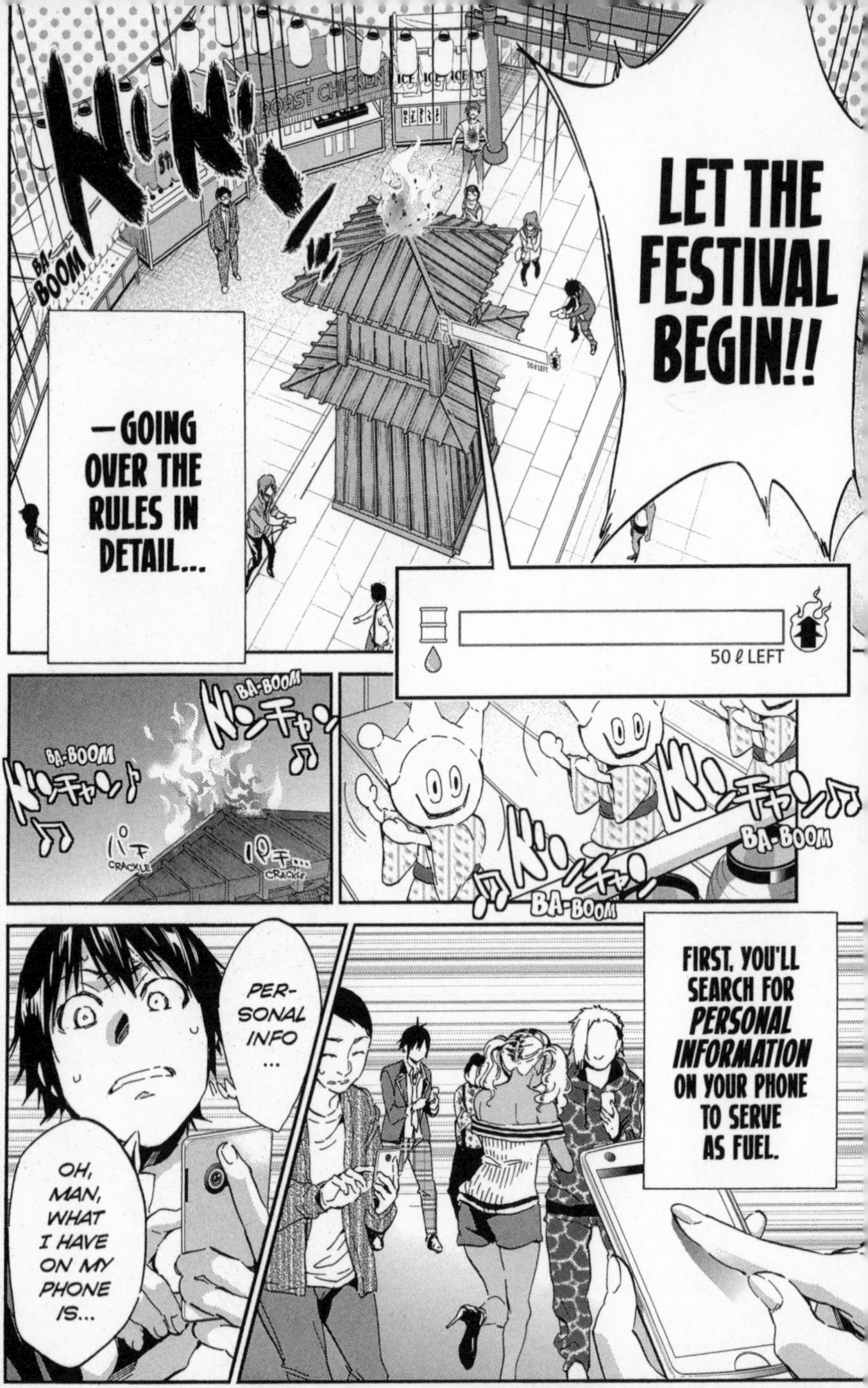
LET THE FESTIVAL BEGIN!!
BA-BOOM
ROAST CHICKEN
ICE ICE ICE
—GOING OVER THE RULES IN DETAIL...
50 ℓ LEFT
BA-BOOM
BA-BOOM
BA-BOOM
BA-BOOM
BA-BOOM
CRACKLE
CRACKLE
FIRST, YOU'LL SEARCH FOR *PERSONAL INFORMATION* ON YOUR PHONE TO SERVE AS FUEL.
PER-SONAL INFO...
OH, MAN, WHAT I HAVE ON MY PHONE IS...

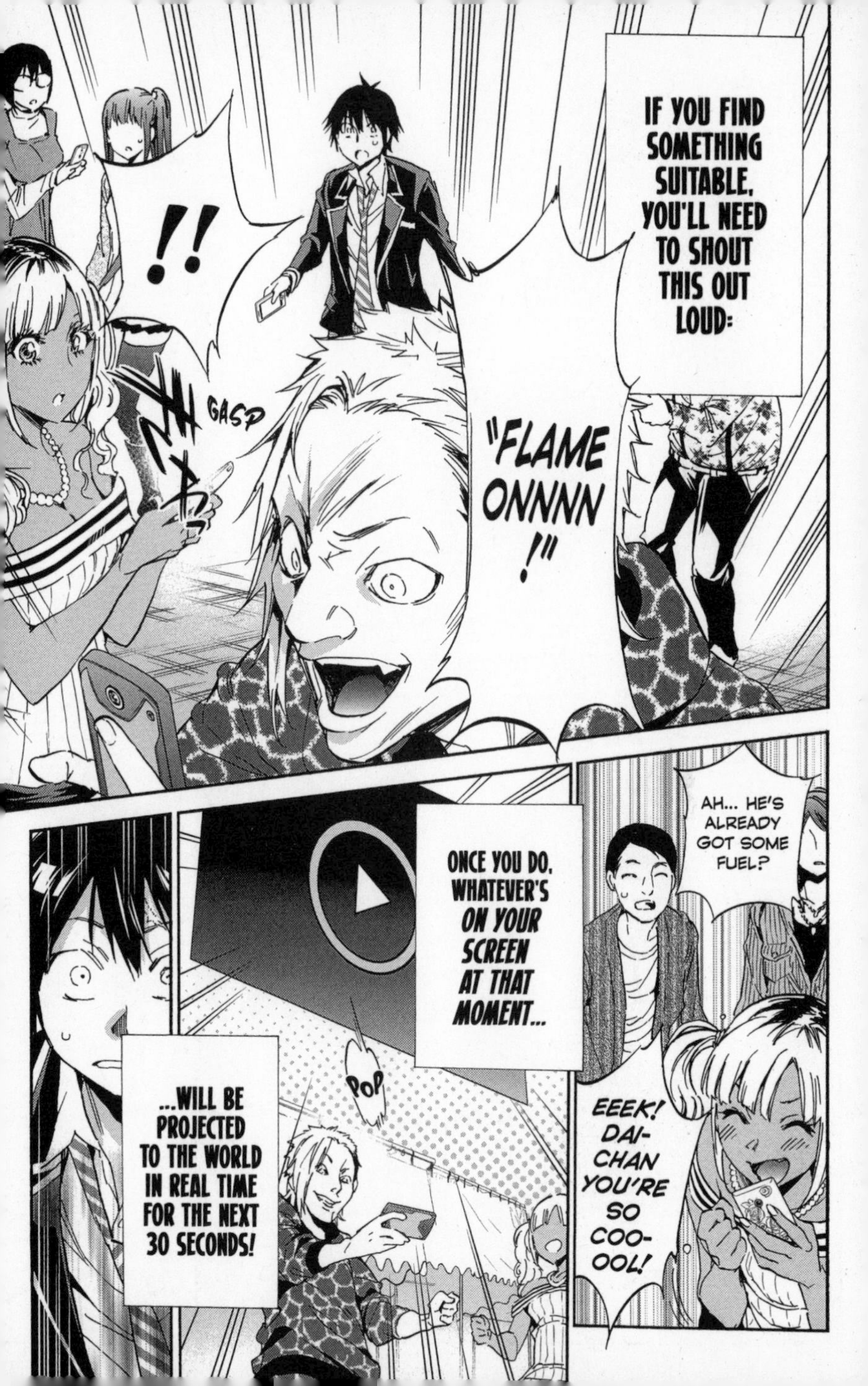
IF YOU FIND SOMETHING SUITABLE, YOU'LL NEED TO SHOUT THIS OUT LOUD:
"FLAME ONNNN!"
!!
GASP
AH... HE'S ALREADY GOT SOME FUEL?
EEEK! DAI-CHAN YOU'RE SO COO-OOL!
ONCE YOU DO, WHATEVER'S *ON YOUR SCREEN AT THAT MOMENT...*
POP
...WILL BE PROJECTED TO THE WORLD IN REAL TIME FOR THE NEXT 30 SECONDS!

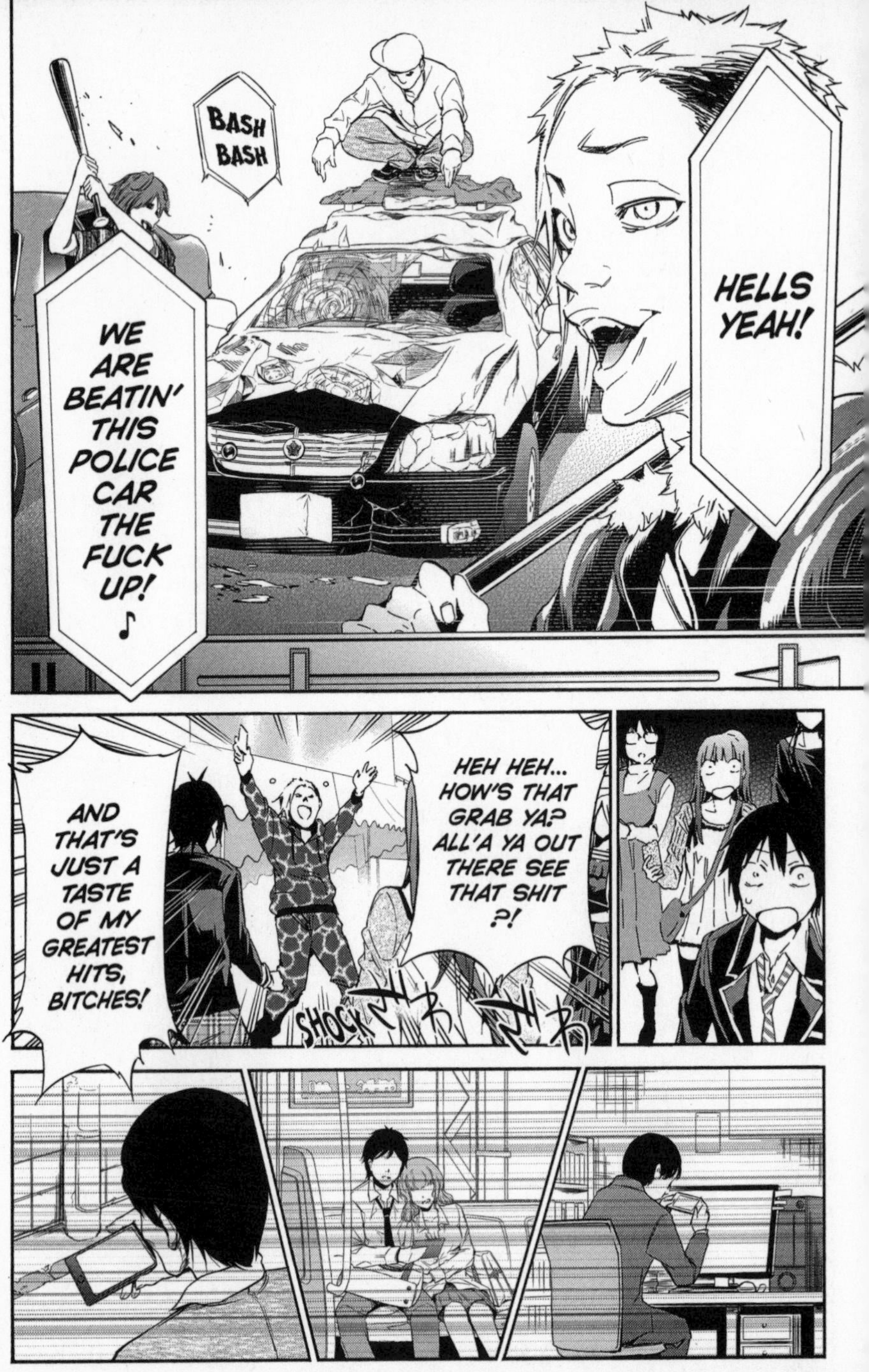
HELLS YEAH!
BASH BASH
WE ARE BEATIN' THIS POLICE CAR THE FUCK UP! ♪
HEH HEH... HOW'S THAT GRAB YA? ALL'A YA OUT THERE SEE THAT SHIT ?!
AND THAT'S JUST A TASTE OF MY GREATEST HITS, BITCHES!
SHOCK

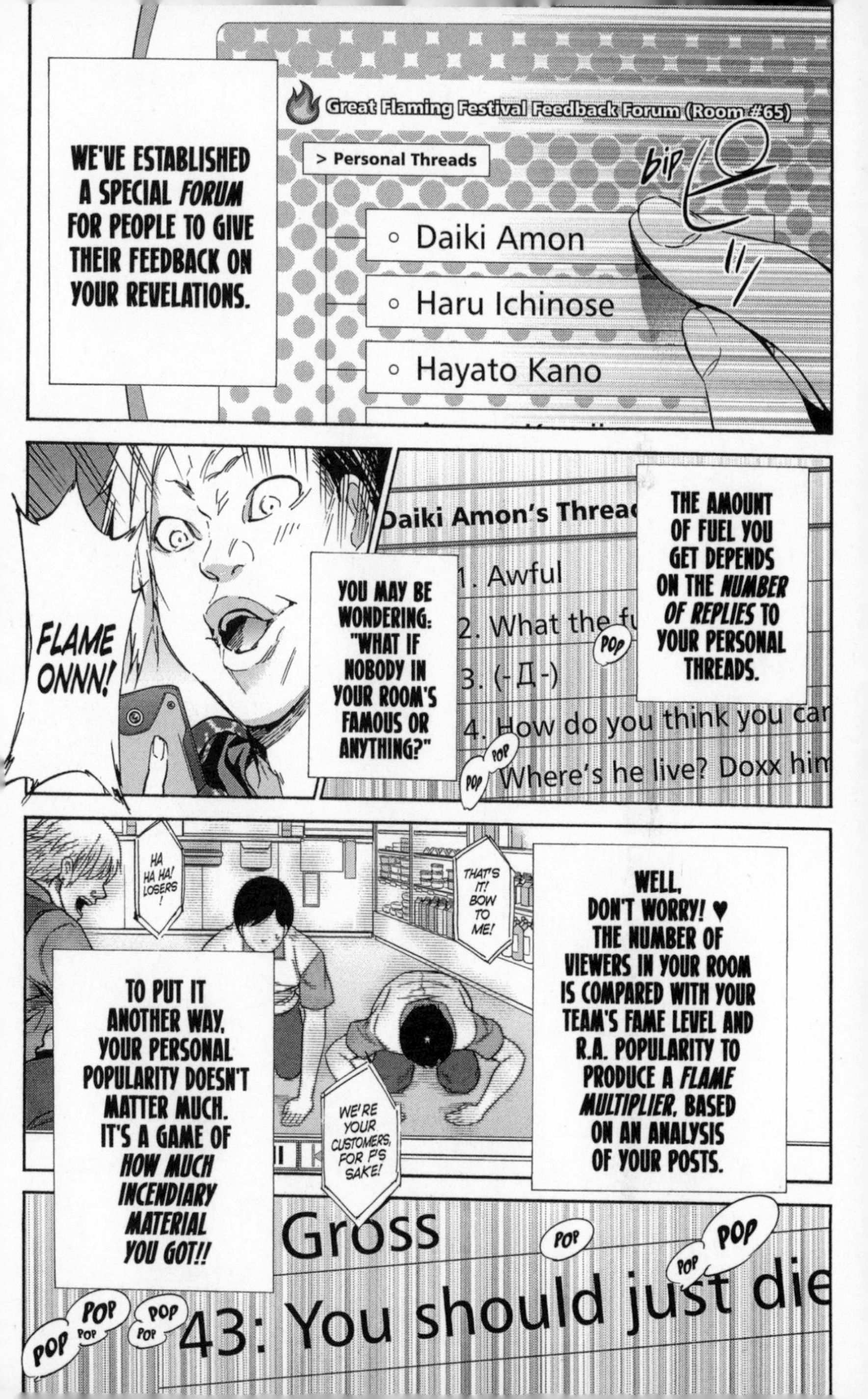

Great Flaming Festival Feedback Forum (Room #65)
bip
> Personal Threads
Daiki Amon
Haru Ichinose
Hayato Kano
WE'VE ESTABLISHED A SPECIAL *FORUM* FOR PEOPLE TO GIVE THEIR FEEDBACK ON YOUR REVELATIONS.
Daiki Amon's Threa
THE AMOUNT OF FUEL YOU GET DEPENDS ON THE *NUMBER OF REPLIES* TO YOUR PERSONAL THREADS.
1. Awful
2. What the fu
POP
3. (-Д-)
4. How do you think you ca
POP POP
Where's he live? Doxx hi
YOU MAY BE WONDERING: "WHAT IF NOBODY IN YOUR ROOM'S FAMOUS OR ANYTHING?"
FLAME ONNN!
WELL, DON'T WORRY! ♥ THE NUMBER OF VIEWERS IN YOUR ROOM IS COMPARED WITH YOUR TEAM'S FAME LEVEL AND R.A. POPULARITY TO PRODUCE A *FLAME MULTIPLIER*, BASED ON AN ANALYSIS OF YOUR POSTS.
THAT'S IT! BOW TO ME!
HA HA HA! LOSERS!
WE'RE YOUR CUSTOMERS, FOR F'S SAKE!
TO PUT IT ANOTHER WAY, YOUR PERSONAL POPULARITY DOESN'T MATTER MUCH. IT'S A GAME OF *HOW MUCH INCENDIARY MATERIAL YOU GOT!!*
POP POP POP
Gross
POP
43: You should just die
POP POP POP POP POP POP

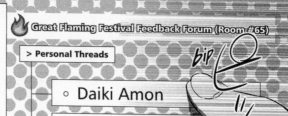

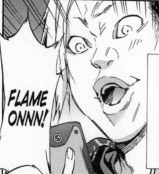

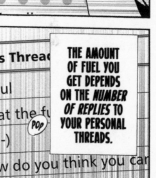

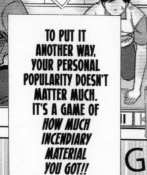

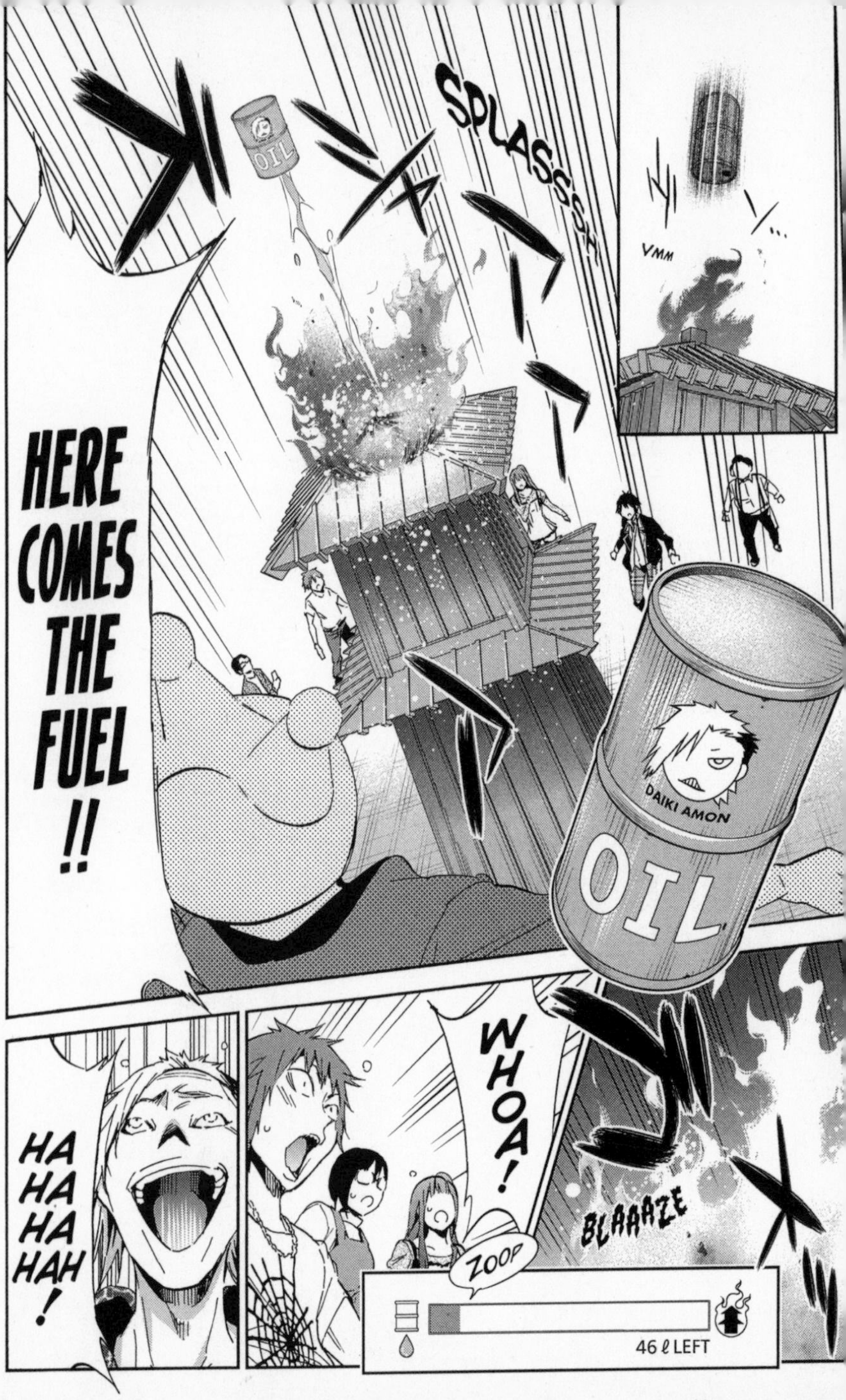
VMM
SPLASSSH
OIL
HERE COMES THE FUEL!!
DAIKI AMON
OIL
BLAAAZE
46 ℓ LEFT
WHOA!
ZOOP
HA HA HA HA HAH!

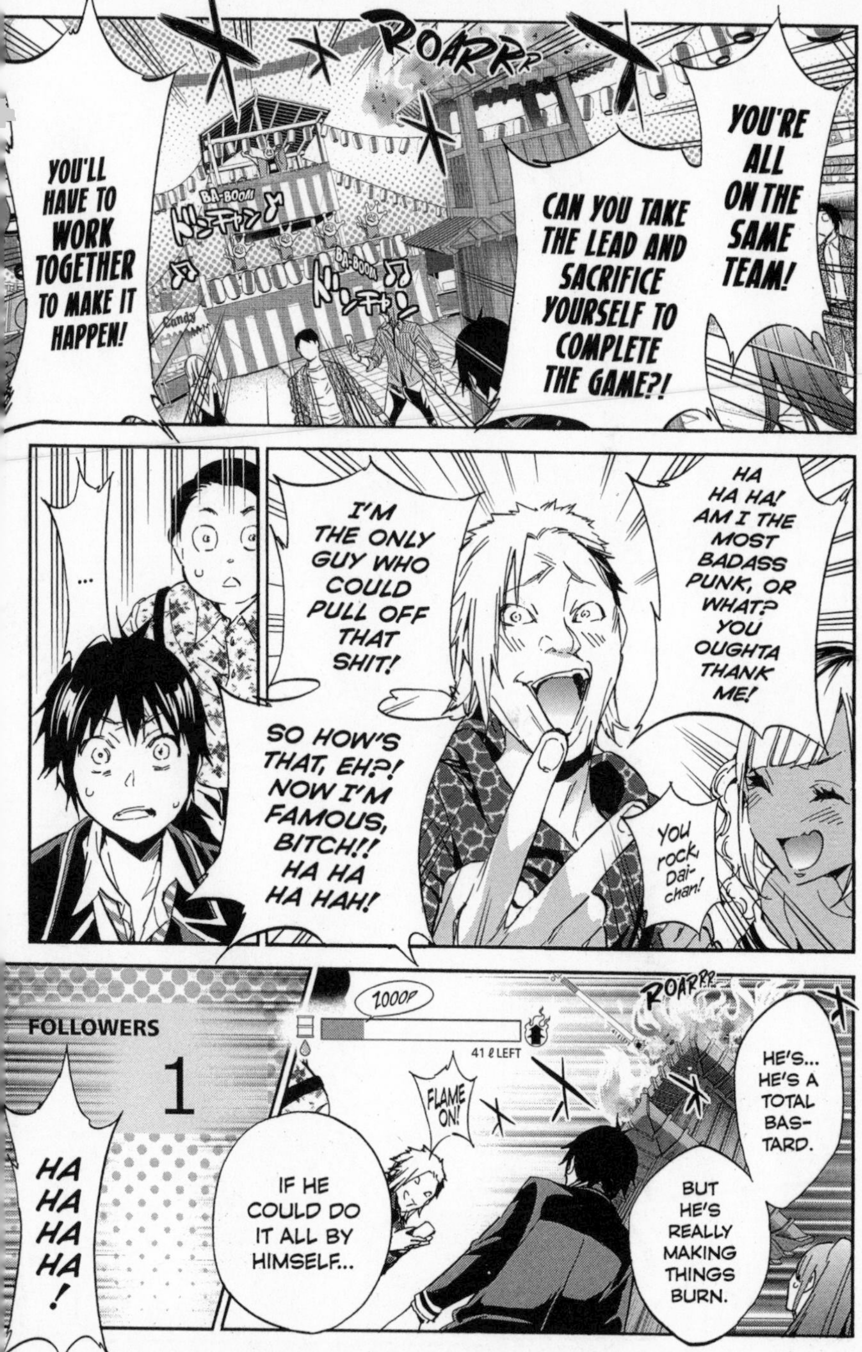
ROARRR
YOU'RE ALL ON THE SAME TEAM!
CAN YOU TAKE THE LEAD AND SACRIFICE YOURSELF TO COMPLETE THE GAME?!
BA-BOOM
ドンチャン♪
BA-BOOM
ドンチャン♪
Candy
YOU'LL HAVE TO WORK TOGETHER TO MAKE IT HAPPEN!
HA HA HA! AM I THE MOST BADASS PUNK, OR WHAT? YOU OUGHTA THANK ME!
I'M THE ONLY GUY WHO COULD PULL OFF THAT SHIT!
You rock, Dai-chan!
SO HOW'S THAT, EH?! NOW I'M FAMOUS, BITCH!! HA HA HA HAH!
...
ROARRR
HE'S... HE'S A TOTAL BASTARD.
BUT HE'S REALLY MAKING THINGS BURN.
FLAME ON!
2000P
41 ℓ LEFT
FOLLOWERS
1
IF HE COULD DO IT ALL BY HIMSELF...
HA HA HA HA!

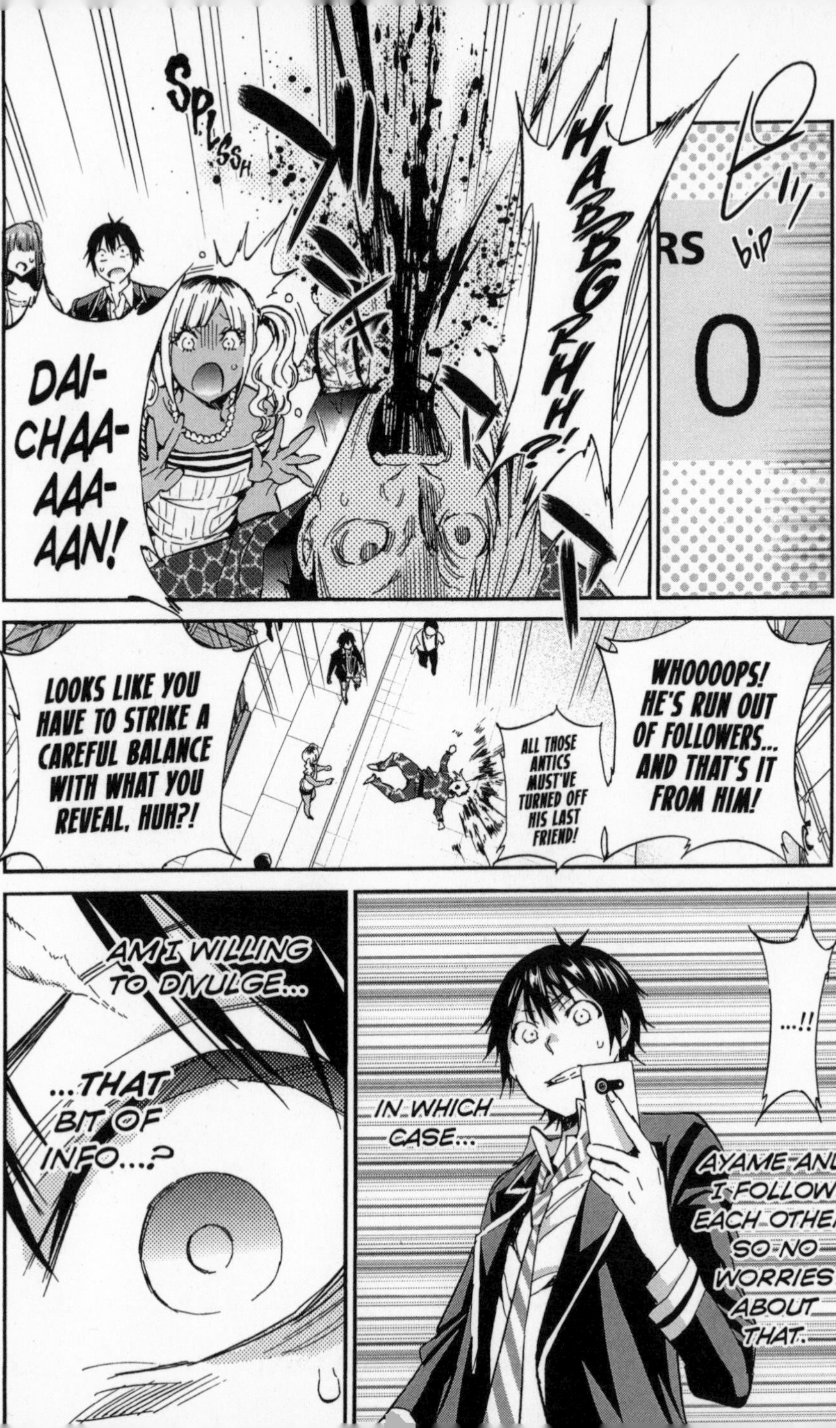
ピッ
bip
RS
0
HABBGRHHH?!
SPLSSH
DAI-CHAAA-AAAA-AAN!
WHOOOOPS! HE'S RUN OUT OF FOLLOWERS... AND THAT'S IT FROM HIM!
ALL THOSE ANTICS MUST'VE TURNED OFF HIS LAST FRIEND!
LOOKS LIKE YOU HAVE TO STRIKE A CAREFUL BALANCE WITH WHAT YOU REVEAL, HUH?!
...!!
IN WHICH CASE...
AYAME AND I FOLLOW EACH OTHER, SO NO WORRIES ABOUT THAT.
AM I WILLING TO DIVULGE...
...THAT BIT OF INFO...?

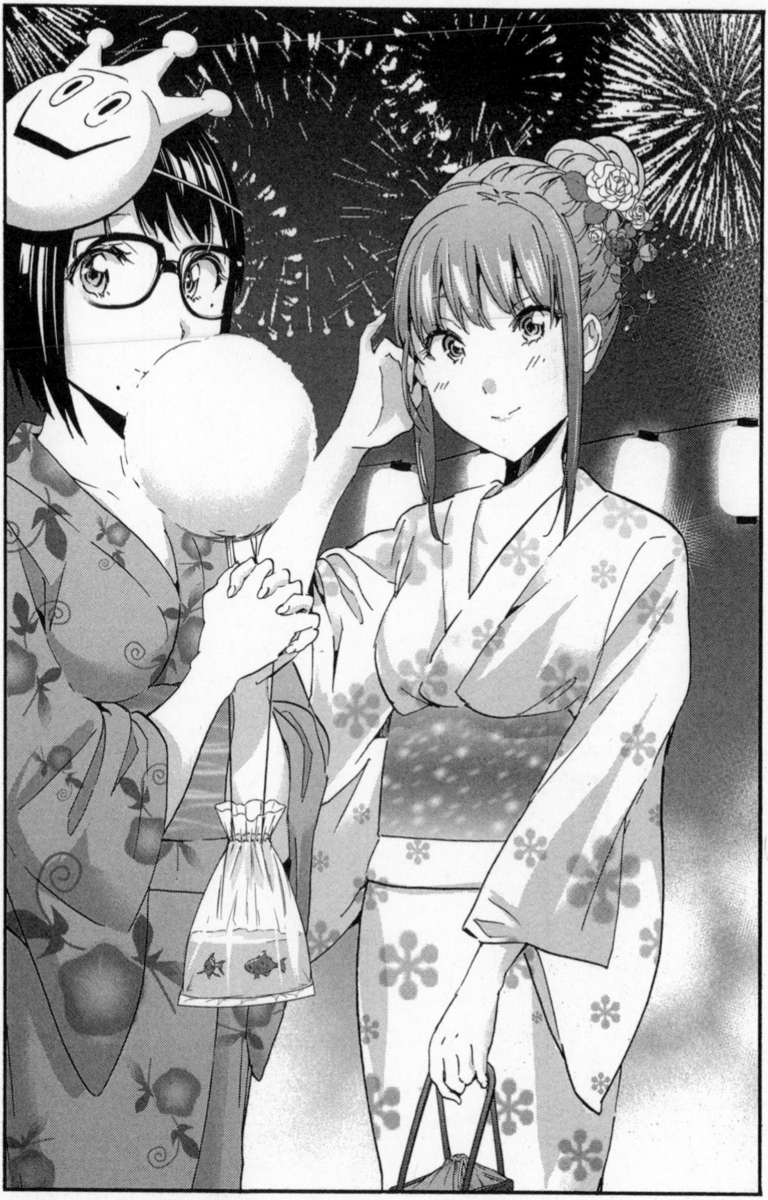

ACCOUNT 24 Flame On!

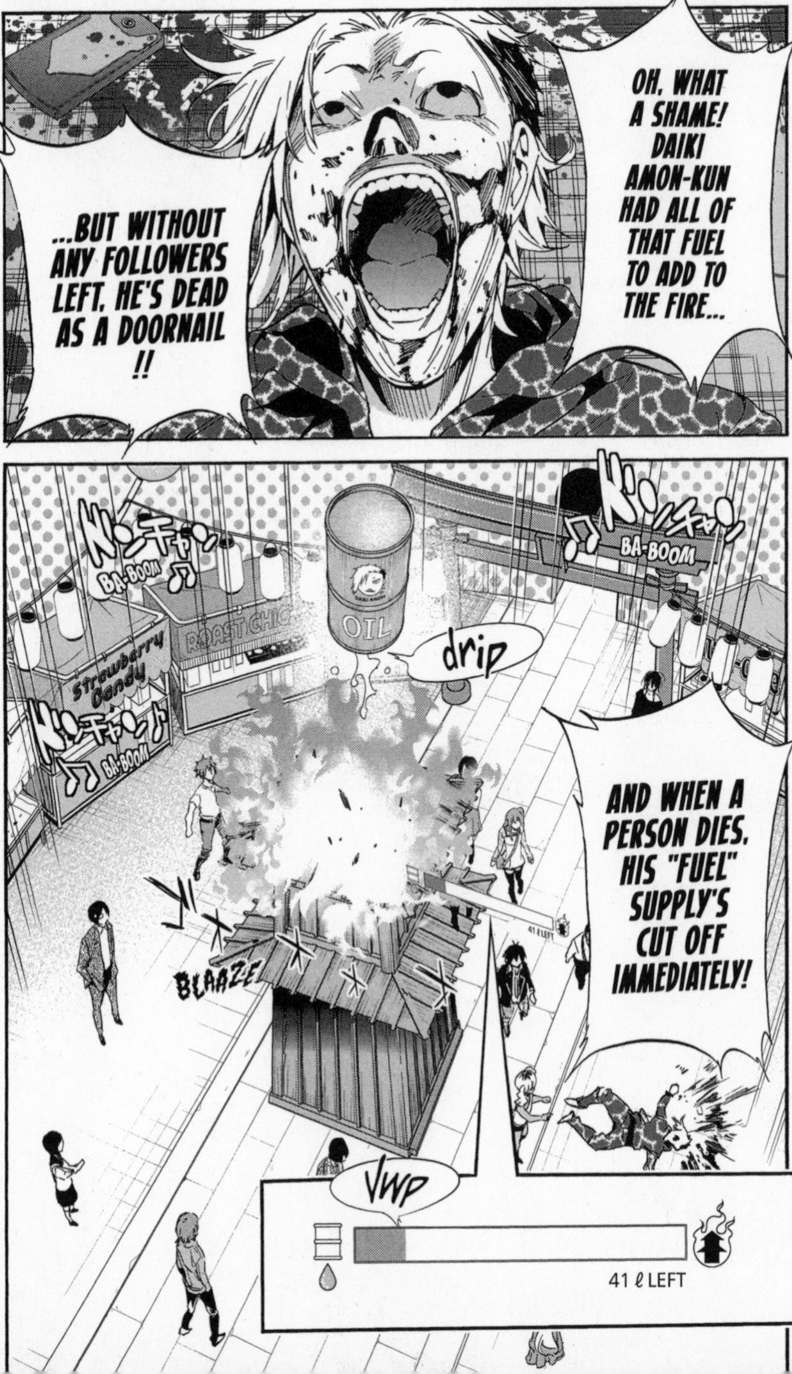
OH, WHAT A SHAME! DAIKI AMON-KUN HAD ALL OF THAT FUEL TO ADD TO THE FIRE...
...BUT WITHOUT ANY FOLLOWERS LEFT, HE'S DEAD AS A DOORNAIL !!
BA-BOOM
BA-BOOM
OIL
drip
AND WHEN A PERSON DIES, HIS "FUEL" SUPPLY'S CUT OFF IMMEDIATELY!
BA-BOOM
BLAAZE
VWP
41 ℓ LEFT

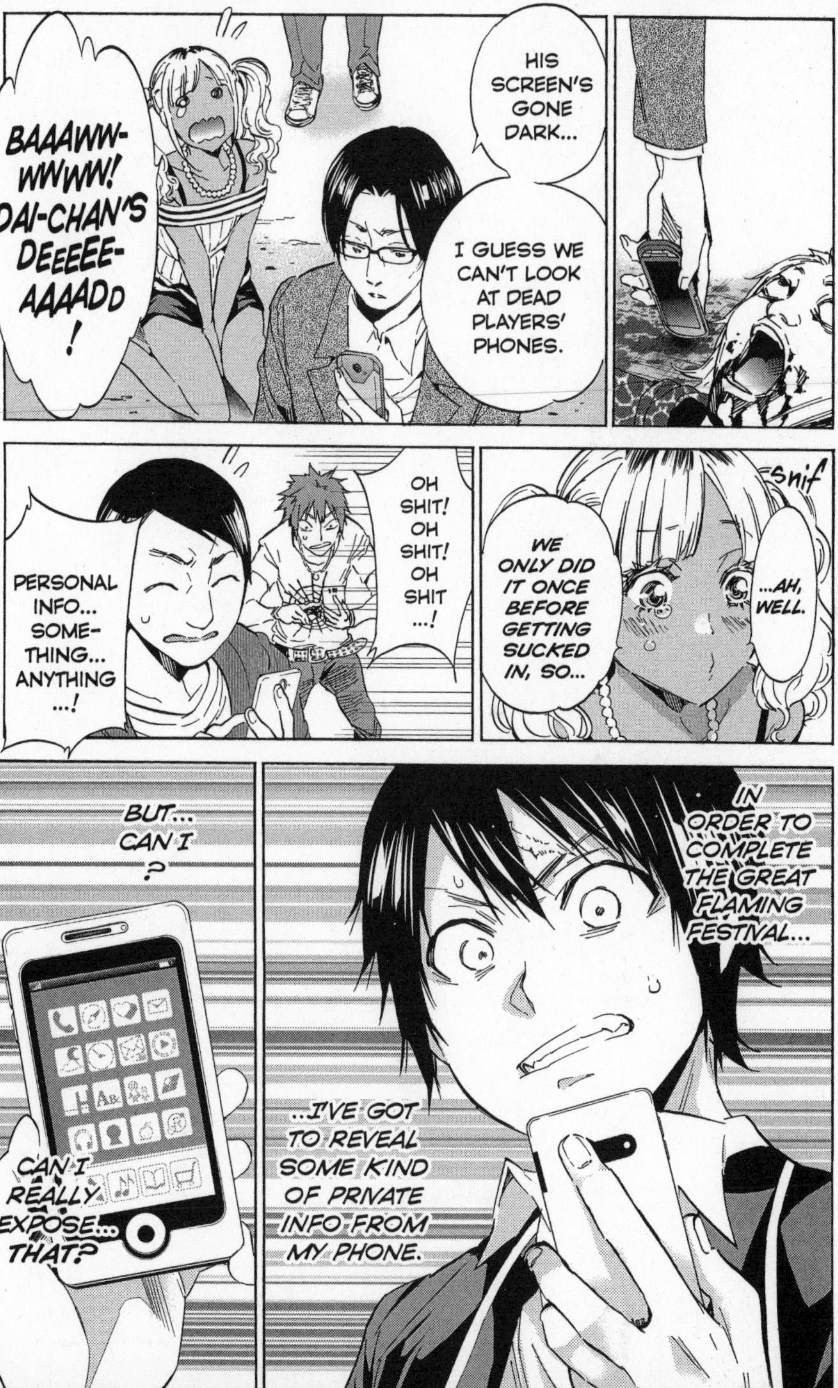
HIS SCREEN'S GONE DARK...
I GUESS WE CAN'T LOOK AT DEAD PLAYERS' PHONES.
BAAAWW-WWWW! DAI-CHAN'S DEEEEE-AAAADD!
snif
...AH, WELL.
WE ONLY DID IT ONCE BEFORE GETTING SUCKED IN, SO...
OH SHIT! OH SHIT! OH SHIT...!
PERSONAL INFO... SOME-THING... ANYTHING...!
IN ORDER TO COMPLETE THE GREAT FLAMING FESTIVAL...
...I'VE GOT TO REVEAL SOME KIND OF PRIVATE INFO FROM MY PHONE.
BUT... CAN I?
CAN I REALLY EXPOSE... THAT?

UH ...

...FLAME ON!

Arata Kiyotani

<IMAGE FILE>

MIHOKO

ARATA

...

OIL

Heh heh...

IT'S A COUPLE'S PHOTO WITH MY WIFE...

...

...

...

WE PRETTY MUCH GO HIS-AND-HERS WITH ALL OUR HOUSEHOLD ITEMS...! ♥

ROARRR

IT'S A NO MAKEUP SELFIE!

...OH, MAN, SO FREAKING EMBARASS-ING!

Riko Kuri
<IMAGE FILE>

ALL RIGHT!

I'LL ADD SOME FUEL, TOO.

34: lulz
35: that face, lol
36: Funny, but all too common
37: I like the "before" shot mor
38: ↑!?Σ(ﾟДﾟ)

POP POP POP

HER FACE IS JACKED UP!

WHAT THE ?!

THIS IS MY PHONE'S SEARCH HISTORY!!

Recent Search Results ▼

mature tits pics

mature porn vid

mature milf cheating

mature spread eagle pics

mature horny chat

F-F-FLAME ON!

blush

42: Oh jeez lol
43: You really like 'em matu
44: Nice keyword experime
45: I've been there
46: Now that's embarrass

POP POP POP

Hayato Kano
<SEARCH HISTORY>

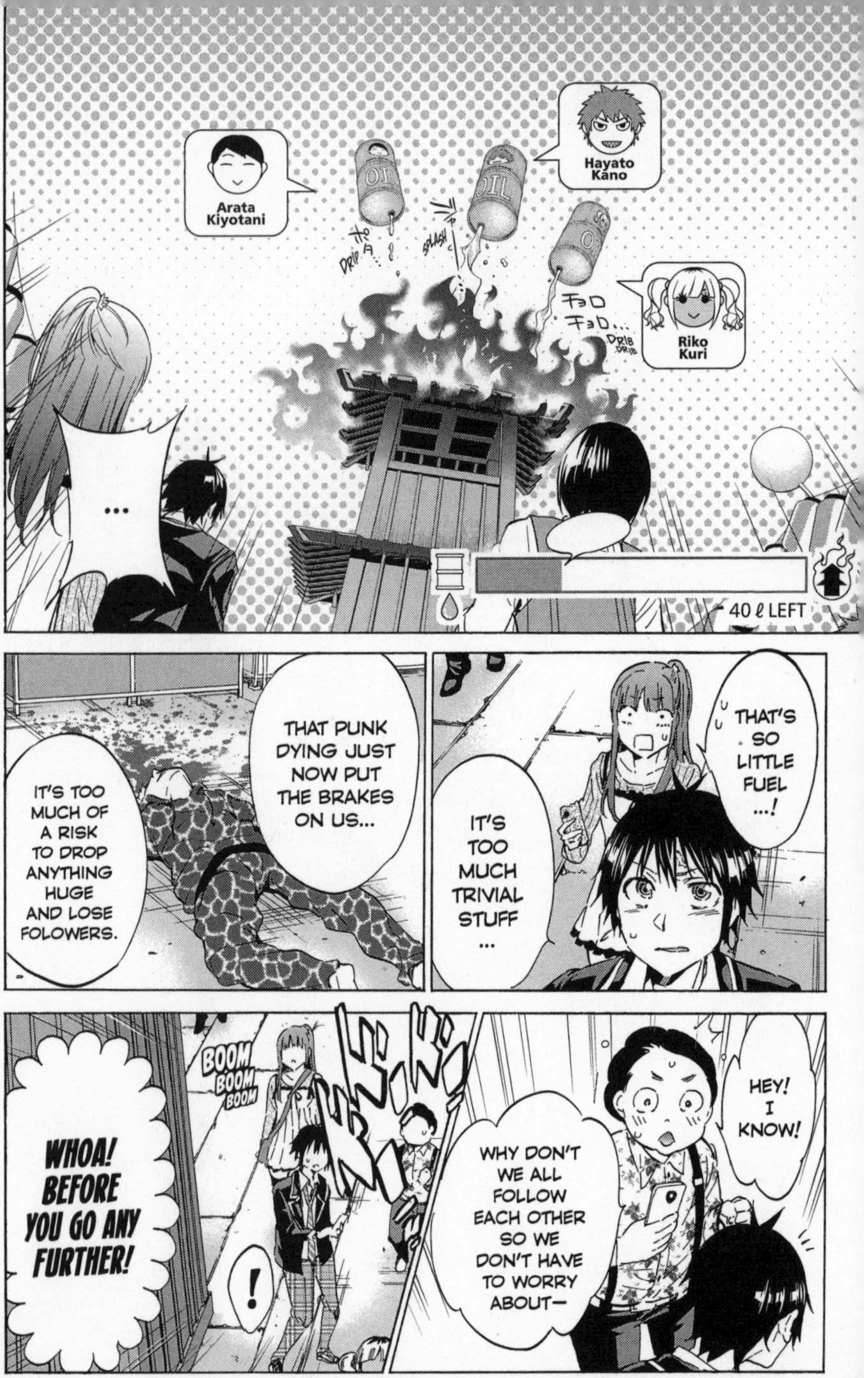
Hayato Kano
Arata Kiyotani
SPLASH
DRIP
Riko Kuri
チョロチョロ…
DRIB DRIB
…
40 ℓ LEFT
THAT'S SO LITTLE FUEL …!
IT'S TOO MUCH TRIVIAL STUFF …
THAT PUNK DYING JUST NOW PUT THE BRAKES ON US…
IT'S TOO MUCH OF A RISK TO DROP ANYTHING HUGE AND LOSE FOLOWERS.
HEY! I KNOW!
WHY DON'T WE ALL FOLLOW EACH OTHER SO WE DON'T HAVE TO WORRY ABOUT—
BOOM BOOM BOOM
!
WHOA! BEFORE YOU GO ANY FURTHER!

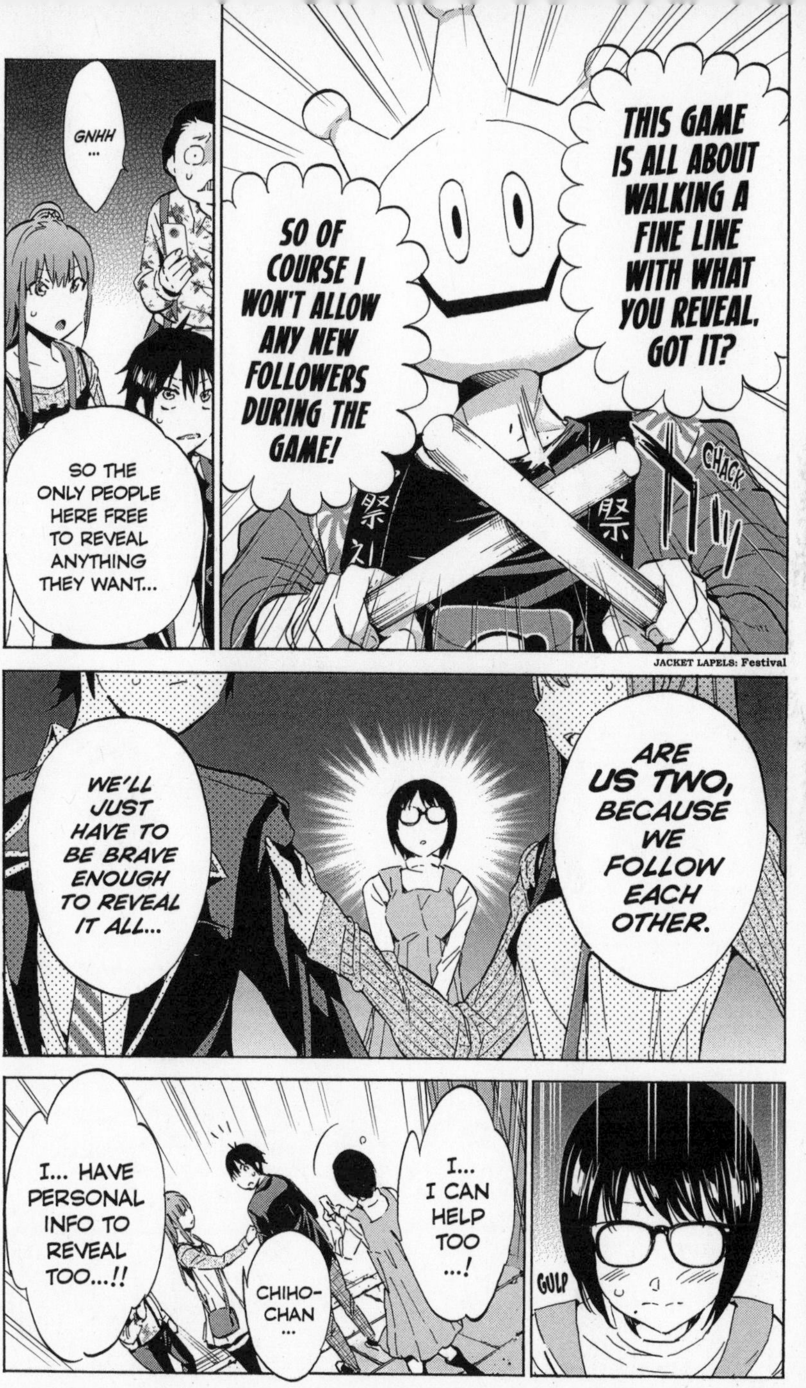
THIS GAME IS ALL ABOUT WALKING A FINE LINE WITH WHAT YOU REVEAL, GOT IT?
SO OF COURSE I WON'T ALLOW ANY NEW FOLLOWERS DURING THE GAME!
CHACK
GNHH ...
SO THE ONLY PEOPLE HERE FREE TO REVEAL ANYTHING THEY WANT...
JACKET LAPELS: Festival
ARE US TWO, BECAUSE WE FOLLOW EACH OTHER.
WE'LL JUST HAVE TO BE BRAVE ENOUGH TO REVEAL IT ALL...
GULP
I... I CAN HELP TOO ...!
CHIHO-CHAN ...
I... HAVE PERSONAL INFO TO REVEAL TOO...!!

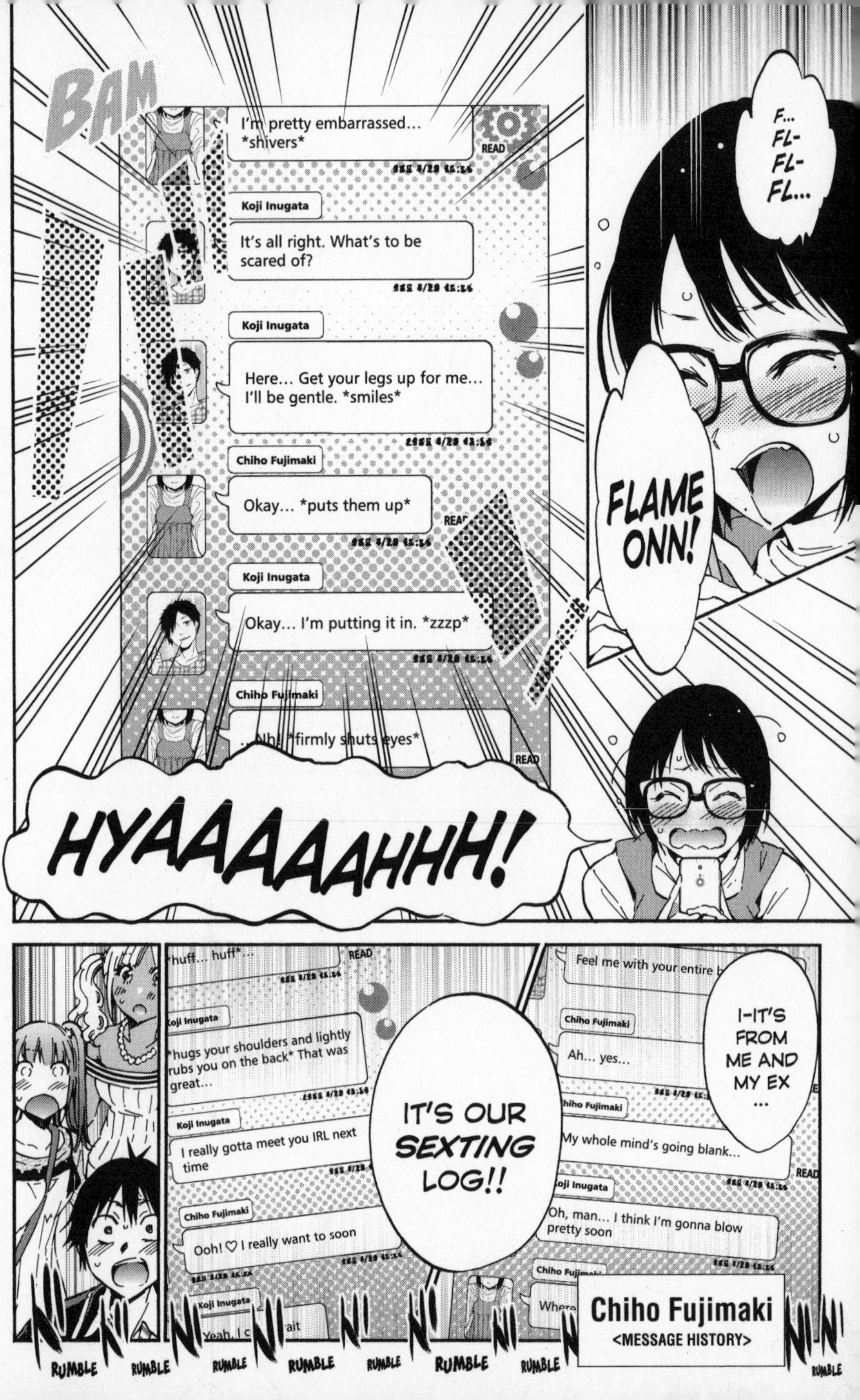
F... FL- FL- FL...
FLAME ONN!
HYAAAAAHHH!
BAM
I'm pretty embarrassed... *shivers*
READ
Koji Inugata
It's all right. What's to be scared of?
Koji Inugata
Here... Get your legs up for me... I'll be gentle. *smiles*
Chiho Fujimaki
Okay... *puts them up*
Koji Inugata
Okay... I'm putting it in. *zzzp*
Chiho Fujimaki
...Nh! *firmly shuts eyes*
READ
I-IT'S FROM ME AND MY EX...
IT'S OUR SEXTING LOG!!
Chiho Fujimaki
<MESSAGE HISTORY>
Feel me with your entire b
Chiho Fujimaki
Ah... yes...
Chiho Fujimaki
My whole mind's going blank...
READ
Koji Inugata
Oh, man... I think I'm gonna blow pretty soon
Where
huff... huff...
READ
Koji Inugata
hugs your shoulders and lightly rubs you on the back That was great...
Koji Inugata
I really gotta meet you IRL next time
Chiho Fujimaki
Ooh! ♡ I really want to soon
Koji Inugata
Yeah, I c ait
RUMBLE RUMBLE RUMBLE RUMBLE RUMBLE RUMBLE RUMBLE RUMBLE

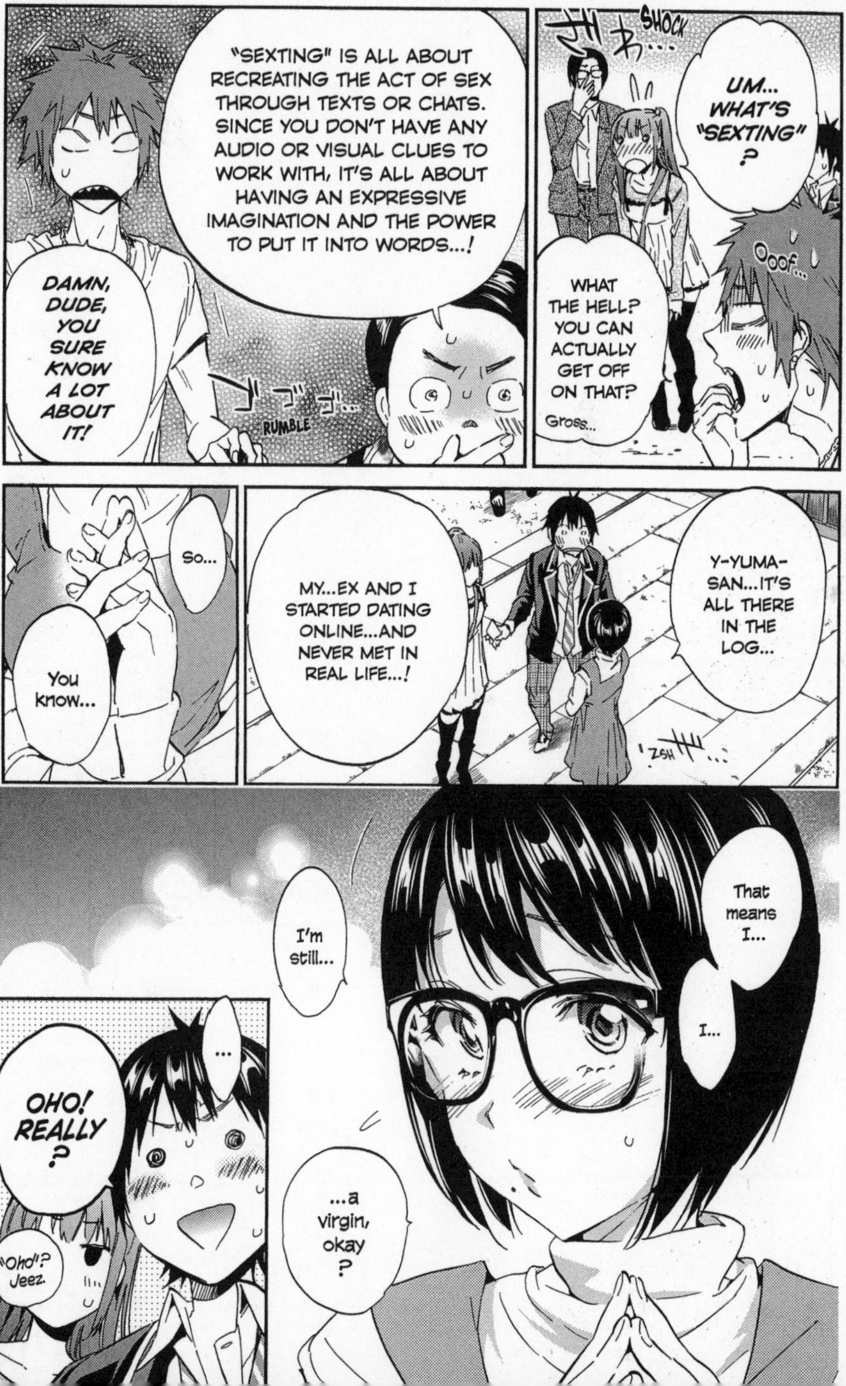
UM... WHAT'S "SEXTING" ?
SHOCK
Ooof...
WHAT THE HELL? YOU CAN ACTUALLY GET OFF ON THAT?
Gross...
"SEXTING" IS ALL ABOUT RECREATING THE ACT OF SEX THROUGH TEXTS OR CHATS. SINCE YOU DON'T HAVE ANY AUDIO OR VISUAL CLUES TO WORK WITH, IT'S ALL ABOUT HAVING AN EXPRESSIVE IMAGINATION AND THE POWER TO PUT IT INTO WORDS...!
DAMN, DUDE, YOU SURE KNOW A LOT ABOUT IT!
RUMBLE
Y-YUMA-SAN...IT'S ALL THERE IN THE LOG...
MY...EX AND I STARTED DATING ONLINE...AND NEVER MET IN REAL LIFE...!
ZSH
So...
You know...
That means I...
I...
I'm still...
...a virgin, okay ?
...
OHO! REALLY ?
"Oho"? Jeez.

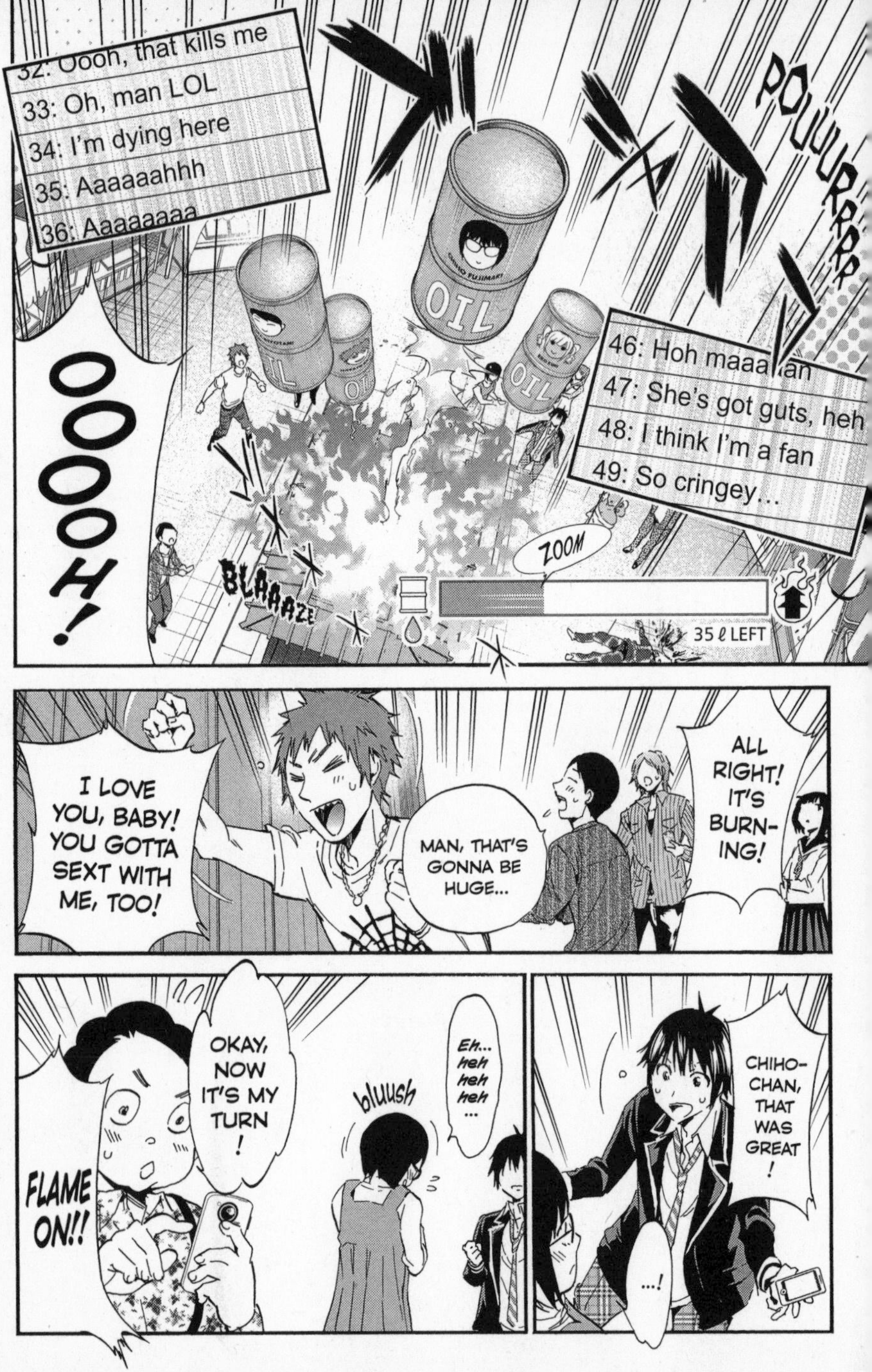
32: Oooh, that kills me
33: Oh, man LOL
34: I'm dying here
35: Aaaaaahhh
36: Aaaaaaaa
POUUURRRR
46: Hoh maaaaaan
47: She's got guts, heh
48: I think I'm a fan
49: So cringey…
ZOOM
35 ℓ LEFT
BLAAAZE
OOOOOH!
ALL RIGHT! IT'S BURNING!
MAN, THAT'S GONNA BE HUGE...
I LOVE YOU, BABY! YOU GOTTA SEXT WITH ME, TOO!
CHIHO-CHAN, THAT WAS GREAT!
...!
Eh... heh heh heh...
bluush
OKAY, NOW IT'S MY TURN!
FLAME ON!!

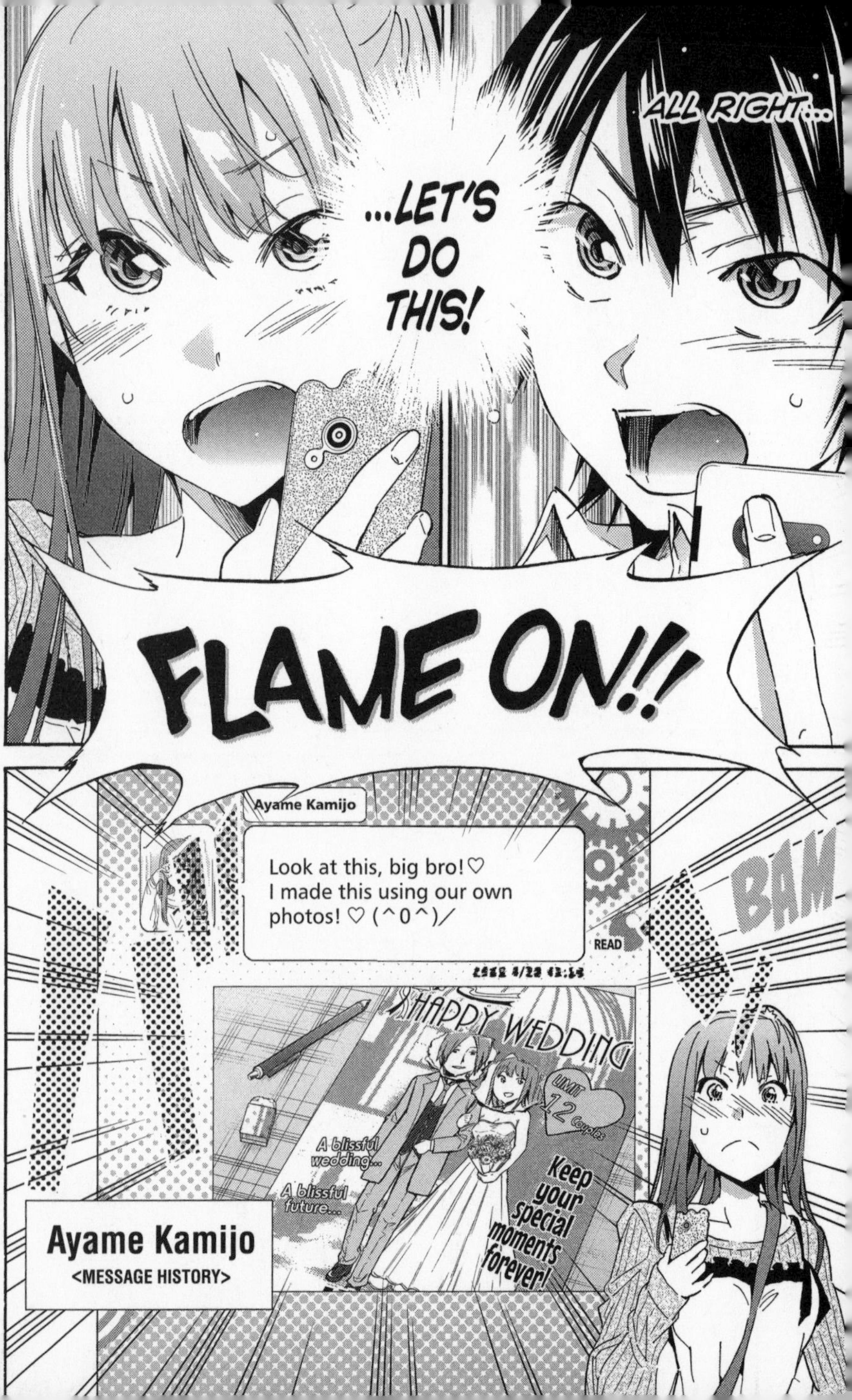
ALL RIGHT...
...LET'S DO THIS!
FLAME ON!!
BAM
Ayame Kamijo
Look at this, big bro! ♡ I made this using our own photos! ♡ (^0^)/
READ
HAPPY WEDDING
LIMIT 12 Couples
Keep your special moments forever!
A blissful wedding...
A blissful future...
Ayame Kamijo
<MESSAGE HISTORY>

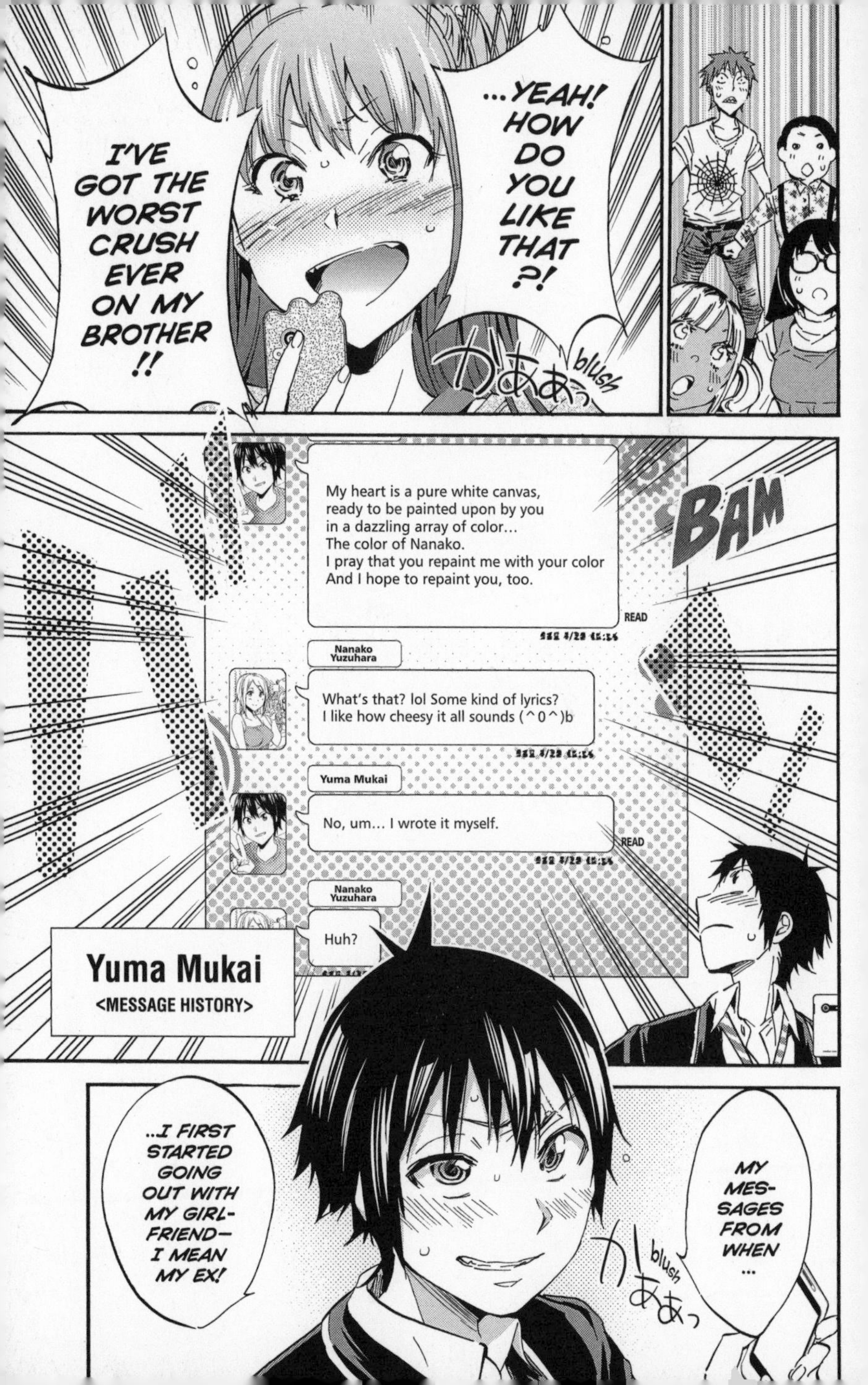
...YEAH! HOW DO YOU LIKE THAT?!
I'VE GOT THE WORST CRUSH EVER ON MY BROTHER!!
blush
BAM
My heart is a pure white canvas, ready to be painted upon by you in a dazzling array of color... The color of Nanako. I pray that you repaint me with your color And I hope to repaint you, too.
READ
Nanako Yuzuhara
What's that? lol Some kind of lyrics? I like how cheesy it all sounds (^0^)b
Yuma Mukai
No, um... I wrote it myself.
READ
Nanako Yuzuhara
Huh?
Yuma Mukai
<MESSAGE HISTORY>
MY MES-SAGES FROM WHEN...
blush
...I FIRST STARTED GOING OUT WITH MY GIRL-FRIEND— I MEAN MY EX!

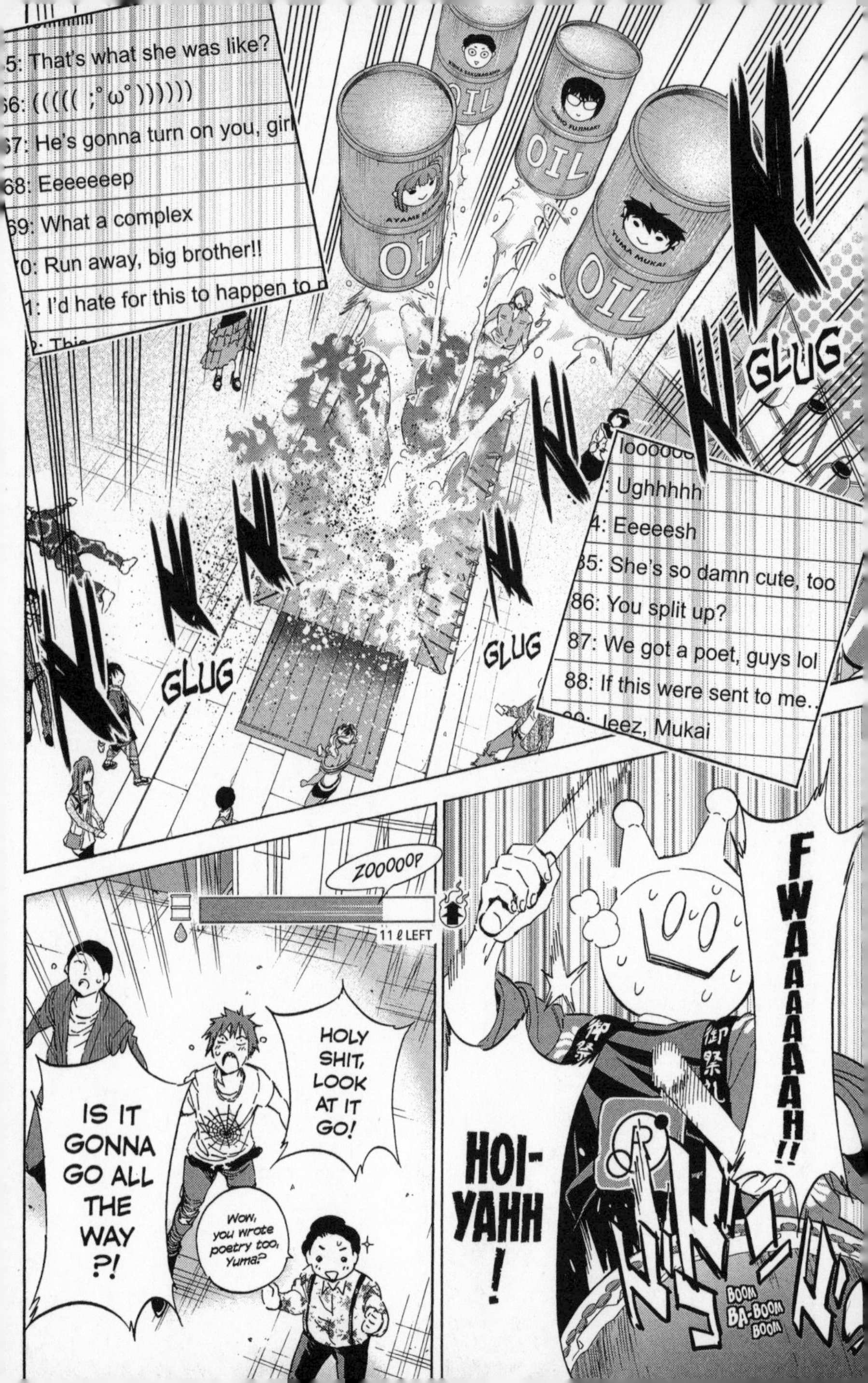
5: That's what she was like?
66: (((((;°ω°))))))
67: He's gonna turn on you, girl
68: Eeeeeeep
69: What a complex
70: Run away, big brother!!
1: I'd hate for this to happen to
OIL
OIL
OIL
OIL
GLUG
GLUG
GLUG
Ughhhhh
4: Eeeeesh
85: She's so damn cute, too
86: You split up?
87: We got a poet, guys lol
88: If this were sent to me...
Jeez, Mukai
FWAAAAAAH!!
HOI-YAHH!
BOOM BA-BOOM BOOM
ZOOOOOP
11 ℓ LEFT
HOLY SHIT, LOOK AT IT GO!
IS IT GONNA GO ALL THE WAY?!
Wow, you wrote poetry too, Yuma?

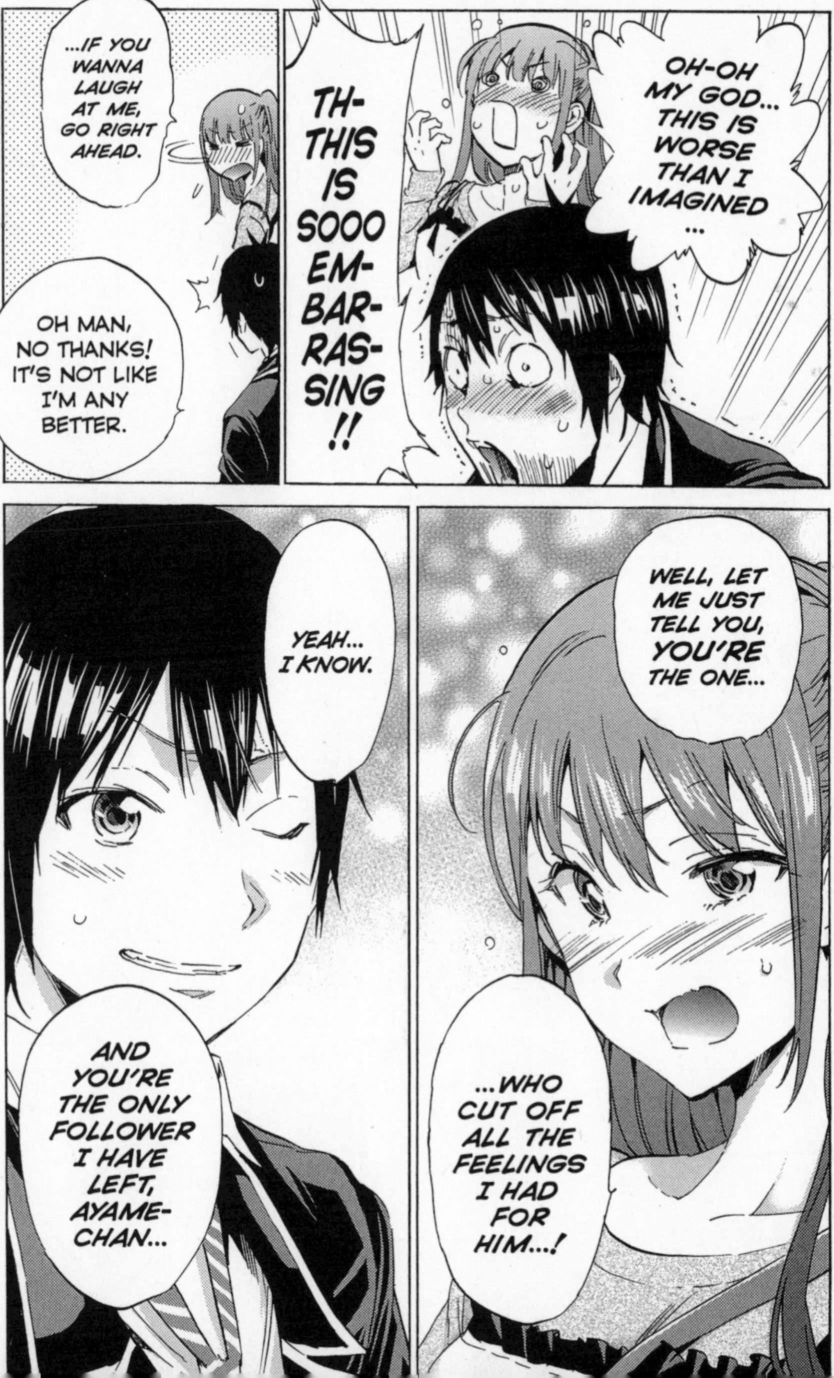
OH-OH MY GOD... THIS IS WORSE THAN I IMAGINED...
TH-THIS IS SOOO EM-BAR-RAS-SING!!
...IF YOU WANNA LAUGH AT ME, GO RIGHT AHEAD.
OH MAN, NO THANKS! IT'S NOT LIKE I'M ANY BETTER.
WELL, LET ME JUST TELL YOU, YOU'RE THE ONE...
...WHO CUT OFF ALL THE FEELINGS I HAD FOR HIM...!
YEAH... I KNOW.
AND YOU'RE THE ONLY FOLLOWER I HAVE LEFT, AYAME-CHAN...

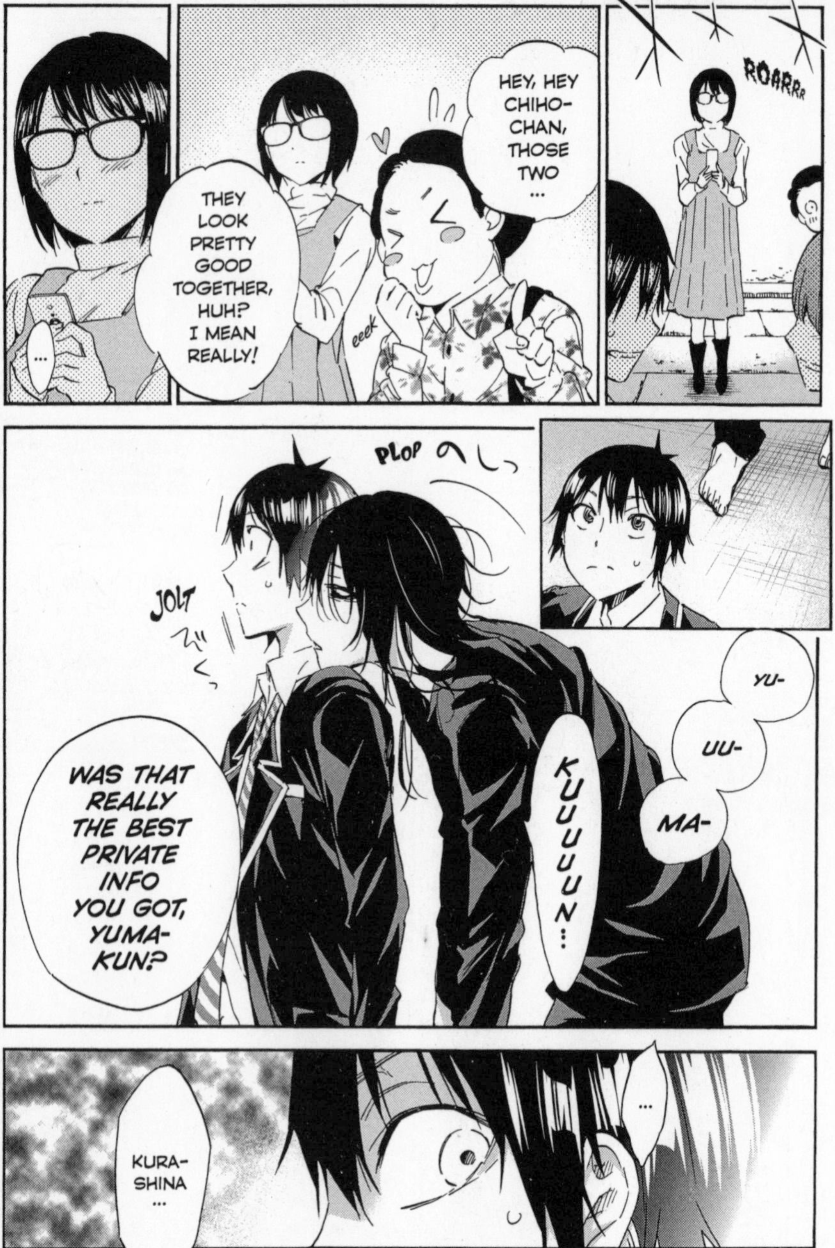
ROARRR
HEY, HEY CHIHO-CHAN, THOSE TWO ...
eeek
THEY LOOK PRETTY GOOD TOGETHER, HUH? I MEAN REALLY!
...
PLOP へしっ
YU- UU- MA-
KUUUUUN...
JOLT びくっ
WAS THAT REALLY THE BEST PRIVATE INFO YOU GOT, YUMA-KUN?
...
KURA-SHINA ...

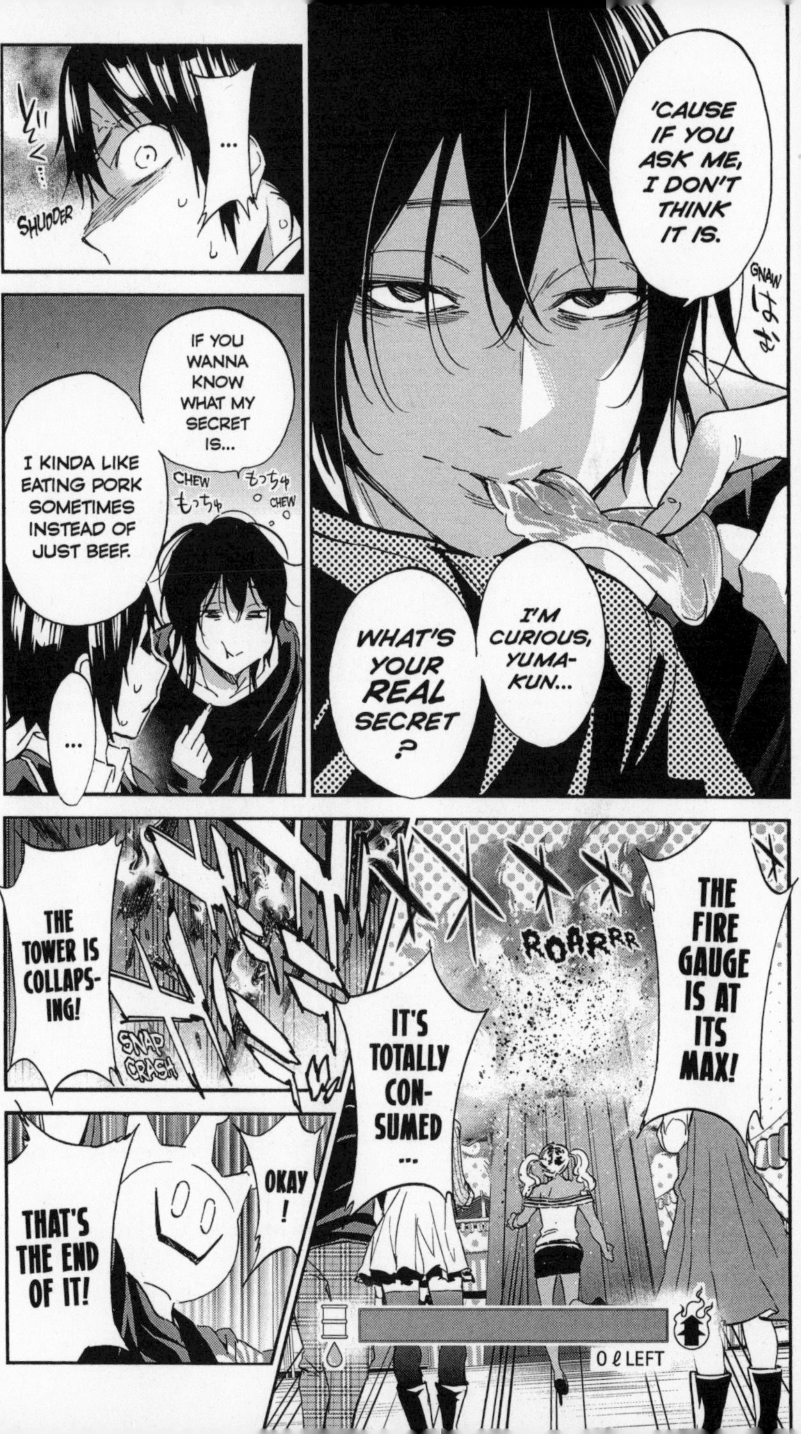
'CAUSE IF YOU ASK ME, I DON'T THINK IT IS.
GNAW
はむ
I'M CURIOUS, YUMA-KUN...
WHAT'S YOUR REAL SECRET?
...
SHUDDER
ぞくっ
IF YOU WANNA KNOW WHAT MY SECRET IS...
I KINDA LIKE EATING PORK SOMETIMES INSTEAD OF JUST BEEF.
CHEW
もっちゅ
CHEW
もっちゅ
...
THE FIRE GAUGE IS AT ITS MAX!
ROARRR
THE TOWER IS COLLAPSING!
SNAP CRASH
IT'S TOTALLY CONSUMED...
OKAY!
THAT'S THE END OF IT!
0 ℓ LEFT

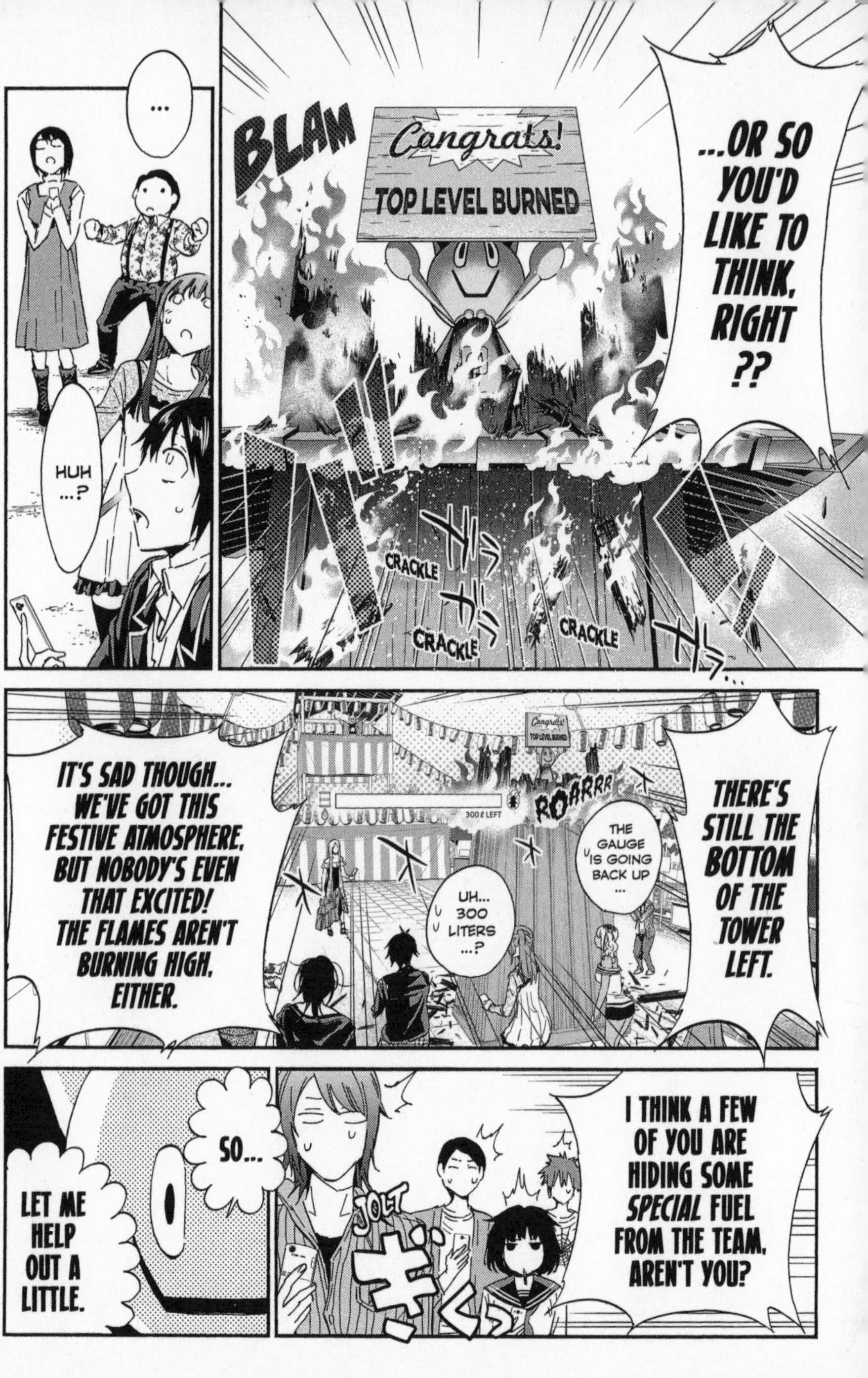
...OR SO YOU'D LIKE TO THINK, RIGHT ??
Congrats!
TOP LEVEL BURNED
BLAM
CRACKLE
CRACKLE
CRACKLE
...
HUH ...?
THERE'S STILL THE BOTTOM OF THE TOWER LEFT.
Congrats!
TOP LEVEL BURNED
ROARRR
THE GAUGE IS GOING BACK UP ...
300ℓ LEFT
UH... 300 LITERS ...?
IT'S SAD THOUGH... WE'VE GOT THIS FESTIVE ATMOSPHERE, BUT NOBODY'S EVEN THAT EXCITED! THE FLAMES AREN'T BURNING HIGH, EITHER.
I THINK A FEW OF YOU ARE HIDING SOME *SPECIAL* FUEL FROM THE TEAM. AREN'T YOU?
JOLT
SO...
LET ME HELP OUT A LITTLE.

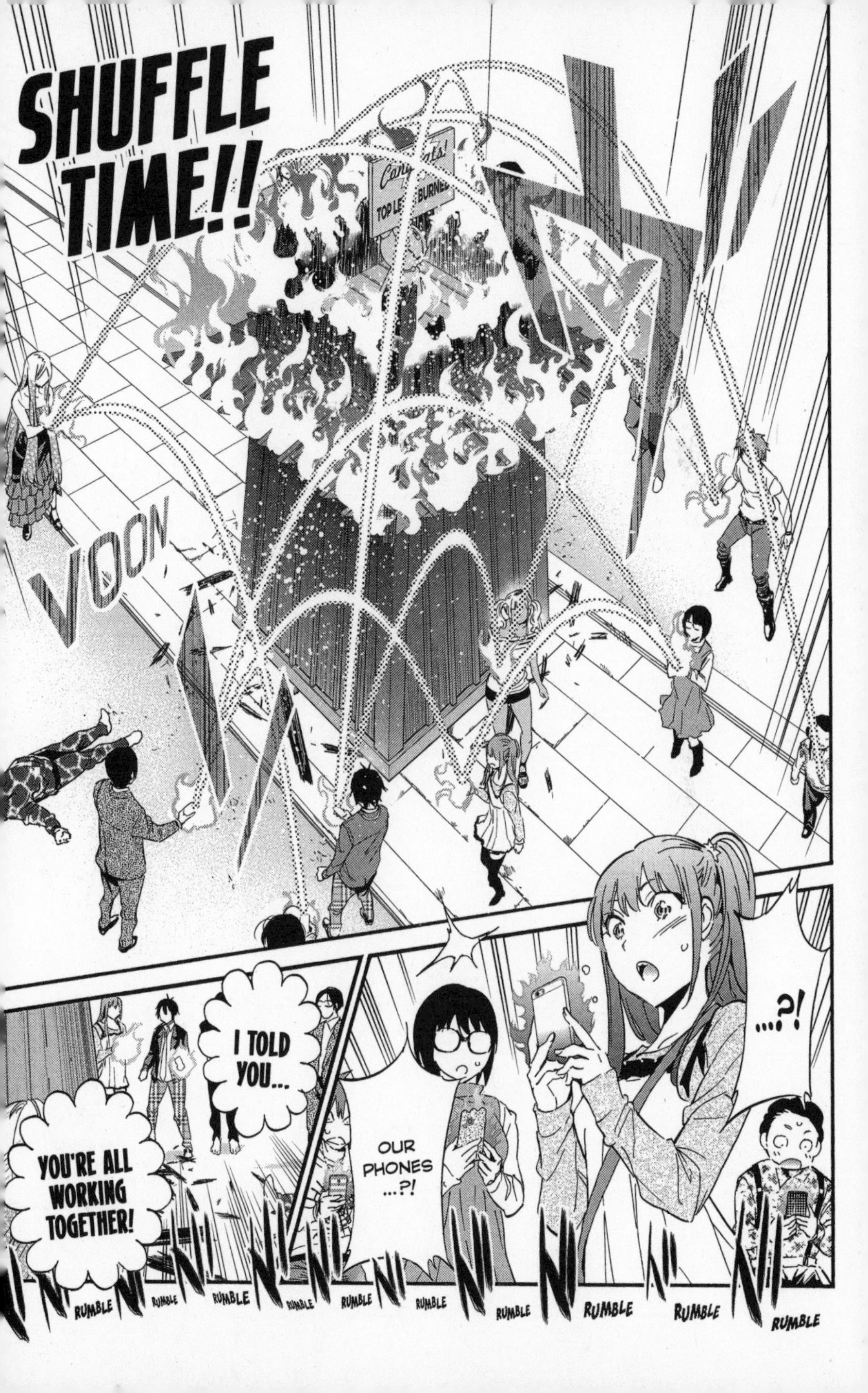
SHUFFLE TIME!!
VOON
...?!
OUR PHONES ...?!
I TOLD YOU...
YOU'RE ALL WORKING TOGETHER!
RUMBLE RUMBLE RUMBLE RUMBLE RUMBLE RUMBLE RUMBLE RUMBLE RUMBLE RUMBLE

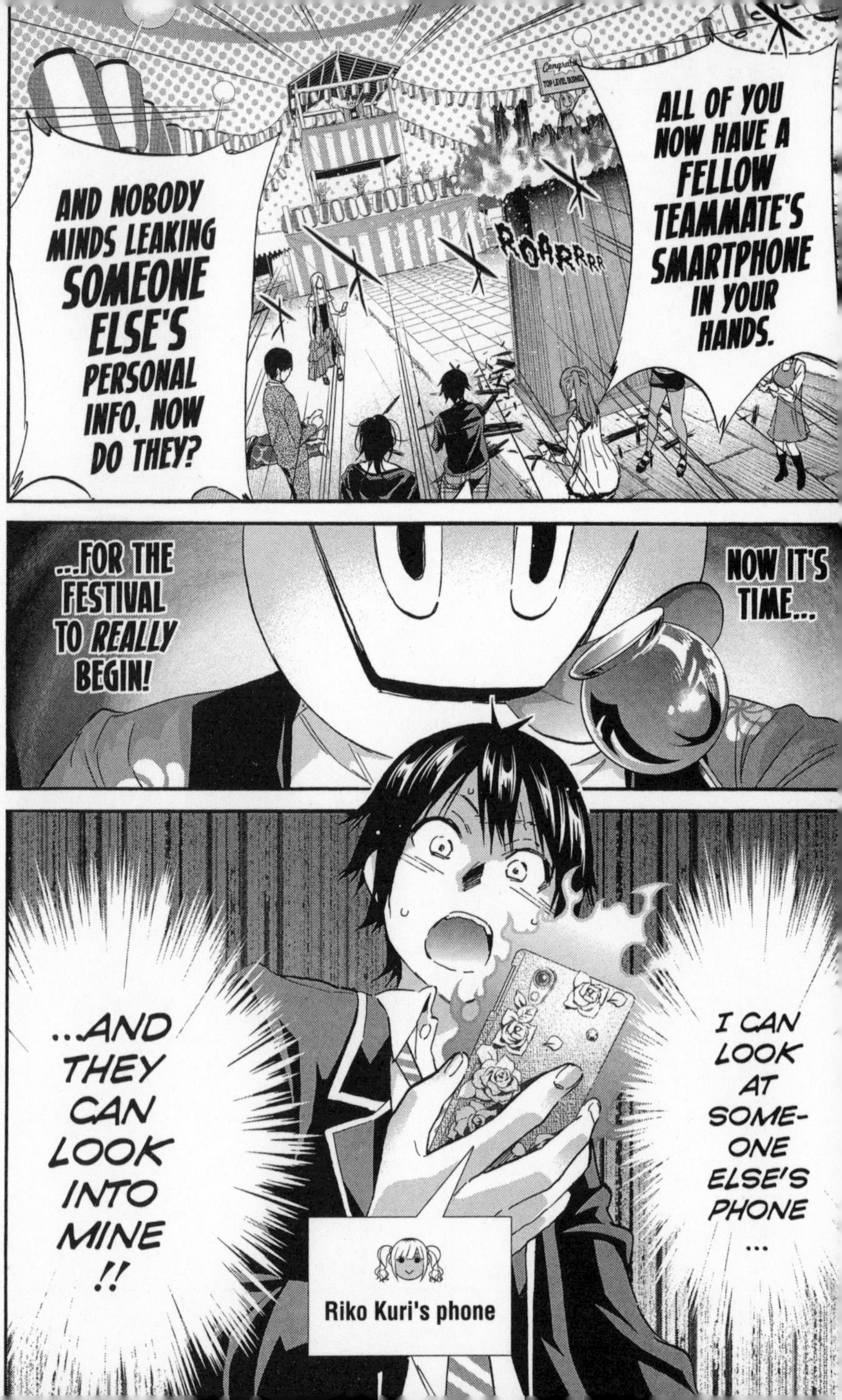
ALL OF YOU NOW HAVE A FELLOW TEAMMATE'S SMARTPHONE IN YOUR HANDS.
ROARRRR
AND NOBODY MINDS LEAKING SOMEONE ELSE'S PERSONAL INFO, NOW DO THEY?
NOW IT'S TIME...
...FOR THE FESTIVAL TO REALLY BEGIN!
I CAN LOOK AT SOME-ONE ELSE'S PHONE...
...AND THEY CAN LOOK INTO MINE!!
Riko Kuri's phone

ACCOUNT 25 The Real Account Leakpocalypse

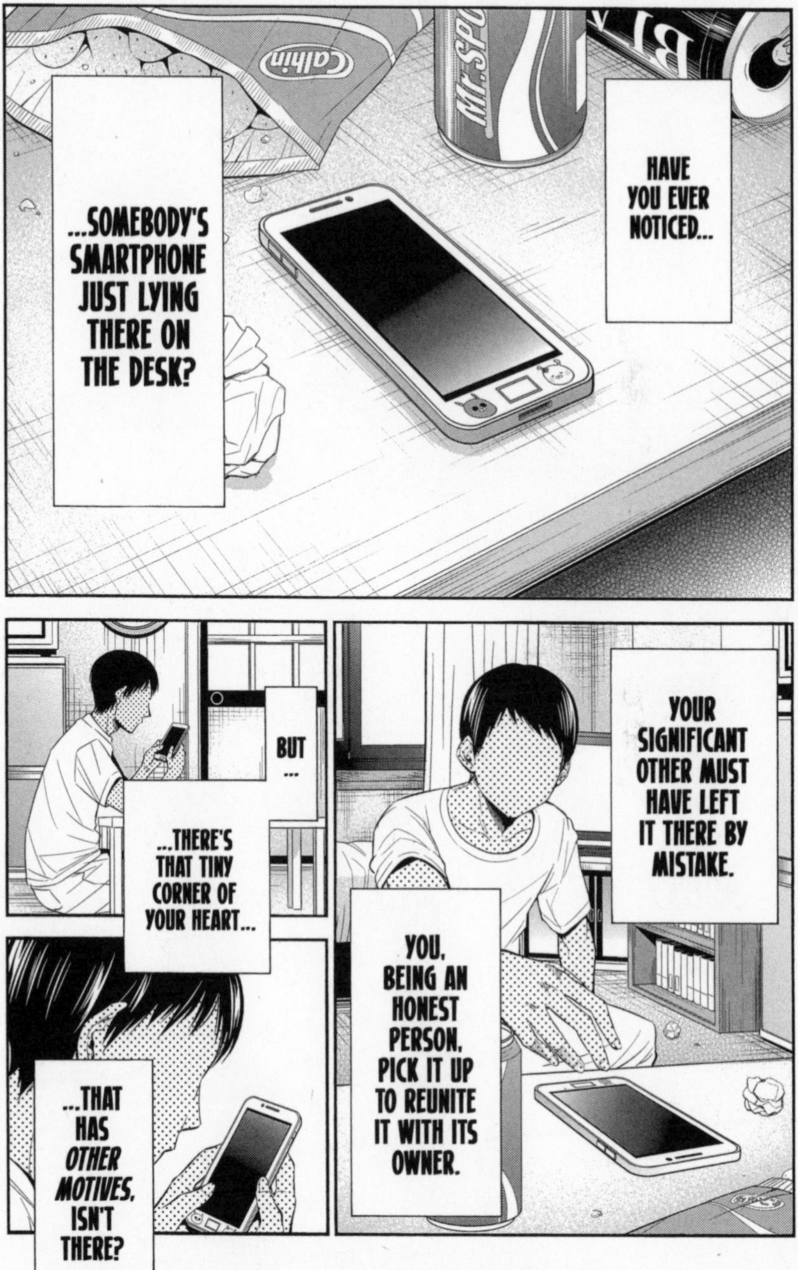
HAVE YOU EVER NOTICED...
...SOMEBODY'S SMARTPHONE JUST LYING THERE ON THE DESK?
YOUR SIGNIFICANT OTHER MUST HAVE LEFT IT THERE BY MISTAKE.
YOU, BEING AN HONEST PERSON, PICK IT UP TO REUNITE IT WITH ITS OWNER.
BUT ...
...THERE'S THAT TINY CORNER OF YOUR HEART...
...THAT HAS *OTHER MOTIVES,* ISN'T THERE?

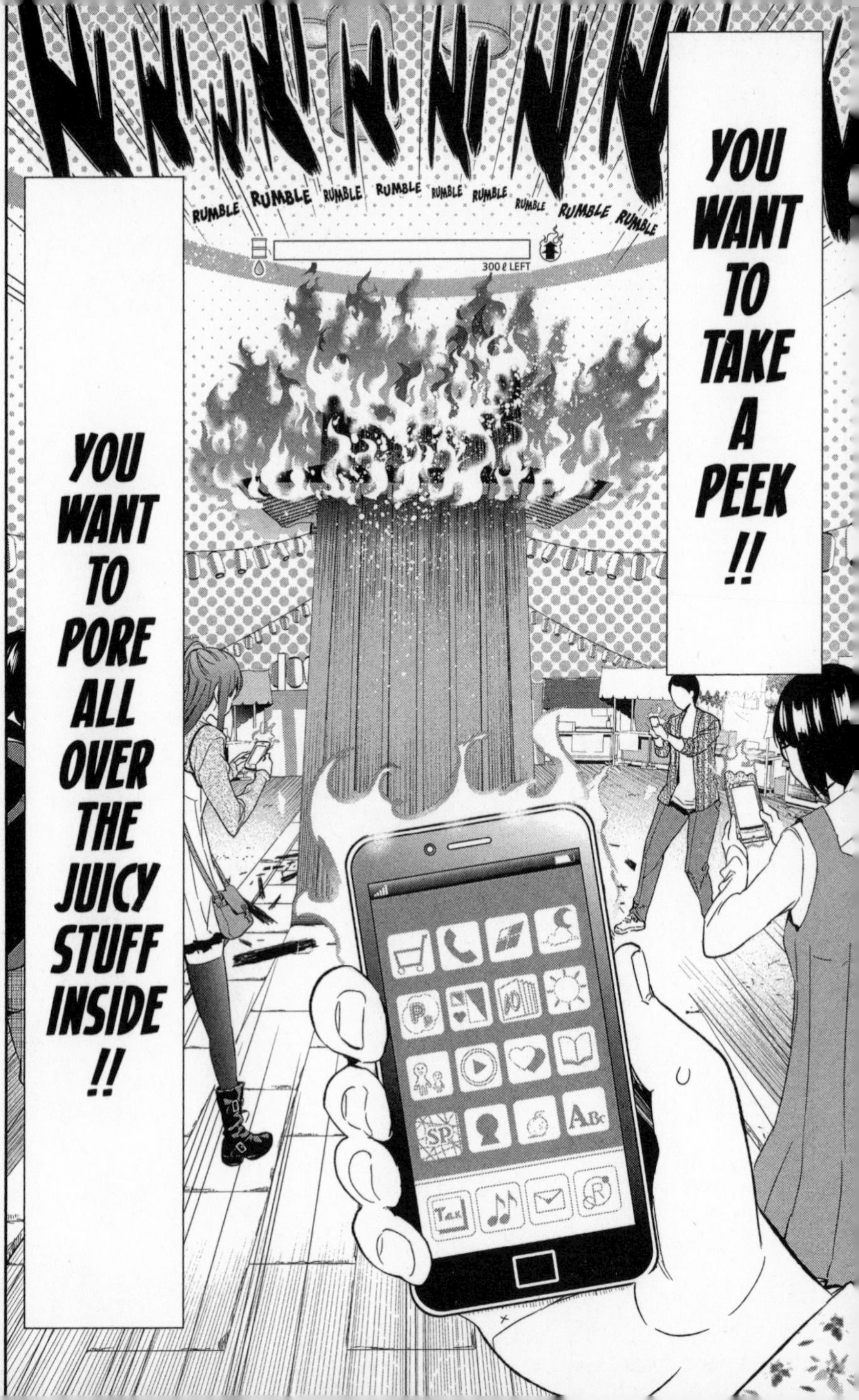
YOU WANT TO TAKE A PEEK!!
RUMBLE RUMBLE RUMBLE RUMBLE RUMBLE RUMBLE RUMBLE RUMBLE RUMBLE
300ℓ LEFT
YOU WANT TO PORE ALL OVER THE JUICY STUFF INSIDE!!

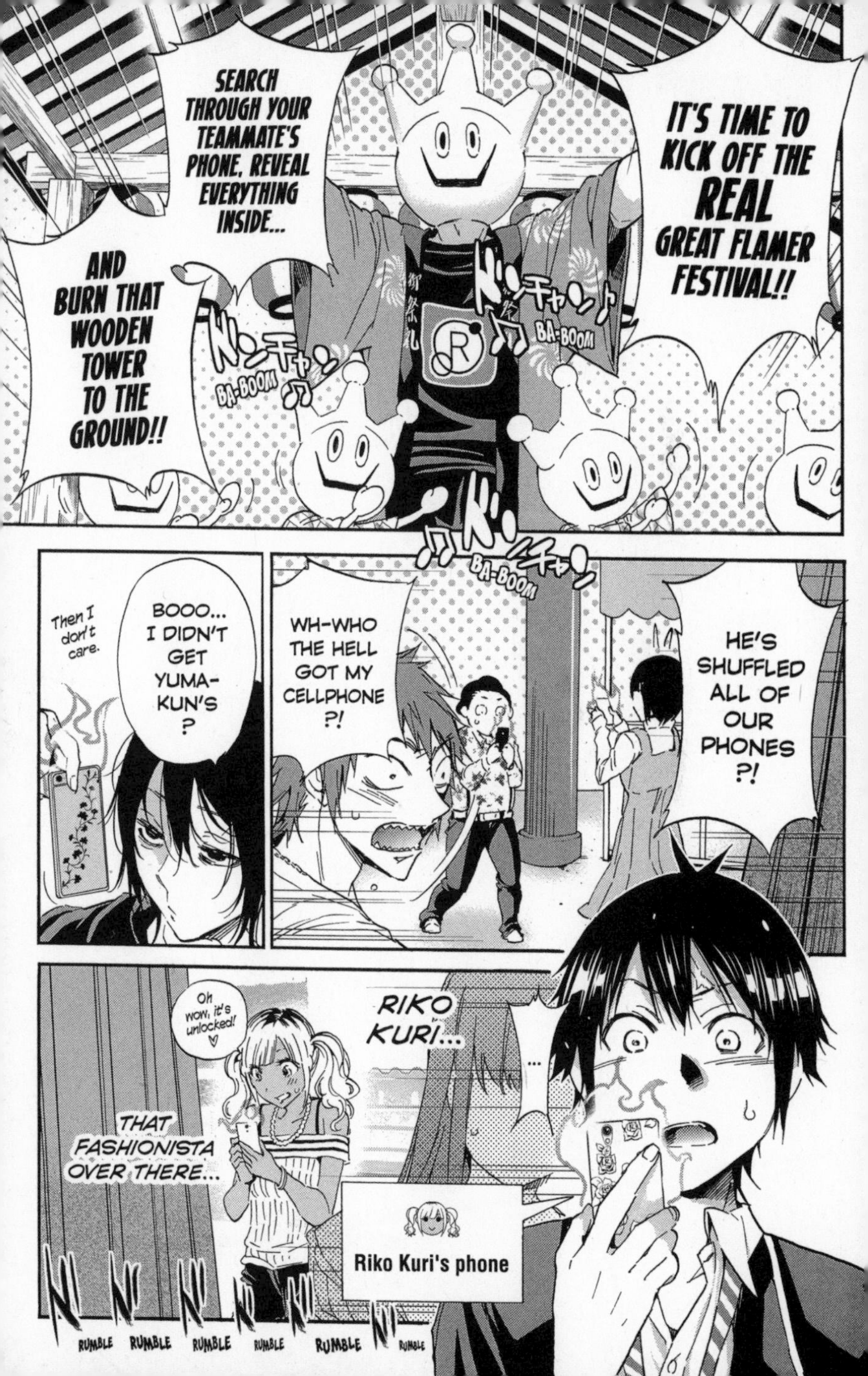
IT'S TIME TO KICK OFF THE REAL GREAT FLAMER FESTIVAL!!
SEARCH THROUGH YOUR TEAMMATE'S PHONE, REVEAL EVERYTHING INSIDE...
AND BURN THAT WOODEN TOWER TO THE GROUND!!
BA-BOOM
BA-BOOM
BA-BOOM
HE'S SHUFFLED ALL OF OUR PHONES?!
WH-WHO THE HELL GOT MY CELLPHONE?!
BOOO... I DIDN'T GET YUMA-KUN'S?
Then I don't care.
RIKO KURI...
...
Riko Kuri's phone
THAT FASHIONISTA OVER THERE...
Oh wow, it's unlocked! ♥
RUMBLE RUMBLE RUMBLE RUMBLE RUMBLE RUMBLE

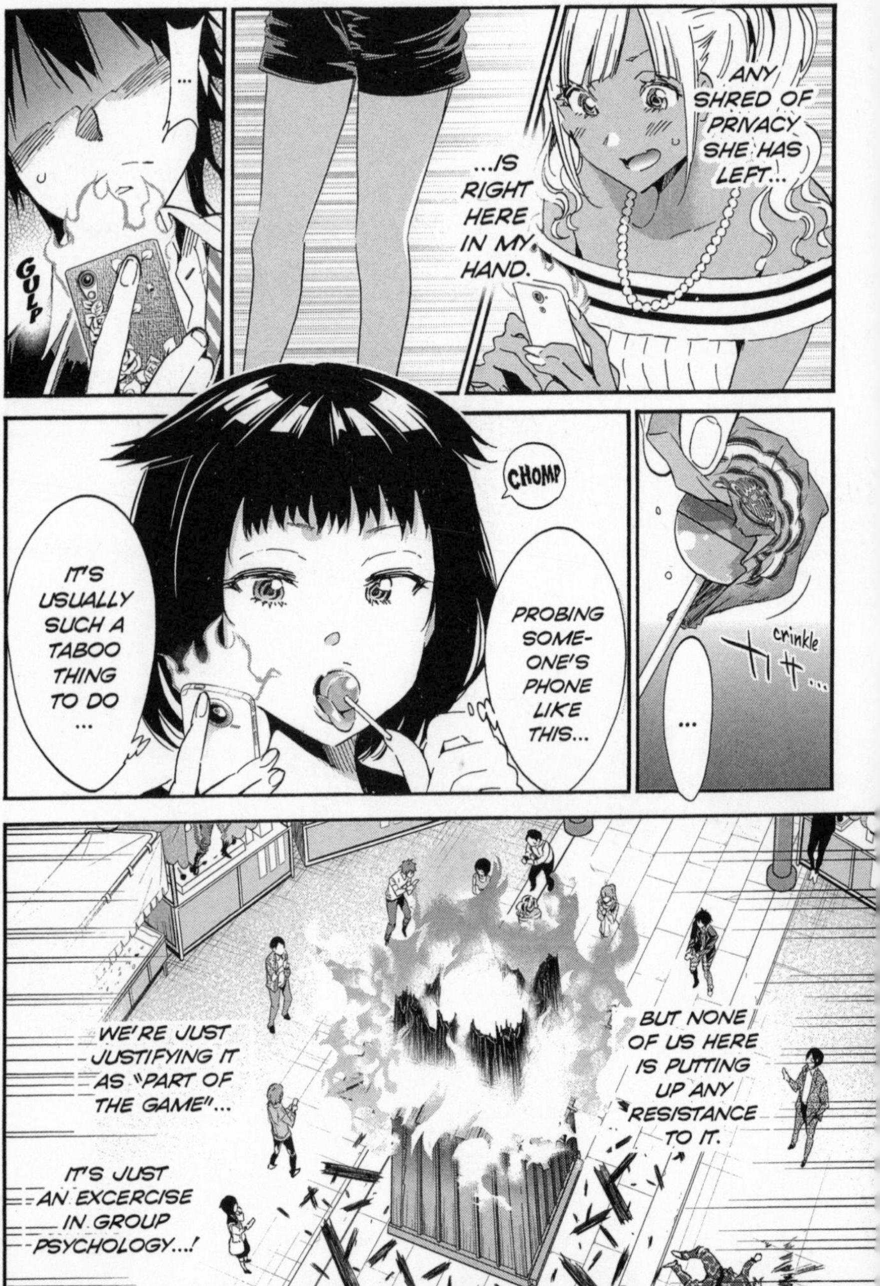

ANY SHRED OF PRIVACY SHE HAS LEFT...
...IS RIGHT HERE IN MY HAND.
...
GULP
crinkle
...
CHOMP
PROBING SOMEONE'S PHONE LIKE THIS...
IT'S USUALLY SUCH A TABOO THING TO DO...
BUT NONE OF US HERE IS PUTTING UP ANY RESISTANCE TO IT.
WE'RE JUST JUSTIFYING IT AS "PART OF THE GAME"...
IT'S JUST AN EXCERCISE IN GROUP PSYCHOLOGY...!

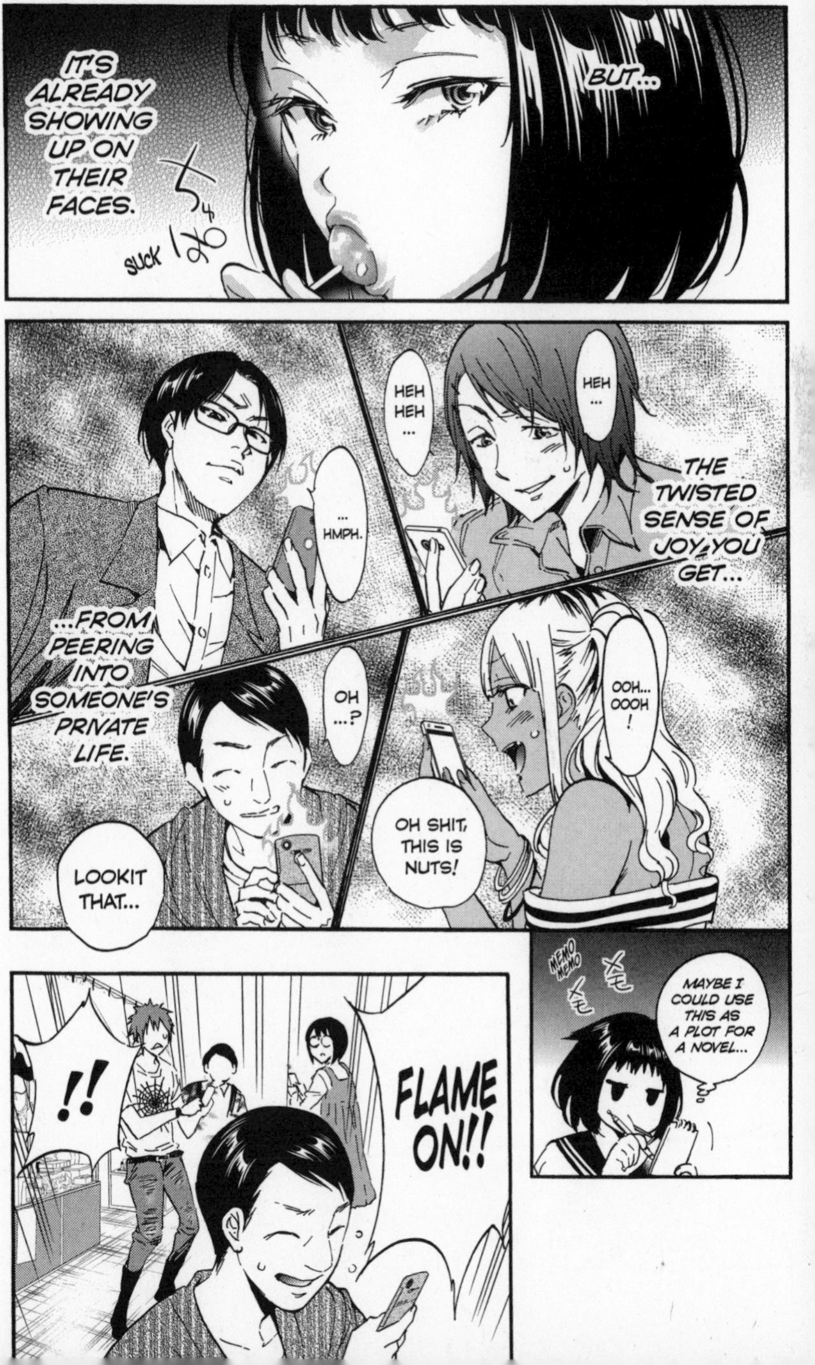
BUT...
IT'S ALREADY SHOWING UP ON THEIR FACES.
SUCK
HEH ...
HEH HEH ...
THE TWISTED SENSE OF JOY YOU GET...
... HMPH.
OOH... OOOH !
OH SHIT, THIS IS NUTS!
OH ...?
...FROM PEERING INTO SOMEONE'S PRIVATE LIFE.
LOOKIT THAT...
MEMO MEMO
MAYBE I COULD USE THIS AS A PLOT FOR A NOVEL...
FLAME ON!!
!!

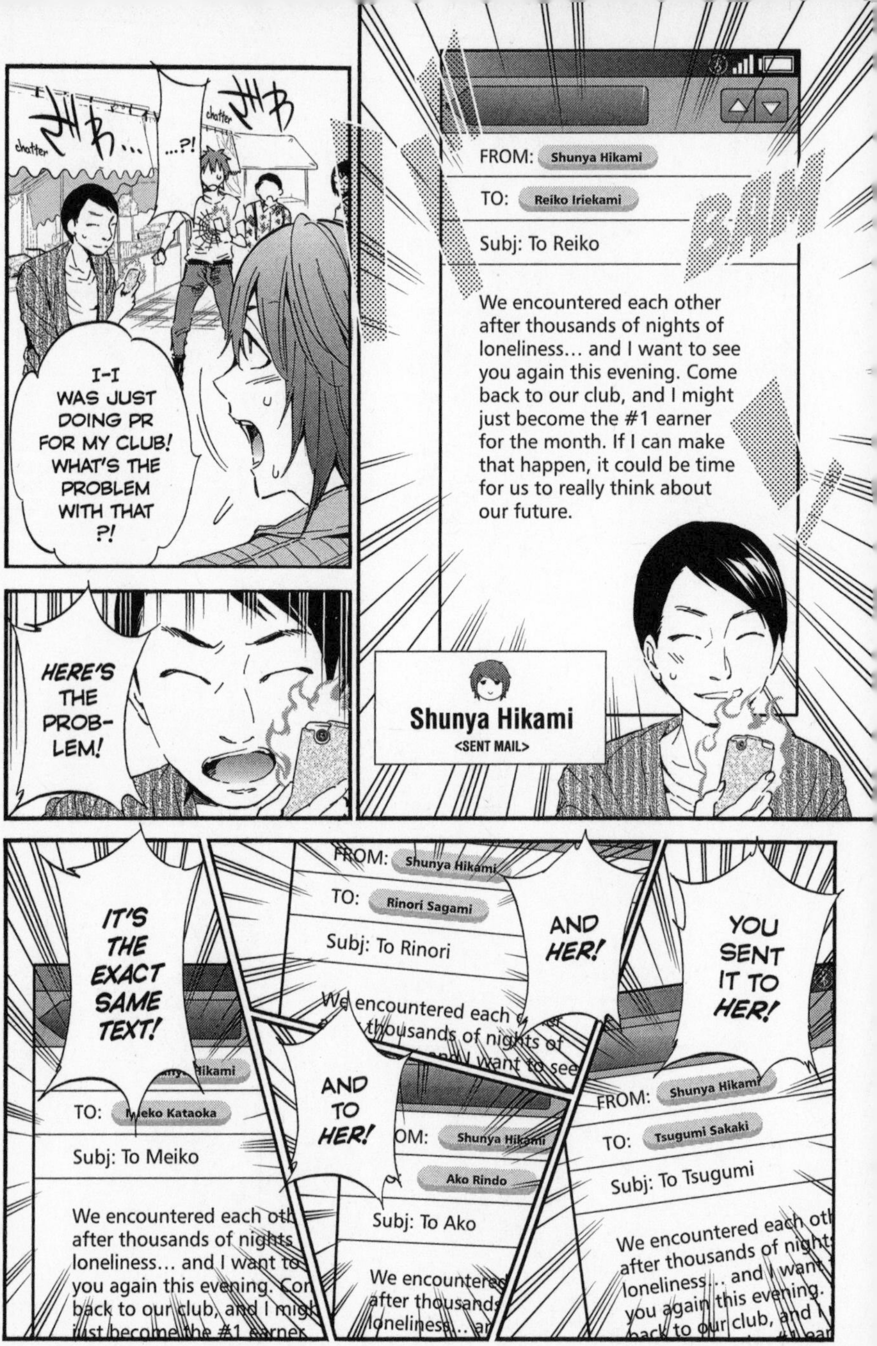
FROM: Shunya Hikami
TO: Reiko Iriekami
Subj: To Reiko
We encountered each other after thousands of nights of loneliness… and I want to see you again this evening. Come back to our club, and I might just become the #1 earner for the month. If I can make that happen, it could be time for us to really think about our future.
BAM
Shunya Hikami
<SENT MAIL>
chatter
chatter
…?!
I-I WAS JUST DOING PR FOR MY CLUB! WHAT'S THE PROBLEM WITH THAT ?!
HERE'S THE PROB-LEM!
YOU SENT IT TO HER!
FROM: Shunya Hikami
TO: Tsugumi Sakaki
Subj: To Tsugumi
AND HER!
FROM: Shunya Hikami
TO: Rinori Sagami
Subj: To Rinori
AND TO HER!
Shunya Hikami
Ako Rindo
Subj: To Ako
IT'S THE EXACT SAME TEXT!
TO: Meiko Kataoka
Subj: To Meiko

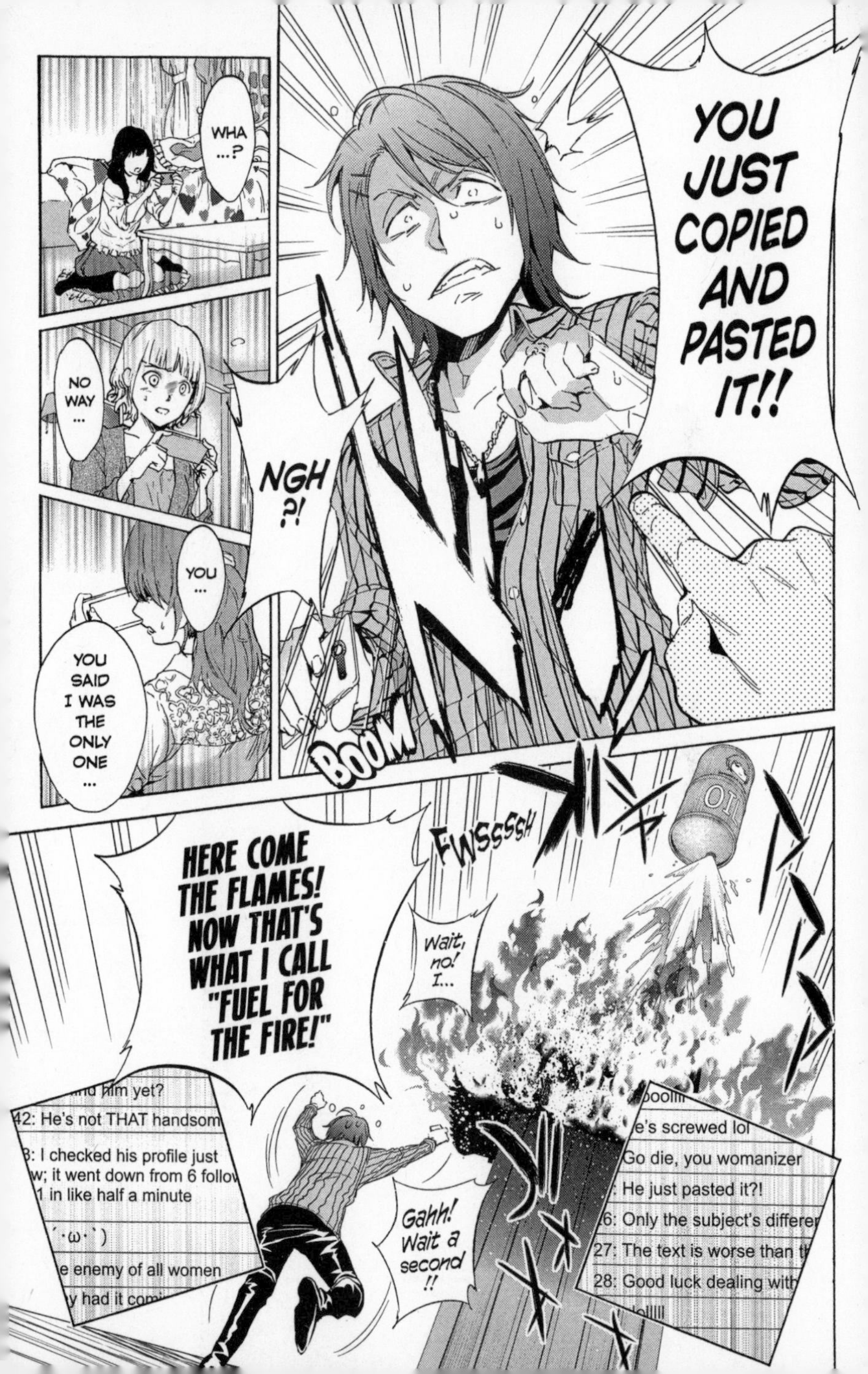
YOU JUST COPIED AND PASTED IT!!
NGH ?!
BOOM
WHA ...?
NO WAY ...
YOU ...
YOU SAID I WAS THE ONLY ONE ...
FWSSSSH
Wait, no! I...
HERE COME THE FLAMES! NOW THAT'S WHAT I CALL "FUEL FOR THE FIRE!"
Gahh! Wait a second !!
e's screwed lol
Go die, you womanizer
: He just pasted it?!
6: Only the subject's differen
27: The text is worse than t
28: Good luck dealing with
lollll
nd him yet?
42: He's not THAT handsom
3: I checked his profile just
w; it went down from 6 follow
1 in like half a minute
(´･ω･`)
e enemy of all women
y had it comi

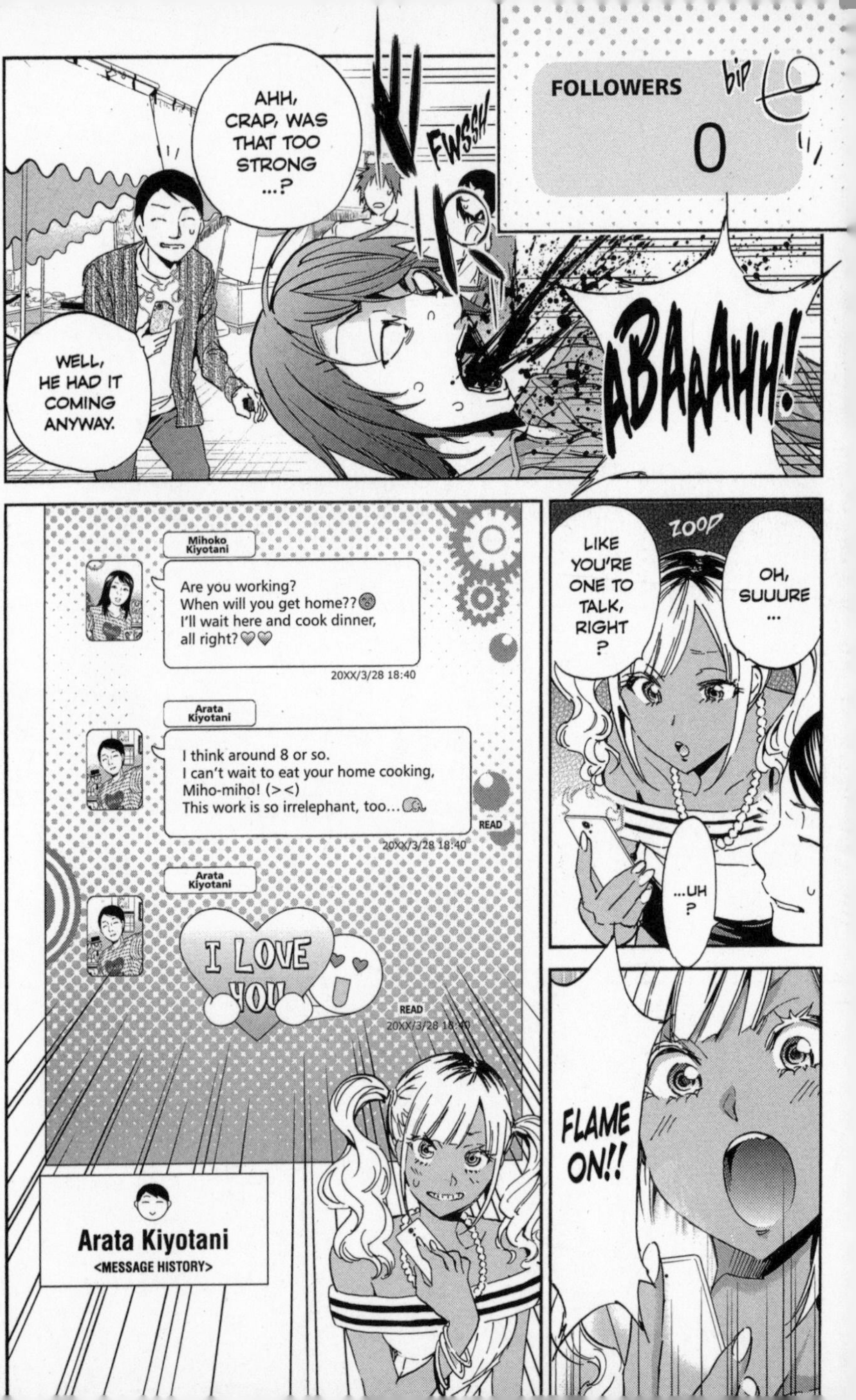
FOLLOWERS
bip
0
ABAAAHH!
FWSSH
AHH, CRAP, WAS THAT TOO STRONG ...?
WELL, HE HAD IT COMING ANYWAY.
ZOOP
OH, SUUURE ...
LIKE YOU'RE ONE TO TALK, RIGHT?
...UH?
FLAME ON!!
Mihoko Kiyotani
Are you working?
When will you get home??
I'll wait here and cook dinner, all right?
20XX/3/28 18:40
Arata Kiyotani
I think around 8 or so.
I can't wait to eat your home cooking, Miho-miho! (><)
This work is so irrelephant, too...
READ
20XX/3/28 18:40
Arata Kiyotani
I LOVE YOU
READ
Arata Kiyotani
<MESSAGE HISTORY>

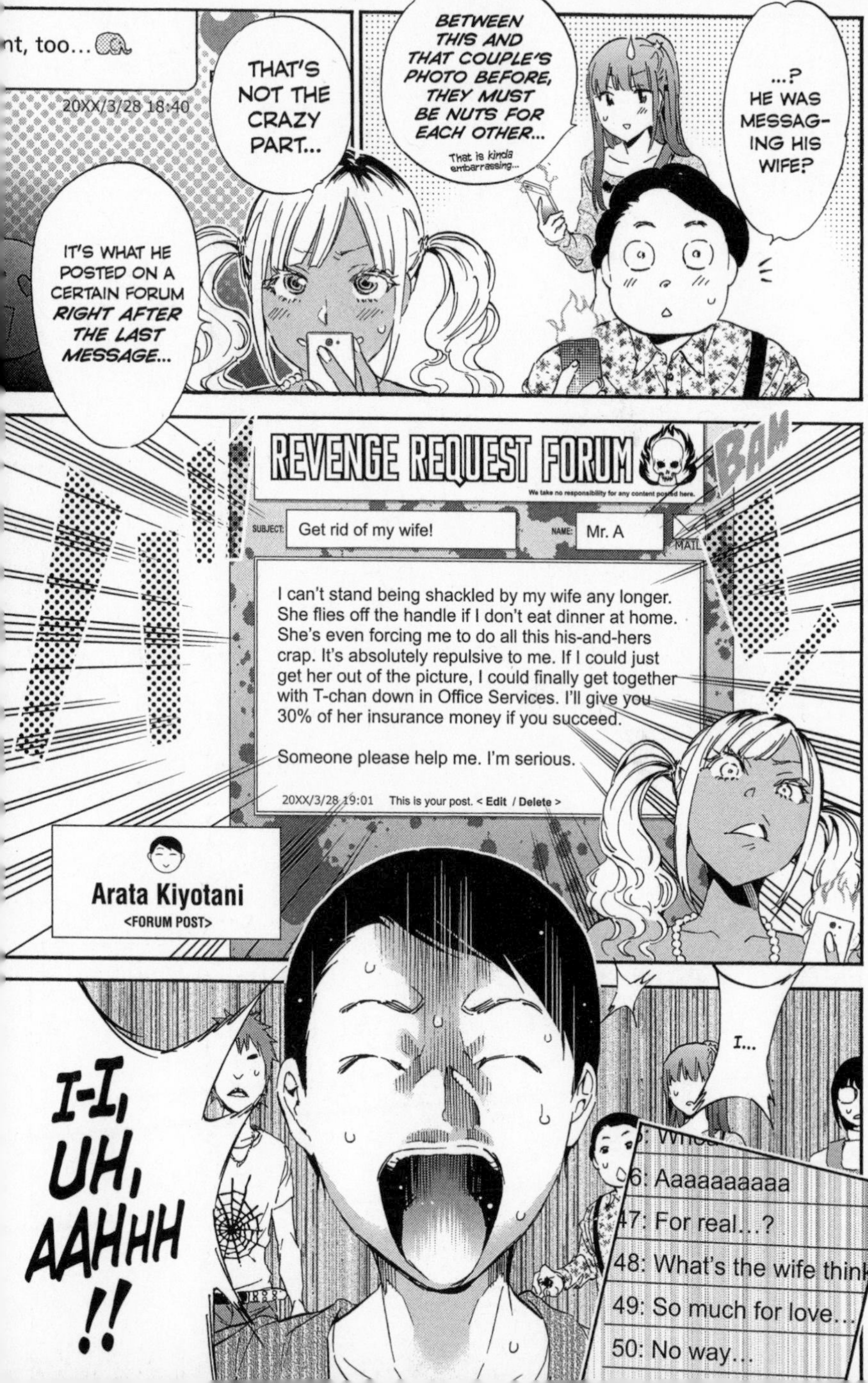
...? HE WAS MESSAGING HIS WIFE?
BETWEEN THIS AND THAT COUPLE'S PHOTO BEFORE, THEY MUST BE NUTS FOR EACH OTHER...
That is kinda embarrassing...
nt, too...
20XX/3/28 18:40
THAT'S NOT THE CRAZY PART...
IT'S WHAT HE POSTED ON A CERTAIN FORUM RIGHT AFTER THE LAST MESSAGE...
BAM
REVENGE REQUEST FORUM
We take no responsibility for any content posted here.
SUBJECT: Get rid of my wife!
NAME: Mr. A
MAIL
I can't stand being shackled by my wife any longer. She flies off the handle if I don't eat dinner at home. She's even forcing me to do all this his-and-hers crap. It's absolutely repulsive to me. If I could just get her out of the picture, I could finally get together with T-chan down in Office Services. I'll give you 30% of her insurance money if you succeed.
Someone please help me. I'm serious.
20XX/3/28 19:01 This is your post. < Edit / Delete >
Arata Kiyotani
<FORUM POST>
I...
6: Aaaaaaaaaa
47: For real...?
48: What's the wife think
49: So much for love...
50: No way...
I-I, UH, AAHHH!!

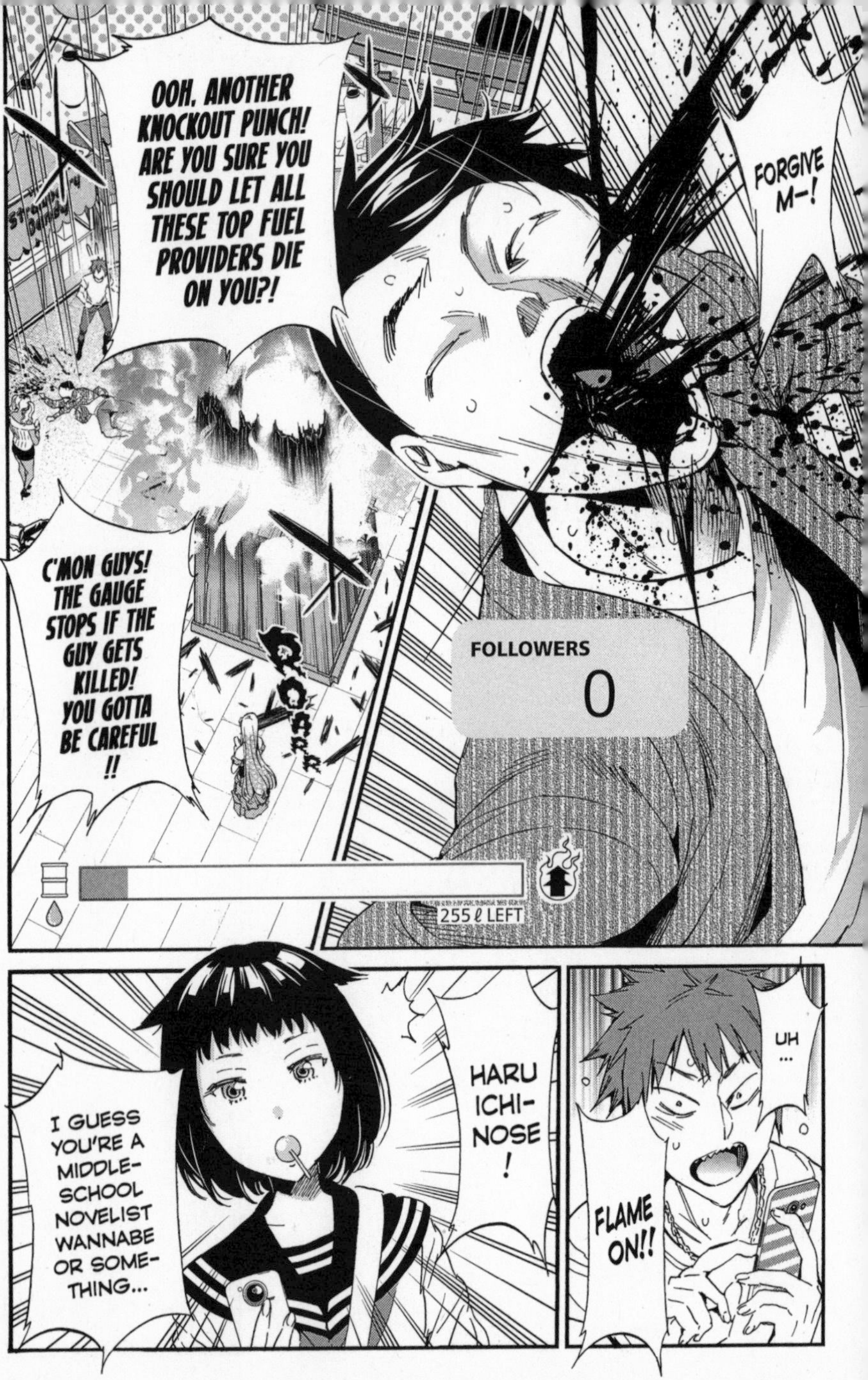
FORGIVE M—!
OOH, ANOTHER KNOCKOUT PUNCH! ARE YOU SURE YOU SHOULD LET ALL THESE TOP FUEL PROVIDERS DIE ON YOU?!
C'MON GUYS! THE GAUGE STOPS IF THE GUY GETS KILLED! YOU GOTTA BE CAREFUL!!
ROARR
FOLLOWERS
0
255 ℓ LEFT
UH ...
FLAME ON!!
HARU ICHINOSE!
I GUESS YOU'RE A MIDDLE-SCHOOL NOVELIST WANNABE OR SOME-THING...

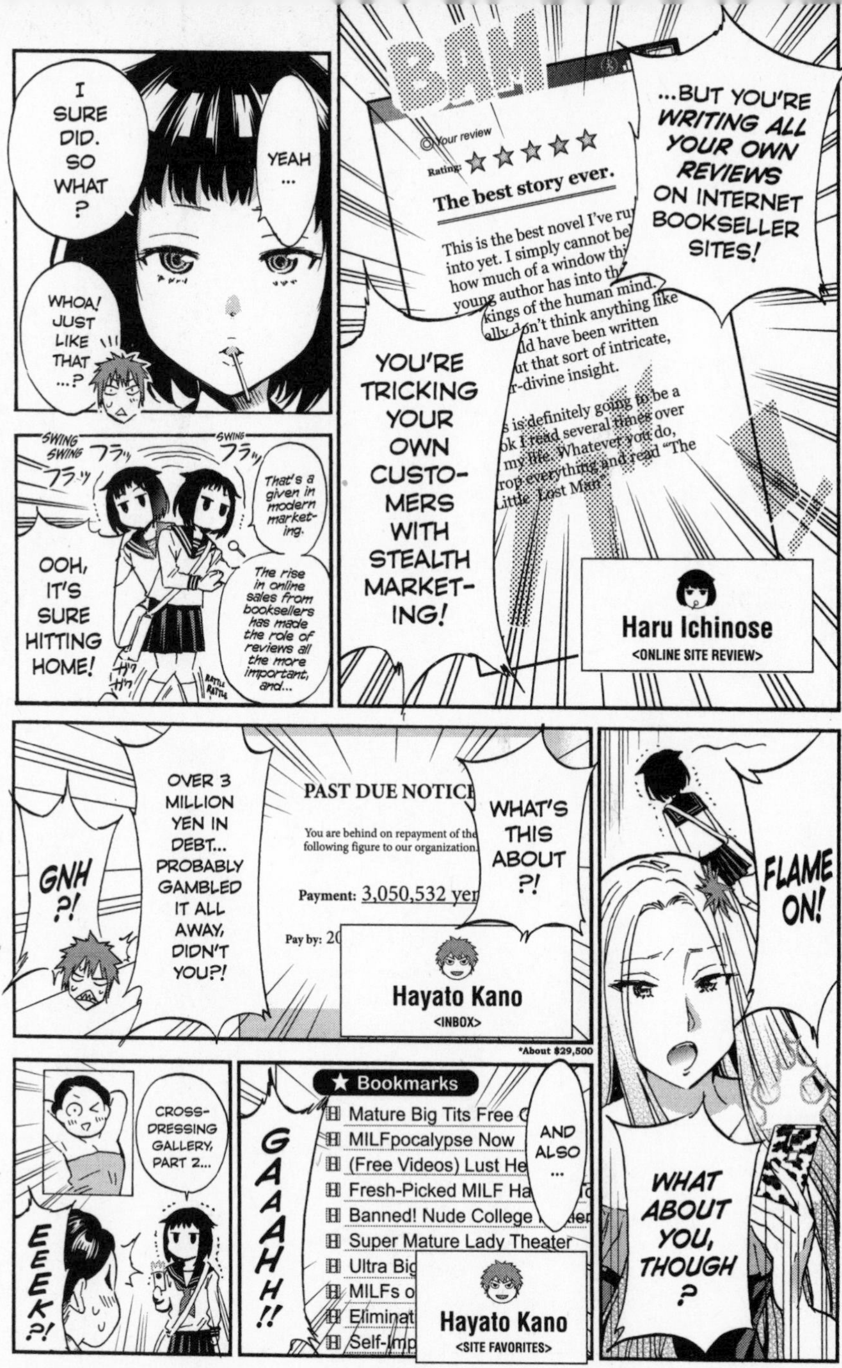
BAM
Your review
Rating:
The best story ever.
This is the best novel I've ru
into yet. I simply cannot be
how much of a window thi
young author has into th
kings of the human mind.
ally don't think anything like
ld have been written
ut that sort of intricate,
r-divine insight.
s is definitely going to be a
ok I read several times over
my life. Whatever you do,
rop everything and read "The
Little Lost Man"
...BUT YOU'RE WRITING ALL YOUR OWN REVIEWS ON INTERNET BOOKSELLER SITES!
YOU'RE TRICKING YOUR OWN CUSTOMERS WITH STEALTH MARKETING!
Haru Ichinose
<ONLINE SITE REVIEW>
YEAH...
I SURE DID. SO WHAT?
WHOA! JUST LIKE THAT...?
SWING SWING
SWING
That's a given in modern marketing.
The rise in online sales from booksellers has made the role of reviews all the more important, and...
OOH, IT'S SURE HITTING HOME!
RATTLE RATTLE
FLAME ON!
WHAT ABOUT YOU, THOUGH?
WHAT'S THIS ABOUT?!
PAST DUE NOTICE
You are behind on repayment of the following figure to our organization.
Payment: 3,050,532 yen
Pay by: 20
Hayato Kano
<INBOX>
OVER 3 MILLION YEN IN DEBT... PROBABLY GAMBLED IT ALL AWAY, DIDN'T YOU?!
GNH?!
*About $29,500
AND ALSO...
Bookmarks
Mature Big Tits Free
MILFpocalypse Now
(Free Videos) Lust He
Fresh-Picked MILF Ha
Banned! Nude College
Super Mature Lady Theater
Ultra Big
MILFs o
Eliminat
Self-Imp
Hayato Kano
<SITE FAVORITES>
GAAAHH!!
CROSS-DRESSING GALLERY, PART 2...
EEEK?!

NOW THINGS ARE GETTING EXCITING!

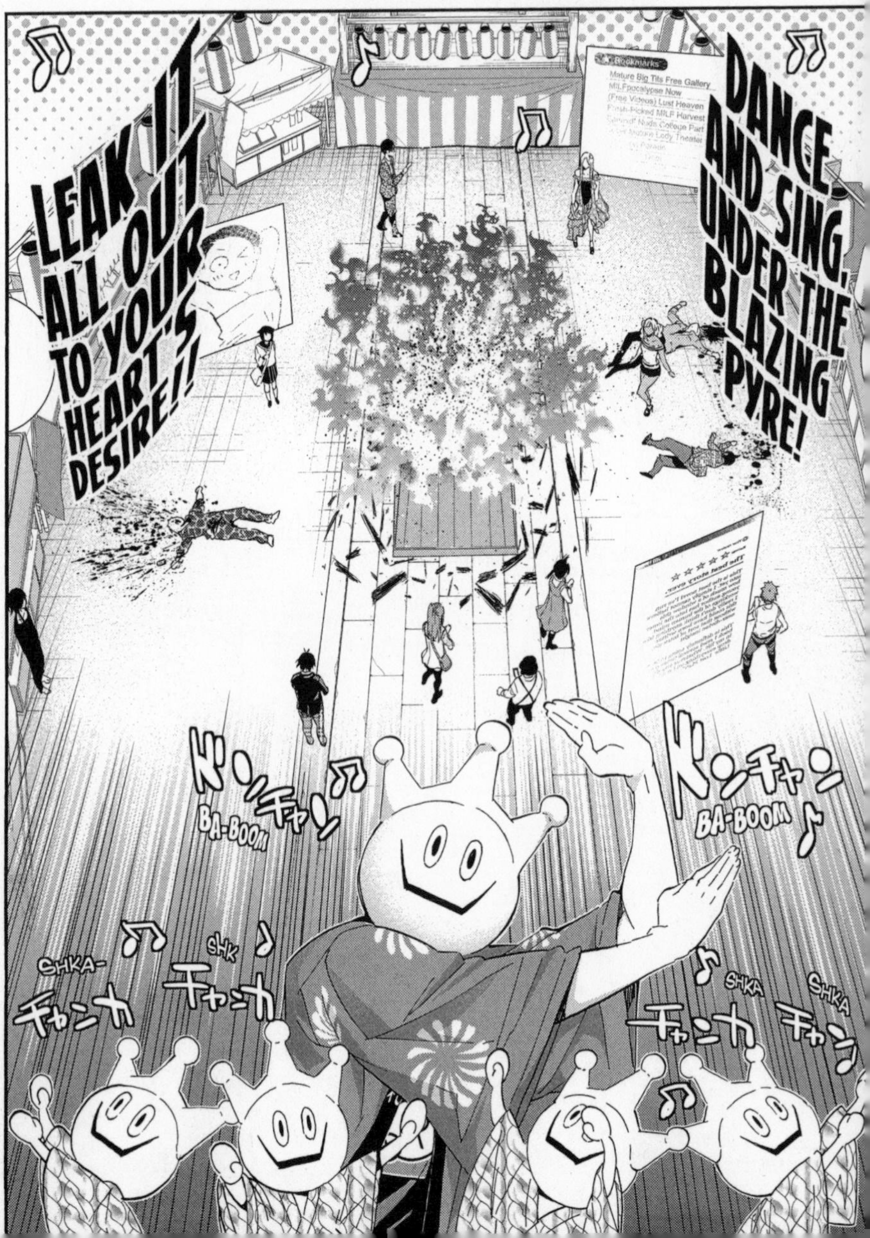
DANCE AND SING UNDER THE BLAZING PYRE!
Bookmarks
Mature Big Tits Free Gallery
MILFpocalypse Now
(Free Videos) Lust Heaven
Fresh-Picked MILF Harvest
LEAK IT ALL OUT TO YOUR HEART'S DESIRE!!
ドンチャン BA-BOOM
ドンチャン BA-BOOM
チャンカ SHKA
チャン SHKA
チャンカ SHK
チャンカ SHKA-

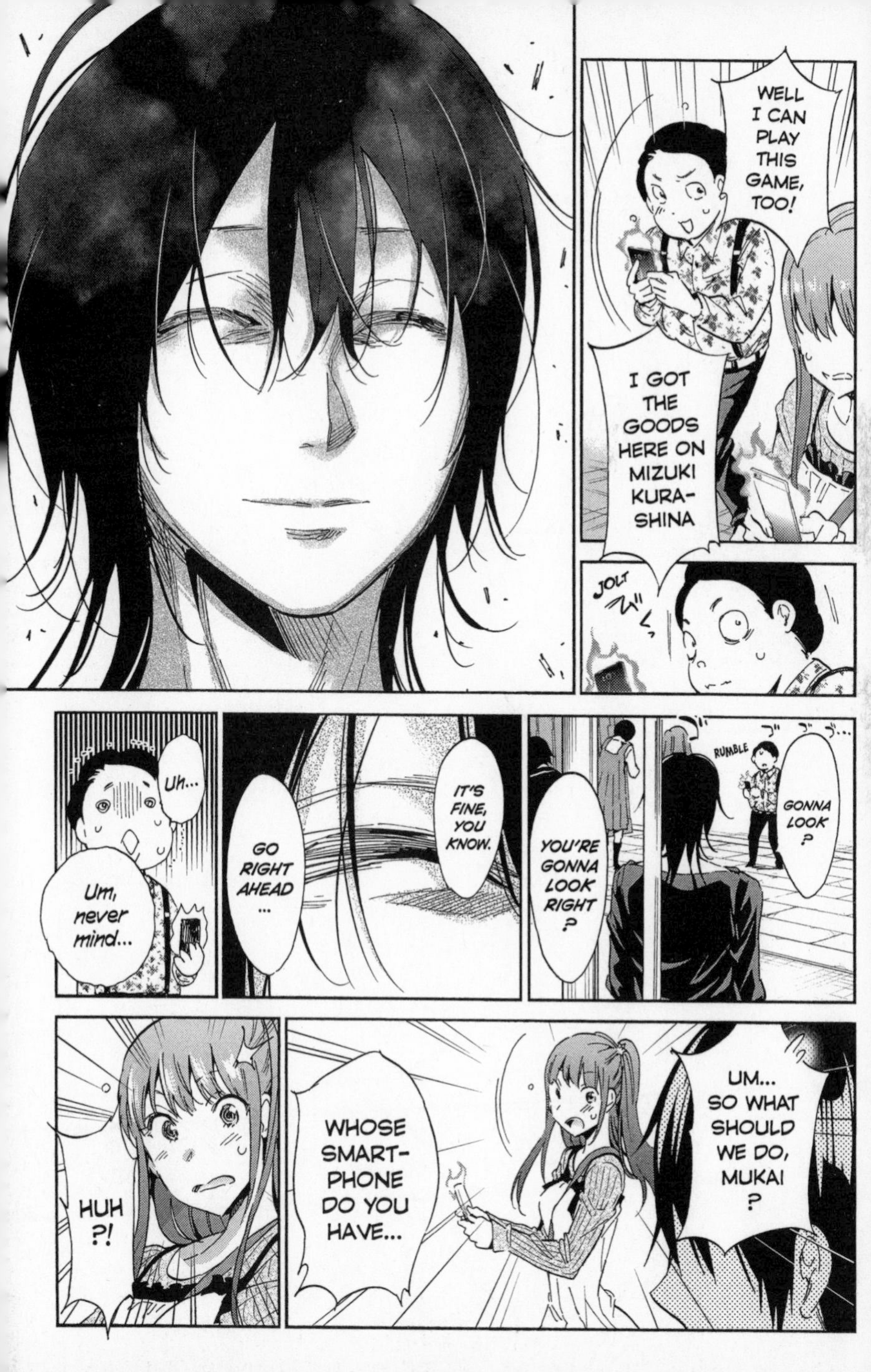
WELL I CAN PLAY THIS GAME, TOO!
I GOT THE GOODS HERE ON MIZUKI KURA-SHINA
JOLT
GONNA LOOK?
RUMBLE
YOU'RE GONNA LOOK RIGHT?
IT'S FINE, YOU KNOW.
GO RIGHT AHEAD...
Uh...
Um, never mind...
UM... SO WHAT SHOULD WE DO, MUKAI?
WHOSE SMART-PHONE DO YOU HAVE...
HUH?!

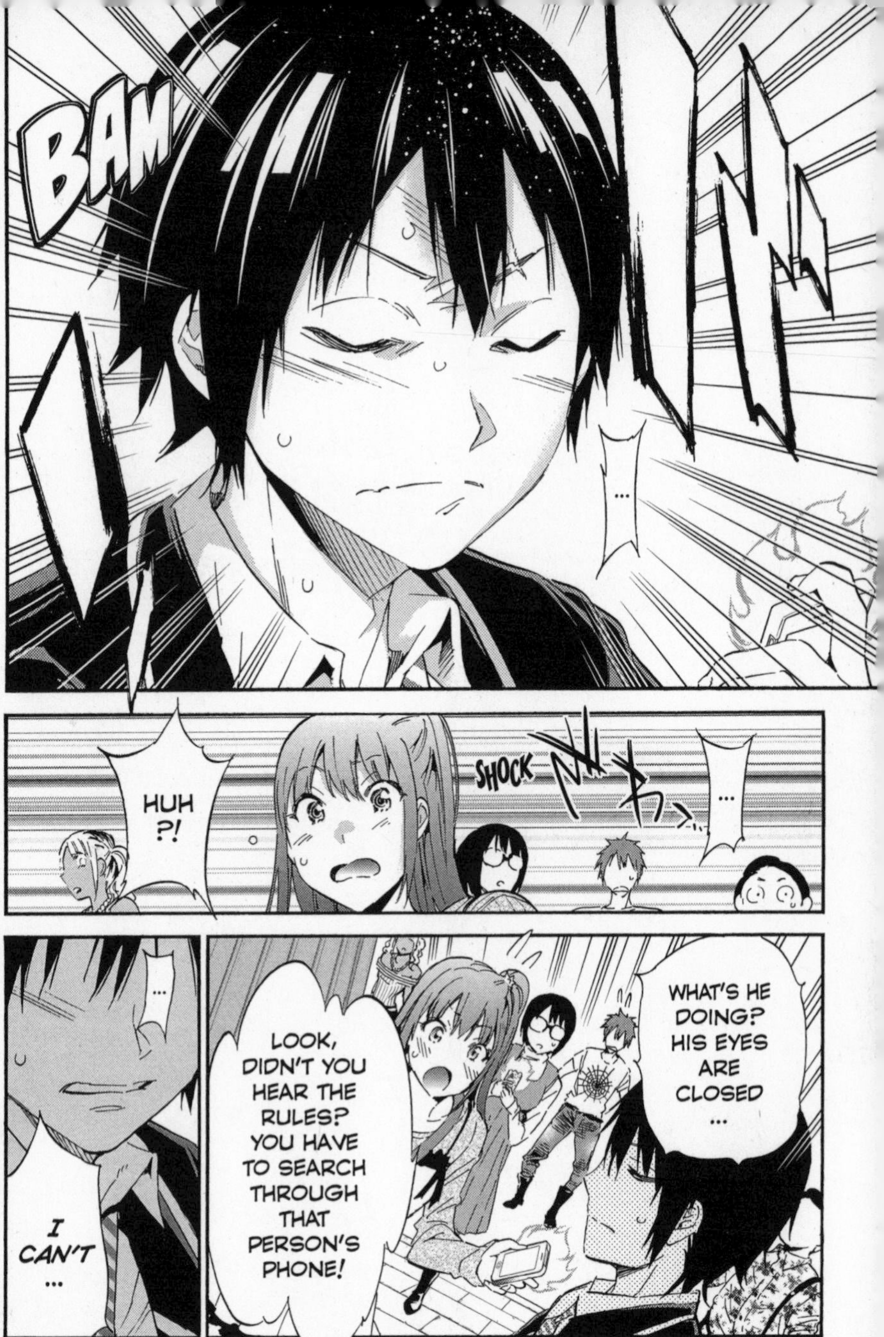
...
BAM
...
SHOCK
HUH ?!
WHAT'S HE DOING? HIS EYES ARE CLOSED ...
LOOK, DIDN'T YOU HEAR THE RULES? YOU HAVE TO SEARCH THROUGH THAT PERSON'S PHONE!
...
I CAN'T ...

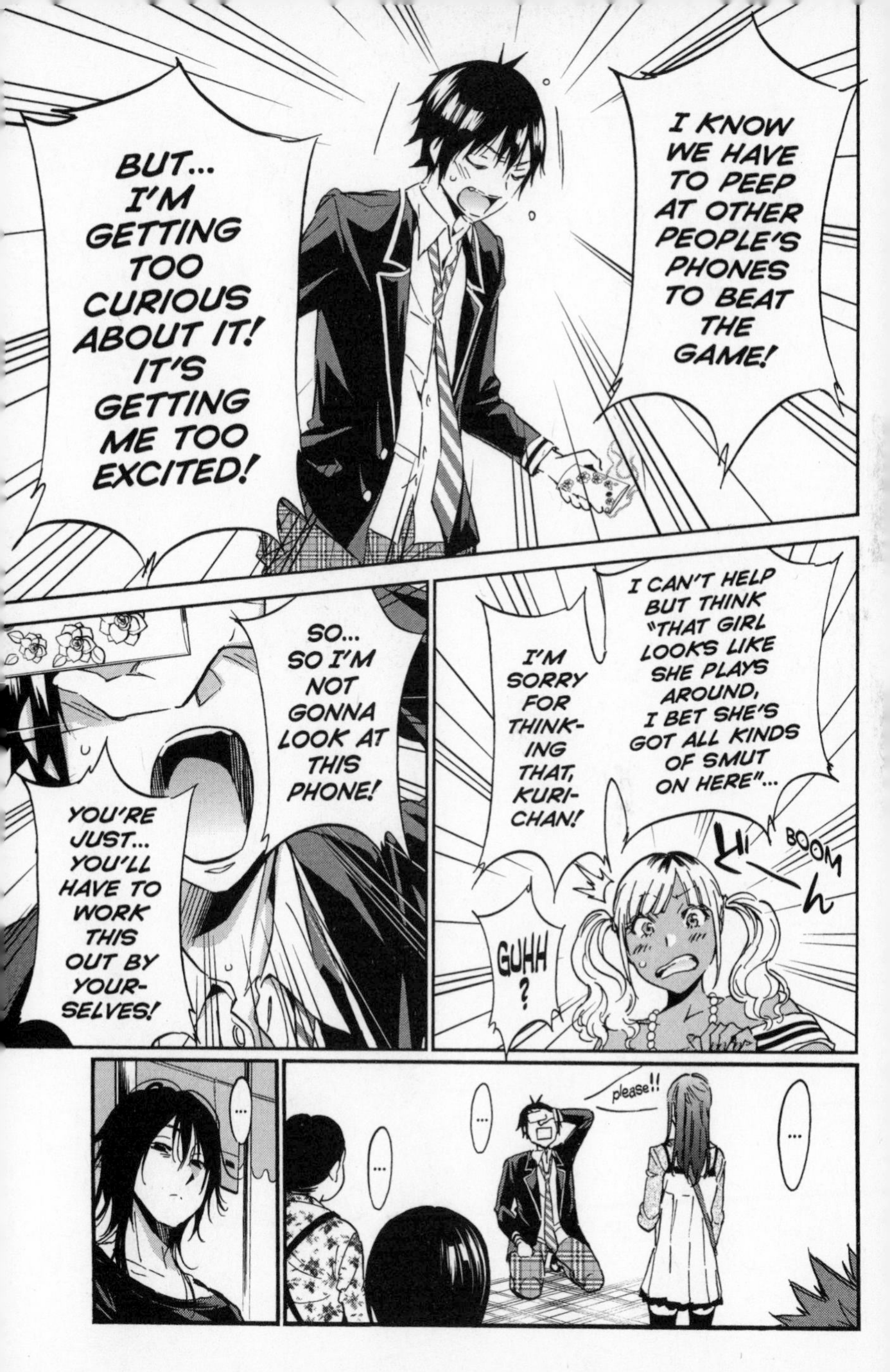
I KNOW WE HAVE TO PEEP AT OTHER PEOPLE'S PHONES TO BEAT THE GAME!
BUT... I'M GETTING TOO CURIOUS ABOUT IT! IT'S GETTING ME TOO EXCITED!
I CAN'T HELP BUT THINK "THAT GIRL LOOKS LIKE SHE PLAYS AROUND, I BET SHE'S GOT ALL KINDS OF SMUT ON HERE"...
I'M SORRY FOR THINKING THAT, KURI-CHAN!
BOOM
GUHH?
SO... SO I'M NOT GONNA LOOK AT THIS PHONE!
YOU'RE JUST... YOU'LL HAVE TO WORK THIS OUT BY YOUR-SELVES!
...
please!!
...
...
...

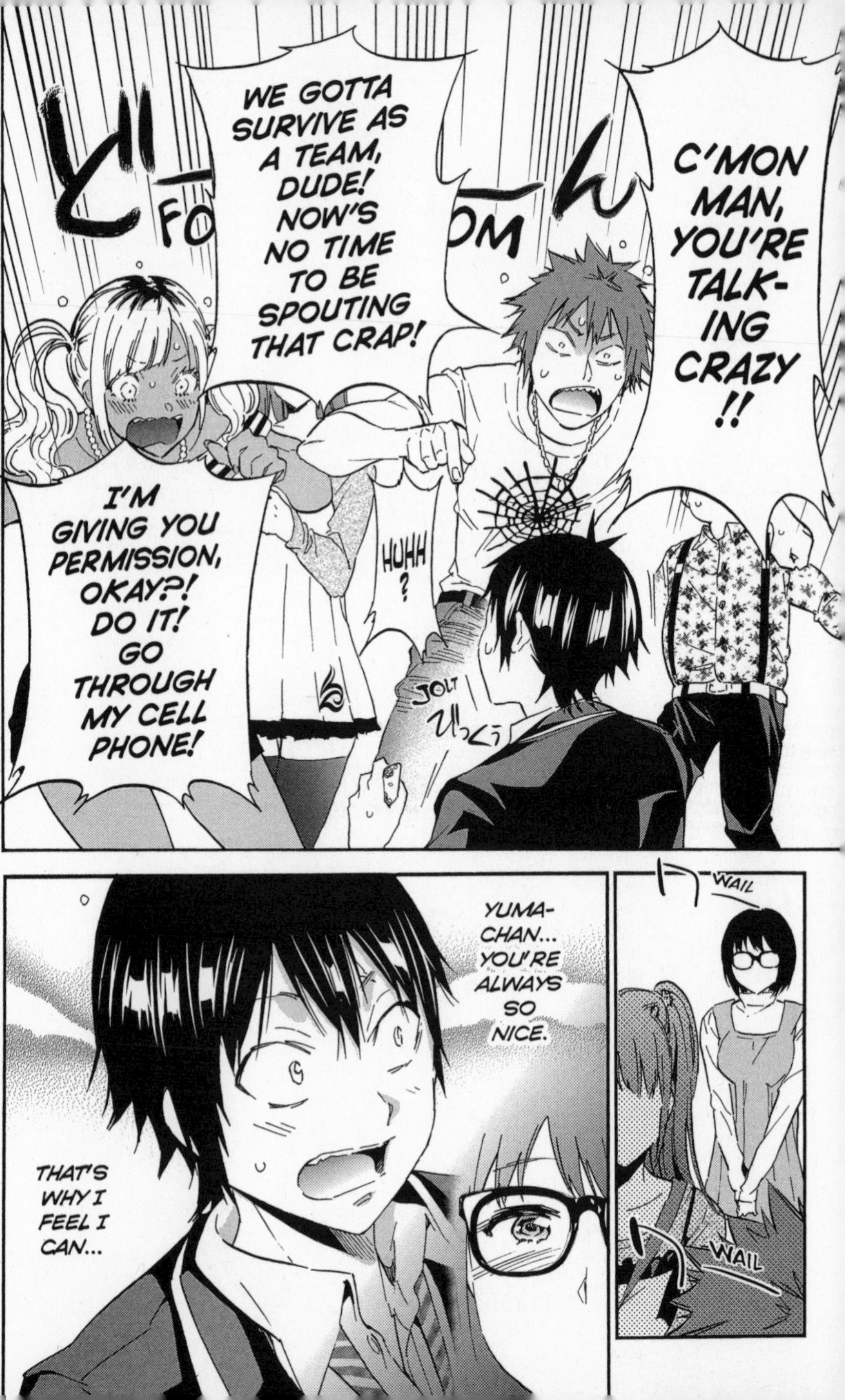
C'MON MAN, YOU'RE TALK-ING CRAZY!!
WE GOTTA SURVIVE AS A TEAM, DUDE! NOW'S NO TIME TO BE SPOUTING THAT CRAP!
HUHH?
I'M GIVING YOU PERMISSION, OKAY?! DO IT! GO THROUGH MY CELL PHONE!
JOLT
WAIL
WAIL
YUMA-CHAN... YOU'RE ALWAYS SO NICE.
THAT'S WHY I FEEL I CAN...

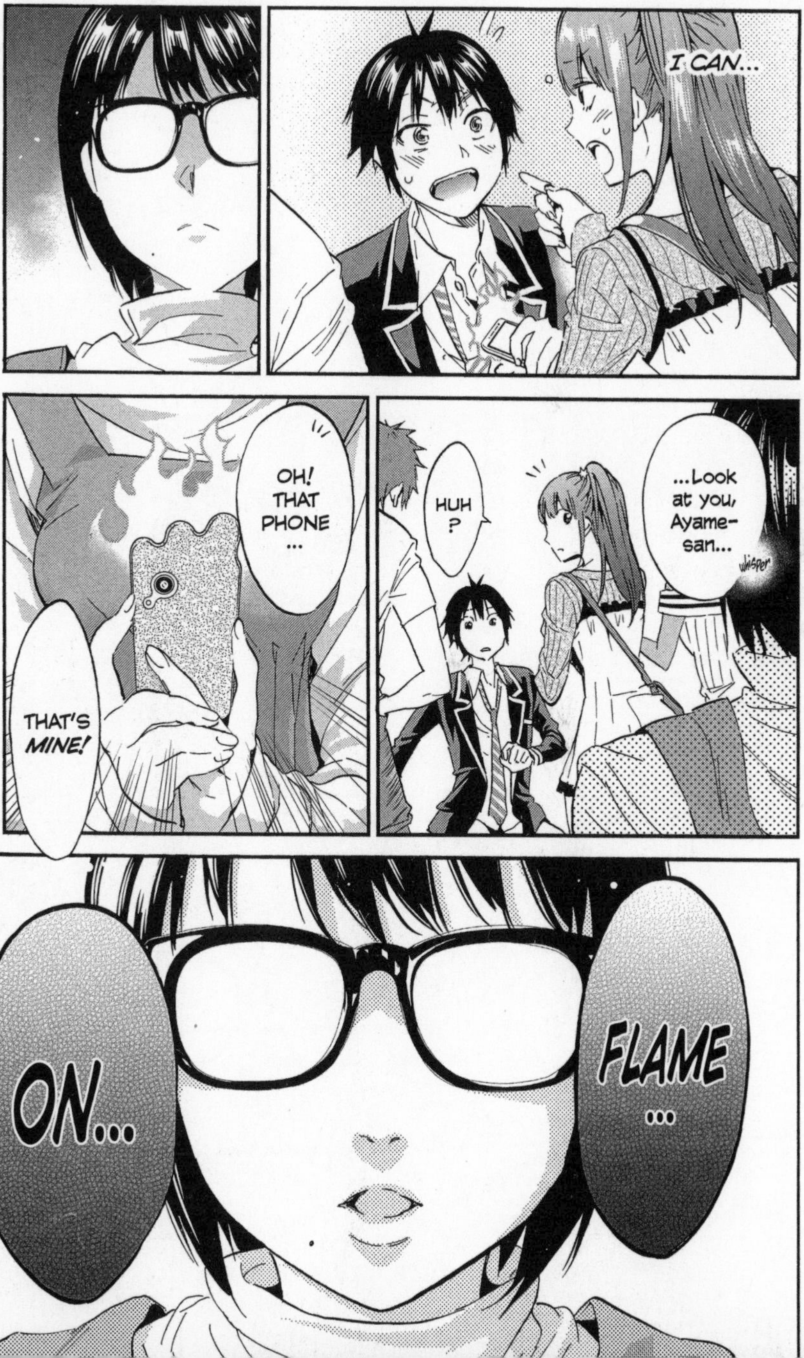

I CAN...
...Look at you, Ayame-san...
whisper
HUH?
OH! THAT PHONE...
THAT'S *MINE!*
FLAME...
ON...

【POISON MOSS CULTIVATION RECORD】

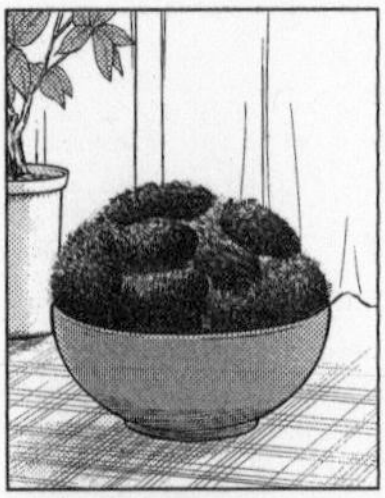

↑ Red soresin moss cultivation in progress. It's so cute, you wouldn't believe there was a lethal poison inside! ♡

I obtained a supply of ***red soresin moss*** from an overseas website. Given that cultivating plants is kind of my hobby, I use this site all the time, so nobody in my family suspects a thing (grin). Mixing this moss with camellia oil in a certain ratio creates a ***lethal poison*** that creates symptoms of dehydration...! It looks almost exactly like food poisoning, and it can't be detected by scientific testing (at least, that's what the net says). One miscalculation, though: there isn't anywhere near enough moss! I am such an idiot... If I keep on ordering more, both my family and the supplier might start suspecting me. I'll have to raise this moss to create more of it. I've done it before. It should be a piece of cake.

*** It's been a month. Things aren't going well. The heat's making the red soresin moss ***start to die out!*** I was so focused on tailing my targets that I stopped paying much attention to it... I quickly moved it under the AC vent, but it'll dry up really quickly under there, so I have to water it over twice as much as usual...

*** My red soresin moss has finally recovered; there's about as much as what I first ordered. If this keeps up, I should have enough by October to make the quantity of extract I need. Just one step away!!

*** It's mission complete for my moss cultivation. With all the work I put into it, I'm sure it's feeling my tender, loving care by now... although given that I'm raising this in order to poison three people, I'm not sure it's the healthiest thing for it. Still cute, though. I'll keep an eye on its progress for a little longer.

Why do people hurt each other?
Why can't we all live with mutual respect for each other, the way that plants do?

MURDER!!!

ANYONE WHO LAYS EYES ON THIS BESIDES ME SHOULD BE PREPARED FOR A QUICK, INEVITABLE DEATH!

【NOTES】

I don't want to hear "goodbye".
I want to hear "see you later".
My tears never dry up, after

SEPTEMBER 8
Something about this operation plan feels so calming to me as I write it. It's a secret belonging to me, and me alone, in the palm of my hand. Whenever I sit back and think to myself "I swear I'll kill all of them!", it's like an enormous weight just floats away, right off of my heart. I know I shouldn't whine too much, but [...] I guess I'm a prett awful girl... know I'm a little too dark a lot of the time for most people. But if I can't keep myself that way, I feel like I'm going to [...] Yeah, you see? I'm not dark at all (late night revelation) ...Let's go to sleep.

SEPTEMBER 14
Sigh... I'm tired of tailing them. (What a way to start this entry, huh?) I'm starting to get the feeling that someone's been repositioning my smartphone on my desk. I take my hands off it and [...] Did my big brother see this file? I mean, I have a password lock on this phone, of course, but [...] If he saw this...he's going to ha me. Maybe I should change my password. Oh, but will he think I'm being weird to do that? Oh, but if he does, that means he's already seen inside. What should I do
Big brother. Big brother. Big brother. Big brother. Big brother. Big brother. Big b
Big brother. Big brother. Big brother. Big brother. Big brother.
Big brother. Big brother. Big brother. Big brother. Big brother.
Big brother. Big brother. Big brother. Big brother. Big brother.
Big brother. Big brother. Big brother. Big brother. Big brother.

Big brother: The closest thing to me, and the furthest away.

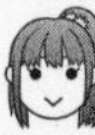

Ayami Kamijo
<MEMO FILE>

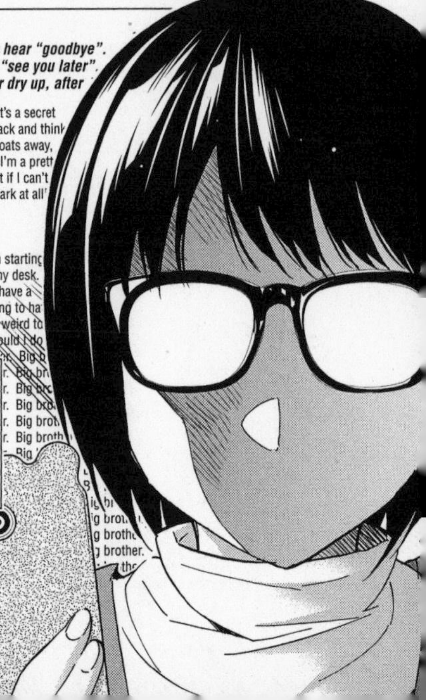

【INTRODUCTION】

This document is my plan for me, Ayame Kamijo, to exact my revenge on the three of my classmates—***Akiho Senda, Sae Hamura, and Yumika Kamada***—who ruined my life with their bullying. On the right, you see Senda sending me that "Verdict: Death" stamp—well, I'm the executioner now, bitch!!!!! (Angry beyond all belief!!!!!)

I'll make all of them pay. Thanks to them, I can no longer sleep at night, and I can't attend school any longer, either. Even now, when I close my eyes, their faces float into my mind, their eyes sneering at me. Their laughing voices. The endless torment they messaged me. There was a while when I couldn't even eat anything; I would just throw all of it back up. I remember reading somewhere that trying to get revenge wasn't a positive way to go through life. But the only thing I know is that this is absolutely necessary for me in order to make any forward progress.
This grudge of mine must be avenged!!!

Of course, I can't show this operation plan to anybody (if I did, it'd kill me!!), so this is just to keep everything ordered in my head and make sure this anger never subsides! I'm using this note-taking app and gradually adding to it over time. It'll be my new life's work, the fodder I use to sustain myself.

DEATH DEATH DEATH DEATH DEATH

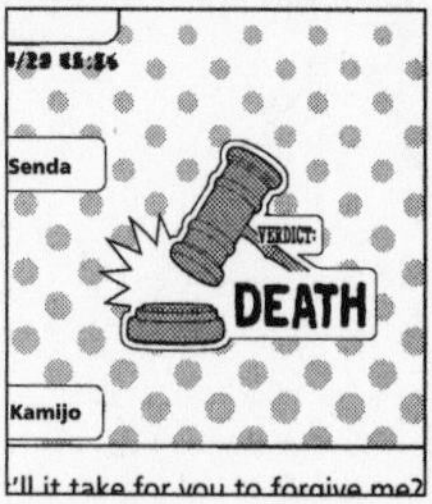
Senda
VERDICT:
DEATH
Kamijo
...'ll it take for you to forgive me?

DEATH DEATH DEATH DEATH DEATH DEATH

Closed girls' communities are a total pain in the ass. I'm never doing it again.

【CAUTIONS】

First off, for all three of them, do a thorough investigation into their movements. Since I'm not going to school, I've got plenty of time on my hands (evil grin) / Change into a new outfit every time I'm tailing them. Be careful with fingerprints and wear gloves whenever I can / I lost my target today when I had to take a bathroom break. Better keep an eye on my liquid intake / Add in more cautions as I think of them. This operation needs to be perfect.

OPERATION:

!!!WARNING!!! THIS GOES WITHOUT SAYING, BUT SINCE THIS IS SUPER A-LEVEL CLASSIFIED MATERIAL,

【MURDER METHOD→POISONING】

My existence. My brother's existence. Other people's existence. Red soresin moss's existence. What does existence really mean?

TARGETS

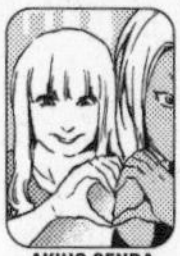

AKIHO SENDA

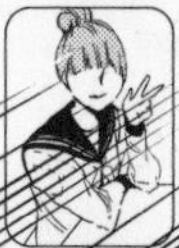

SAE HAMURA

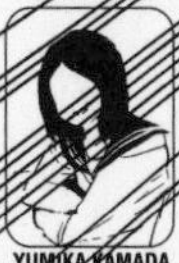

YUMIKA KAMADA

After careful scrutiny of all possible methods (having little in the way of strength, I immediately discounted anything involving a weapon), I came to the conclusion that poisoning would be ideal. For the poison, I decided to take ***an extract made from poison moss*** and make it look like a bad case of food poisoning. The raising of this moss will be covered in the "Poison Moss Cultivation Record" section.

There are two issues to tackle. First off, it'd be unnatural for all three of them to get sickened in separate incidents, so I'll need to find a situation where they're all eating or drinking at the same time and place. Second, the poison made from red soresin moss is a very dark red in color, emits a foul odor, and is bitter to the point that it numbs your tongue. I'll need to mix it with something just as bitter (something like coffee) to make sure they fully digest it.

Following dogged research, I now have a general picture of the activity patterns of all three. They drink tea together pretty often (I used to be part of that group. Now they're all just sitting there, having fun, acting sooooooooooooooooooooooo[...]oooooooo happy as if I wasn't even there in the past. They probably think of hurting me and scaring me away from school as, like, ***"Ha ha ha, oh yeah, I guess we did that, huh? That was hilarious!"*** Well, thanks a lot for instilling the urge to kill in me, you bastards!).

Anyway... Yumika takes her coffee black because she's ***soooo*** grown up, but Sae and Akiho are still little kids, so they drink all this girlish sweet stuff like macchiatos and iced frappes and so on. More to the point, I don't know how I'm going to mix poison into something prepared at the café. I can't be identifiable on the scene. What about a way to make them absorb it through the skin instead of orally? (Forget about injecting it)? That'll make it tougher to pursue the food poisoning cover, but I'm sure there are poisons that work on a time delay, so it might just work. Akiko got some moisturizing cream from her boyfriend (that fancy-ass, self-absorbed dick. I couldn't say it at the time, but I'll say it here: ***Your boyfriend is a lame-ass piece of shit!!!***).

Anyway... She rubs that cream from her boyfriend on her hands a lot, so maybe I could replace that with a little something of my own making. That won't be as effective as an oral dose, but it should probably take its toll as she rubs it on her. Sae always uses the same brand of lip balm, and Yumika's got her favorite gum, too. Gum, huh... If I gave out poisoned gum samples in disguise on the street, maybe she could get an oral dose that way... They already know my face, though, so I don't think hand anything over to them would work... I probably need to consider this a little longer. There's no need to hurry things along...

Crap. I read an article on the net that if the extract from red soresin moss is exposed to oxygen for too long, the poison effect starts to wear out... That means I'm pretty limited in my approach. It might be time to consider other types of poison. It looks like mixing two parts egg-yolk moss with eight parts of bamboo-peel moss forms a type of nerve poison. It's illegal to cultivate that in Japan and pretty much everywhere else, though, so there's no way a high-school teen like me could ever get her hands on that.

There are apparently examples of bamboo-peel moss growing on elm-tree bonsai plants if they're raised the right away. That might be another path to pursue...

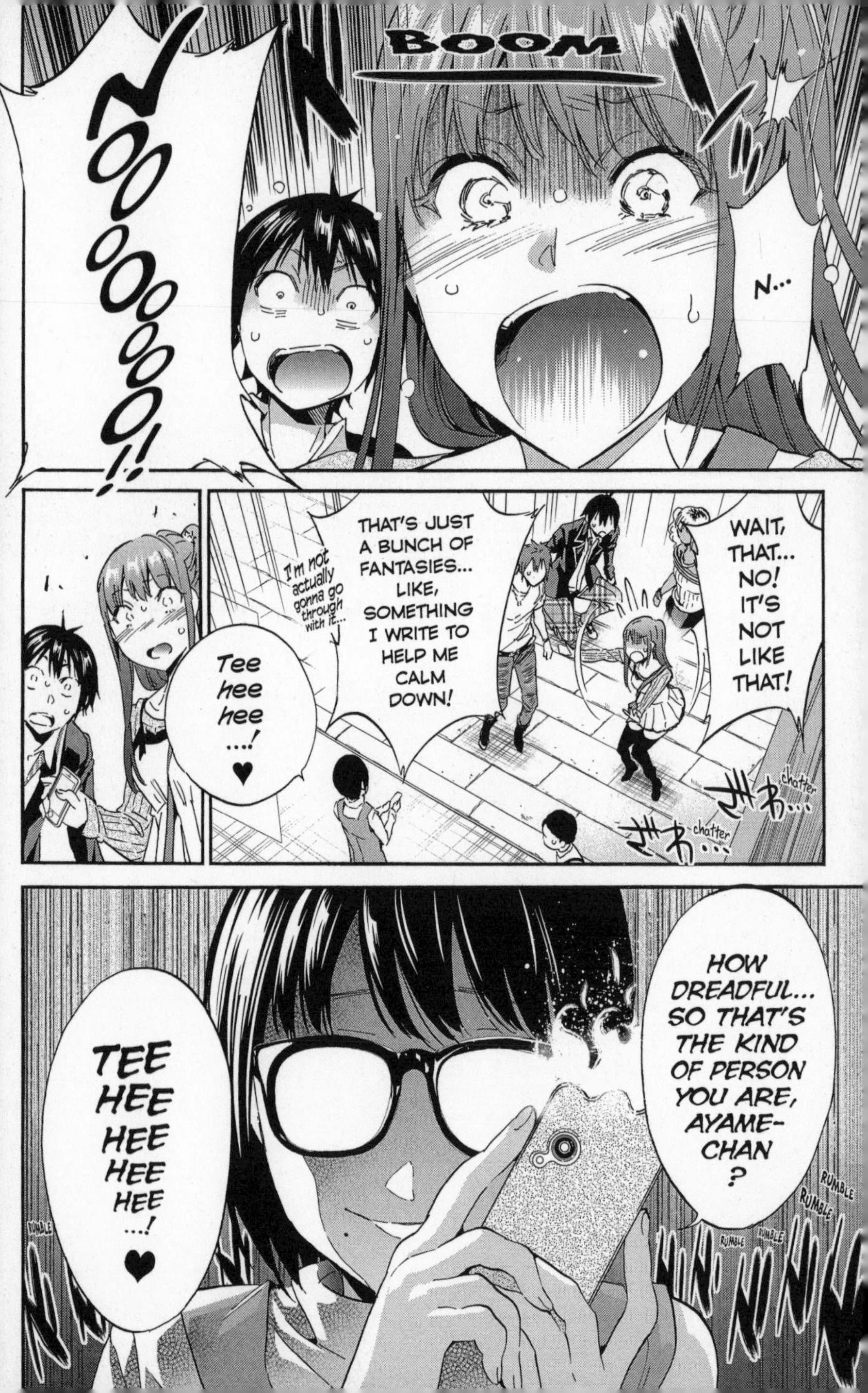
BOOM
N...
NOOOOOOOO!!
WAIT, THAT... NO! IT'S NOT LIKE THAT!
THAT'S JUST A BUNCH OF FANTASIES... LIKE, SOMETHING I WRITE TO HELP ME CALM DOWN!
I'm not actually gonna go through with it...
ざわ… chatter
ざわ… chatter
Tee hee hee ...! ♥
HOW DREADFUL... SO THAT'S THE KIND OF PERSON YOU ARE, AYAME-CHAN?
RUMBLE RUMBLE
RUMBLE RUMBLE
RUMBLE
TEE HEE HEE HEE HEE ...! ♥

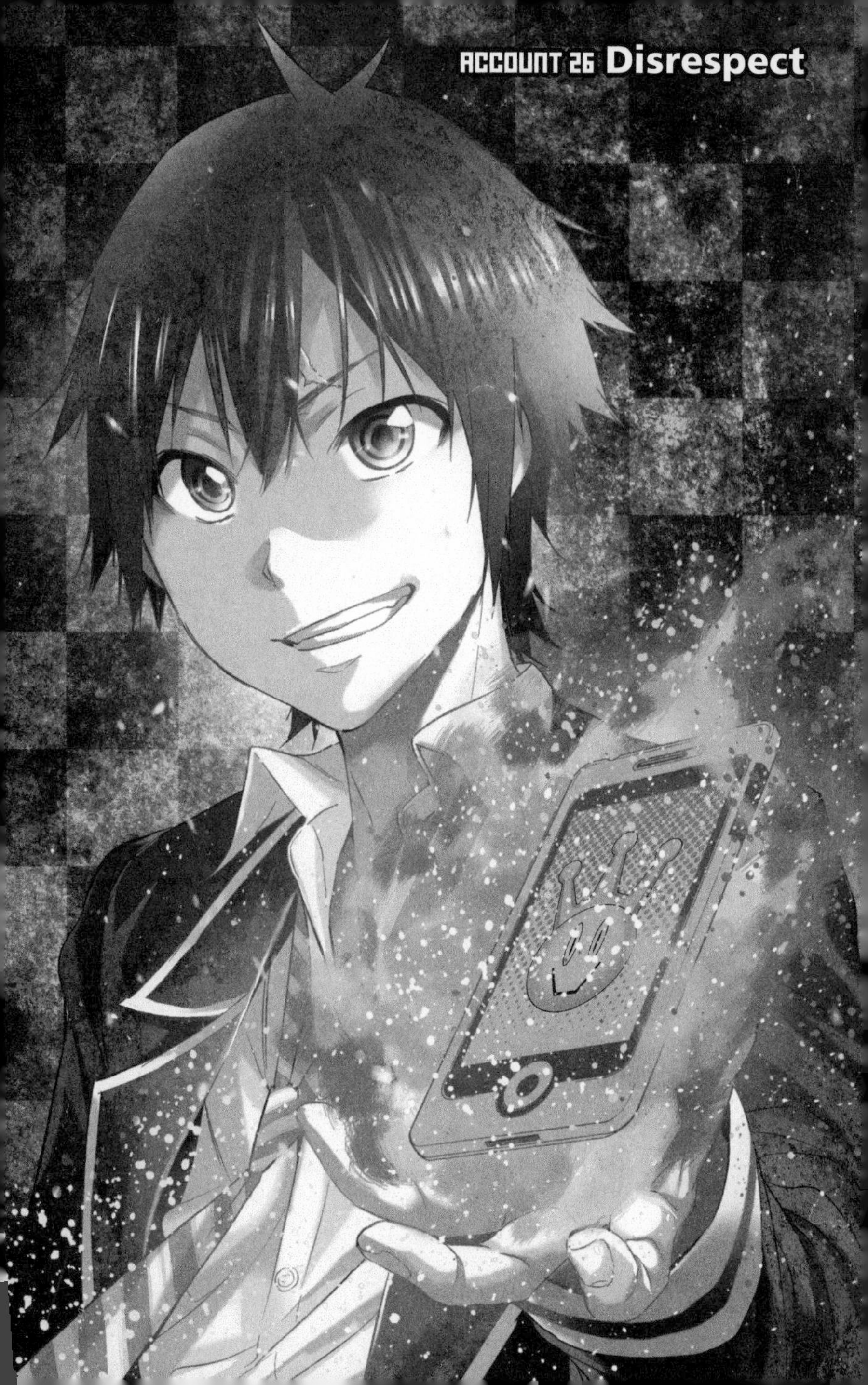
ACCOUNT 26 Disrespect

REAL ACCOUNT

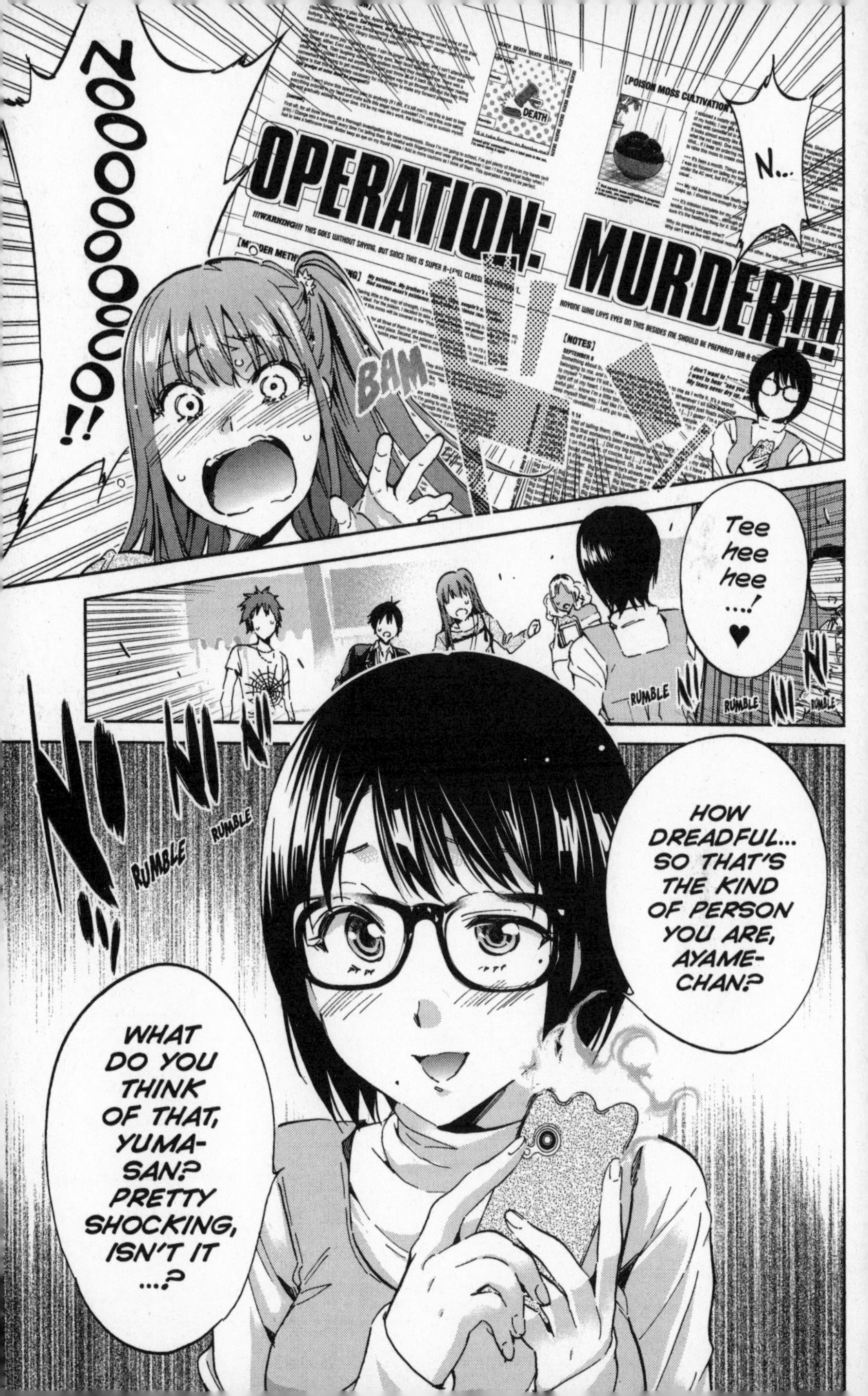
N...
OPERATION: MURDER!!!
BAM
NOOOOOOOOO!!
Tee hee hee ...! ♥
RUMBLE
RUMBLE
RUMBLE
HOW DREADFUL... SO THAT'S THE KIND OF PERSON YOU ARE, AYAME-CHAN?
WHAT DO YOU THINK OF THAT, YUMA-SAN? PRETTY SHOCKING, ISN'T IT ...?
RUMBLE
RUMBLE

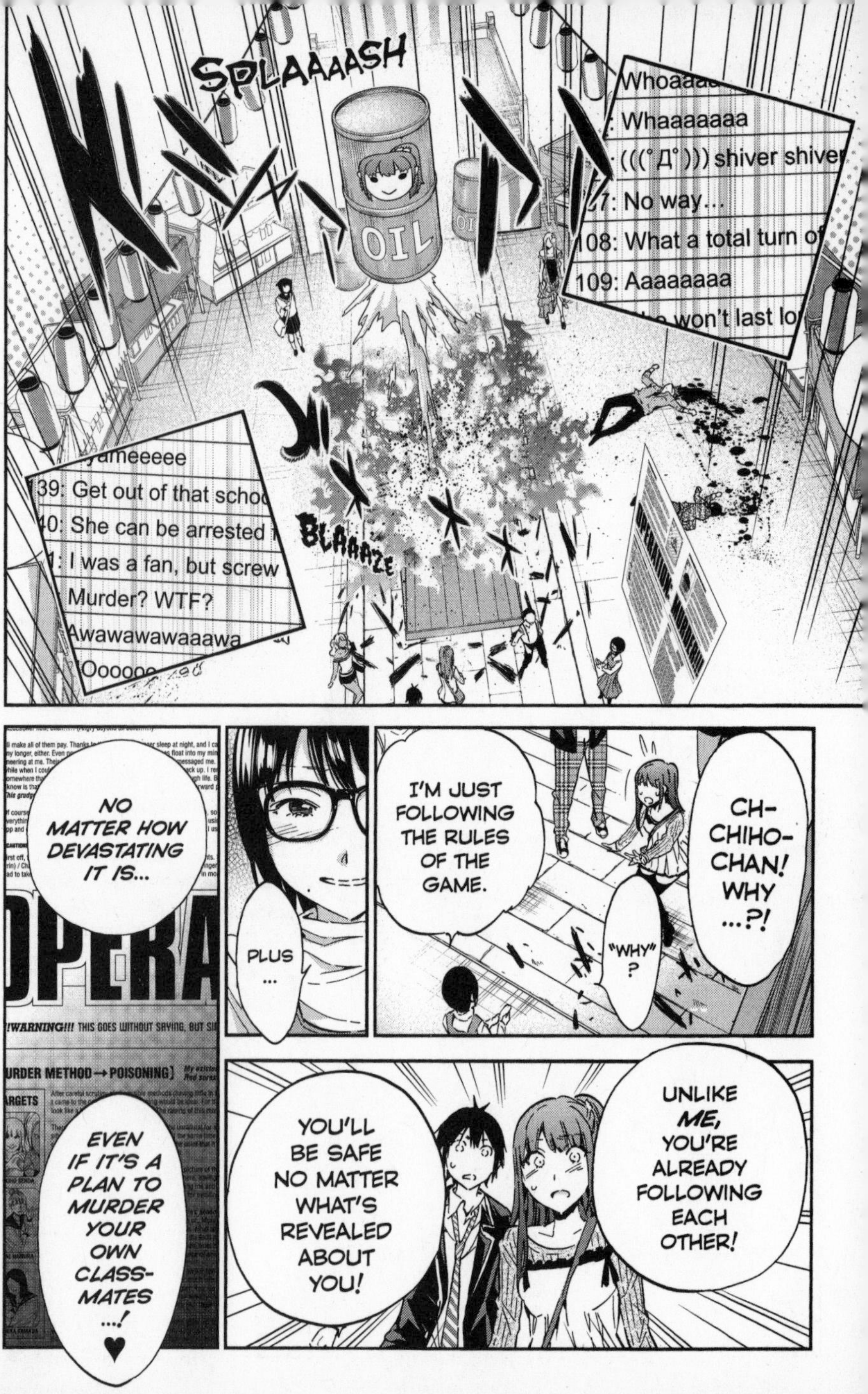
Whoaa
Whaaaaaaa
(((゚Д゚))) shiver shive
27: No way...
108: What a total turn o
109: Aaaaaaaa
won't last lo
SPLAAAASH
OIL
yameeeee
39: Get out of that schoo
40: She can be arrested
I was a fan, but screw
Murder? WTF?
Awawawawaaawa
Ooooo
BLAAAZE
CH-CHIHO-CHAN! WHY ...?!
"WHY"?
I'M JUST FOLLOWING THE RULES OF THE GAME.
PLUS ...
NO MATTER HOW DEVASTATING IT IS...
OPERA
!!WARNING!!! THIS GOES WITHOUT SAYING, BUT SI
URDER METHOD → POISONING]
ARGETS
UNLIKE ME, YOU'RE ALREADY FOLLOWING EACH OTHER!
YOU'LL BE SAFE NO MATTER WHAT'S REVEALED ABOUT YOU!
EVEN IF IT'S A PLAN TO MURDER YOUR OWN CLASSMATES ...! ♥

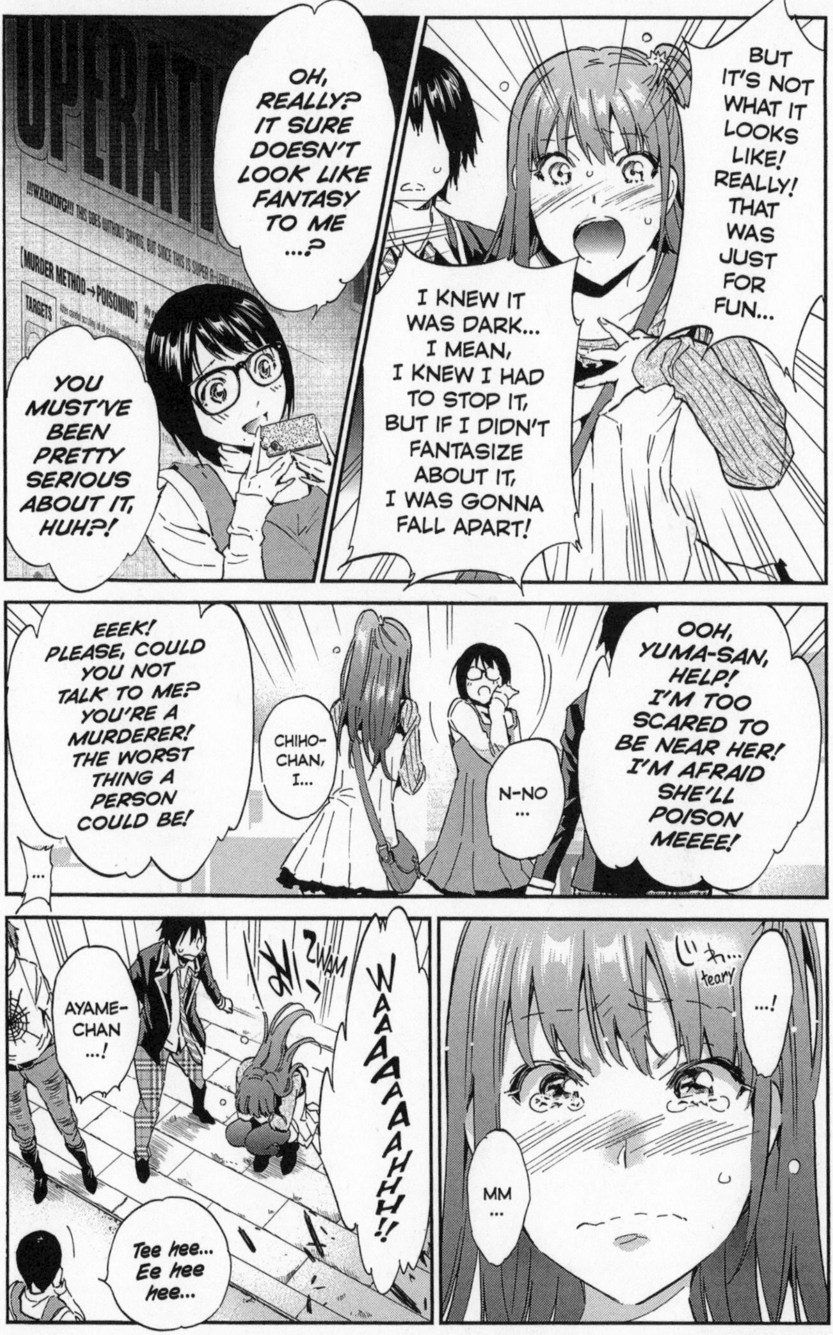
BUT IT'S NOT WHAT IT LOOKS LIKE! REALLY! THAT WAS JUST FOR FUN...
I KNEW IT WAS DARK... I MEAN, I KNEW I HAD TO STOP IT, BUT IF I DIDN'T FANTASIZE ABOUT IT, I WAS GONNA FALL APART!
OH, REALLY? IT SURE DOESN'T LOOK LIKE FANTASY TO ME ...?
OPERATI
MURDER METHOD → POISONING
TARGETS
YOU MUST'VE BEEN PRETTY SERIOUS ABOUT IT, HUH?!
OOH, YUMA-SAN, HELP! I'M TOO SCARED TO BE NEAR HER! I'M AFRAID SHE'LL POISON MEEEE!
N-NO ...
CHIHO-CHAN, I...
EEEK! PLEASE, COULD YOU NOT TALK TO ME? YOU'RE A MURDERER! THE WORST THING A PERSON COULD BE!
...
じわ...
teary
...!
MM ...
WAAAAAAAAHHH!!
ZWAM
AYAME-CHAN ...!
Tee hee... Ee hee hee...

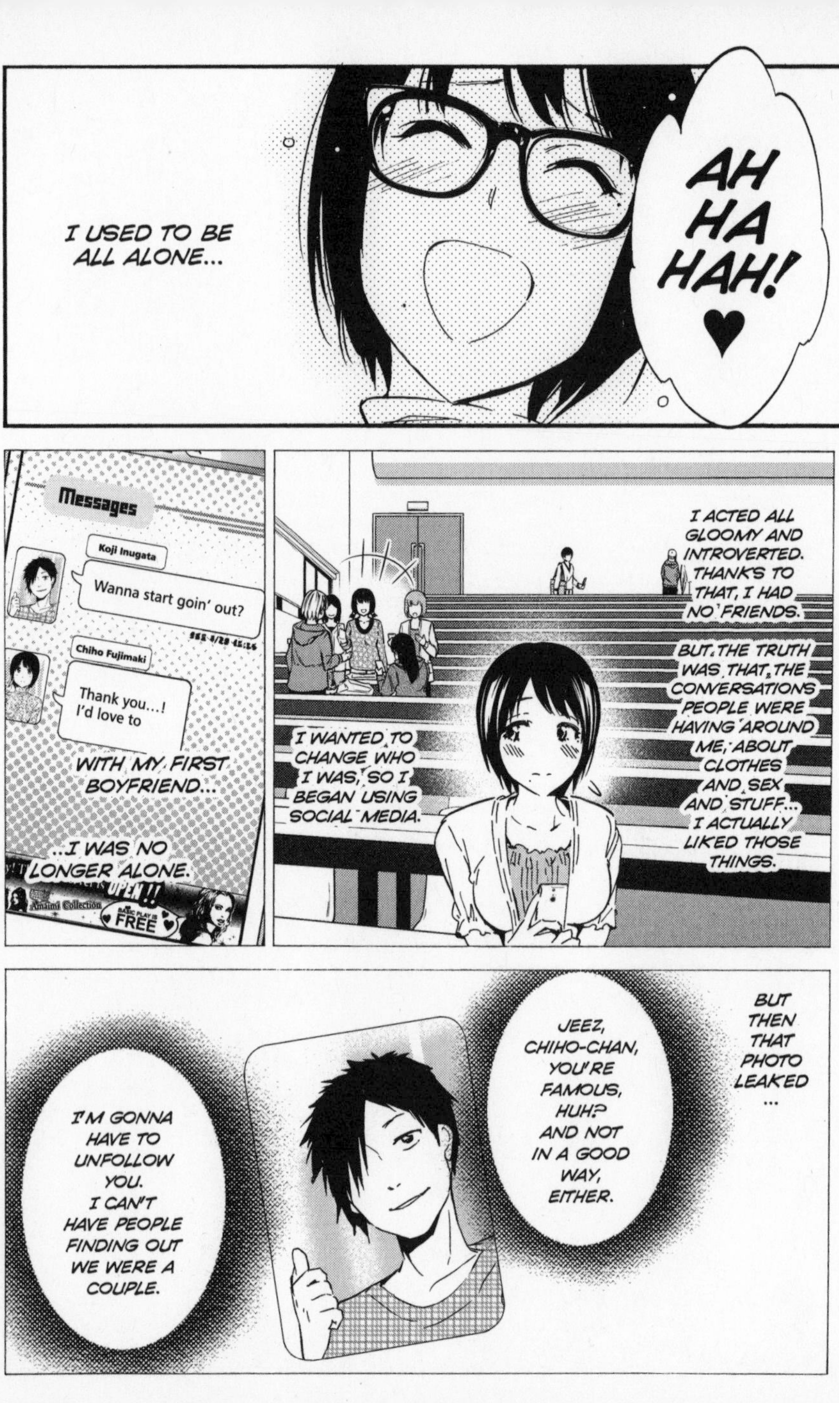
AH HA HAH! ♥
I USED TO BE ALL ALONE...
I ACTED ALL GLOOMY AND INTROVERTED. THANKS TO THAT, I HAD NO FRIENDS.
BUT THE TRUTH WAS THAT THE CONVERSATIONS PEOPLE WERE HAVING AROUND ME, ABOUT CLOTHES AND SEX AND STUFF... I ACTUALLY LIKED THOSE THINGS.
I WANTED TO CHANGE WHO I WAS, SO I BEGAN USING SOCIAL MEDIA.
Messages
Koji Inugata
Wanna start goin' out?
Chiho Fujimaki
Thank you...! I'd love to
WITH MY FIRST BOYFRIEND...
...I WAS NO LONGER ALONE.
OPEN!!
Amaimi Collection
BASIC PLAY IS FREE
BUT THEN THAT PHOTO LEAKED...
JEEZ, CHIHO-CHAN, YOU'RE FAMOUS, HUH? AND NOT IN A GOOD WAY, EITHER.
I'M GONNA HAVE TO UNFOLLOW YOU. I CAN'T HAVE PEOPLE FINDING OUT WE WERE A COUPLE.

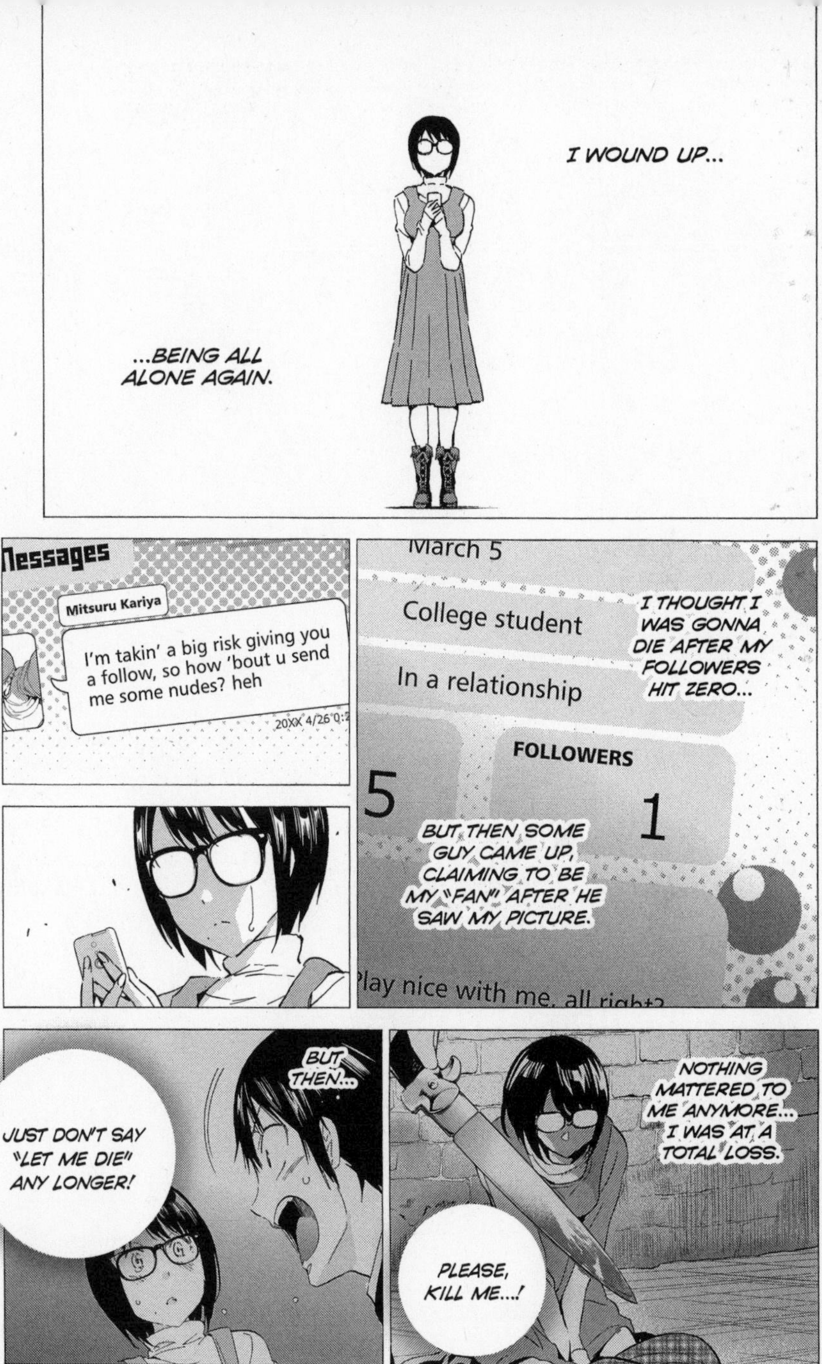

I WOUND UP...
...BEING ALL ALONE AGAIN.
March 5
College student
In a relationship
FOLLOWERS
5
1
Play nice with me, all right?
I THOUGHT I WAS GONNA DIE AFTER MY FOLLOWERS HIT ZERO...
BUT THEN SOME GUY CAME UP, CLAIMING TO BE MY "FAN" AFTER HE SAW MY PICTURE.
Mitsuru Kariya
I'm takin' a big risk giving you a follow, so how 'bout u send me some nudes? heh
20XX 4/26 0:2
NOTHING MATTERED TO ME ANYMORE... I WAS AT A TOTAL LOSS.
PLEASE, KILL ME...!
BUT THEN...
JUST DON'T SAY "LET ME DIE" ANY LONGER!

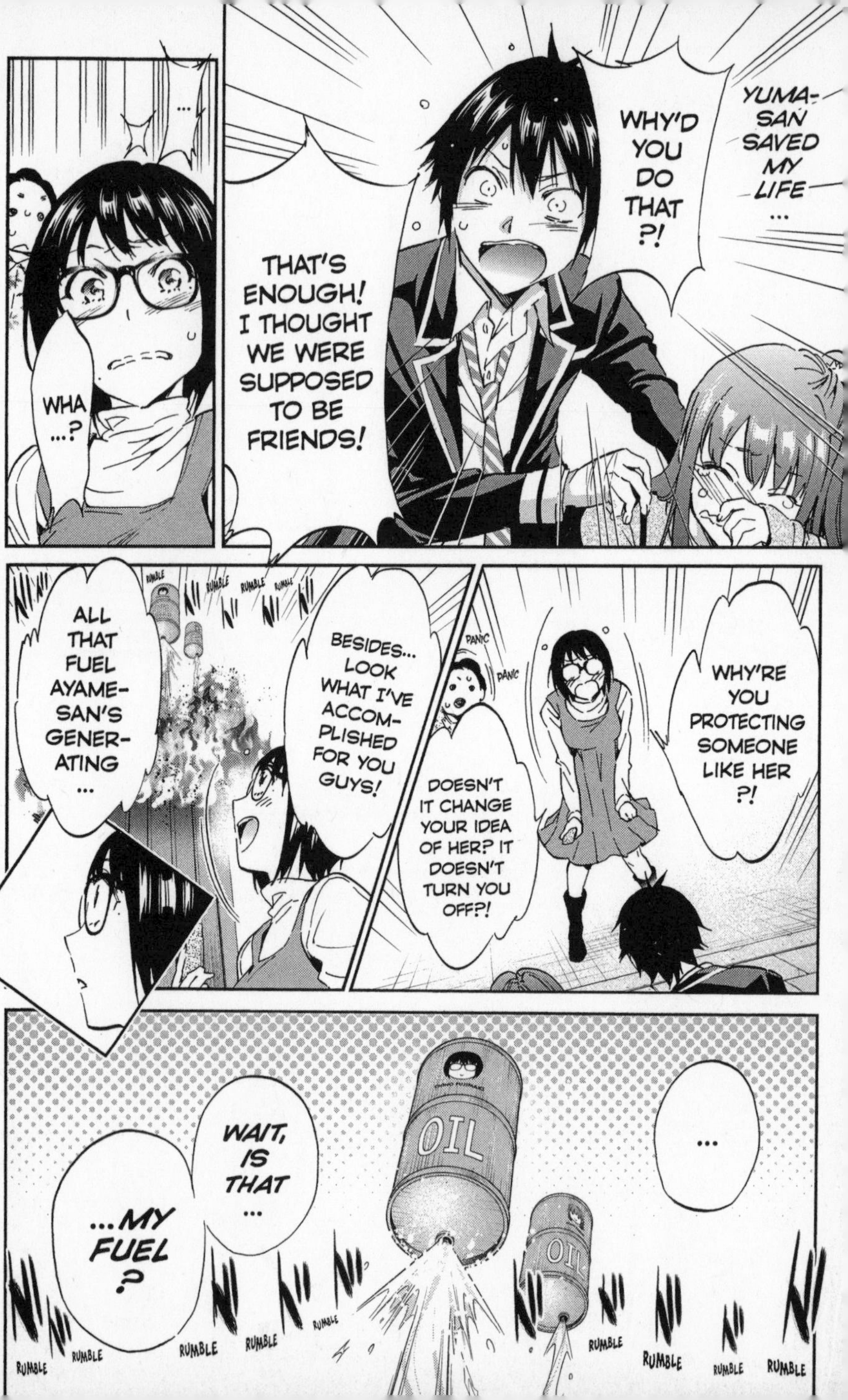
YUMA-SAN SAVED MY LIFE...
WHY'D YOU DO THAT?!
THAT'S ENOUGH! I THOUGHT WE WERE SUPPOSED TO BE FRIENDS!
...
WHA...?
WHY'RE YOU PROTECTING SOMEONE LIKE HER?!
PANIC
PANIC
DOESN'T IT CHANGE YOUR IDEA OF HER? IT DOESN'T TURN YOU OFF?!
BESIDES... LOOK WHAT I'VE ACCOMPLISHED FOR YOU GUYS!
RUMBLE RUMBLE RUMBLE RUMBLE
ALL THAT FUEL AYAME-SAN'S GENERATING...
...
OIL
OIL
WAIT, IS THAT...
...MY FUEL?
RUMBLE RUMBLE RUMBLE RUMBLE RUMBLE RUMBLE RUMBLE RUMBLE RUMBLE RUMBLE

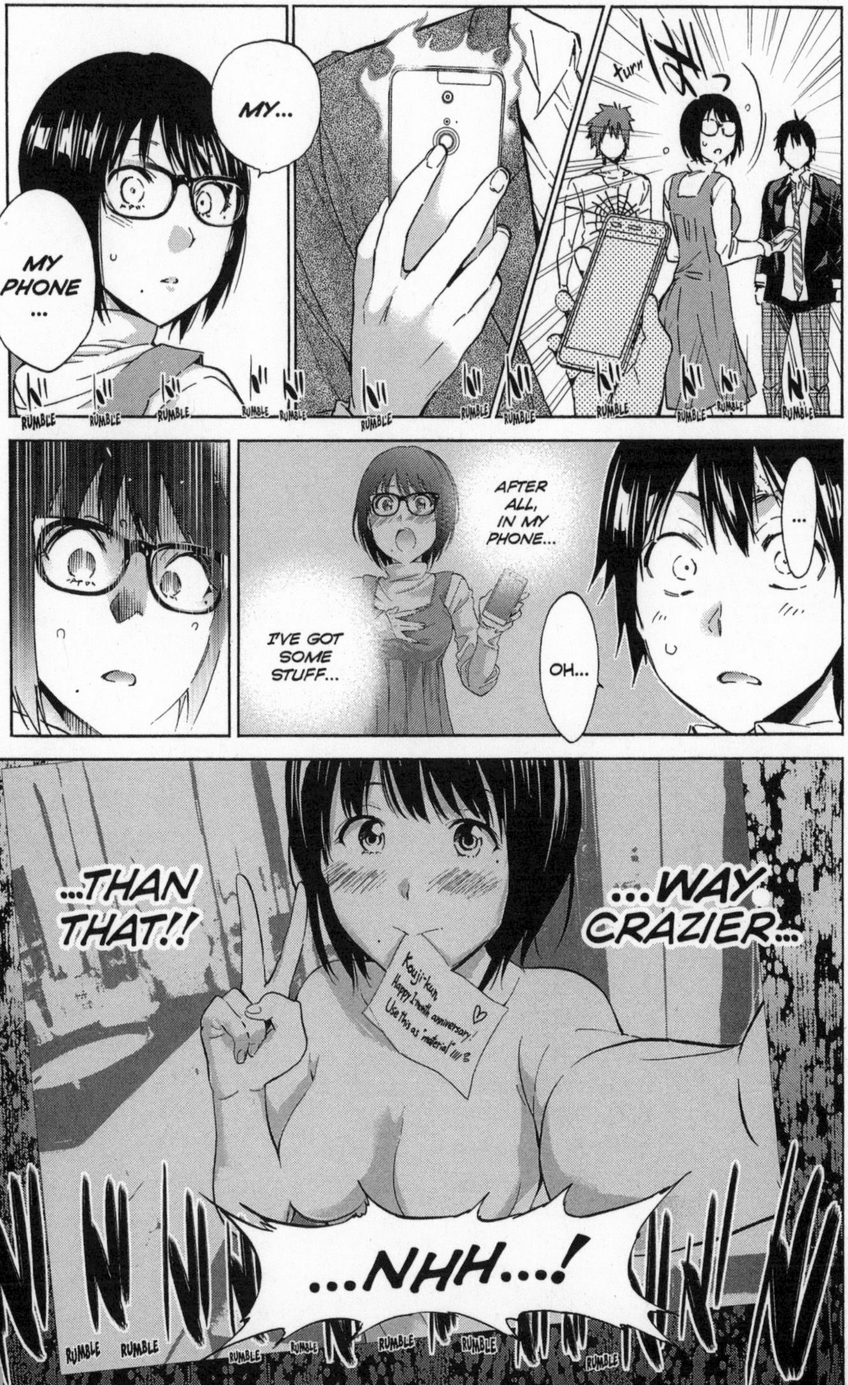
turn
MY...
MY PHONE ...
RUMBLE RUMBLE RUMBLE RUMBLE RUMBLE RUMBLE RUMBLE RUMBLE RUMBLE RUMBLE RUMBLE RUMBLE
...
OH...
AFTER ALL, IN MY PHONE...
I'VE GOT SOME STUFF...
...WAY CRAZIER...
...THAN THAT!!
Kouji-kun
Happy 1-month anniversary!
Use this as "material"
...NHH...!
RUMBLE RUMBLE RUMBLE RUMBLE RUMBLE RUMBLE RUMBLE

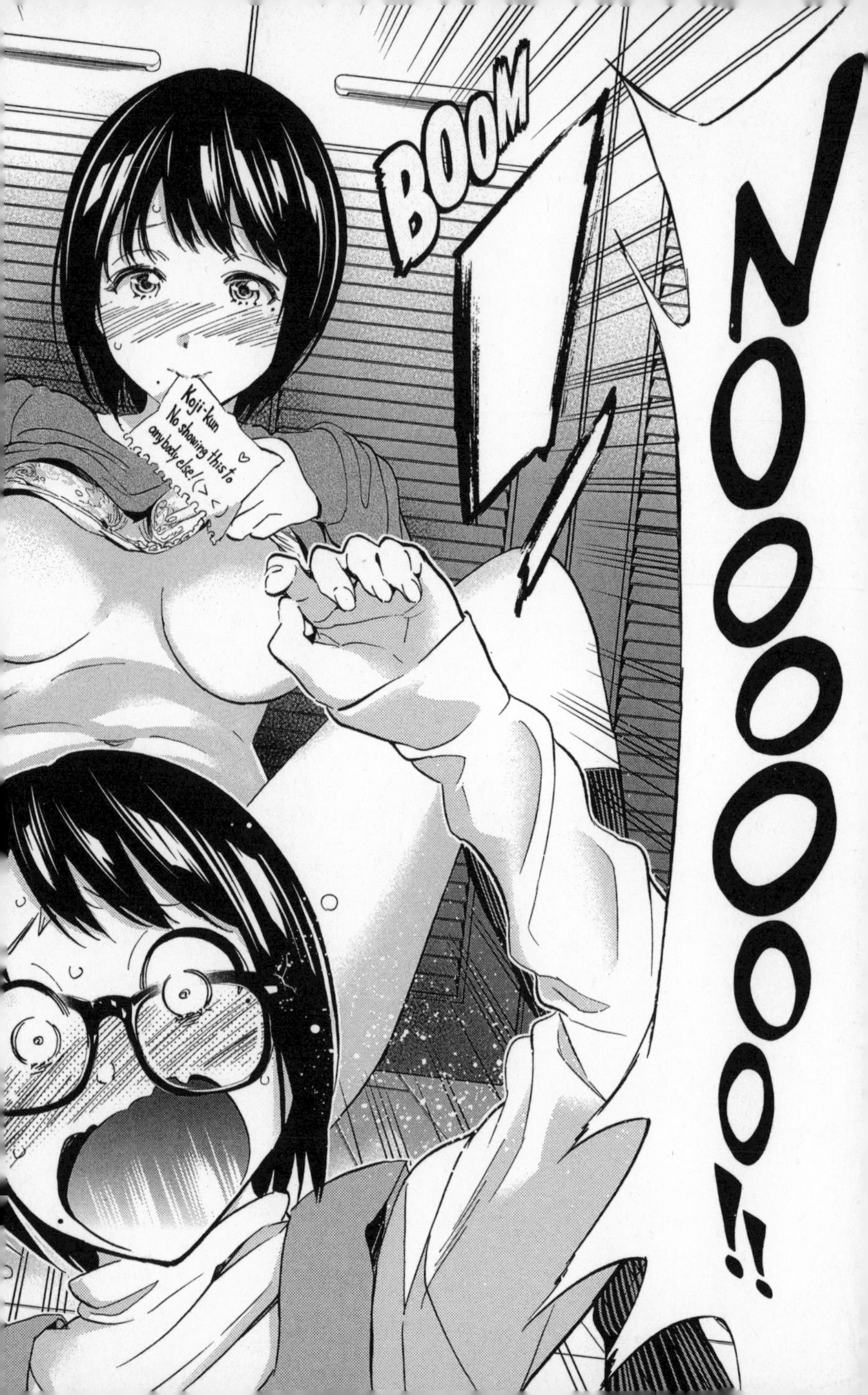
NOOOOOO!!
BOOM
Koji-kun ♡
No showing this to
anybody else! (> <

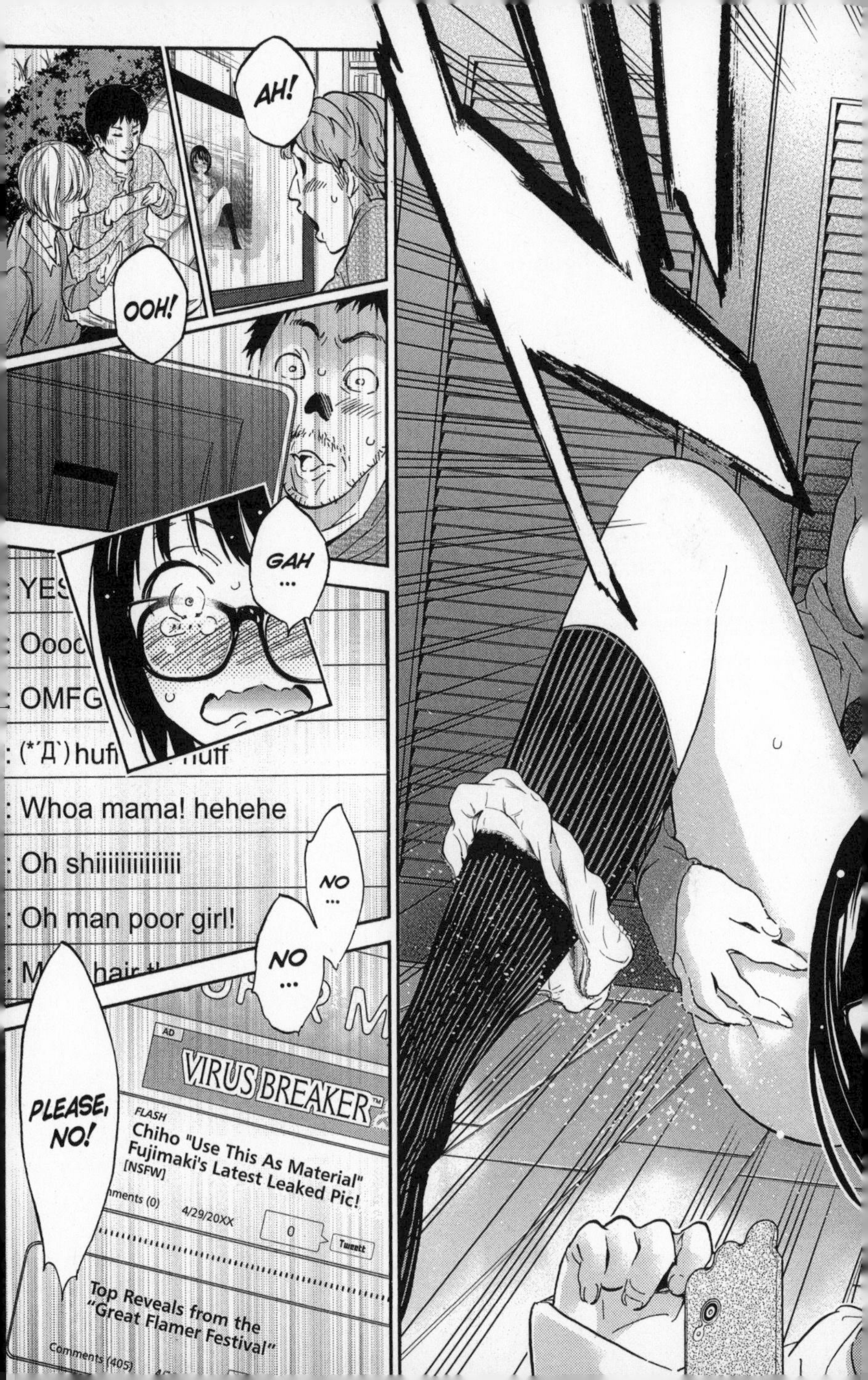
AH!
OOH!
GAH ...
YES
OMFG
Whoa mama! hehehe
Oh shiiiiiiiiiiiii
Oh man poor girl!
NO ...
NO ...
PLEASE, NO!
AD
VIRUS BREAKER™
FLASH
Chiho "Use This As Material" Fujimaki's Latest Leaked Pic!
[NSFW]
4/29/20XX
0
Tweet
Top Reveals from the "Great Flamer Festival"
Comments (405)

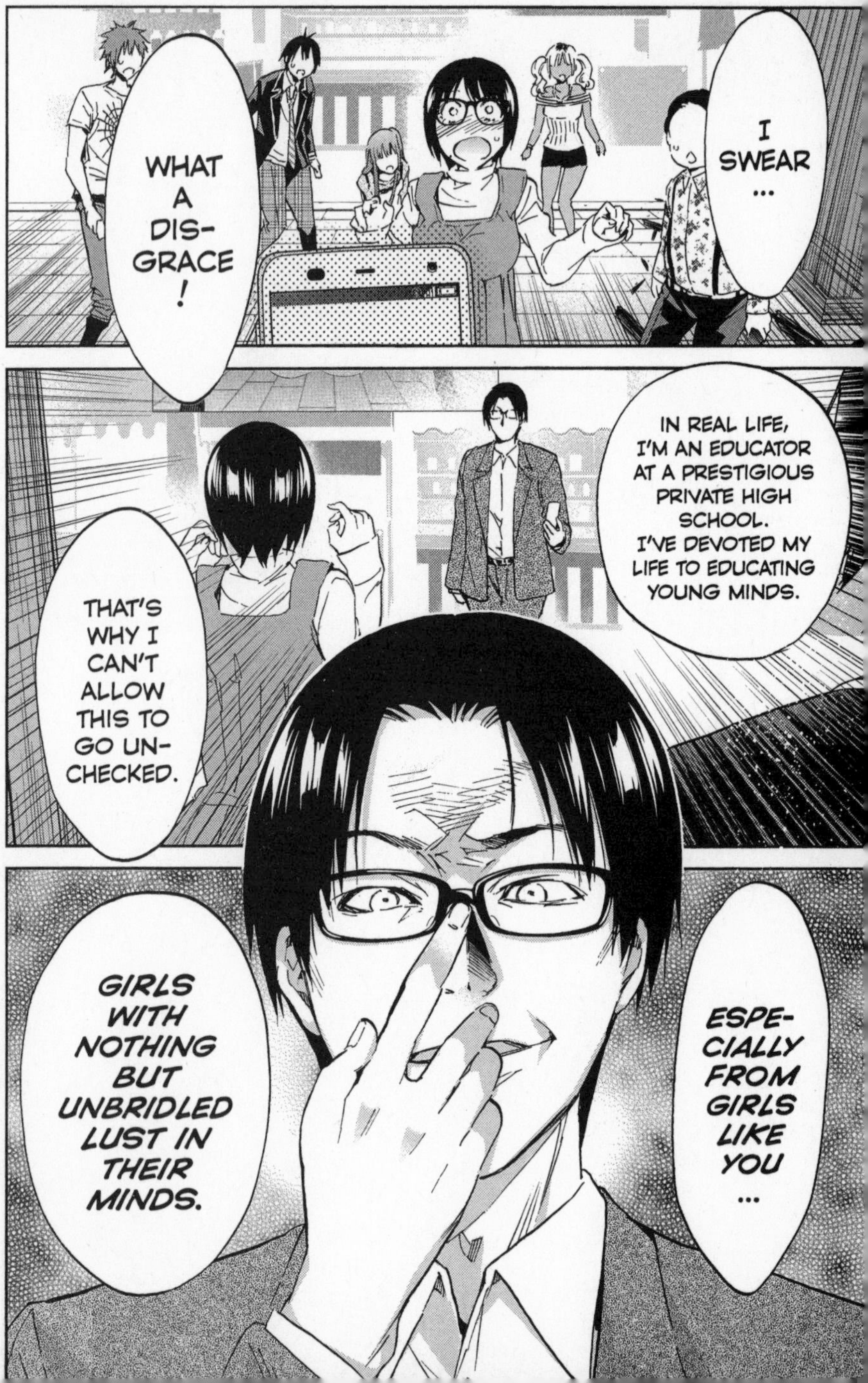
I SWEAR ...
WHAT A DIS-GRACE !
IN REAL LIFE, I'M AN EDUCATOR AT A PRESTIGIOUS PRIVATE HIGH SCHOOL. I'VE DEVOTED MY LIFE TO EDUCATING YOUNG MINDS.
THAT'S WHY I CAN'T ALLOW THIS TO GO UN-CHECKED.
ESPE-CIALLY FROM GIRLS LIKE YOU ...
GIRLS WITH NOTHING BUT UNBRIDLED LUST IN THEIR MINDS.

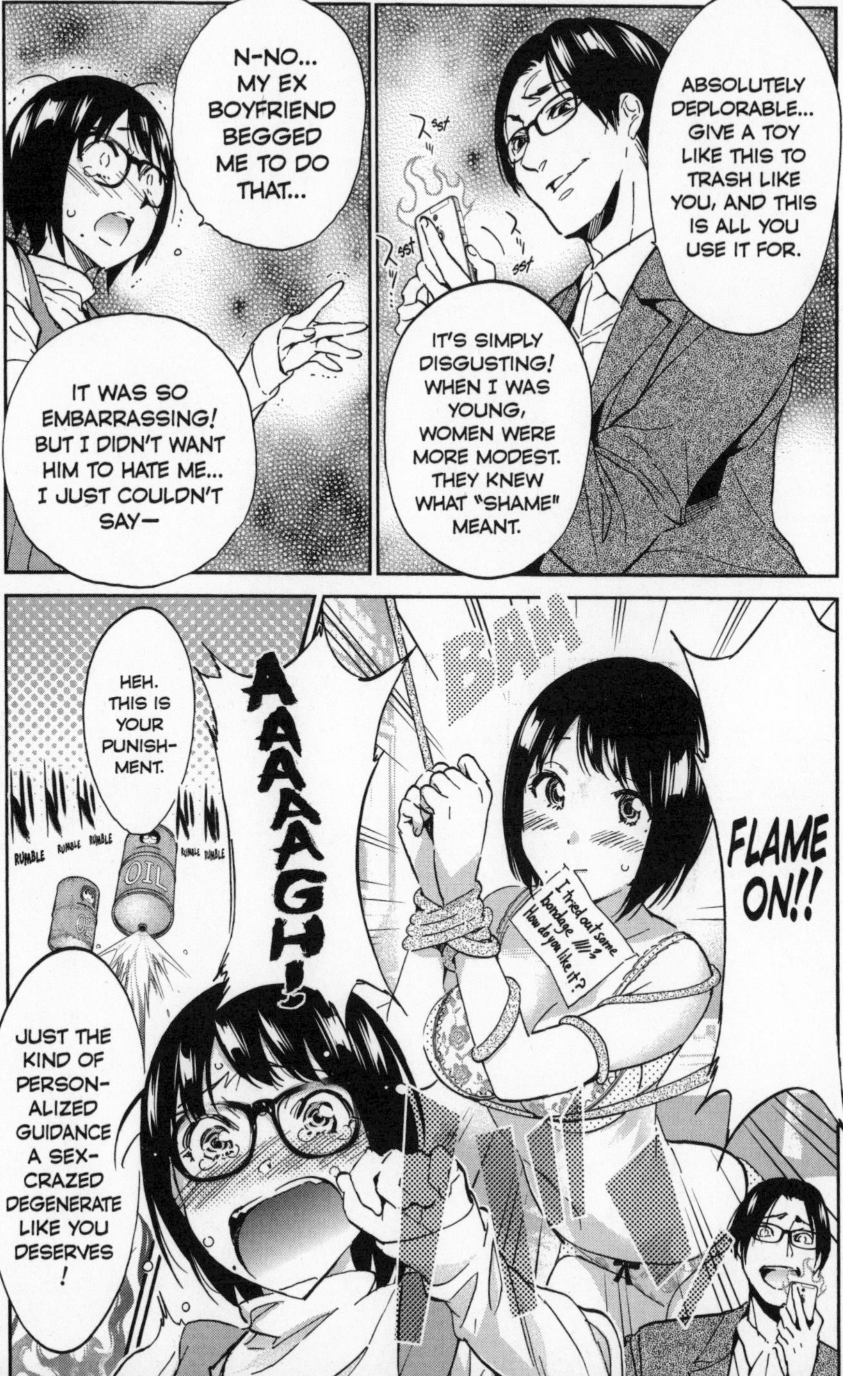
ABSOLUTELY DEPLORABLE... GIVE A TOY LIKE THIS TO TRASH LIKE YOU, AND THIS IS ALL YOU USE IT FOR.
sst
sst
sst
IT'S SIMPLY DISGUSTING! WHEN I WAS YOUNG, WOMEN WERE MORE MODEST. THEY KNEW WHAT "SHAME" MEANT.
N-NO... MY EX BOYFRIEND BEGGED ME TO DO THAT...
IT WAS SO EMBARRASSING! BUT I DIDN'T WANT HIM TO HATE ME... I JUST COULDN'T SAY—
FLAME ON!!
I tried out some bondage ////♪ How do you like it?
BAM
AAAAAGH!
HEH. THIS IS YOUR PUNISHMENT.
RUMBLE RUMBLE RUMBLE
RUMBLE RUMBLE
OIL
JUST THE KIND OF PERSON-ALIZED GUIDANCE A SEX-CRAZED DEGENERATE LIKE YOU DESERVES!

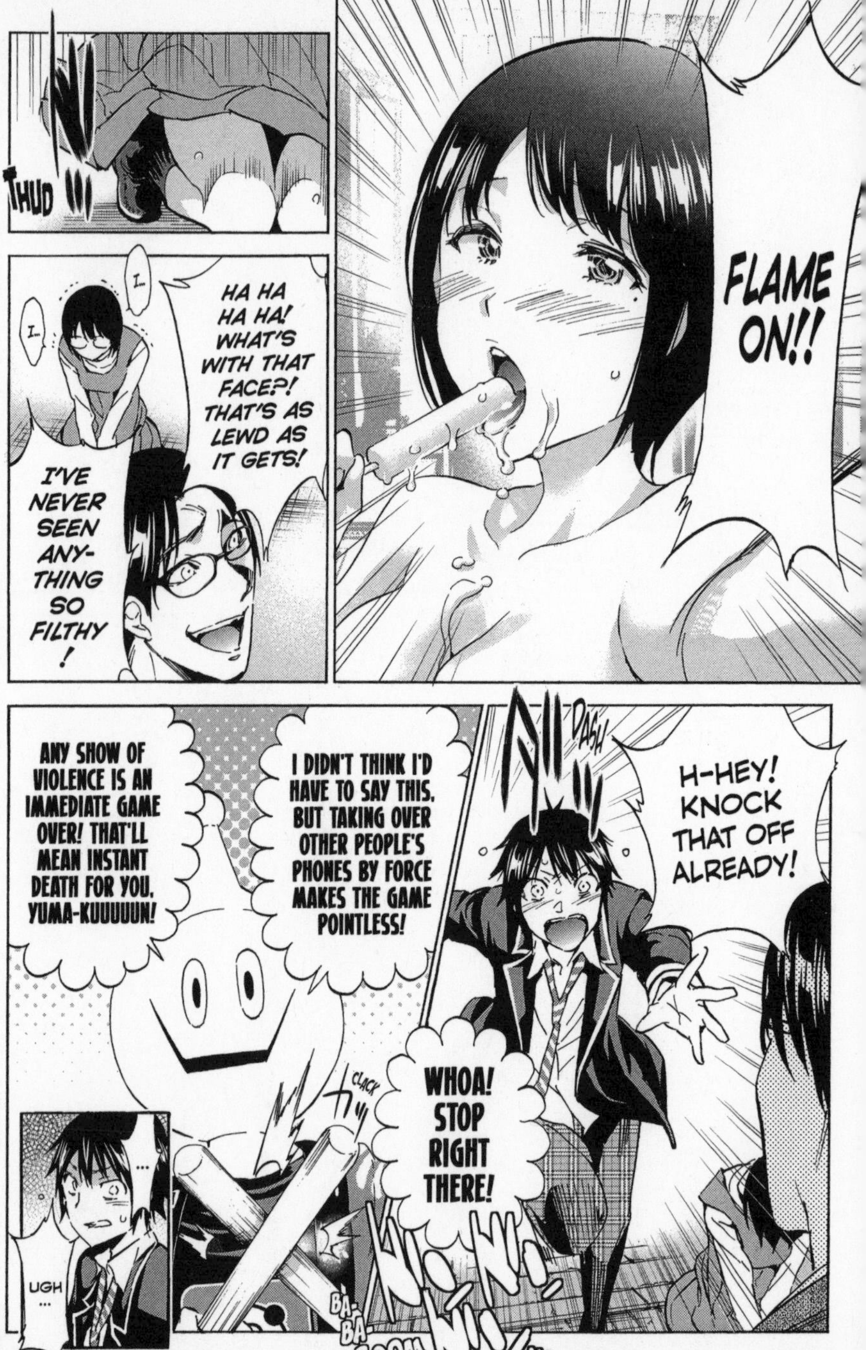
FLAME ON!!
THUD
I...
I...
HA HA HA HA! WHAT'S WITH THAT FACE?! THAT'S AS LEWD AS IT GETS!
I'VE NEVER SEEN ANYTHING SO FILTHY!
DASH
H-HEY! KNOCK THAT OFF ALREADY!
I DIDN'T THINK I'D HAVE TO SAY THIS, BUT TAKING OVER OTHER PEOPLE'S PHONES BY FORCE MAKES THE GAME POINTLESS!
ANY SHOW OF VIOLENCE IS AN IMMEDIATE GAME OVER! THAT'LL MEAN INSTANT DEATH FOR YOU, YUMA-KUUUUUN!
WHOA! STOP RIGHT THERE!
CLACK
BA-BA-BOOM
...
UGH ...

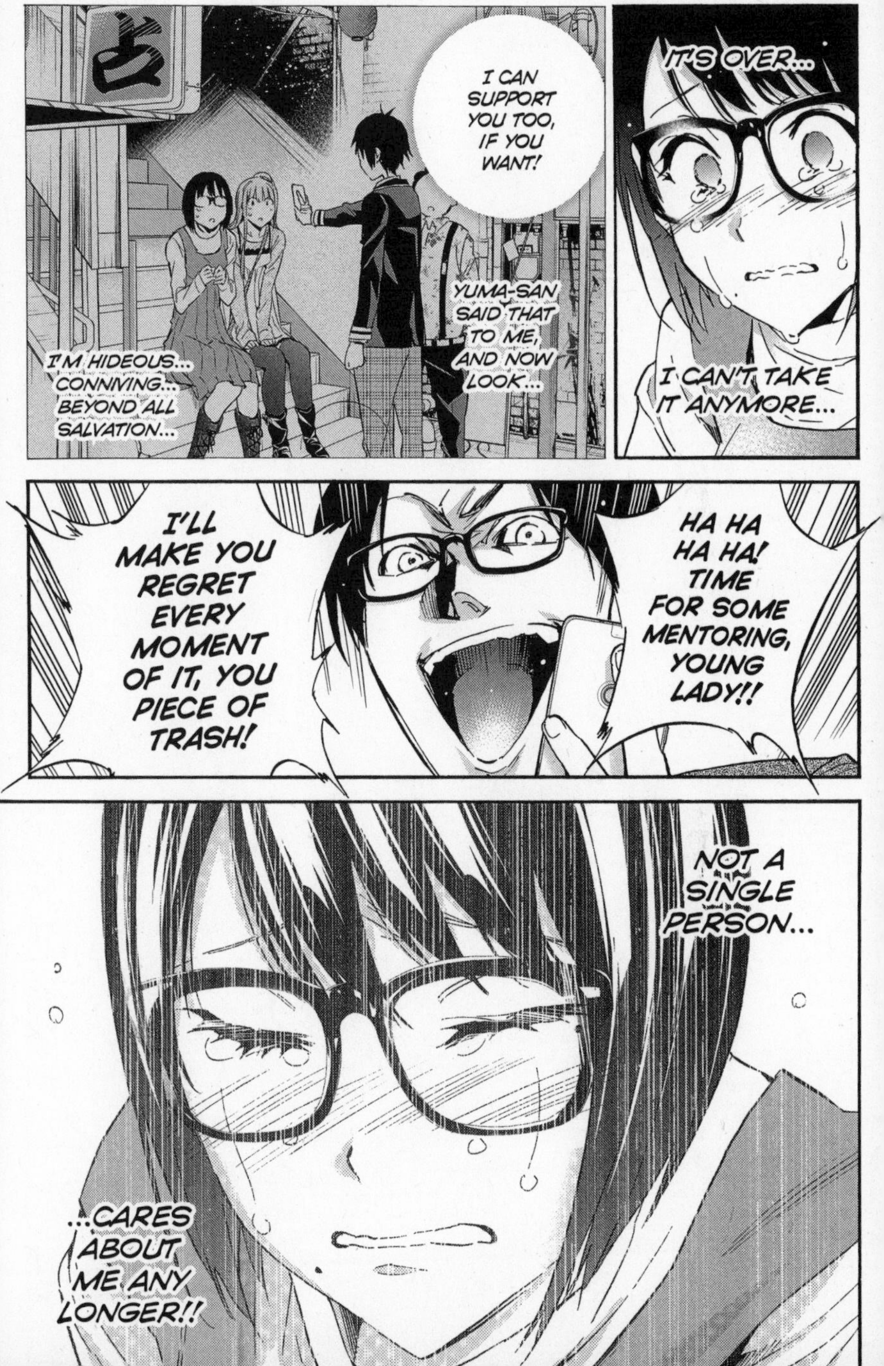
IT'S OVER...
I CAN'T TAKE IT ANYMORE...
I CAN SUPPORT YOU TOO, IF YOU WANT!
YUMA-SAN SAID THAT TO ME, AND NOW LOOK...
I'M HIDEOUS... CONNIVING... BEYOND ALL SALVATION...
HA HA HA HA! TIME FOR SOME MENTORING, YOUNG LADY!!
I'LL MAKE YOU REGRET EVERY MOMENT OF IT, YOU PIECE OF TRASH!
NOT A SINGLE PERSON...
...CARES ABOUT ME ANY LONGER!!

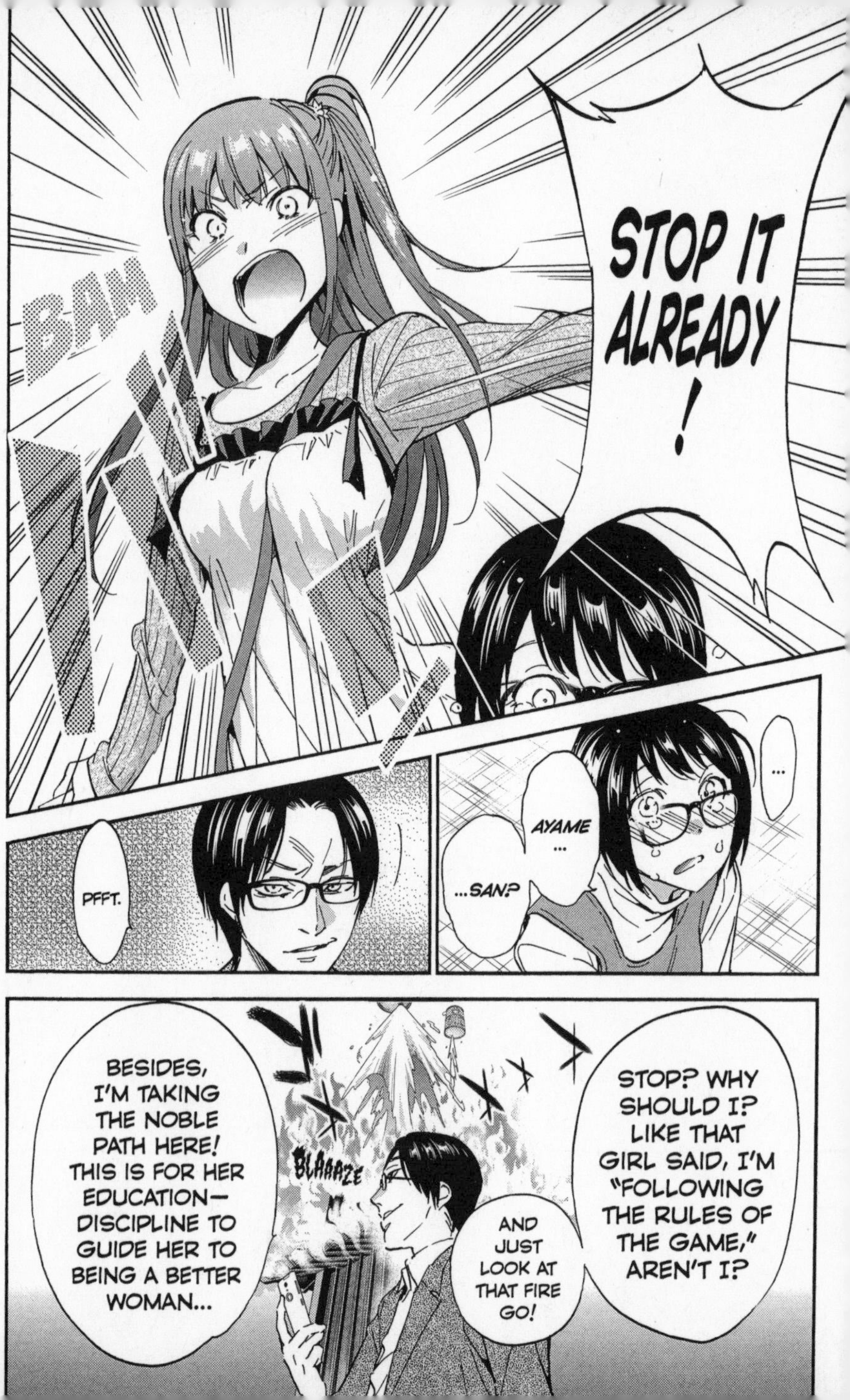
STOP IT ALREADY!
...
AYAME ...
...SAN?
PFFT.
STOP? WHY SHOULD I? LIKE THAT GIRL SAID, I'M "FOLLOWING THE RULES OF THE GAME," AREN'T I?
AND JUST LOOK AT THAT FIRE GO!
BLAAAZE
BESIDES, I'M TAKING THE NOBLE PATH HERE! THIS IS FOR HER EDUCATION—DISCIPLINE TO GUIDE HER TO BEING A BETTER WOMAN...

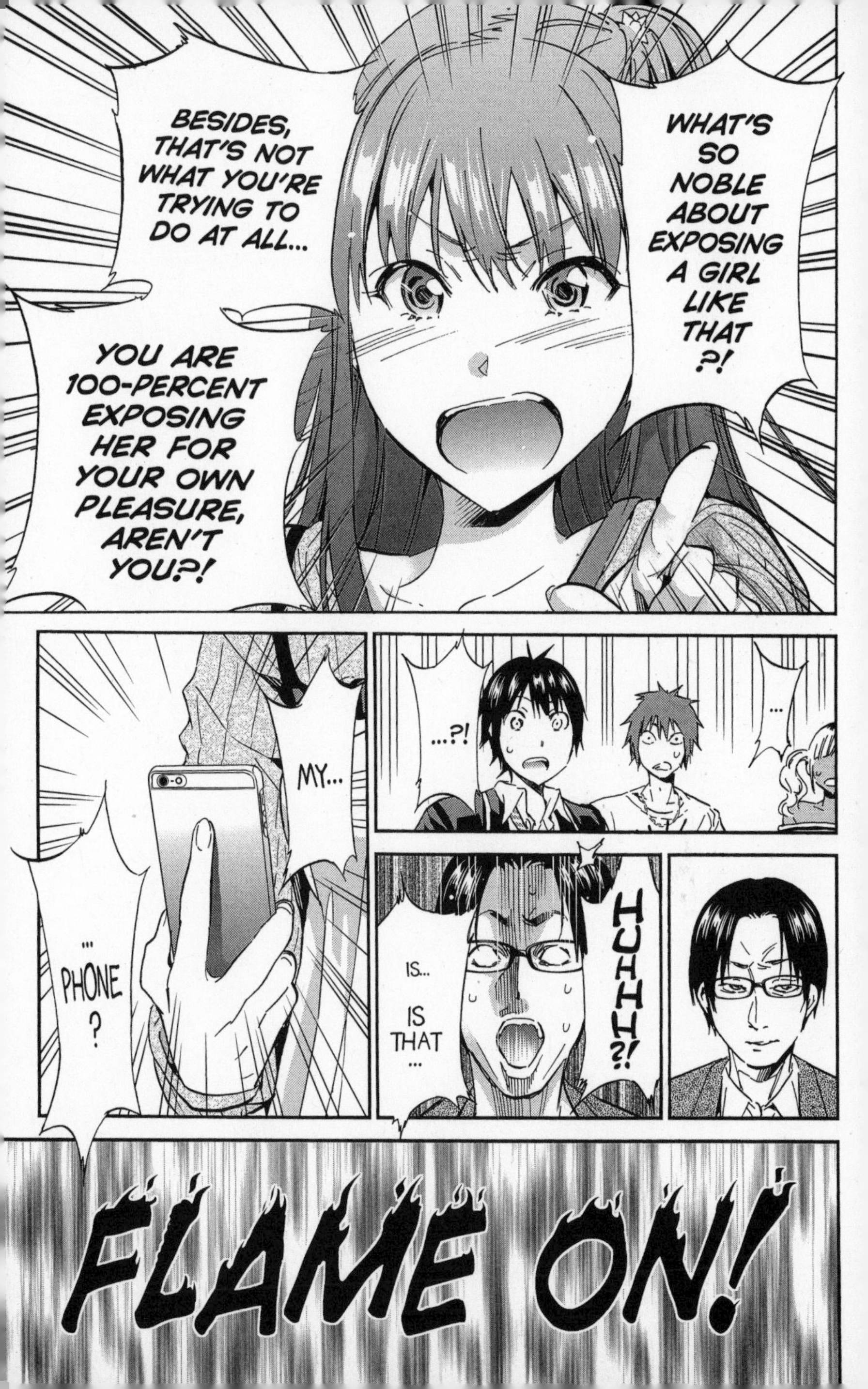
WHAT'S SO NOBLE ABOUT EXPOSING A GIRL LIKE THAT?!
BESIDES, THAT'S NOT WHAT YOU'RE TRYING TO DO AT ALL...
YOU ARE 100-PERCENT EXPOSING HER FOR YOUR OWN PLEASURE, AREN'T YOU?!
...
...?!
HUHHH?!
IS... IS THAT...
MY...
...PHONE?
FLAME ON!

SPECIAL PERSONAL GUIDANCE RESULTS, SEPTEMBER

	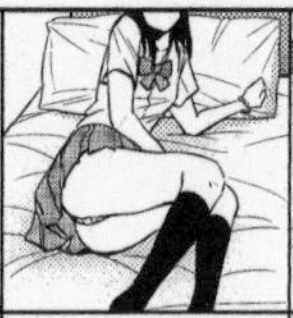	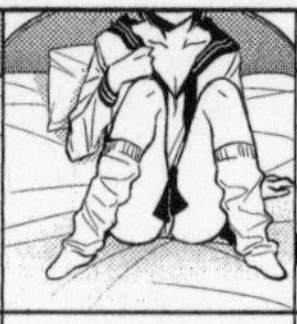	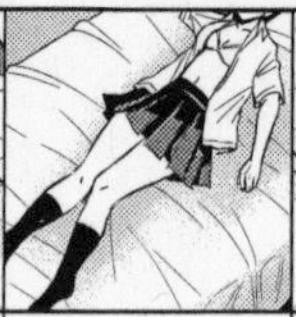	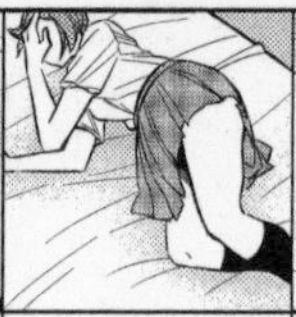	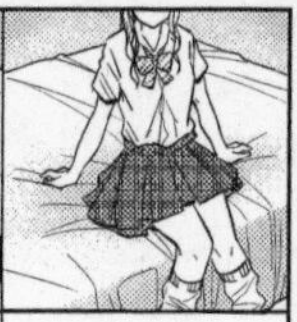
NAME	Chisa	Kaoru	Aika	Rino	Miruku
SCHOOL	Tsubakigaoka Girls'	Sokyu Academy	Mikuri University Affiliated	Tsuyukusa Academy	Urei Girls'
DATE	9/5	9/12	9/20	9/23	9/30
LOCATION	Shibuya hotel "Honey Life"	Shinjuku hotel "Love Sweet"	Shibuya hotel "Party Zone"	Shinjuku hotel "One-Night Dream"	Shibuya hotel "Couples' Kingdom"
COST	35,000	30,000	45,000	30,000	35,000
LOOKS	B	A	C	B	C
EXCITEMENT LEVEL	B	A	D	B	A
BUST SIZE	82B	89F	85C	79B	85D
KISSING	B	A	C	C	C
HAND SKILLS	B	B	C	B	B
ORAL SKILLS	A	B	D	C	
OPTIONS	Swallowing	Dirty talk	None		
RESULTS	B She contacted me first. A completely dirty girl, not at all what you'd expect from a place as prestigious as Tsubakigaoka. Her speech indicates she's no stranger to this, and her oral tehnique is master-class.	A+ One of the greatest finds in the past year of guidance. Her breasts are like mountains, her skin as pale as a pearl. During guidance, she finished me off with her mouth. I couldn't believe it. She definitely needs ...ore guidance.	C Not proactive at all; balks at everything I suggest. She also asked for full payment in advance and at a high price. Considering how great it was last time, this is a major drop-off... You'd think at least a kiss would be nice, but noooo. Not coming back.	She... I thi... perl... if w... big... de...	...t okay. ...: It is ...good ...g time ...highs ...n up ...ful ...haps ...bite
SUMM... FOR T... MONT... GUID...	...k the day off, which ... health ... g advantage of my g... an... ...u really deserves sp... this ... ...viting eyes, and the a... belie... ...g up and down, right ... bec... ...ness right on the sp... In fa... me a whole new outlook on life. There are so many lowlife g... an... my guidance. For now, Kaoru needs more guidance immediat... I'd like to get to her as soon as I can next month.				

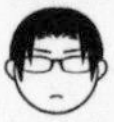

Osamu Tanejima

<DOCUMENT FILE>

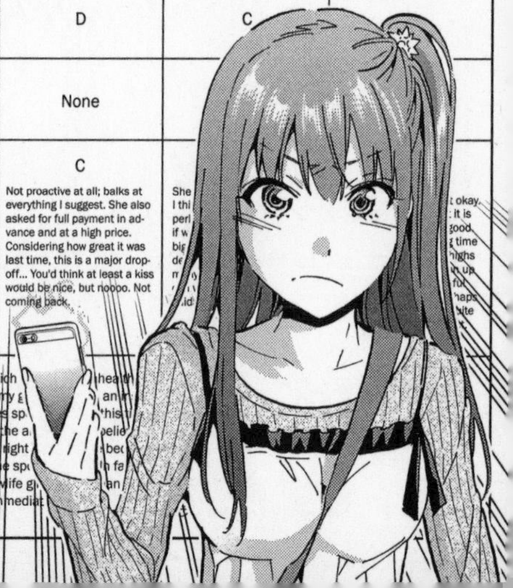

?!

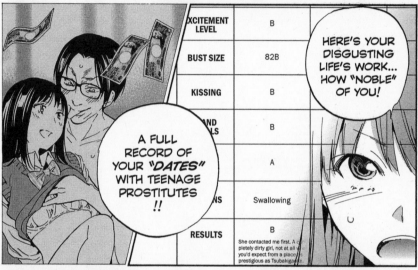

XCITEMENT LEVEL	B
BUST SIZE	82B
KISSING	B
[H]AND [SKI]LLS	B
	A
[?]NS	Swallowing
RESULTS	B

She contacted me first. A completely dirty girl, not at all ...you'd expect from a place ...prestigious as Tsubakigaoka...

HERE'S YOUR DISGUSTING LIFE'S WORK... HOW *"NOBLE"* OF YOU!

A FULL RECORD OF YOUR *"DATES"* WITH TEENAGE PROSTITUTES !!

HOW DARE YOU ACT ALL HIGH AND MIGHTY...

BERATING CHIHO-SAN INCESSANTLY, MAKING HER BREAK DOWN LIKE THAT.

THWUMP

H-HOW DID YOU GET TO THAT ...?!

AH—

AH—

AH...

...I'M THE BEST EXPERT YOU'LL FIND!

WHEN IT COMES TO HIDING FILES ON YOUR SMART-PHONE...

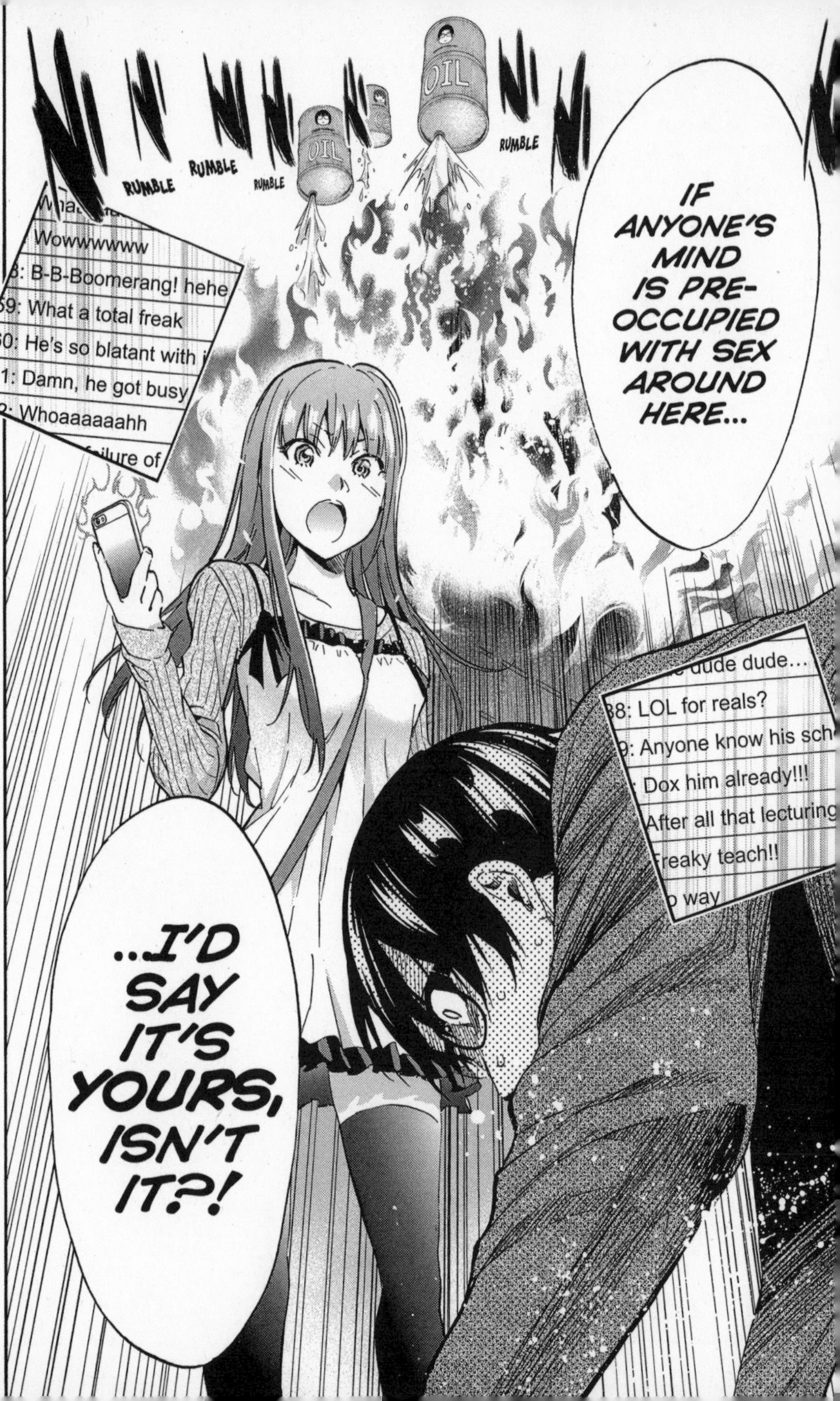
RUMBLE
RUMBLE
RUMBLE
RUMBLE
OIL
OIL
IF ANYONE'S MIND IS PRE-OCCUPIED WITH SEX AROUND HERE...
Wowwwwwww
B-B-Boomerang! hehe
59: What a total freak
60: He's so blatant with
61: Damn, he got busy
Whoaaaaaahh
failure of
dude dude...
38: LOL for reals?
Anyone know his sch
Dox him already!!!
After all that lecturing
Freaky teach!!
way
...I'D SAY IT'S YOURS, ISN'T IT?!

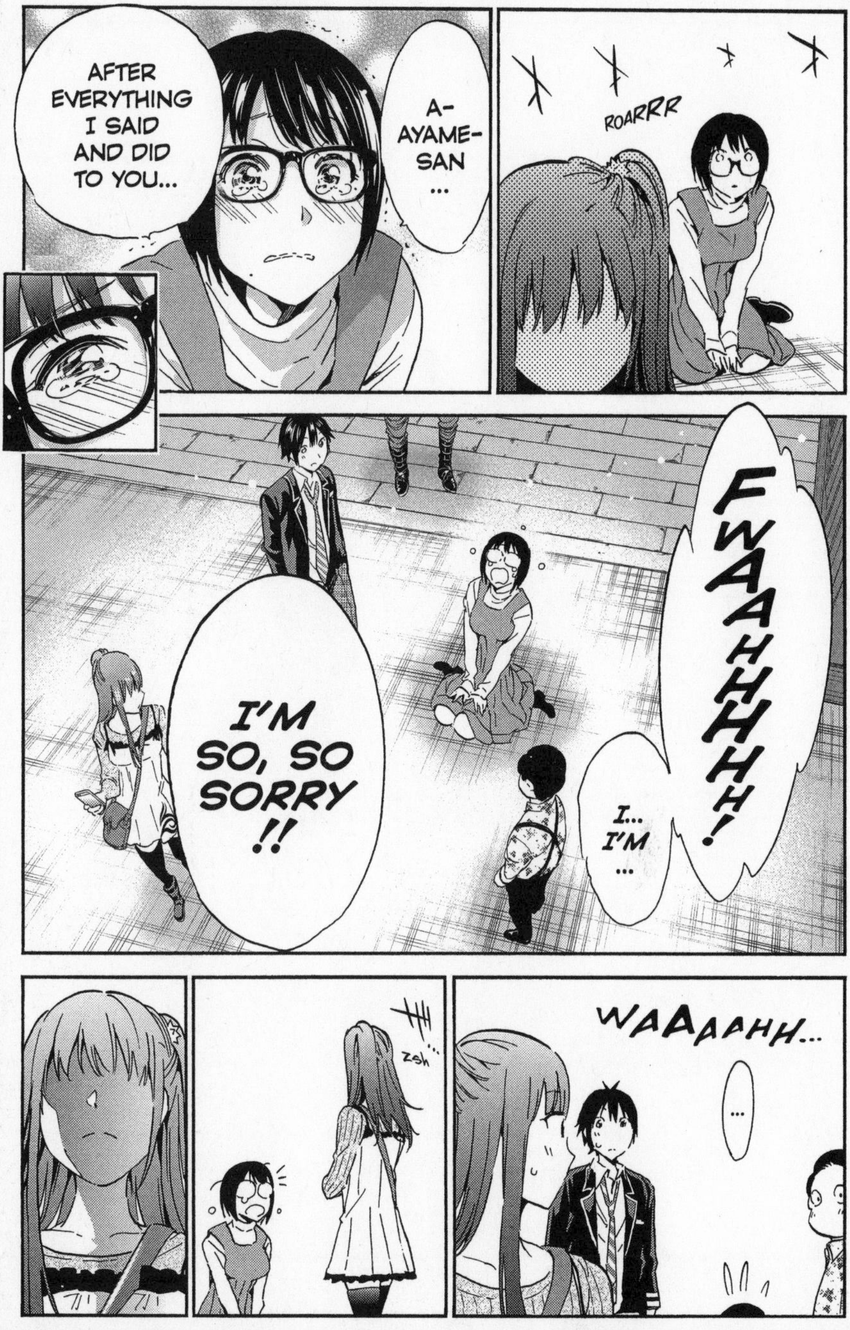
ROARRR
A-AYAME-SAN ...
AFTER EVERYTHING I SAID AND DID TO YOU...
FWAAHHHHHH!
I... I'M ...
I'M SO, SO SORRY !!
WAAAAHH...
...
zsh

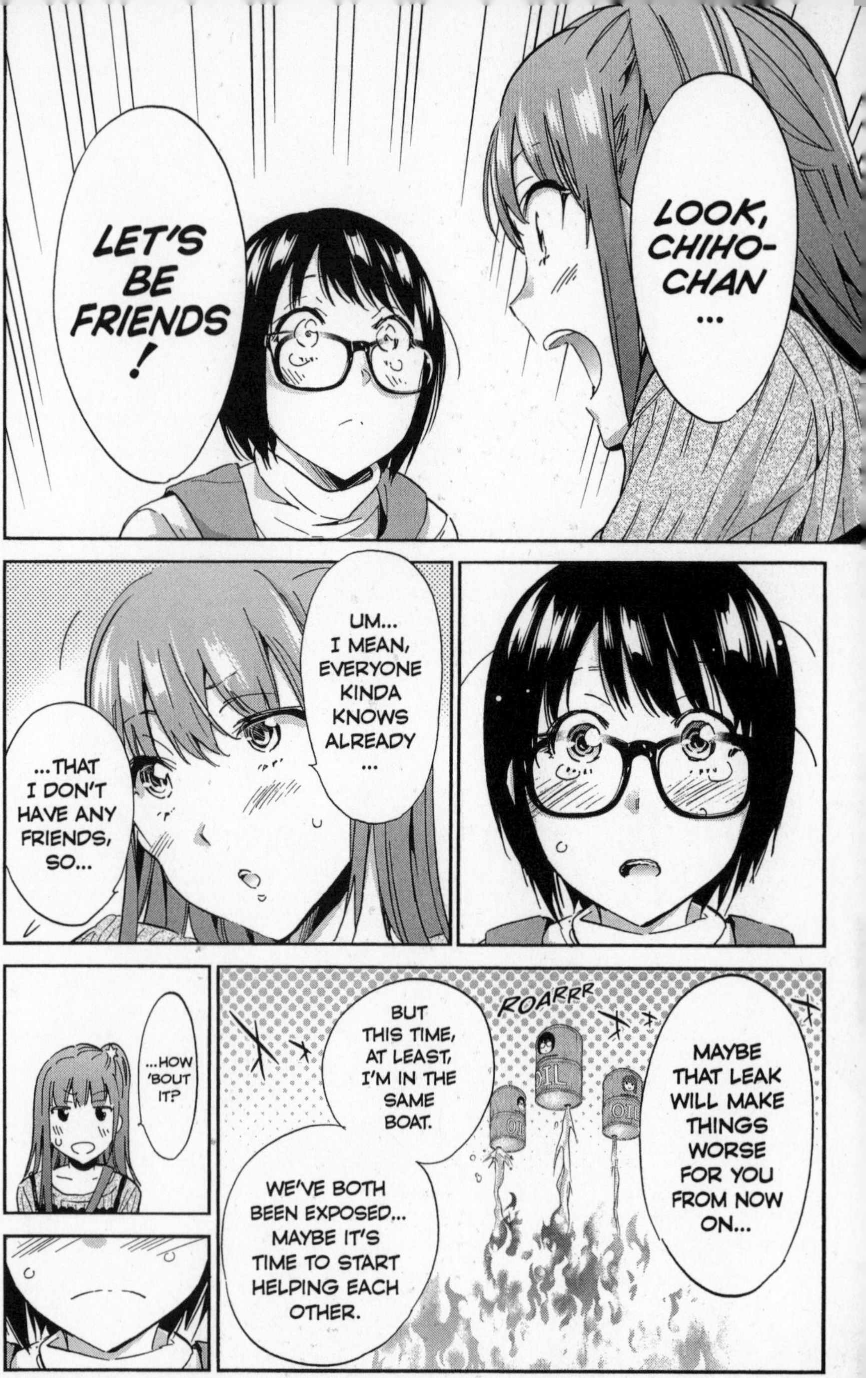
LOOK, CHIHO-CHAN...
LET'S BE FRIENDS!
UM... I MEAN, EVERYONE KINDA KNOWS ALREADY...
...THAT I DON'T HAVE ANY FRIENDS, SO...
ROARRR
MAYBE THAT LEAK WILL MAKE THINGS WORSE FOR YOU FROM NOW ON...
BUT THIS TIME, AT LEAST, I'M IN THE SAME BOAT.
OIL
OIL
WE'VE BOTH BEEN EXPOSED... MAYBE IT'S TIME TO START HELPING EACH OTHER.
...HOW 'BOUT IT?

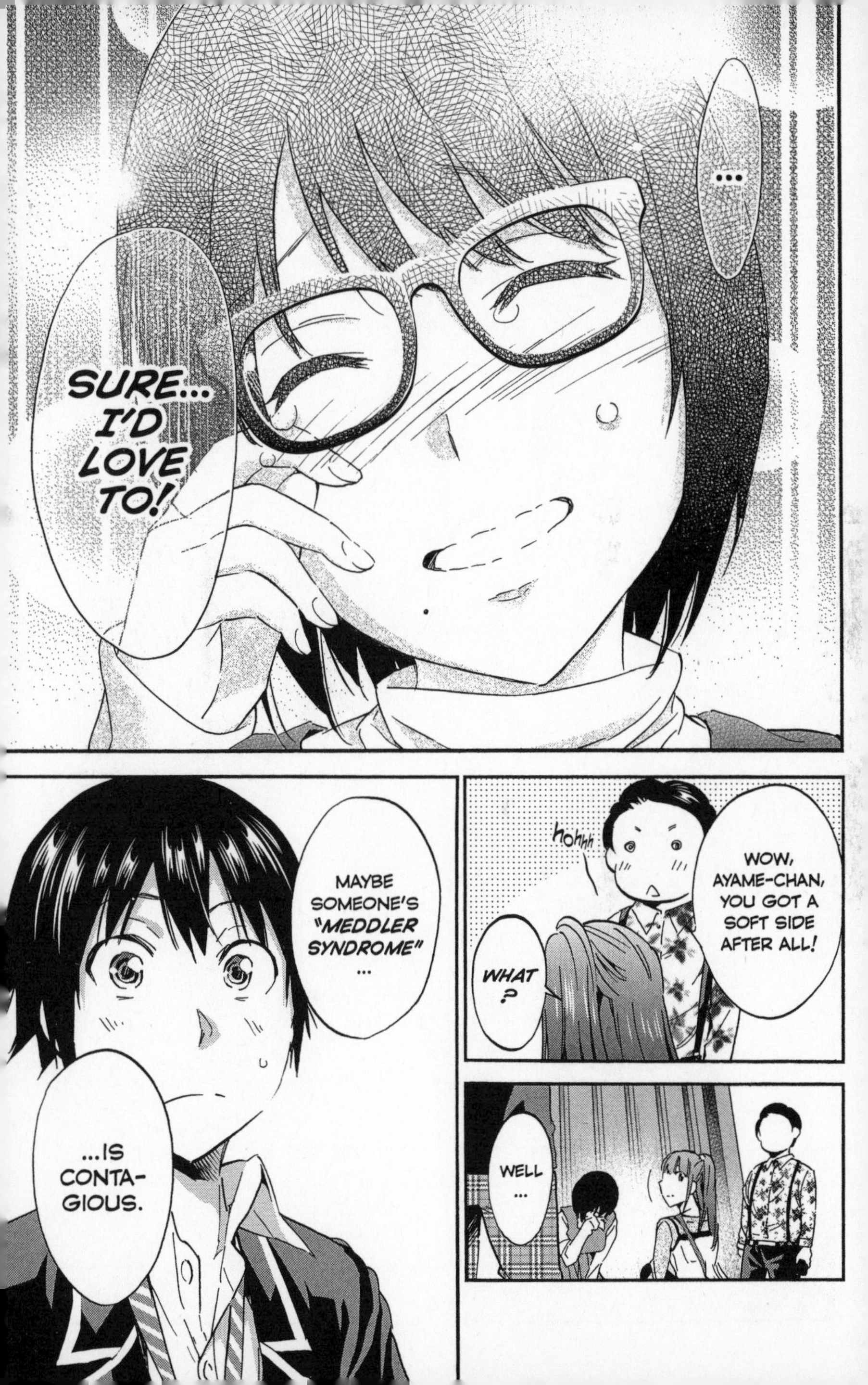
...
SURE... I'D LOVE TO!
WOW, AYAME-CHAN, YOU GOT A SOFT SIDE AFTER ALL!
hohhh
WHAT?
WELL...
MAYBE SOMEONE'S "MEDDLER SYNDROME"...
...IS CONTA-GIOUS.

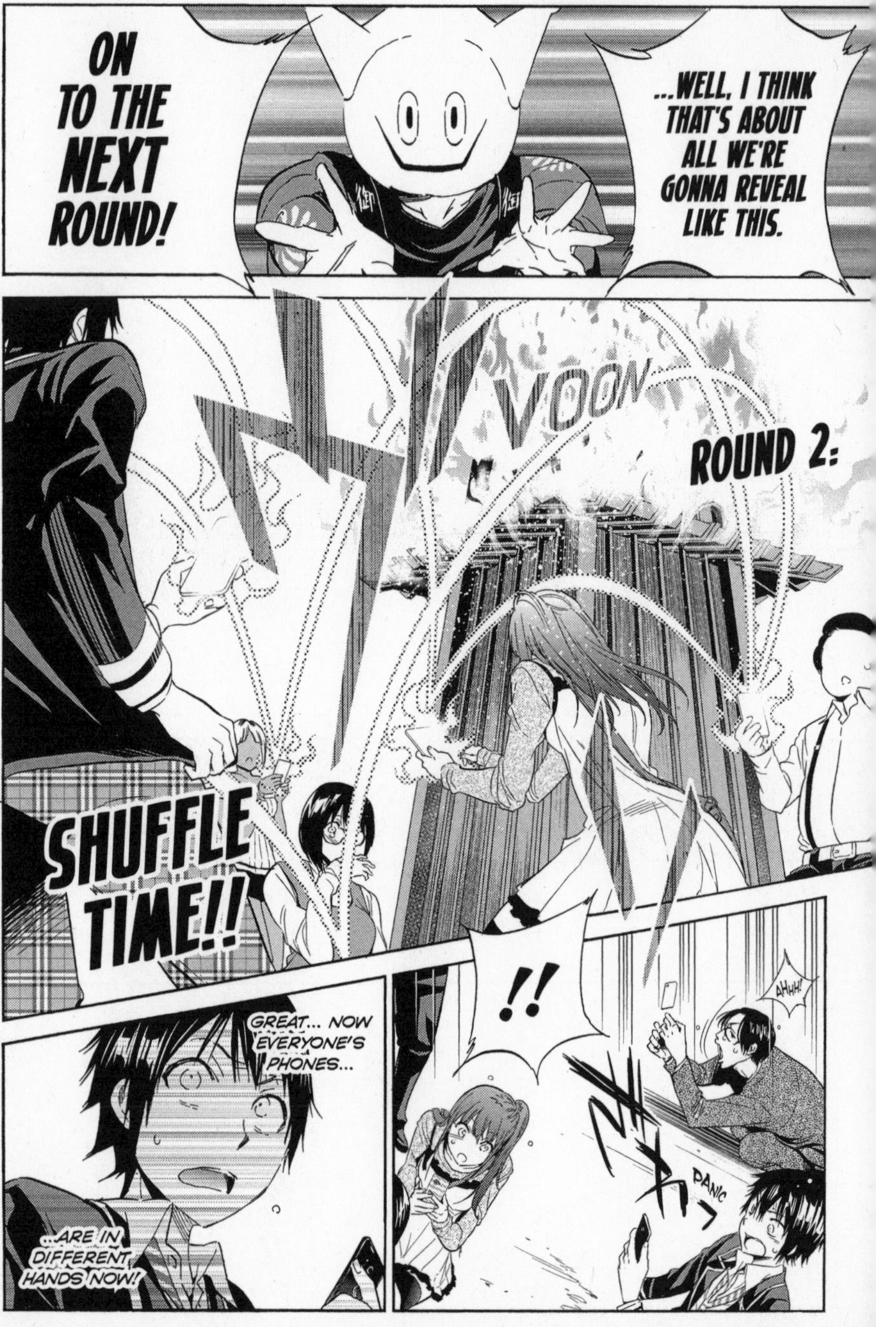
...WELL, I THINK THAT'S ABOUT ALL WE'RE GONNA REVEAL LIKE THIS.
ON TO THE NEXT ROUND!
VOON
ROUND 2:
SHUFFLE TIME!!
AHHH!
!!
PANIC
GREAT... NOW EVERYONE'S PHONES...
...ARE IN DIFFERENT HANDS NOW!

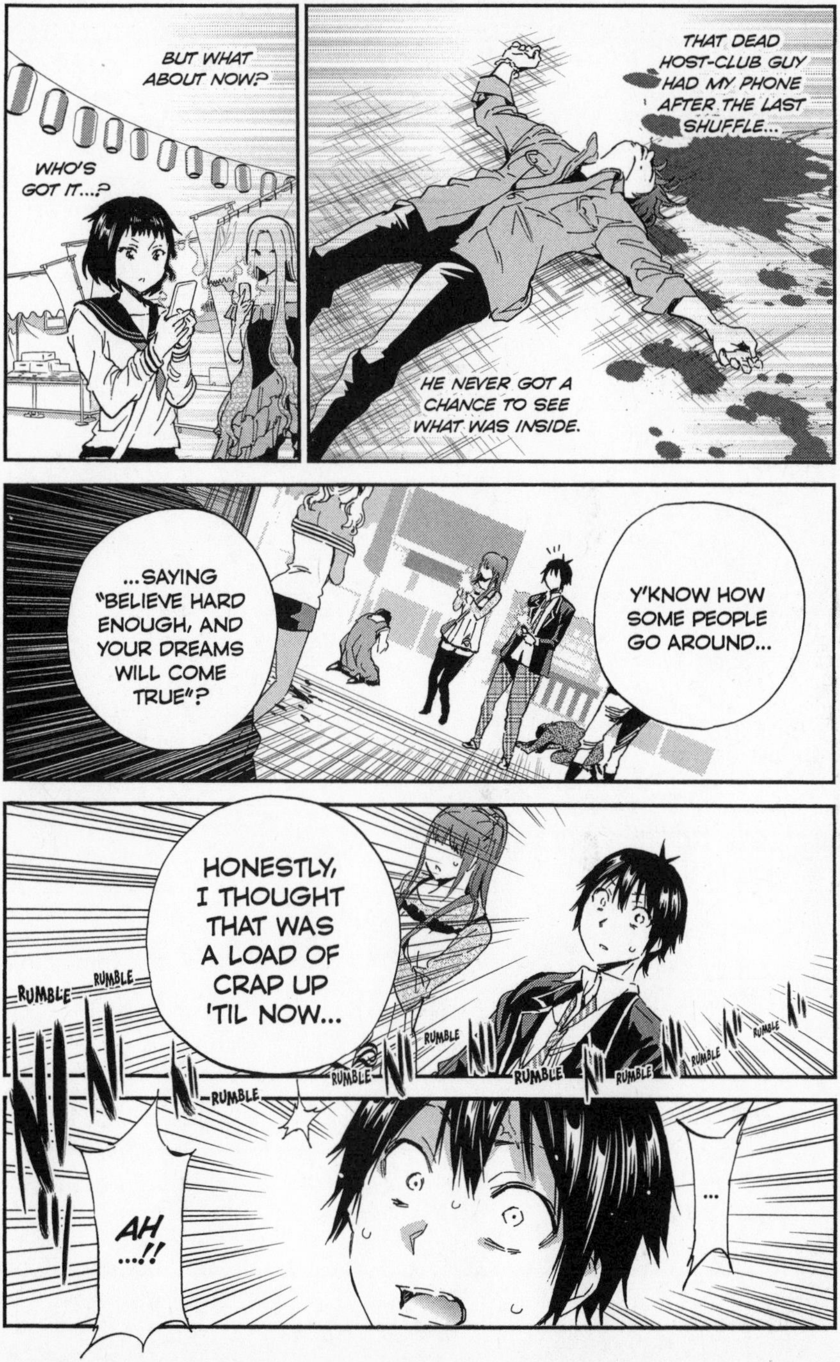
THAT DEAD HOST-CLUB GUY HAD MY PHONE AFTER THE LAST SHUFFLE...
HE NEVER GOT A CHANCE TO SEE WHAT WAS INSIDE.
BUT WHAT ABOUT NOW?
WHO'S GOT IT...?
Y'KNOW HOW SOME PEOPLE GO AROUND...
...SAYING "BELIEVE HARD ENOUGH, AND YOUR DREAMS WILL COME TRUE"?
HONESTLY, I THOUGHT THAT WAS A LOAD OF CRAP UP 'TIL NOW...
RUMBLE RUMBLE RUMBLE RUMBLE RUMBLE RUMBLE RUMBLE RUMBLE
RUMBLE RUMBLE
...
AH ...!!

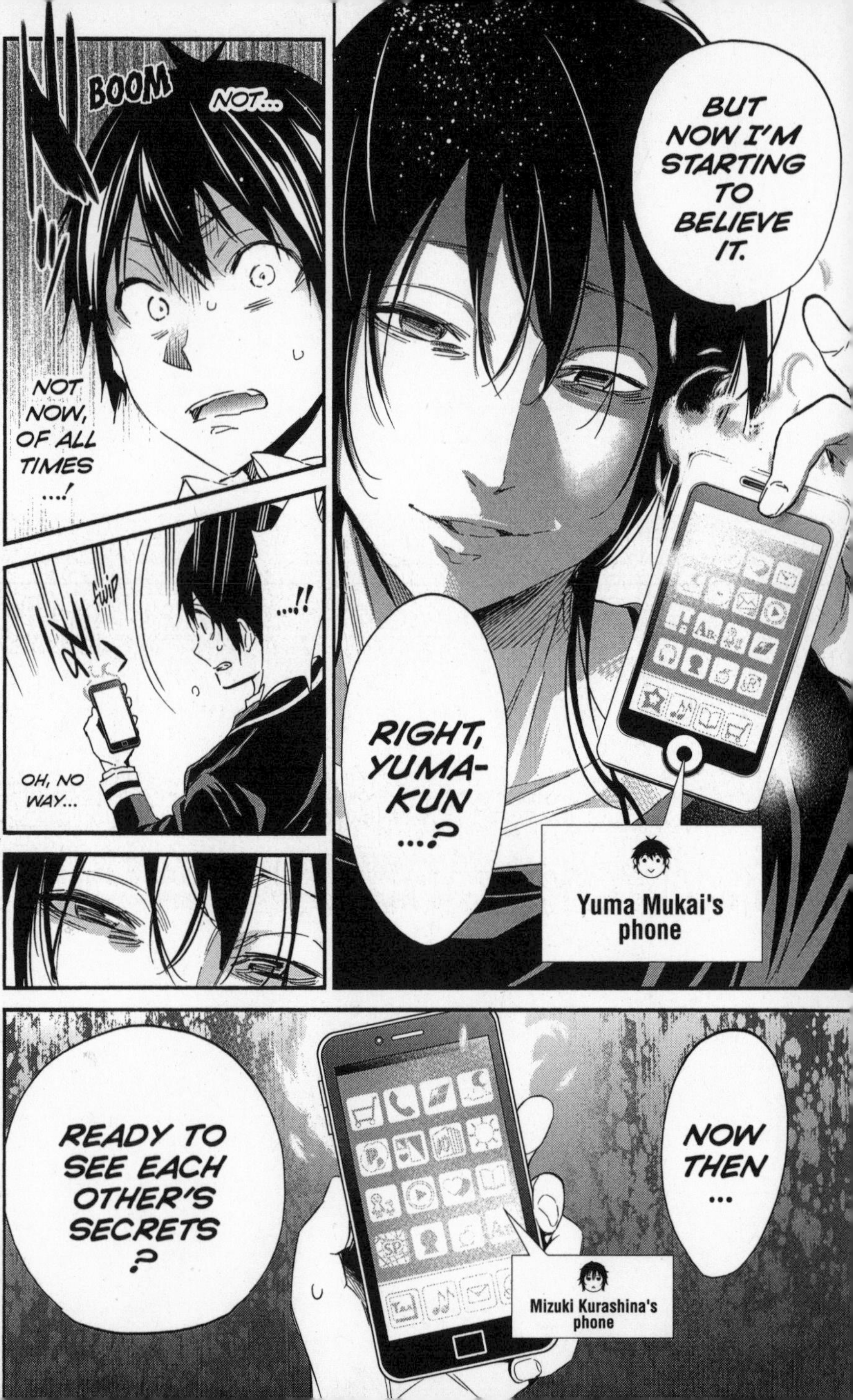
BUT NOW I'M STARTING TO BELIEVE IT.
RIGHT, YUMA-KUN ...?
Yuma Mukai's phone
BOOM
NOT...
NOT NOW, OF ALL TIMES ...!
FWIP
...!!
OH, NO WAY...
NOW THEN ...
READY TO SEE EACH OTHER'S SECRETS?
Mizuki Kurashina's phone

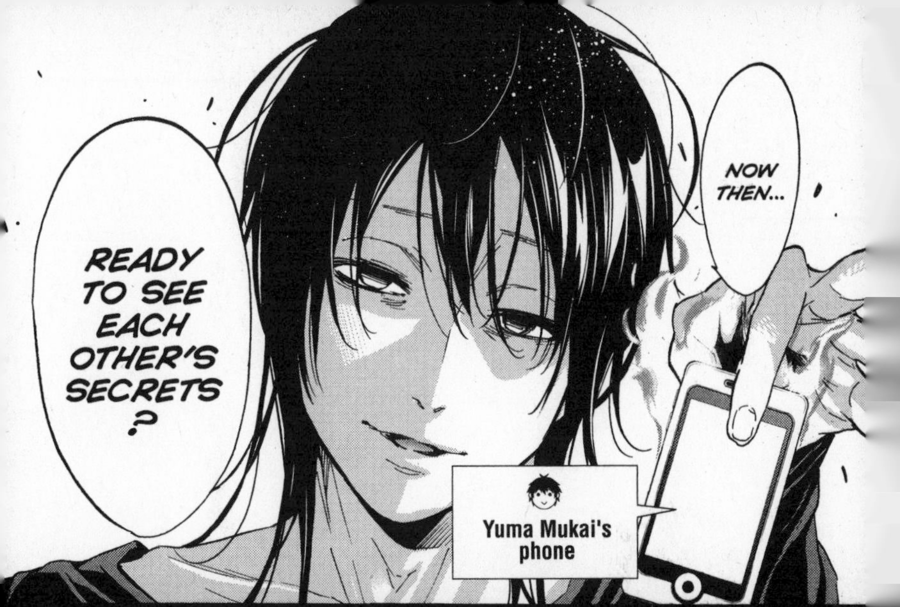
NOW THEN...
READY TO SEE EACH OTHER'S SECRETS?
Yuma Mukai's phone

REAL ACCOUNT

ACCOUNT 27 All a Lie?

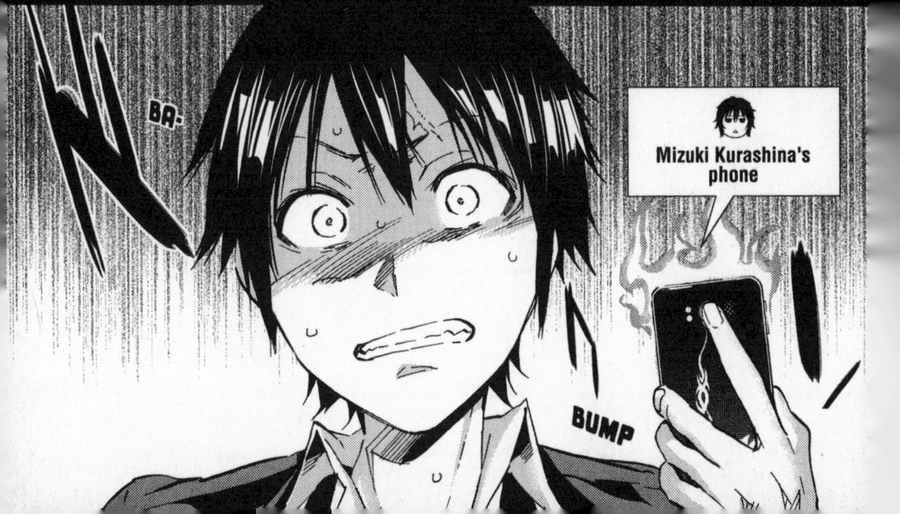
Mizuki Kurashina's phone
BUMP
BA-

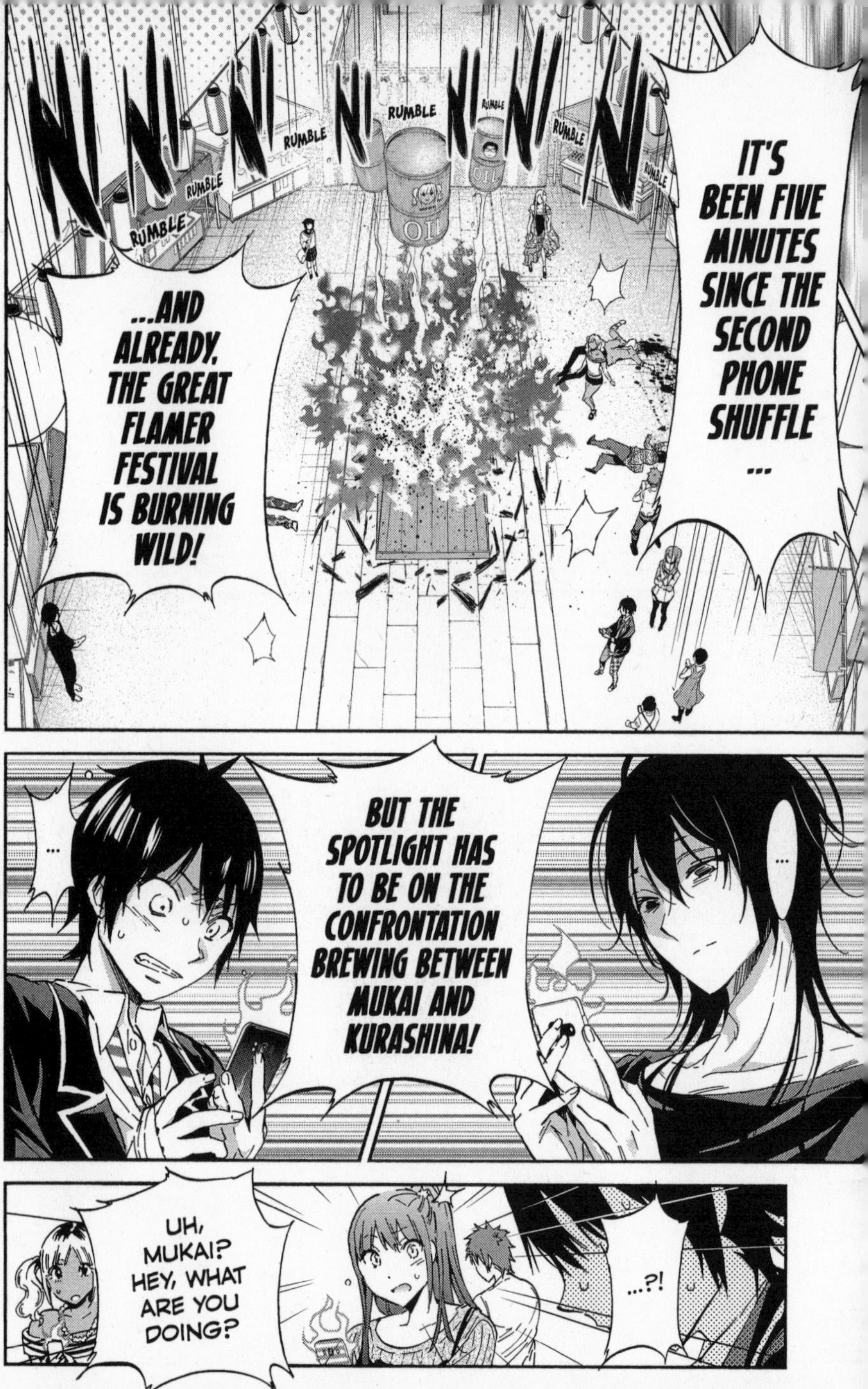
RUMBLE
RUMBLE
RUMBLE
RUMBLE
RUMBLE
RUMBLE
IT'S BEEN FIVE MINUTES SINCE THE SECOND PHONE SHUFFLE ...
...AND ALREADY, THE GREAT FLAMER FESTIVAL IS BURNING WILD!
...
BUT THE SPOTLIGHT HAS TO BE ON THE CONFRONTATION BREWING BETWEEN MUKAI AND KURASHINA!
...
...?!
UH, MUKAI? HEY, WHAT ARE YOU DOING?

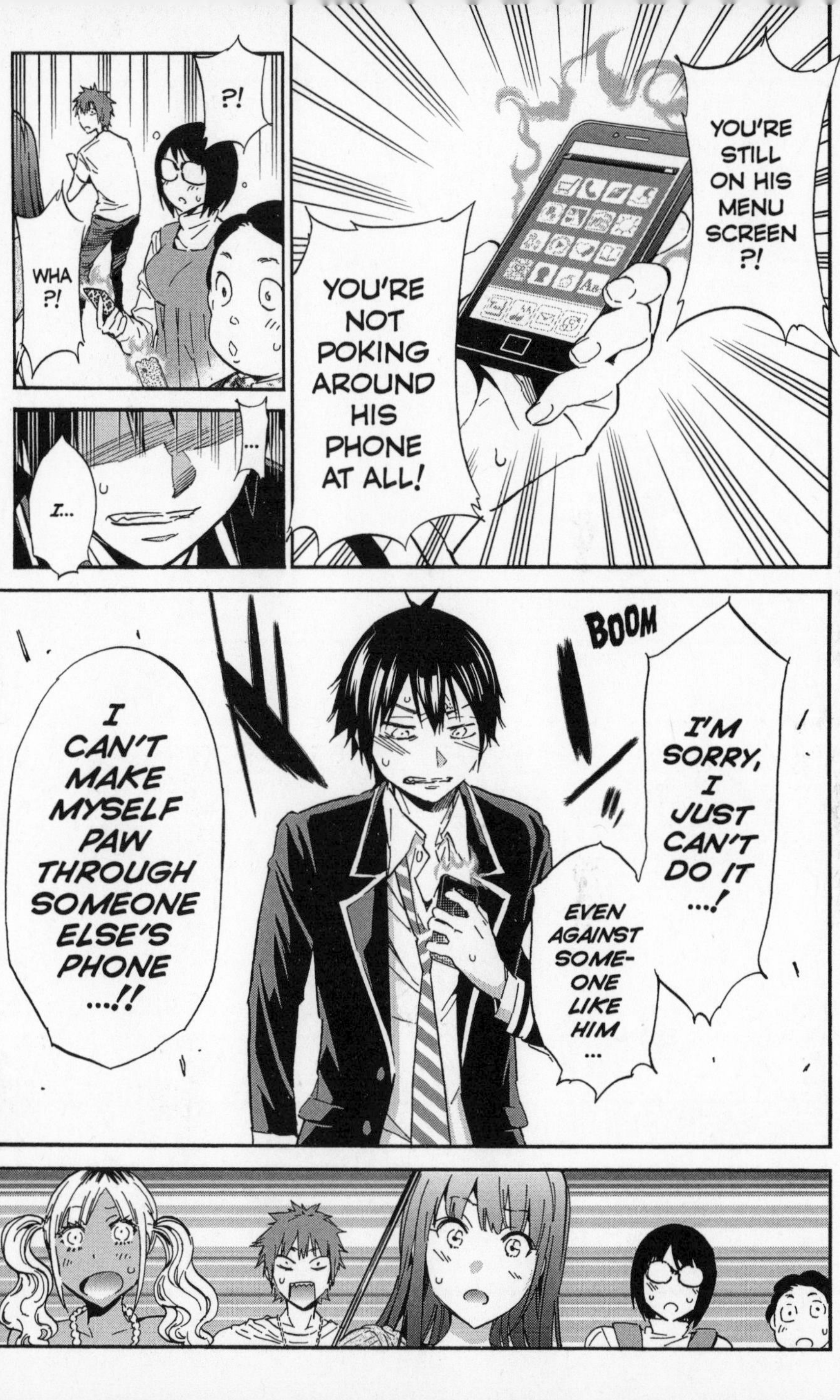
YOU'RE STILL ON HIS MENU SCREEN ?!
YOU'RE NOT POKING AROUND HIS PHONE AT ALL!
?!
WHA ?!
...
I...
BOOM
I'M SORRY, I JUST CAN'T DO IT ...!
EVEN AGAINST SOME-ONE LIKE HIM ...
I CAN'T MAKE MYSELF PAW THROUGH SOMEONE ELSE'S PHONE ...!!

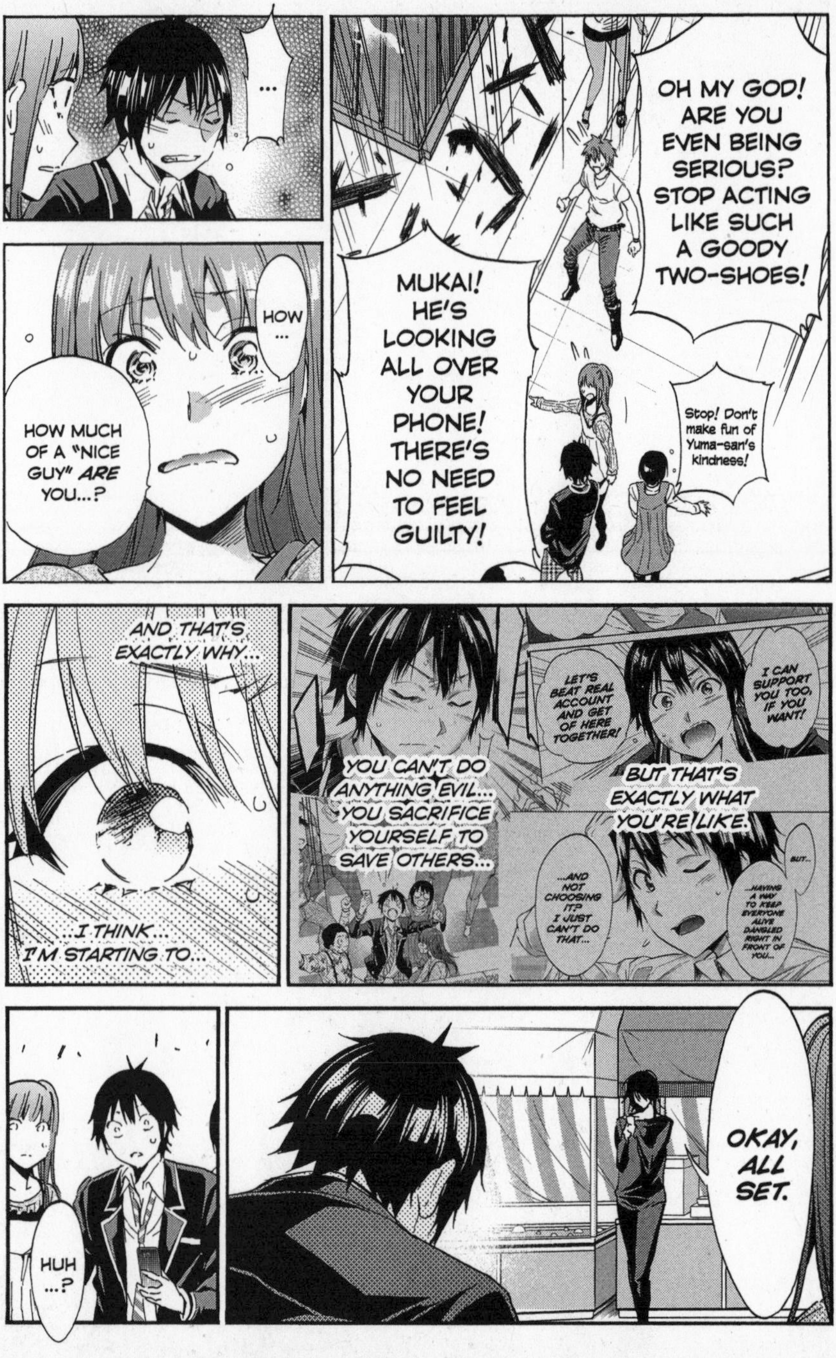
OH MY GOD! ARE YOU EVEN BEING SERIOUS? STOP ACTING LIKE SUCH A GOODY TWO-SHOES!
MUKAI! HE'S LOOKING ALL OVER YOUR PHONE! THERE'S NO NEED TO FEEL GUILTY!
Stop! Don't make fun of Yuma-san's kindness!
...
HOW ...
HOW MUCH OF A "NICE GUY" ARE YOU...?
I CAN SUPPORT YOU TOO, IF YOU WANT!
LET'S BEAT REAL ACCOUNT AND GET OF HERE TOGETHER!
BUT THAT'S EXACTLY WHAT YOU'RE LIKE.
YOU CAN'T DO ANYTHING EVIL... YOU SACRIFICE YOURSELF TO SAVE OTHERS...
BUT...
...HAVING A WAY TO KEEP EVERYONE ALIVE DANGLED RIGHT IN FRONT OF YOU...
...AND NOT CHOOSING IT? I JUST CAN'T DO THAT...
AND THAT'S EXACTLY WHY...
...I THINK... I'M STARTING TO...
OKAY, ALL SET.
HUH ...?

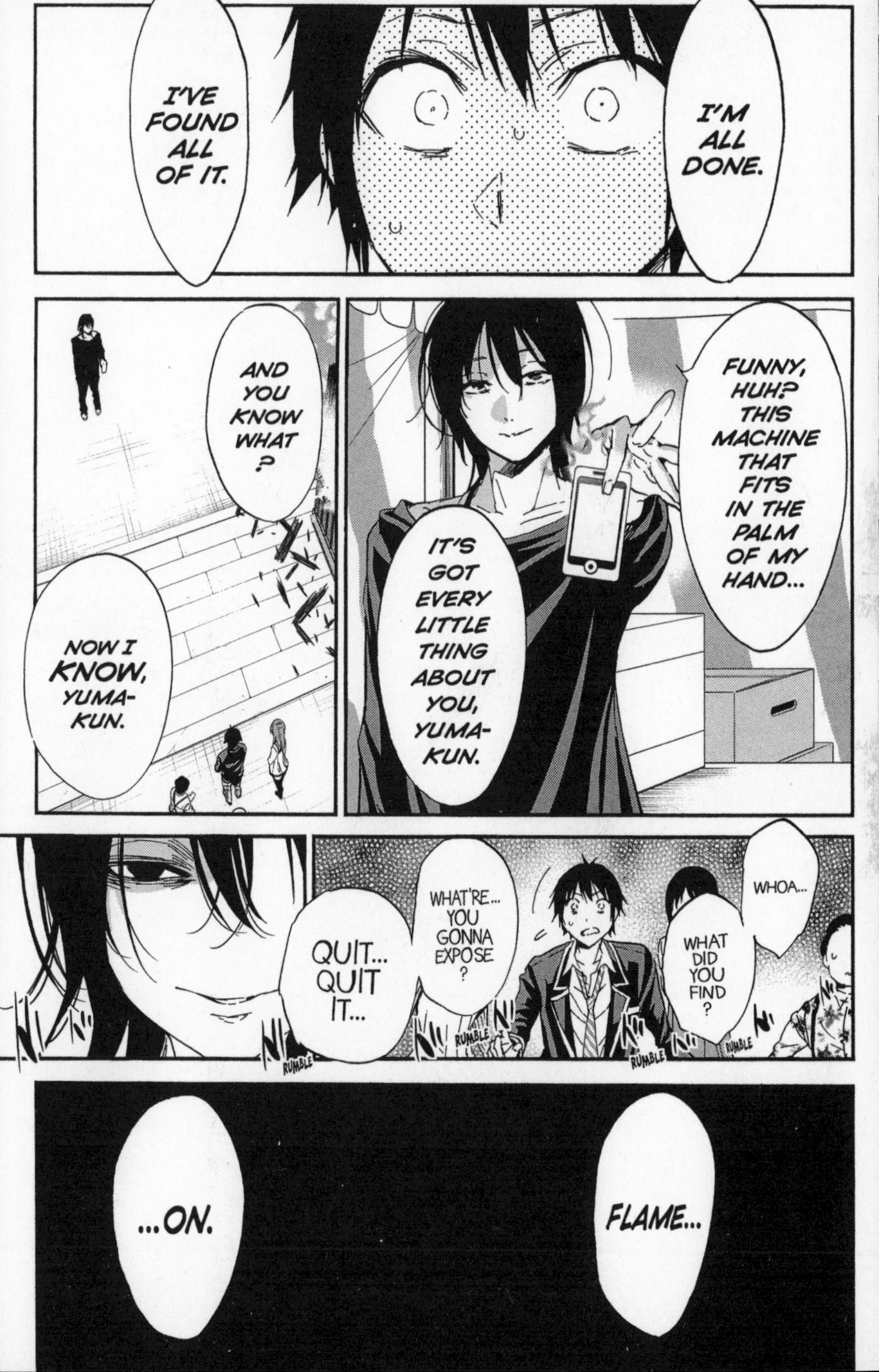
I'M ALL DONE.
I'VE FOUND ALL OF IT.
FUNNY, HUH? THIS MACHINE THAT FITS IN THE PALM OF MY HAND...
IT'S GOT EVERY LITTLE THING ABOUT YOU, YUMA-KUN.
AND YOU KNOW WHAT?
NOW I KNOW, YUMA-KUN.
WHOA...
WHAT DID YOU FIND?
WHAT'RE... YOU GONNA EXPOSE?
RUMBLE
RUMBLE
RUMBLE
QUIT... QUIT IT...
RUMBLE
FLAME...
...ON.

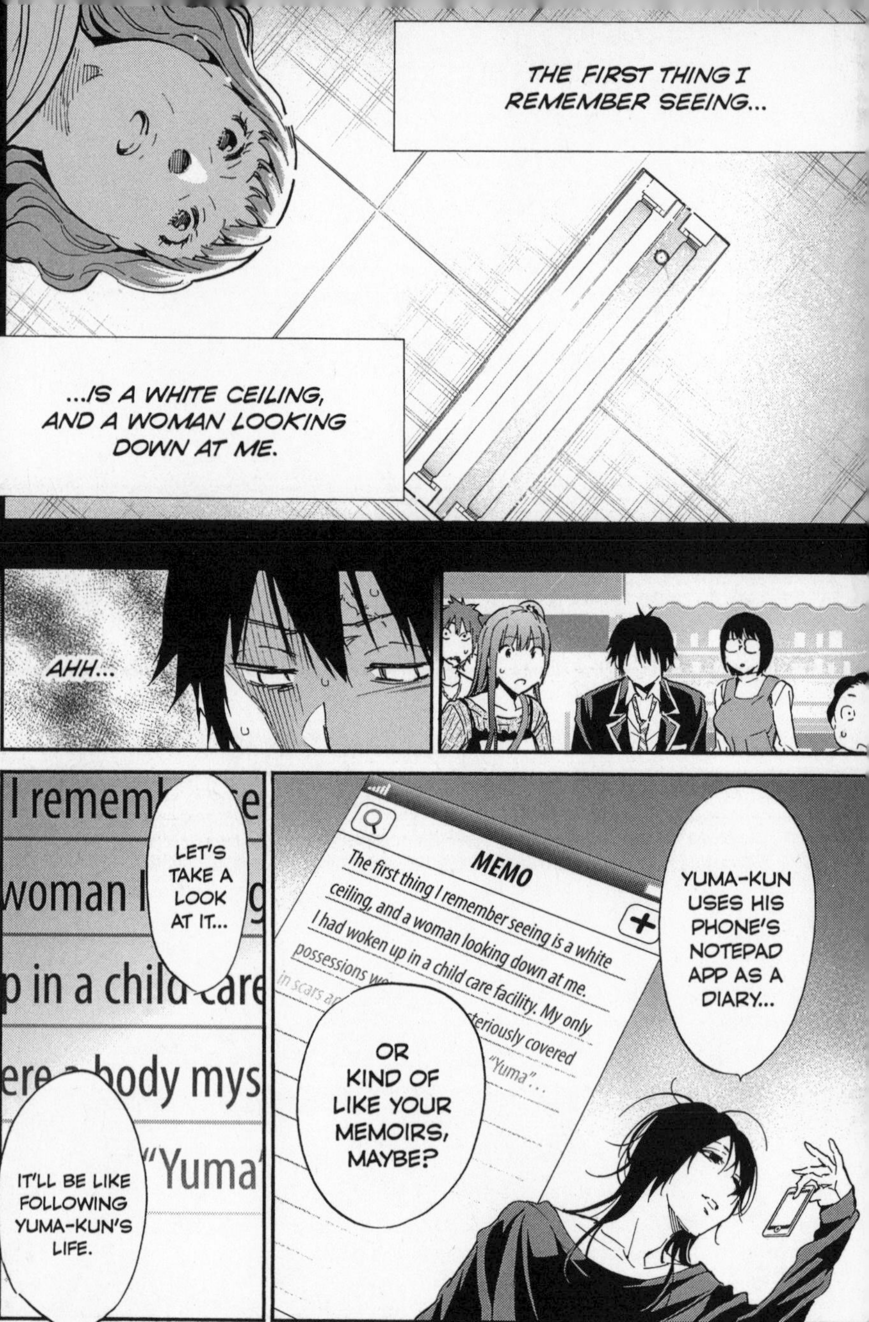
THE FIRST THING I REMEMBER SEEING...
...IS A WHITE CEILING, AND A WOMAN LOOKING DOWN AT ME.
AHH...
YUMA-KUN USES HIS PHONE'S NOTEPAD APP AS A DIARY...
MEMO
The first thing I remember seeing is a white ceiling, and a woman looking down at me.
I had woken up in a child care facility. My only
"Yuma"...
OR KIND OF LIKE YOUR MEMOIRS, MAYBE?
LET'S TAKE A LOOK AT IT...
IT'LL BE LIKE FOLLOWING YUMA-KUN'S LIFE.

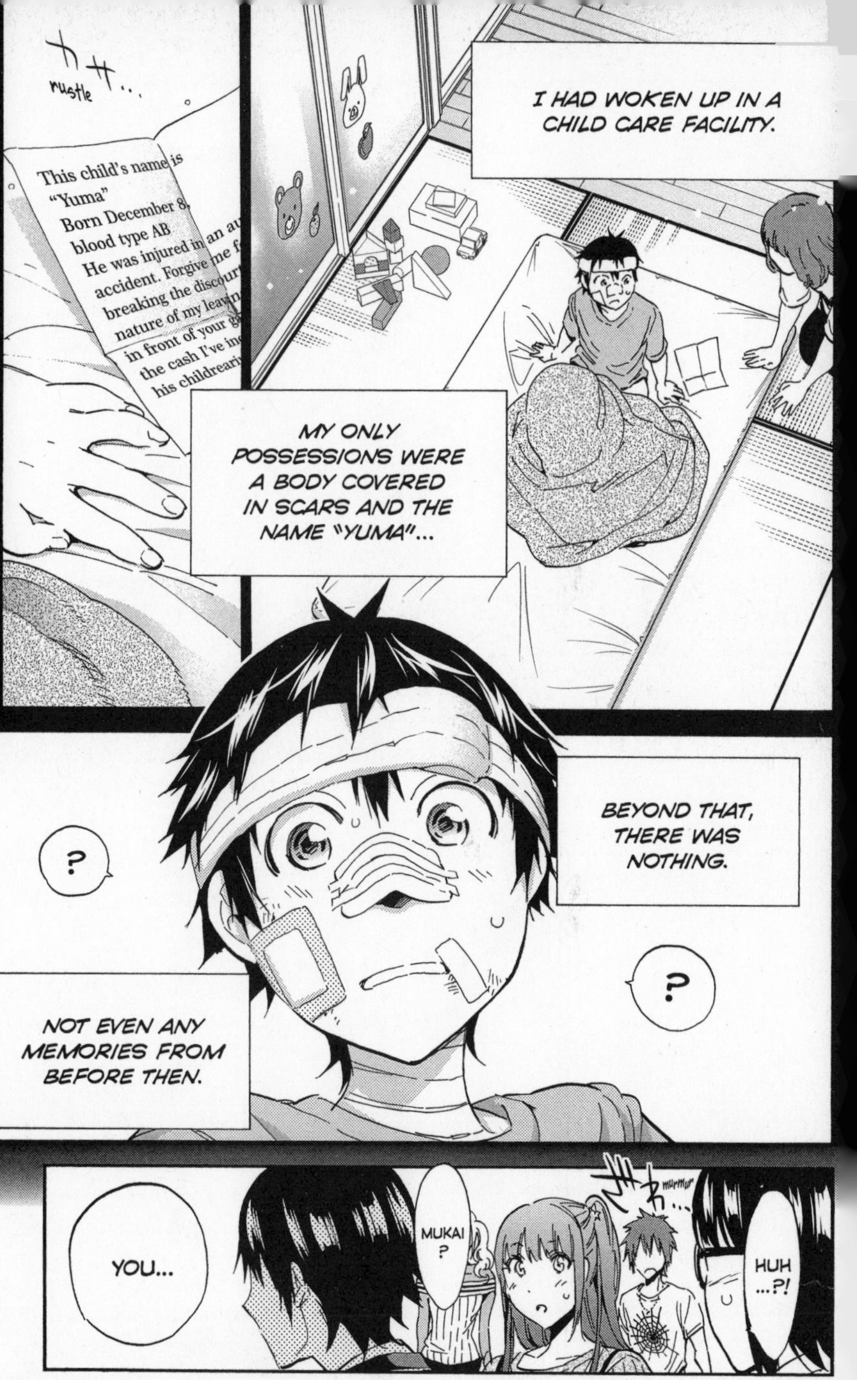
I HAD WOKEN UP IN A CHILD CARE FACILITY.
MY ONLY POSSESSIONS WERE A BODY COVERED IN SCARS AND THE NAME "YUMA"...
rustle...
This child's name is
"Yuma"
Born December 8,
blood type AB
He was injured in an au
accident. Forgive me f
breaking the discou
nature of my leavin
in front of your g
the cash I've in
his childreari
BEYOND THAT, THERE WAS NOTHING.
?
?
NOT EVEN ANY MEMORIES FROM BEFORE THEN.
HUH ...?!
murmur
MUKAI ?
YOU...

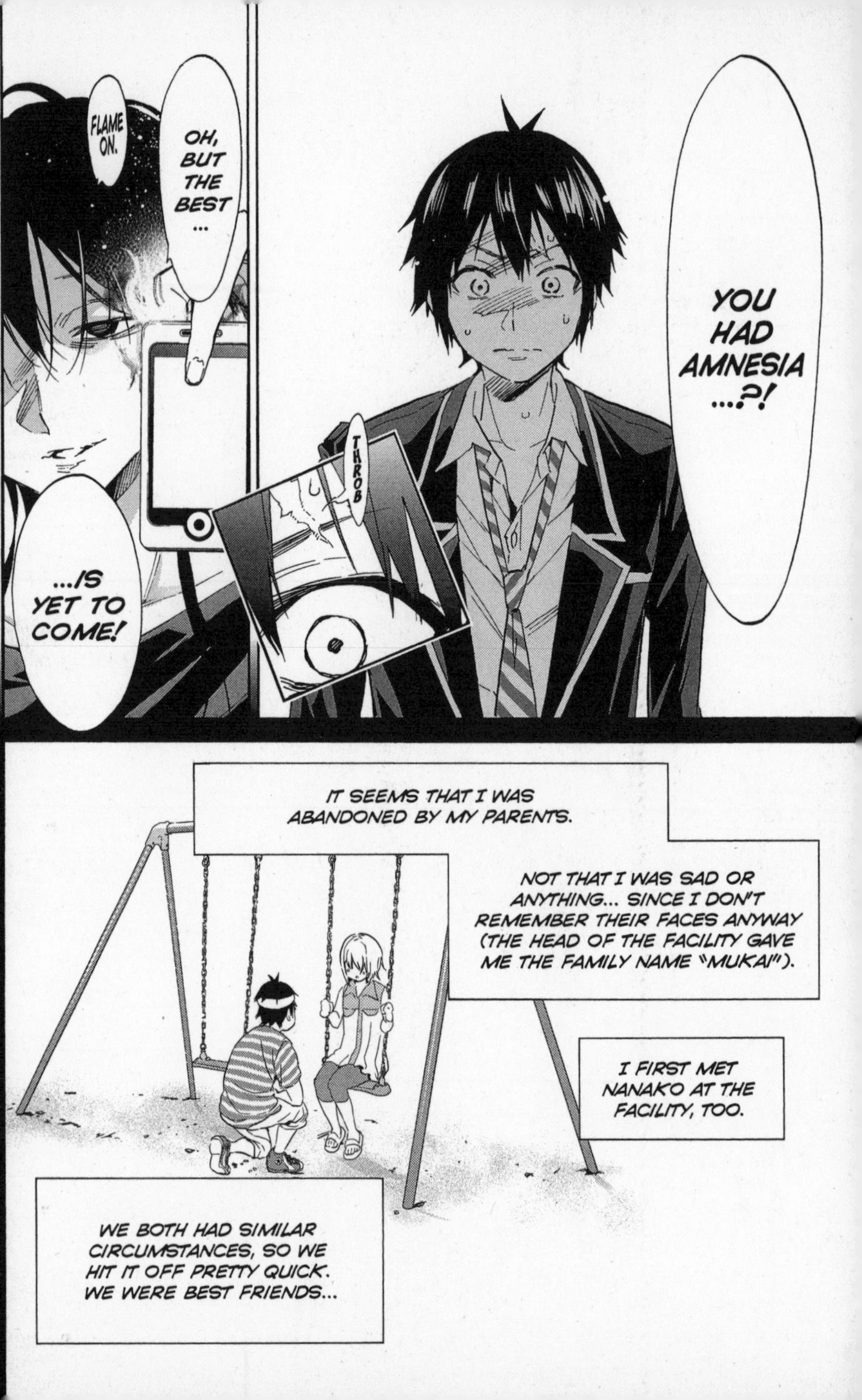

YOU HAD AMNESIA ...?!
THROB
OH, BUT THE BEST ...
FLAME ON.
...IS YET TO COME!
IT SEEMS THAT I WAS ABANDONED BY MY PARENTS.
NOT THAT I WAS SAD OR ANYTHING... SINCE I DON'T REMEMBER THEIR FACES ANYWAY (THE HEAD OF THE FACILITY GAVE ME THE FAMILY NAME "MUKAI").
I FIRST MET NANAKO AT THE FACILITY, TOO.
WE BOTH HAD SIMILAR CIRCUMSTANCES, SO WE HIT IT OFF PRETTY QUICK. WE WERE BEST FRIENDS...

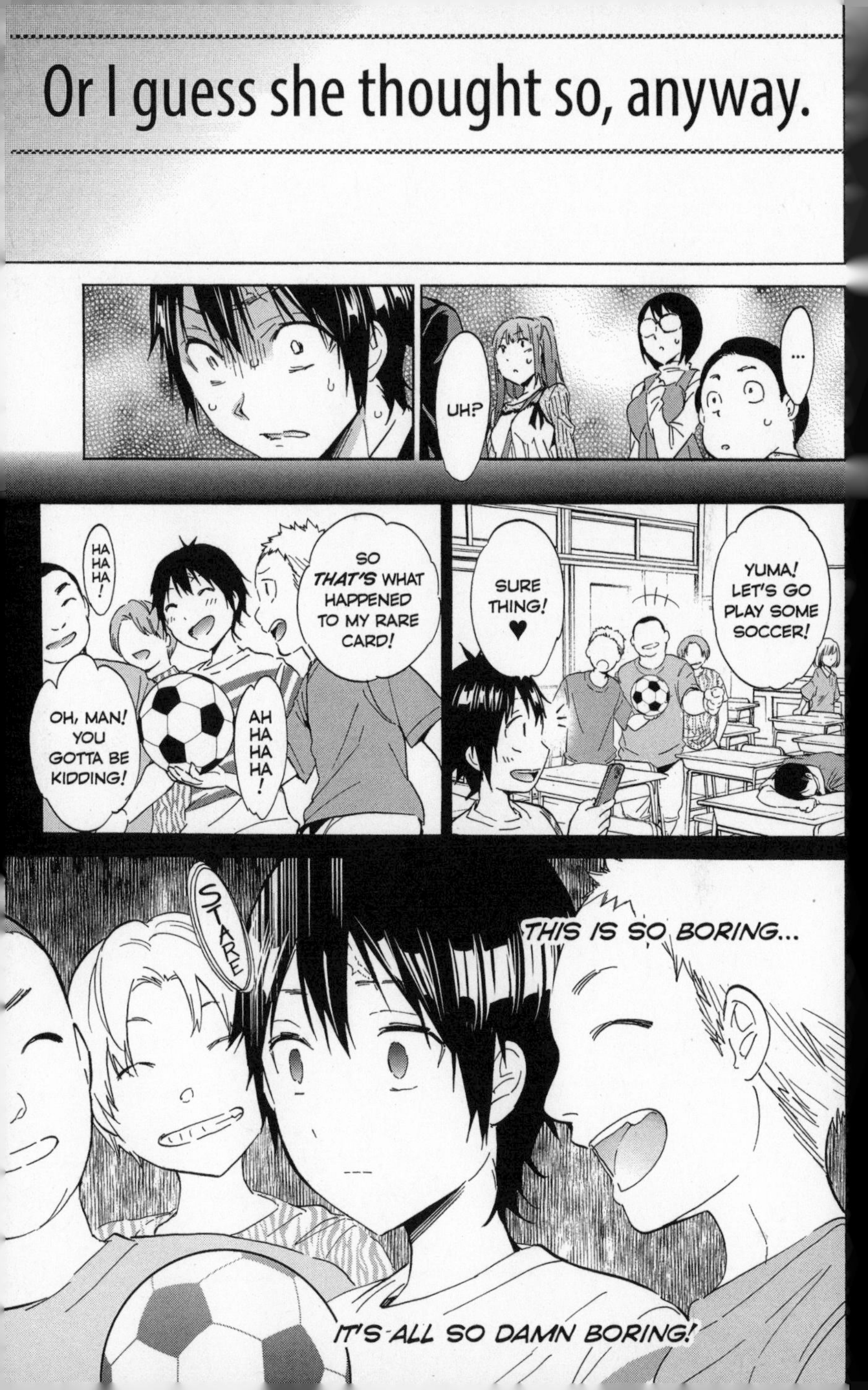
Or I guess she thought so, anyway.
...
UH?
YUMA! LET'S GO PLAY SOME SOCCER!
SURE THING! ♥
SO *THAT'S* WHAT HAPPENED TO MY RARE CARD!
HA HA HA!
AH HA HA HA!
OH, MAN! YOU GOTTA BE KIDDING!
STARE
THIS IS SO BORING...
IT'S ALL SO DAMN BORING!

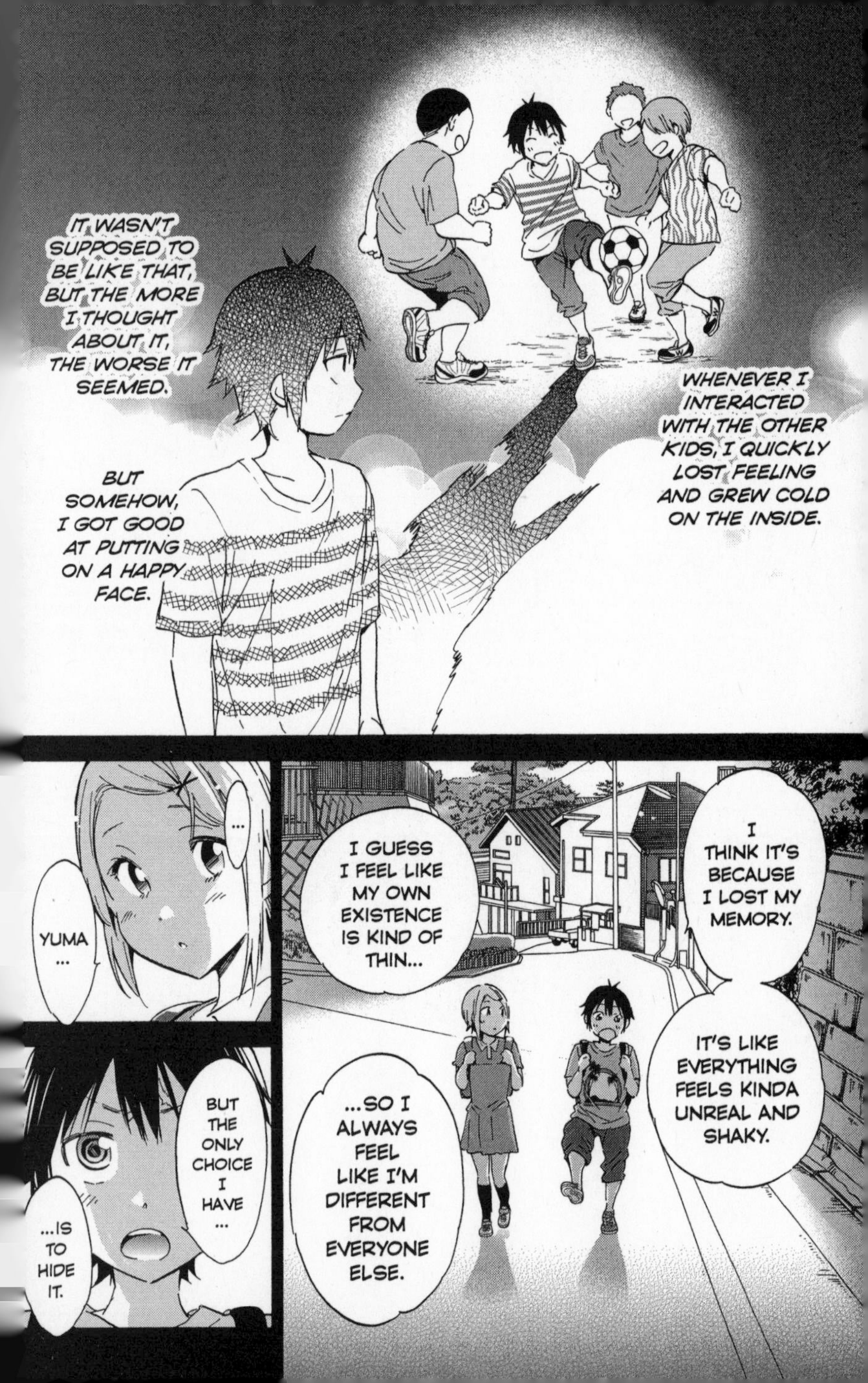
WHENEVER I INTERACTED WITH THE OTHER KIDS, I QUICKLY LOST FEELING AND GREW COLD ON THE INSIDE.
IT WASN'T SUPPOSED TO BE LIKE THAT, BUT THE MORE I THOUGHT ABOUT IT, THE WORSE IT SEEMED.
BUT SOMEHOW, I GOT GOOD AT PUTTING ON A HAPPY FACE.
I THINK IT'S BECAUSE I LOST MY MEMORY.
I GUESS I FEEL LIKE MY OWN EXISTENCE IS KIND OF THIN...
IT'S LIKE EVERYTHING FEELS KINDA UNREAL AND SHAKY.
...SO I ALWAYS FEEL LIKE I'M DIFFERENT FROM EVERYONE ELSE.
...
YUMA...
BUT THE ONLY CHOICE I HAVE...
...IS TO HIDE IT.

Really, I didn't care about

anyone else around me.

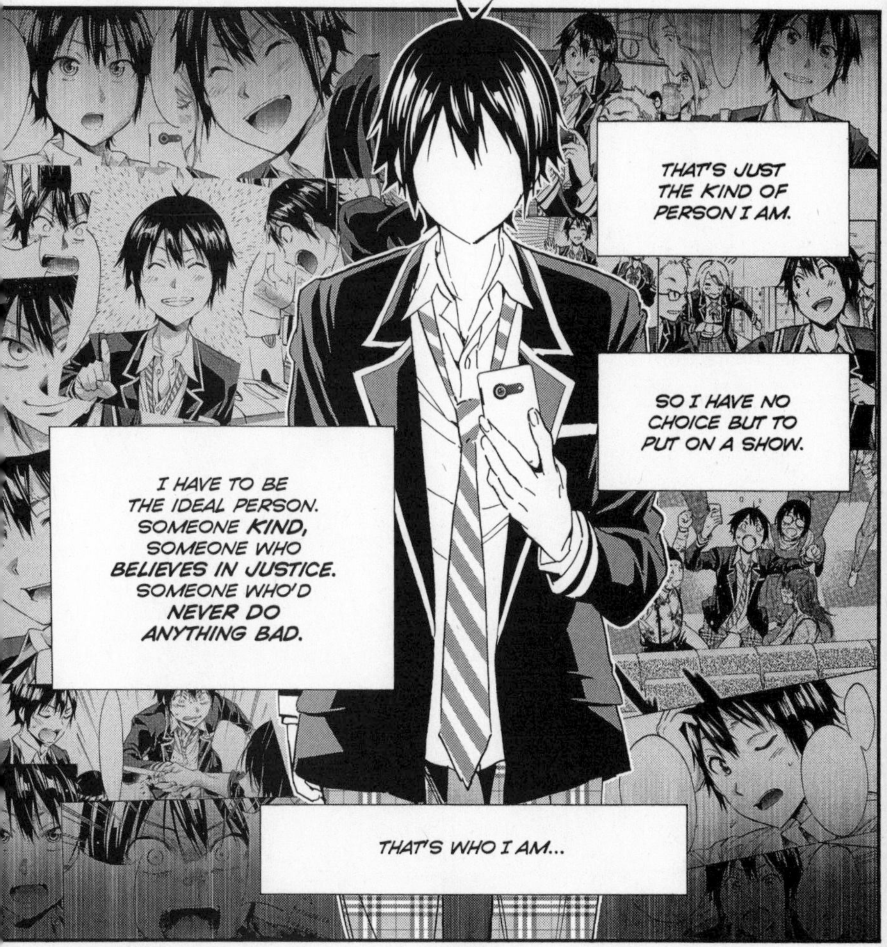
THAT'S JUST THE KIND OF PERSON I AM.
SO I HAVE NO CHOICE BUT TO PUT ON A SHOW.
I HAVE TO BE THE IDEAL PERSON. SOMEONE **KIND**, SOMEONE WHO **BELIEVES IN JUSTICE**. SOMEONE WHO'D **NEVER DO ANYTHING BAD**.
THAT'S WHO I AM...

That's what "Yuma Mukai" is.

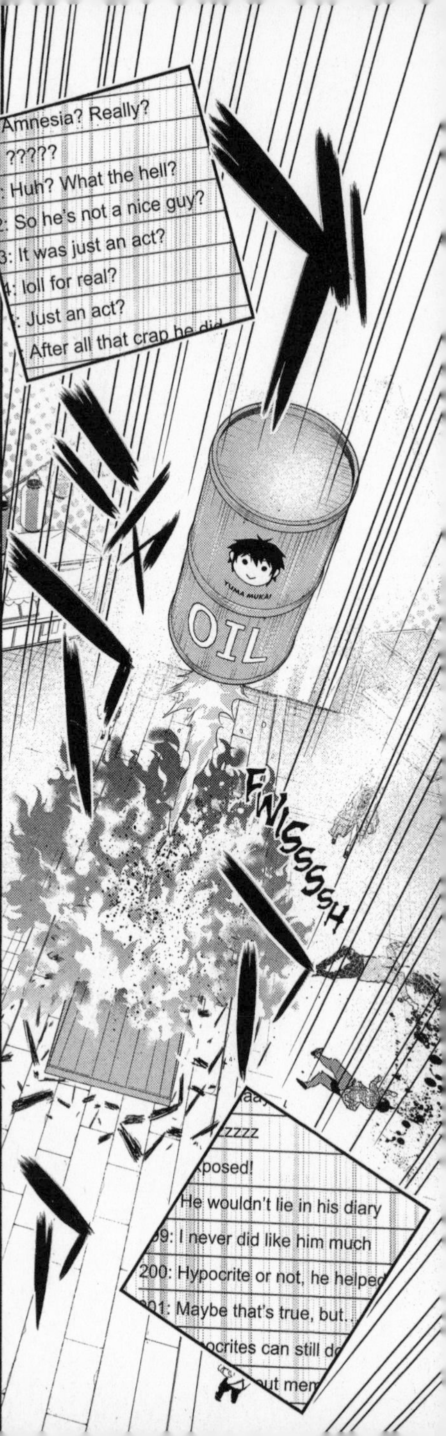
59: Amnesia? Really?
60: ?????
61: Huh? What the hell?
62: So he's not a nice guy?
3: It was just an act?
4: loll for real?
: Just an act?
After all that crap he did
YUMA MUKAI
OIL
FWISSSSH
zzzzz
xposed!
He wouldn't lie in his diary
99: I never did like him much
200: Hypocrite or not, he helped
201: Maybe that's true, but...
pocrites can still do
out mem
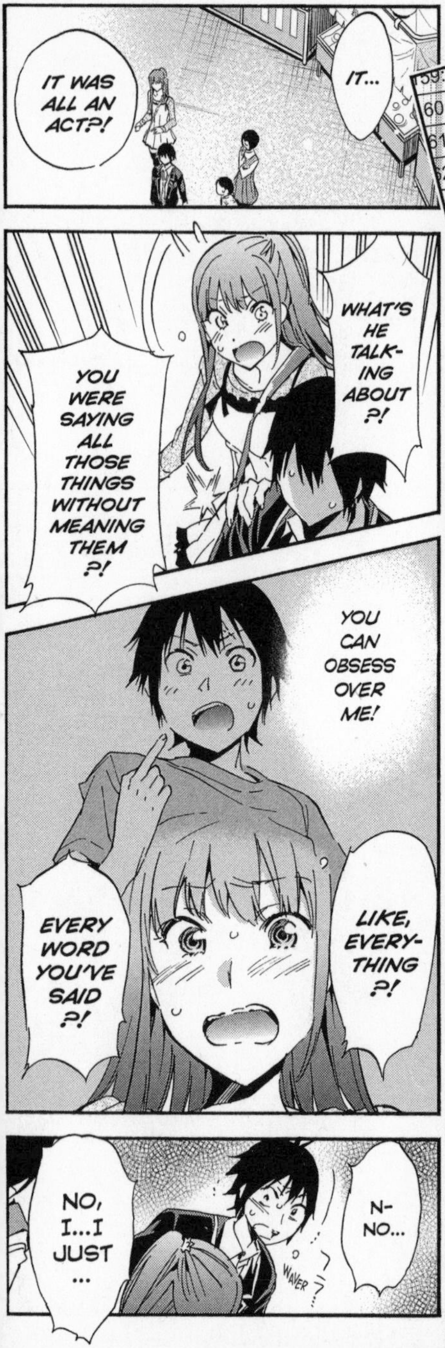
IT...
IT WAS ALL AN ACT?!
WHAT'S HE TALKING ABOUT?!
YOU WERE SAYING ALL THOSE THINGS WITHOUT MEANING THEM?!
YOU CAN OBSESS OVER ME!
LIKE, EVERYTHING?!
EVERY WORD YOU'VE SAID?!
N-NO...
WAVER
NO, I...I JUST...

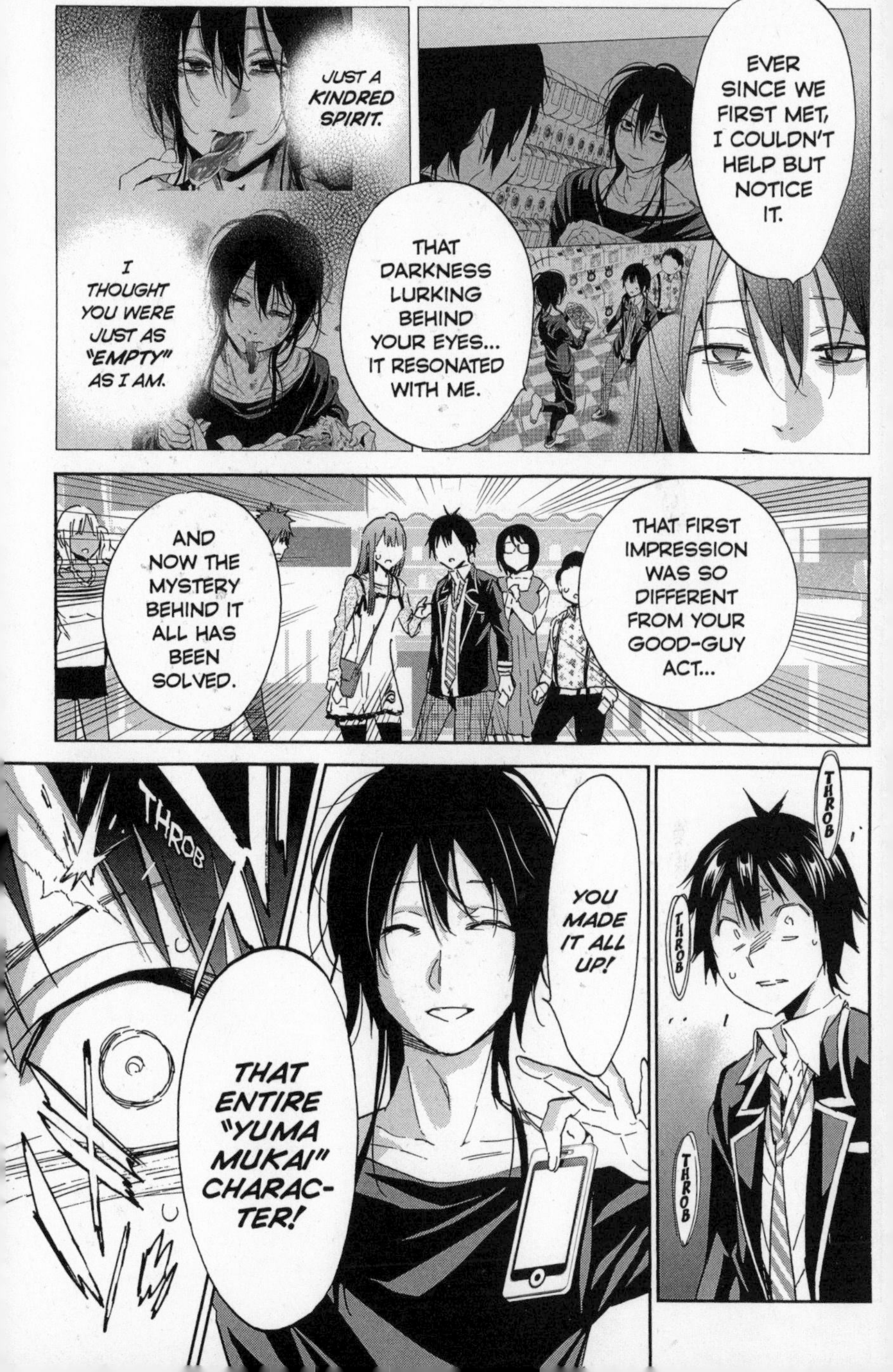
EVER SINCE WE FIRST MET, I COULDN'T HELP BUT NOTICE IT.
THAT DARKNESS LURKING BEHIND YOUR EYES... IT RESONATED WITH ME.
I THOUGHT YOU WERE JUST AS "EMPTY" AS I AM.
JUST A KINDRED SPIRIT.
THAT FIRST IMPRESSION WAS SO DIFFERENT FROM YOUR GOOD-GUY ACT...
AND NOW THE MYSTERY BEHIND IT ALL HAS BEEN SOLVED.
THROB
THROB
THROB
YOU MADE IT ALL UP!
THAT ENTIRE "YUMA MUKAI" CHARACTER!
THROB

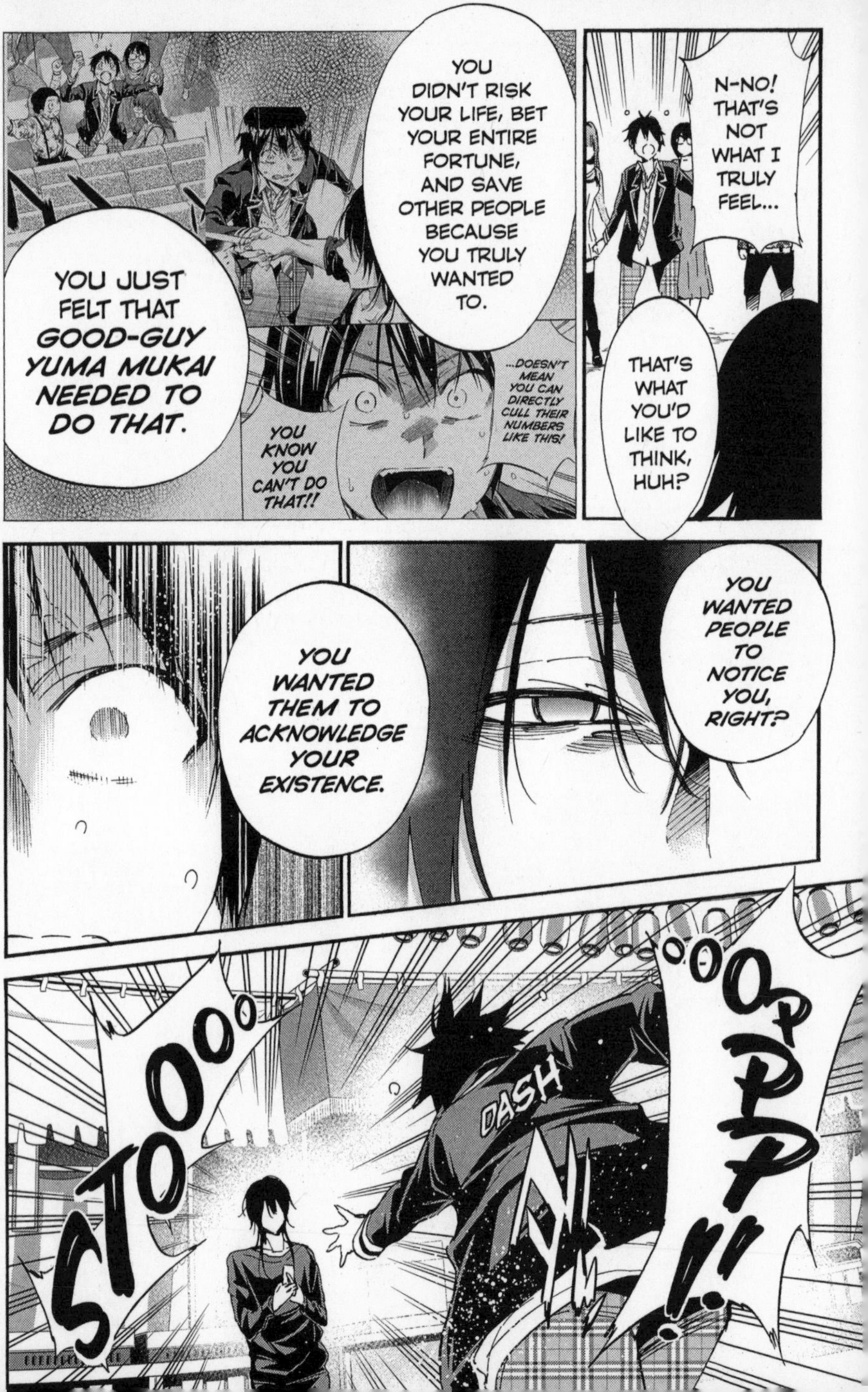
N-NO! THAT'S NOT WHAT I TRULY FEEL...
THAT'S WHAT YOU'D LIKE TO THINK, HUH?
YOU DIDN'T RISK YOUR LIFE, BET YOUR ENTIRE FORTUNE, AND SAVE OTHER PEOPLE BECAUSE YOU TRULY WANTED TO.
YOU JUST FELT THAT *GOOD-GUY YUMA MUKAI* NEEDED TO DO THAT.
...DOESN'T MEAN YOU CAN DIRECTLY CULL THEIR NUMBERS LIKE THIS!
YOU KNOW YOU CAN'T DO THAT!!
YOU WANTED PEOPLE TO NOTICE YOU, RIGHT?
YOU WANTED THEM TO ACKNOWLEDGE YOUR EXISTENCE.
STOOOO
OOOOPP!!
DASH

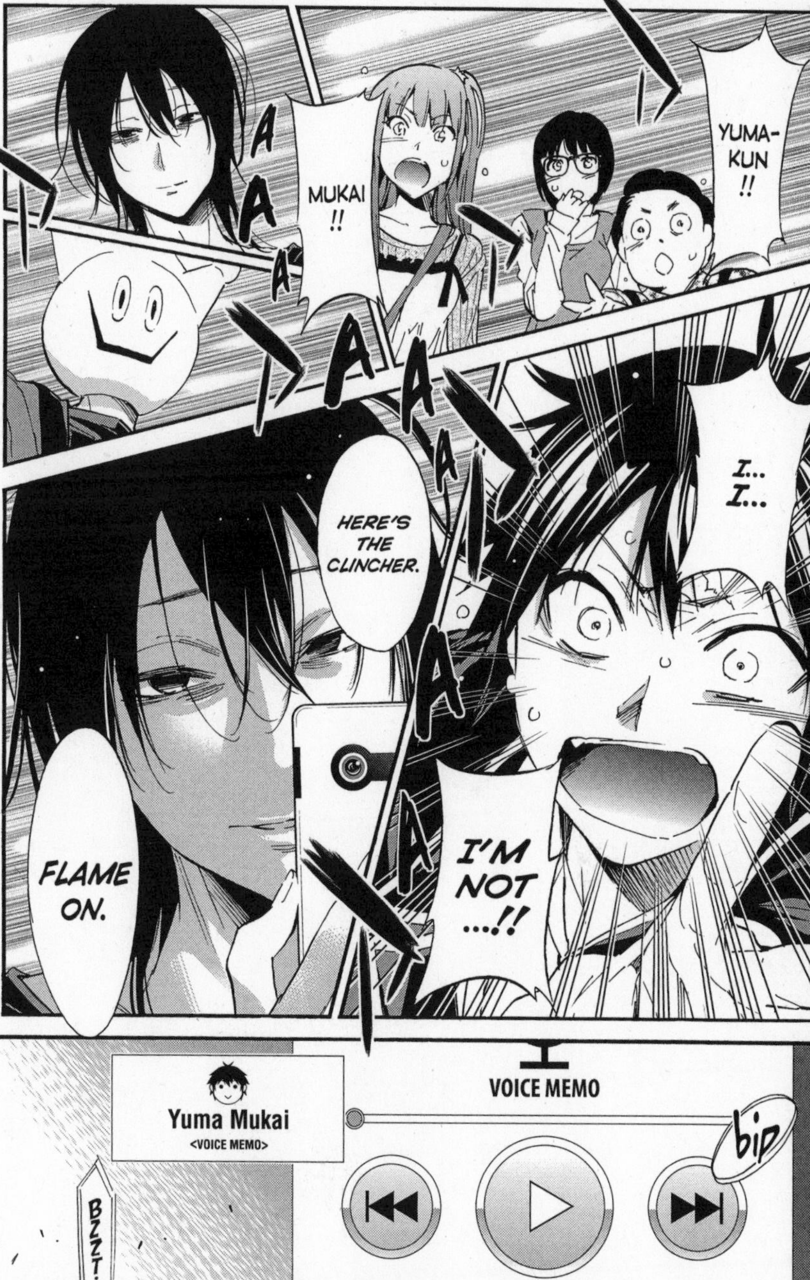
YUMA-KUN!!
MUKAI!!
I... I...
HERE'S THE CLINCHER.
I'M NOT ...!!
FLAME ON.
VOICE MEMO
bip
Yuma Mukai
<VOICE MEMO>
REPEAT
BZZT...

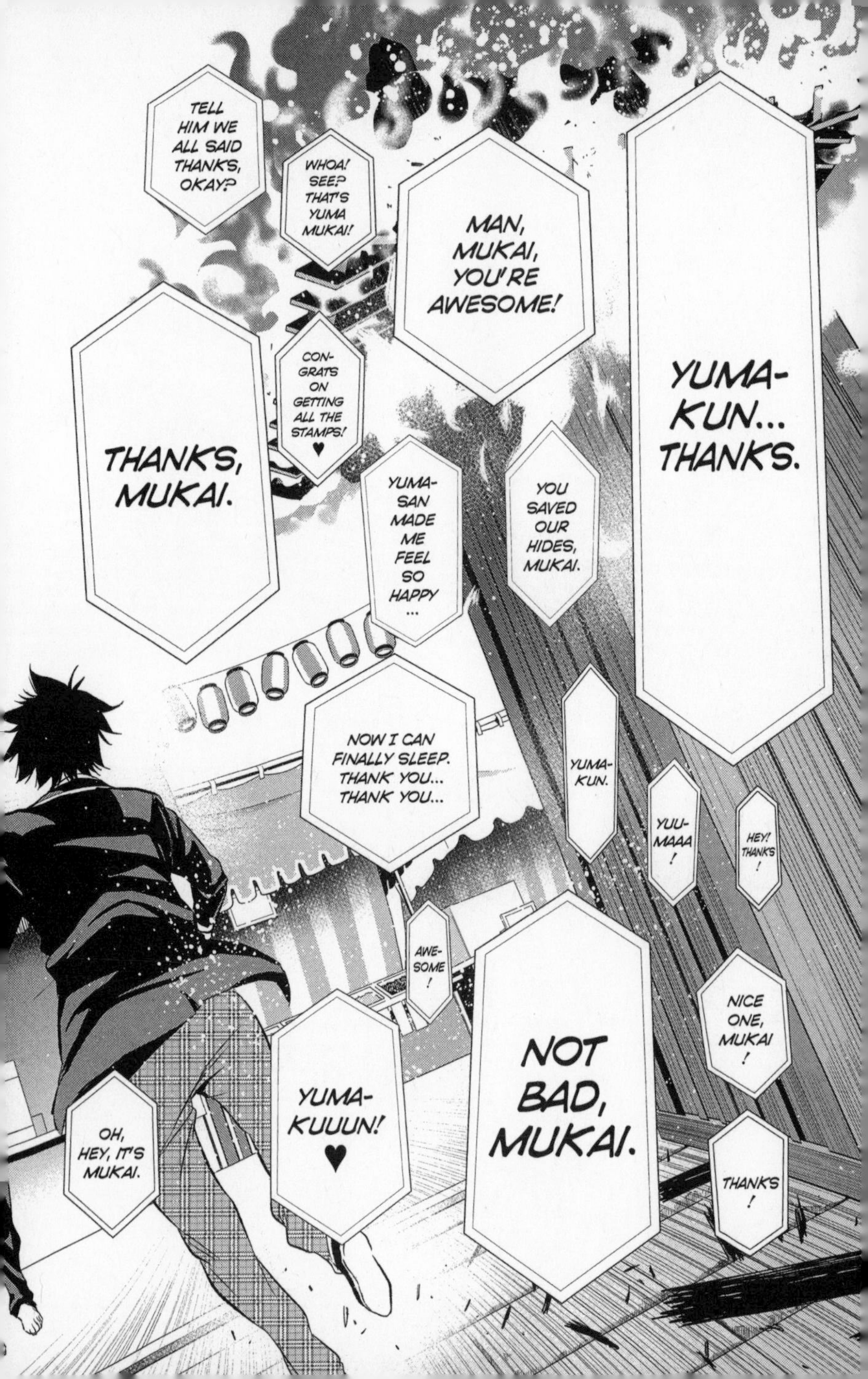
YUMA-KUN... THANKS.
MAN, MUKAI, YOU'RE AWESOME!
WHOA! SEE? THAT'S YUMA MUKAI!
TELL HIM WE ALL SAID THANKS, OKAY?
YOU SAVED OUR HIDES, MUKAI.
YUMA-SAN MADE ME FEEL SO HAPPY ...
CON-GRATS ON GETTING ALL THE STAMPS! ♥
THANKS, MUKAI.
HEY! THANKS!
YUU-MAAA!
YUMA-KUN.
NOW I CAN FINALLY SLEEP. THANK YOU... THANK YOU...
NICE ONE, MUKAI!
THANKS!
NOT BAD, MUKAI.
AWE-SOME!
YUMA-KUUUN! ♥
OH, HEY, IT'S MUKAI.

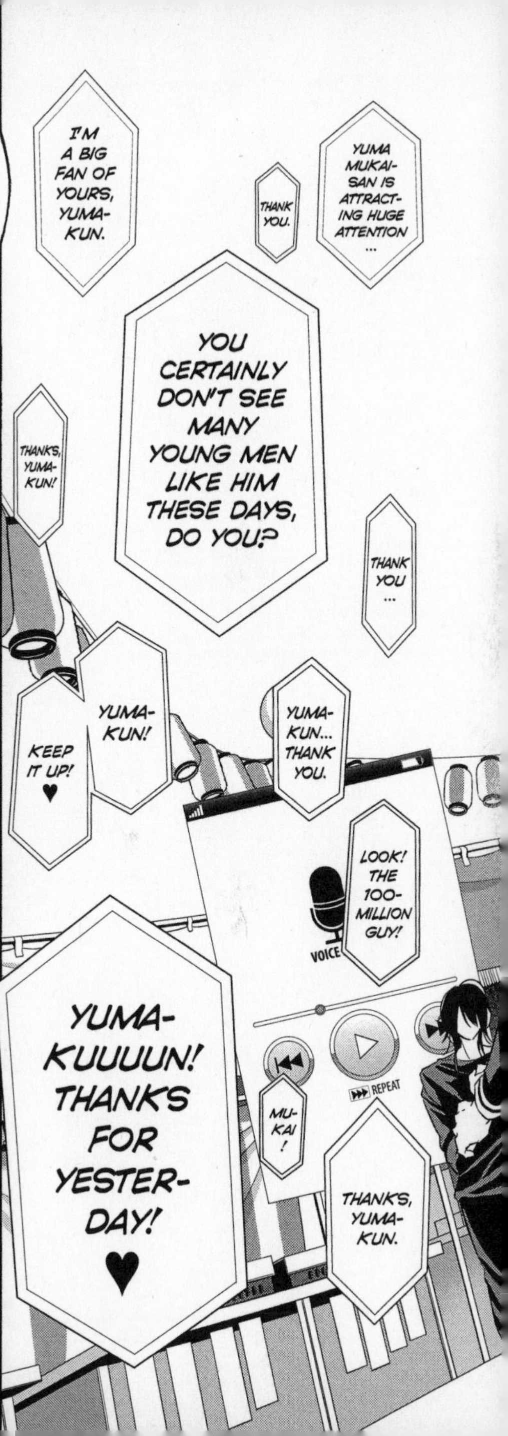
YUMA MUKAI-SAN IS ATTRACTING HUGE ATTENTION...
THANK YOU.
I'M A BIG FAN OF YOURS, YUMA-KUN.
THANK YOU...
YOU CERTAINLY DON'T SEE MANY YOUNG MEN LIKE HIM THESE DAYS, DO YOU?
THANKS, YUMA-KUN!
YUMA-KUN... THANK YOU.
YUMA-KUN!
KEEP IT UP! ♥
LOOK! THE 100-MILLION GUY!
VOICE
REPEAT
THANKS, YUMA-KUN.
MU-KAI!
YUMA-KUUUUN! THANKS FOR YESTERDAY! ♥

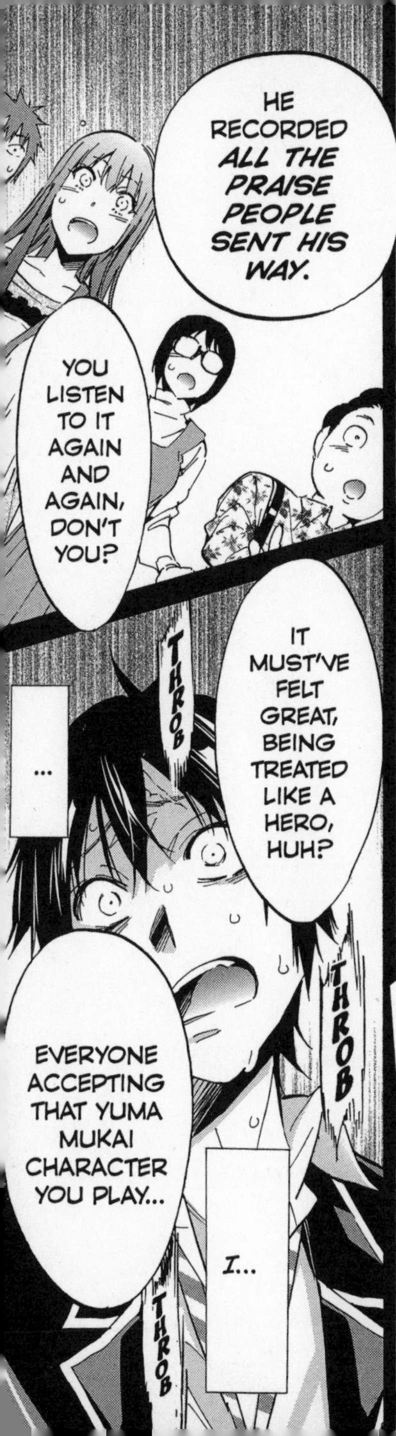
HE RECORDED ALL THE PRAISE PEOPLE SENT HIS WAY.
YOU LISTEN TO IT AGAIN AND AGAIN, DON'T YOU?
IT MUST'VE FELT GREAT, BEING TREATED LIKE A HERO, HUH?
THROB
...
THROB
EVERYONE ACCEPTING THAT YUMA MUKAI CHARACTER YOU PLAY...
I...
THROB

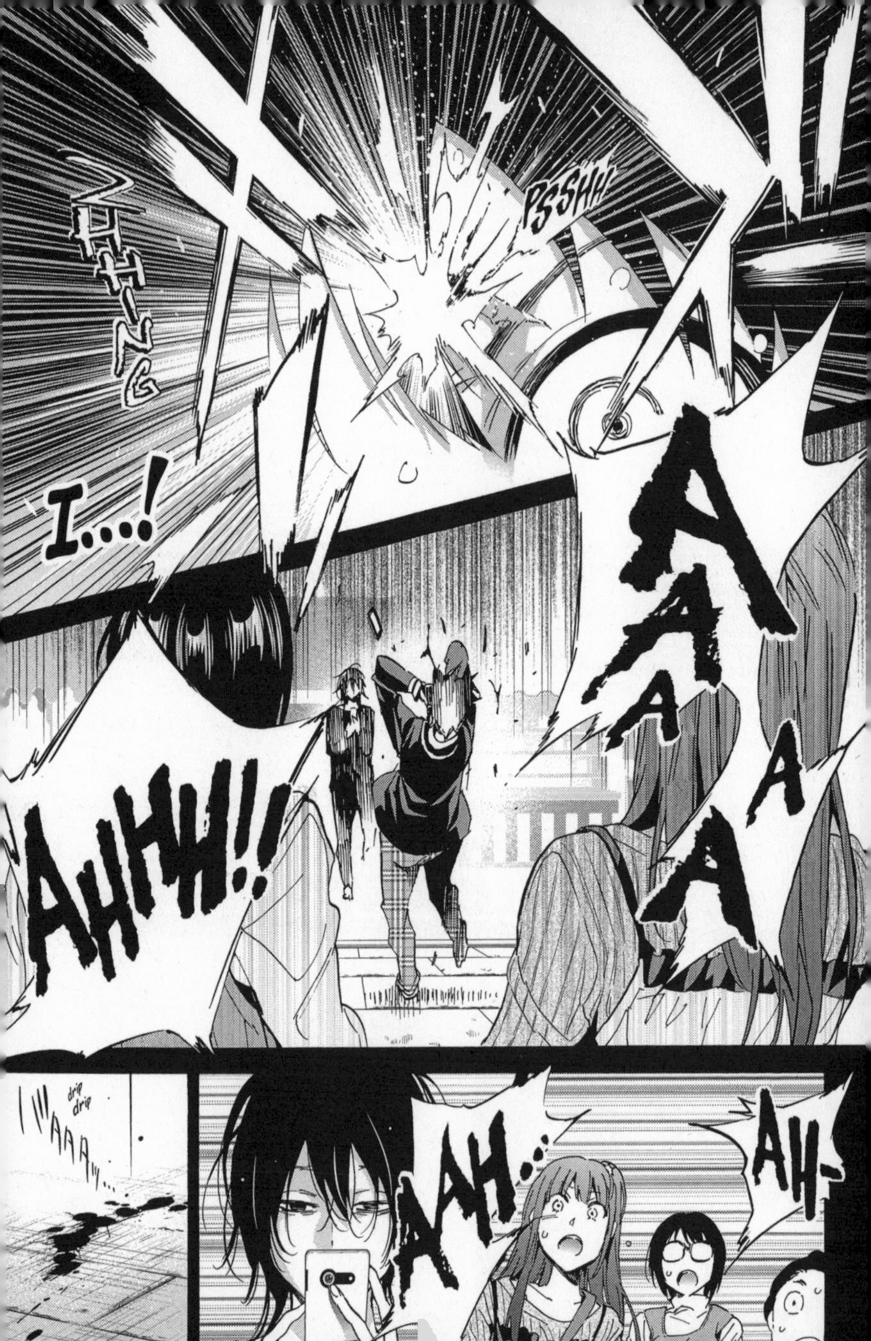
PSSHH
VHHHNG
I...!
AAAAAA
AHHH!!
AH-
AH...
drip drip
AAAA...

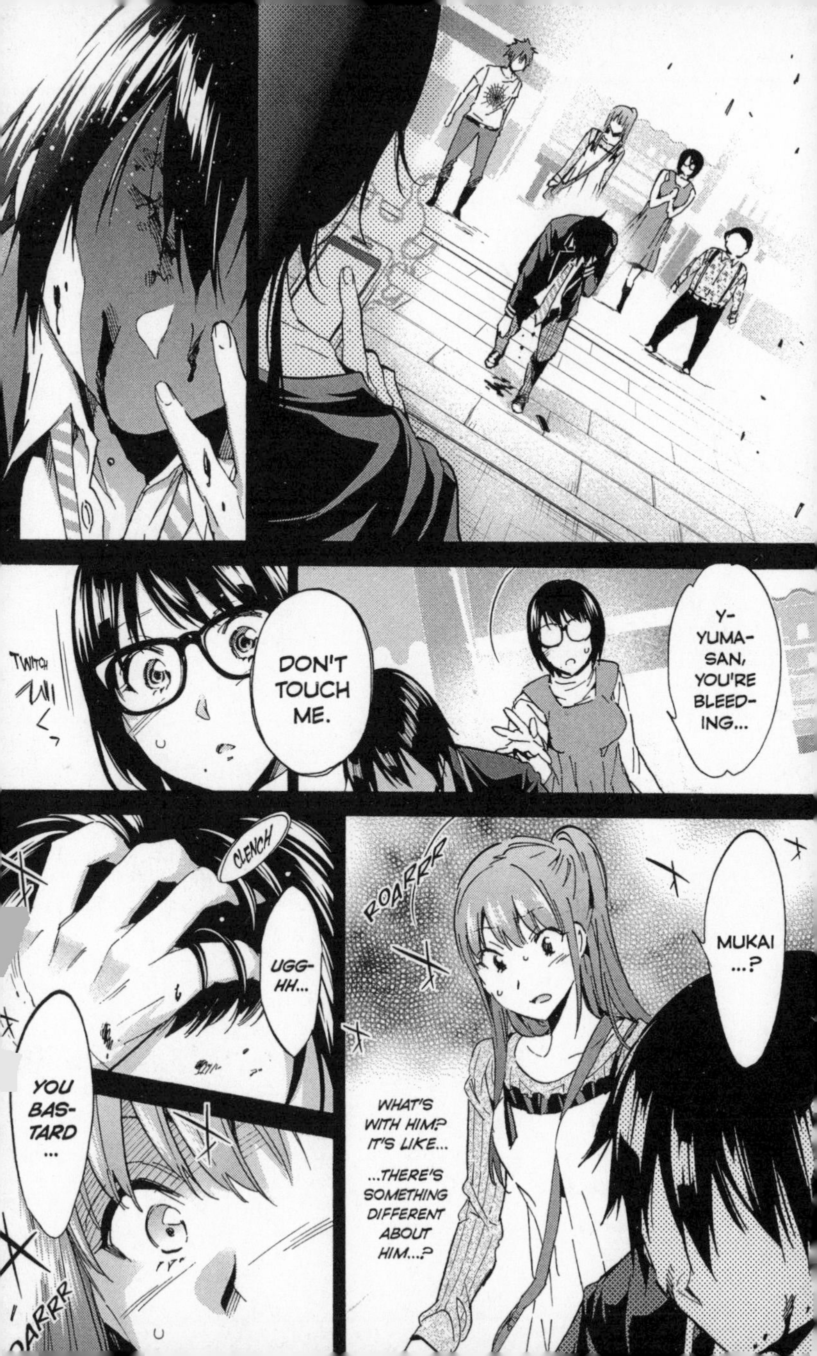
Y-YUMA-SAN, YOU'RE BLEEDING...
DON'T TOUCH ME.
TWITCH
MUKAI...?
ROARRR
WHAT'S WITH HIM? IT'S LIKE...
...THERE'S SOMETHING DIFFERENT ABOUT HIM...?
CLENCH
UGG-HH...
YOU BASTARD...

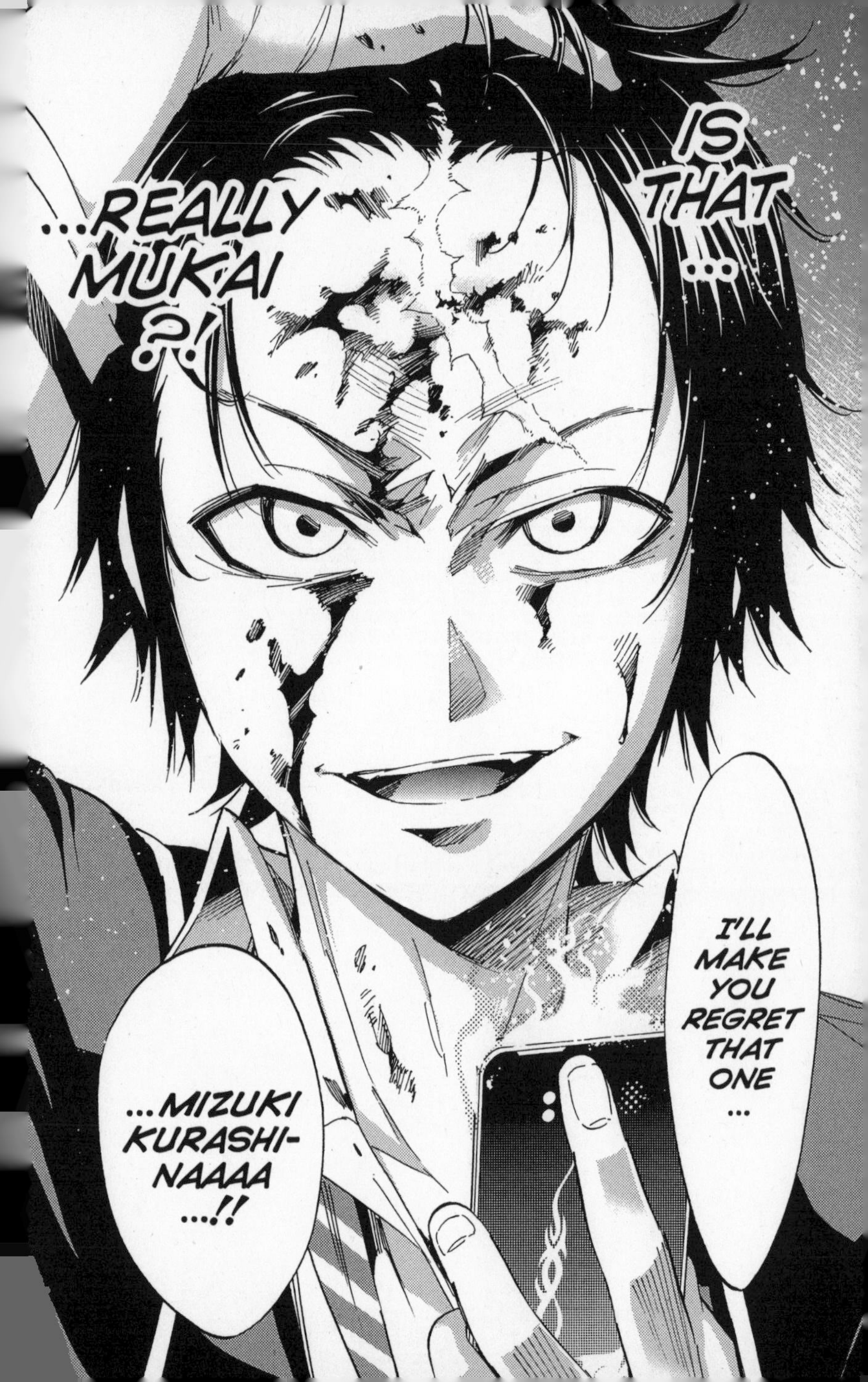
IS THAT ...
...REALLY MUKAI ?!
I'LL MAKE YOU REGRET THAT ONE ...
...MIZUKI KURASHI-NAAAA ...!!

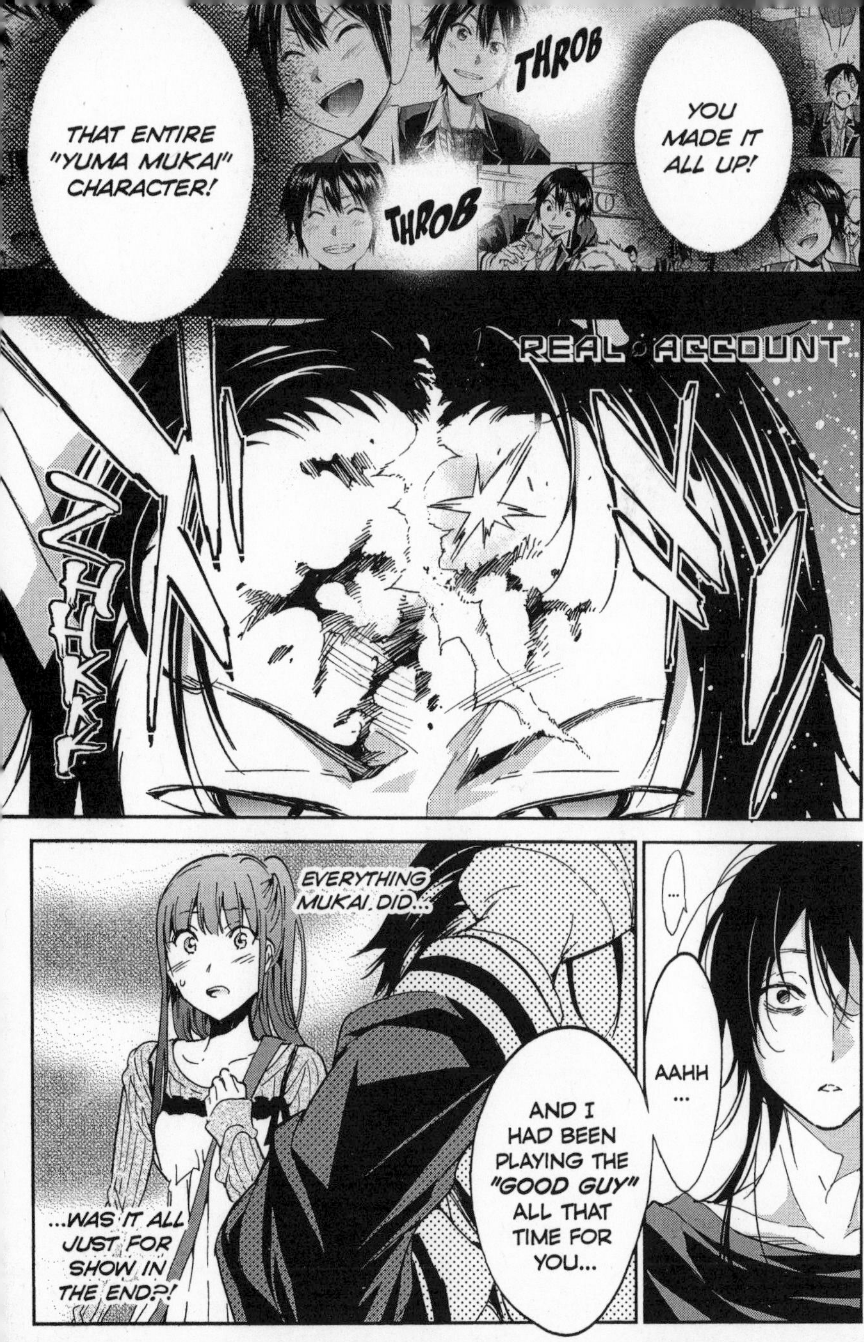
YOU MADE IT ALL UP!
THROB
THROB
THAT ENTIRE "YUMA MUKAI" CHARACTER!
REAL ACCOUNT
...
AAHH ...
AND I HAD BEEN PLAYING THE "GOOD GUY" ALL THAT TIME FOR YOU...
EVERYTHING MUKAI DID...
...WAS IT ALL JUST FOR SHOW IN THE END?!

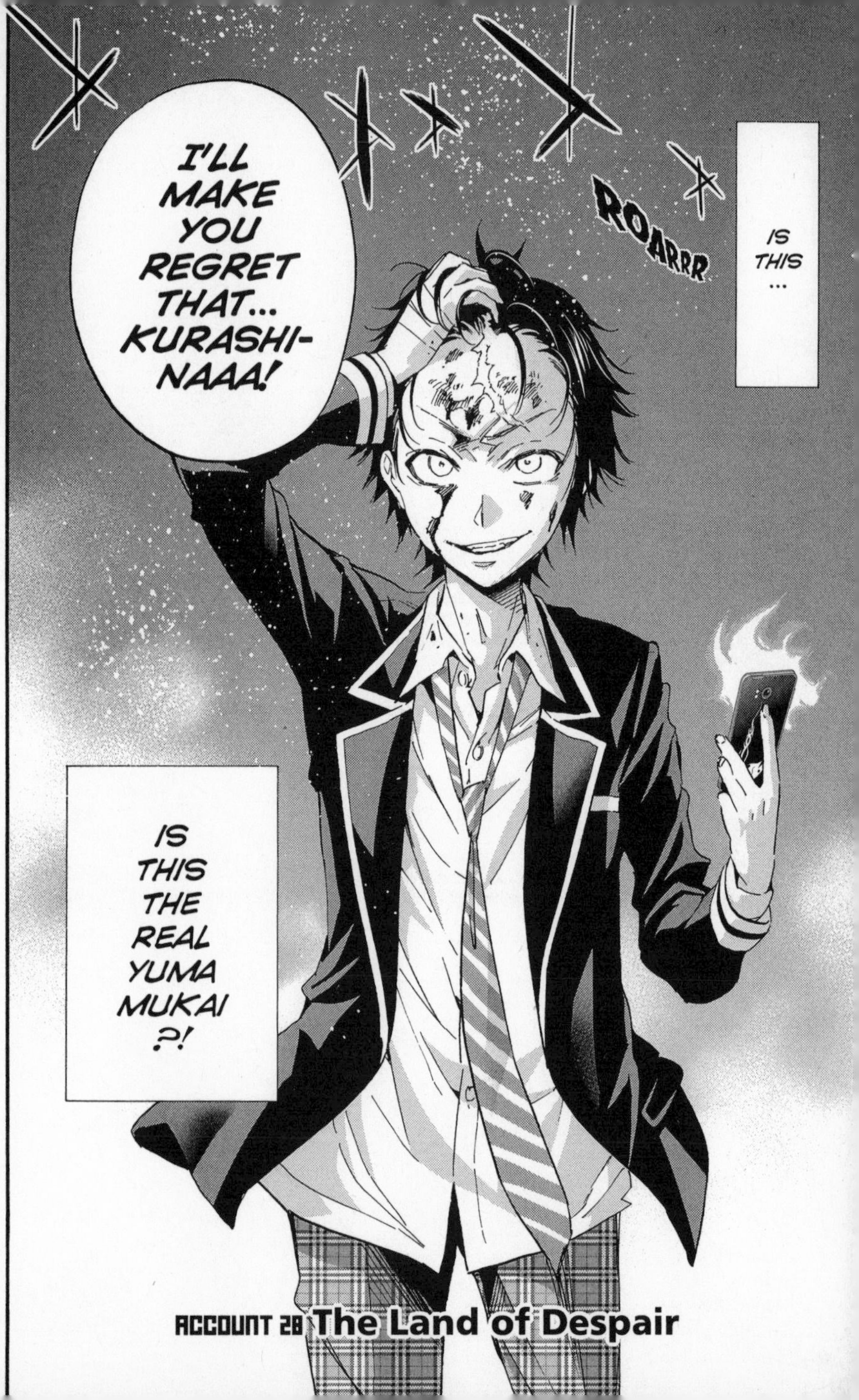
IS THIS ...
ROARRR
I'LL MAKE YOU REGRET THAT... KURASHI-NAAA!
IS THIS THE REAL YUMA MUKAI ?!
ACCOUNT 28 The Land of Despair

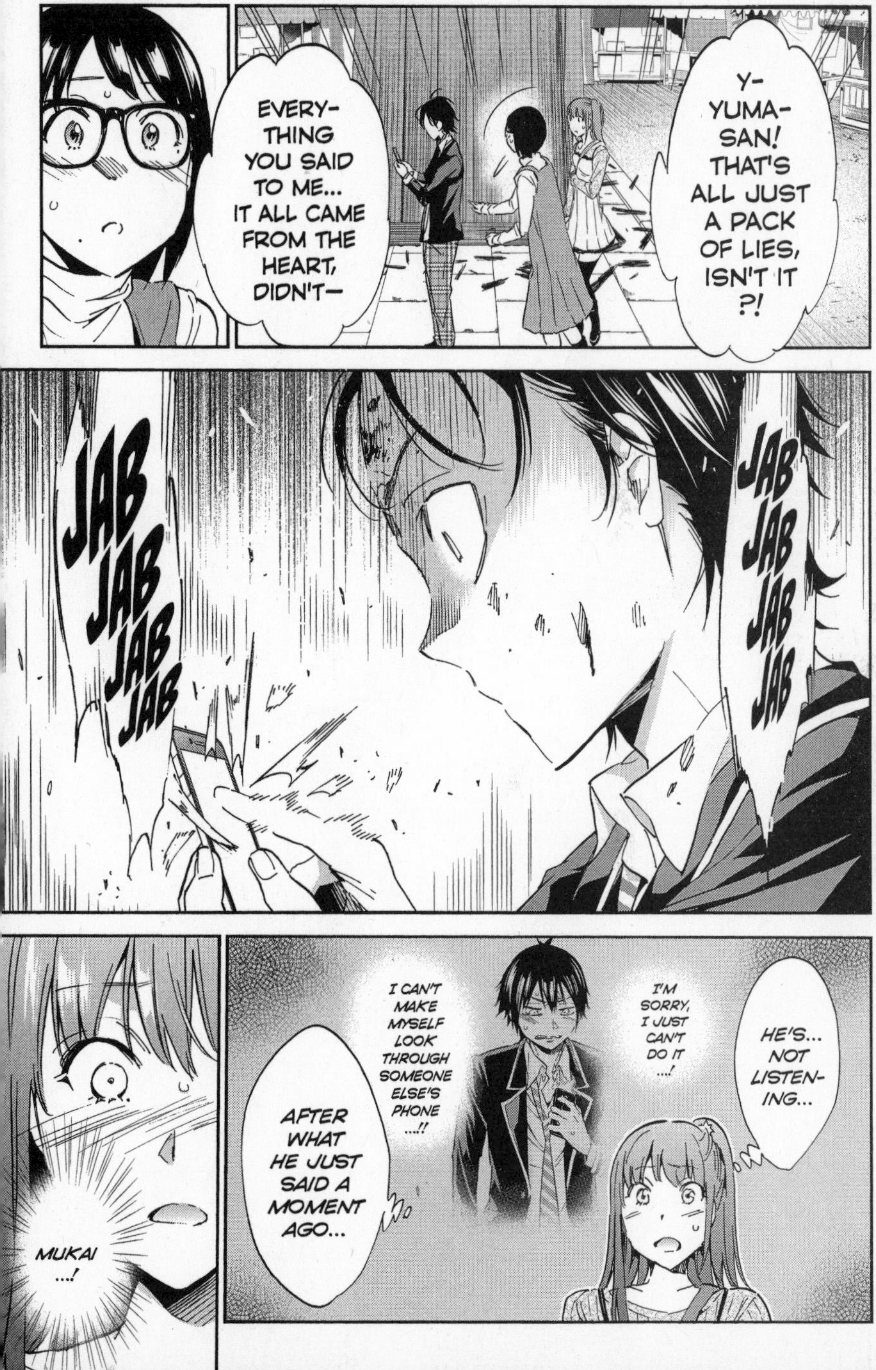

Y-YUMA-SAN! THAT'S ALL JUST A PACK OF LIES, ISN'T IT ?!
EVERY-THING YOU SAID TO ME... IT ALL CAME FROM THE HEART, DIDN'T—
JAB JAB JAB JAB JAB
JAB JAB JAB JAB
HE'S... NOT LISTEN-ING...
I'M SORRY, I JUST CAN'T DO IT ...!
I CAN'T MAKE MYSELF LOOK THROUGH SOMEONE ELSE'S PHONE ...!!
AFTER WHAT HE JUST SAID A MOMENT AGO...
MUKAI ...!

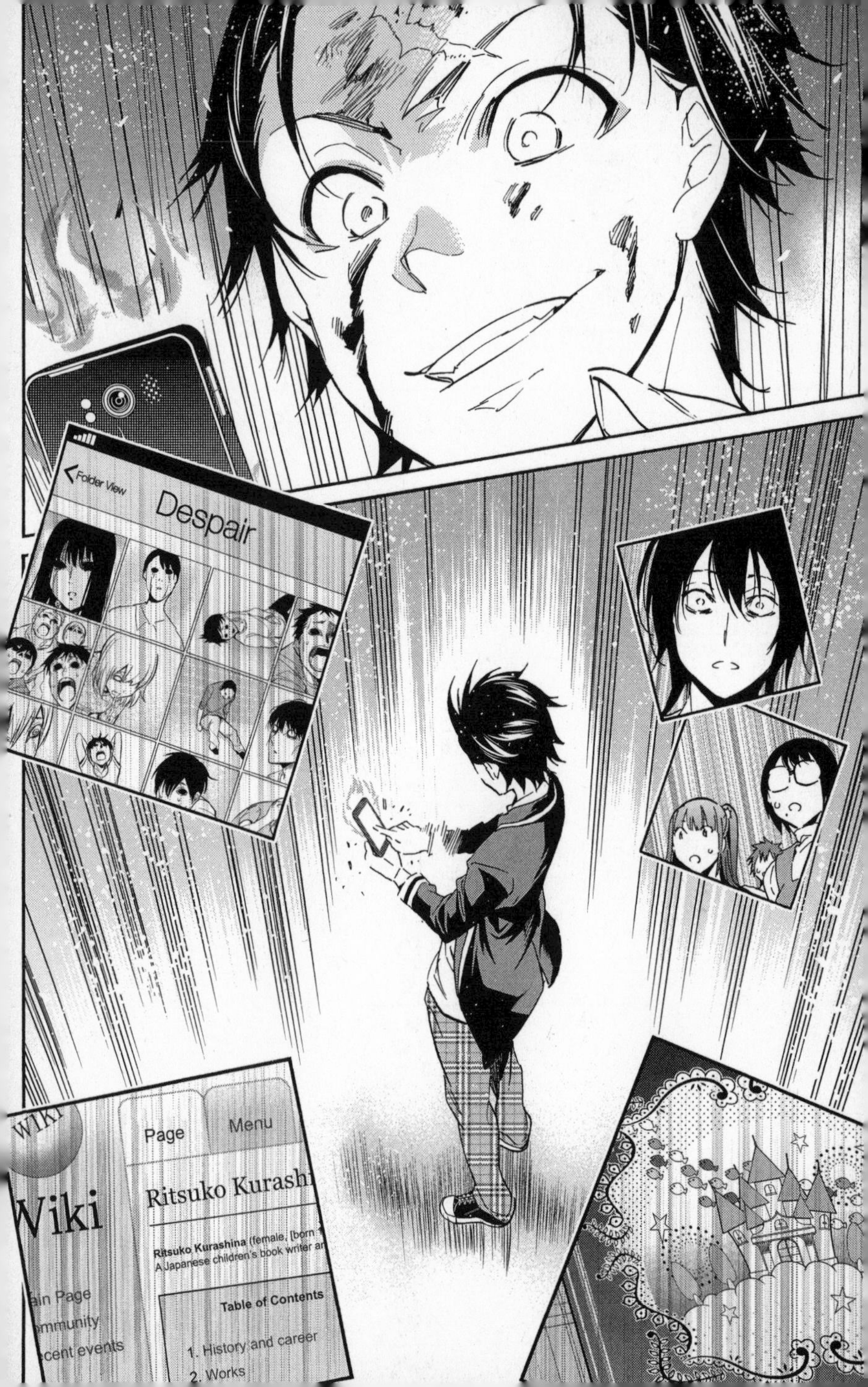

Folder View
Despair
WIKI
Wiki
Page
Menu
Ritsuko Kurashi
Ritsuko Kurashina (female, [born
A Japanese children's book writer an
ain Page
mmunity
cent events
Table of Contents
1. History and career
2. Works

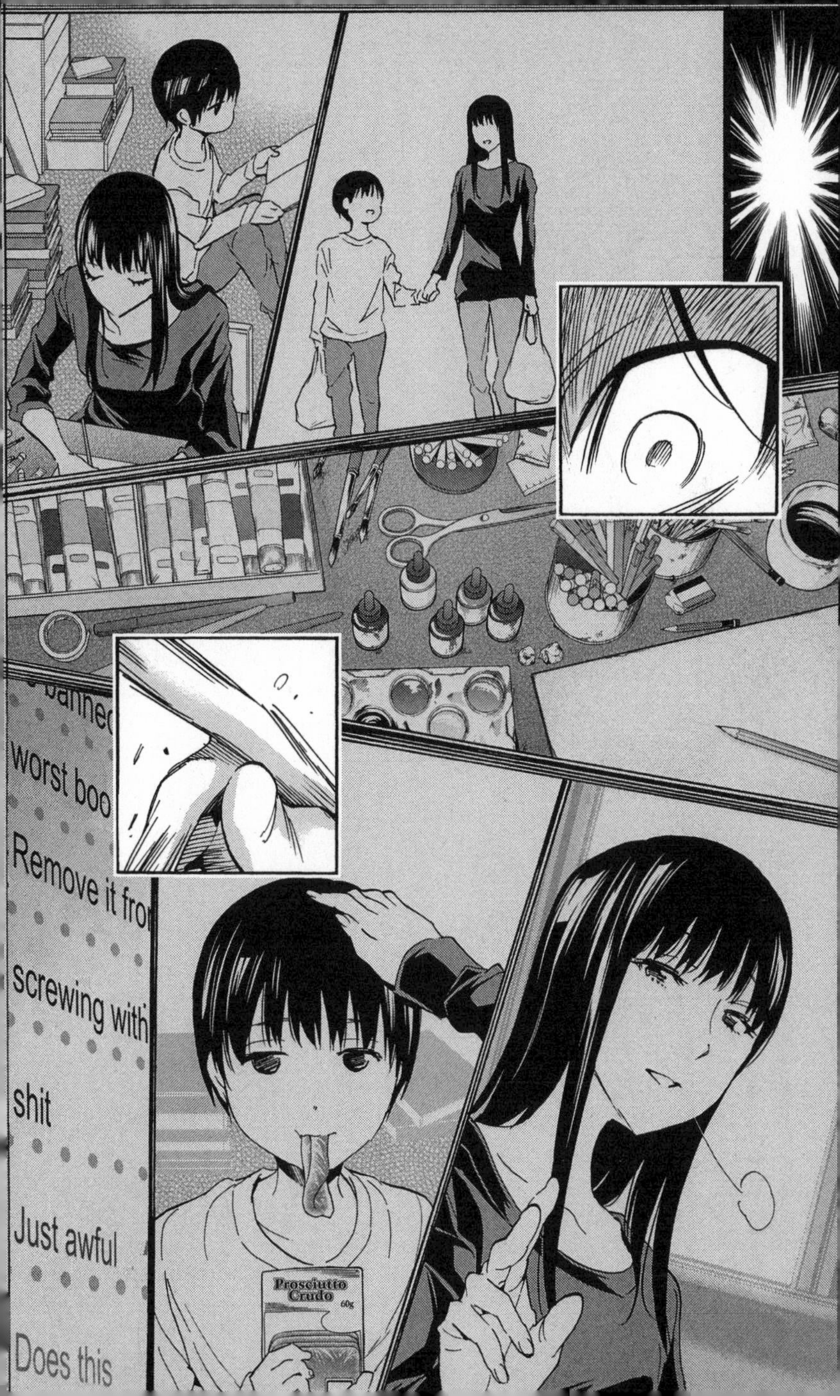
Prosciutto Crudo
60g
worst boo
Remove it fro
screwing with
shit
Just awful
Does this

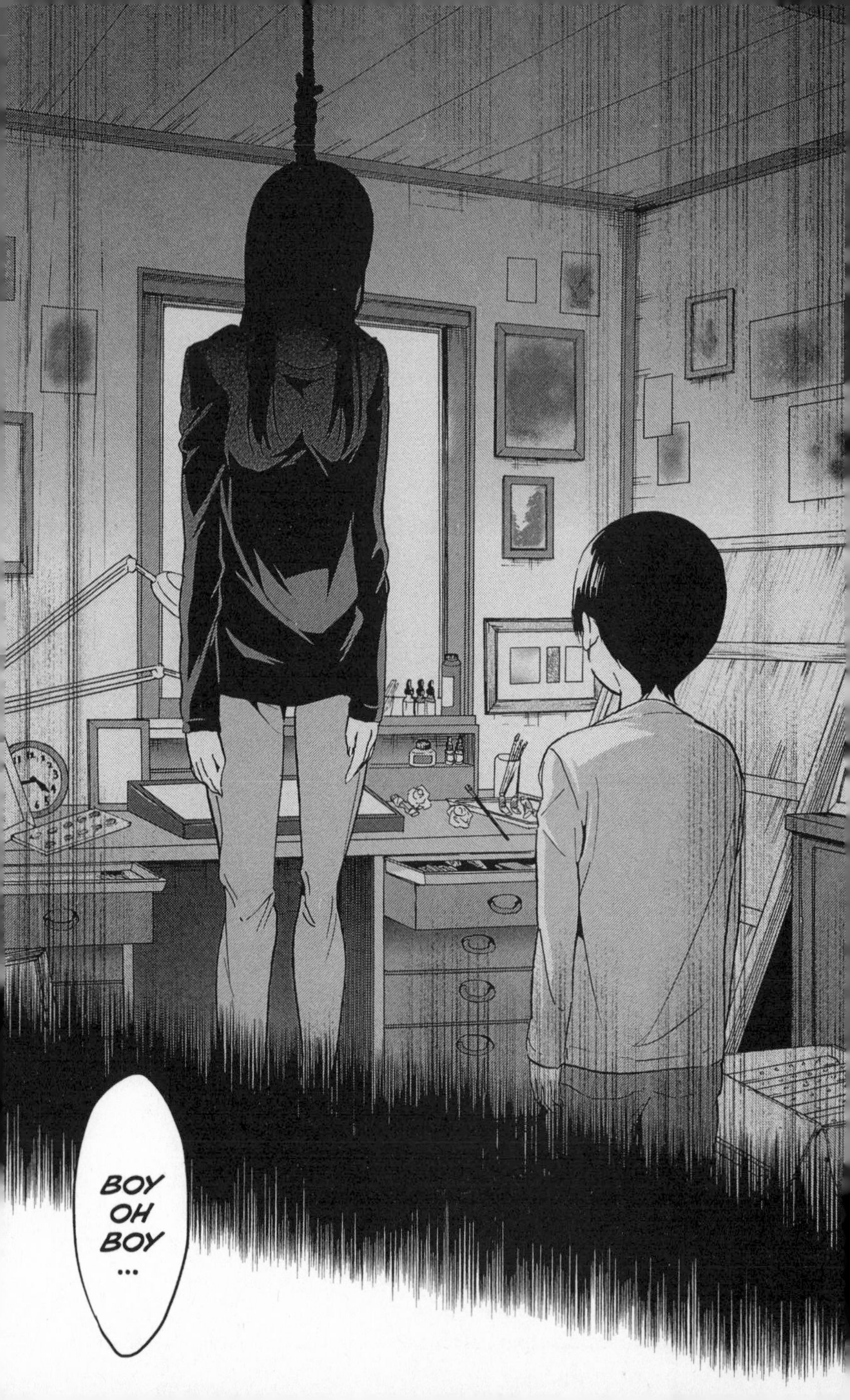
BOY OH BOY ...

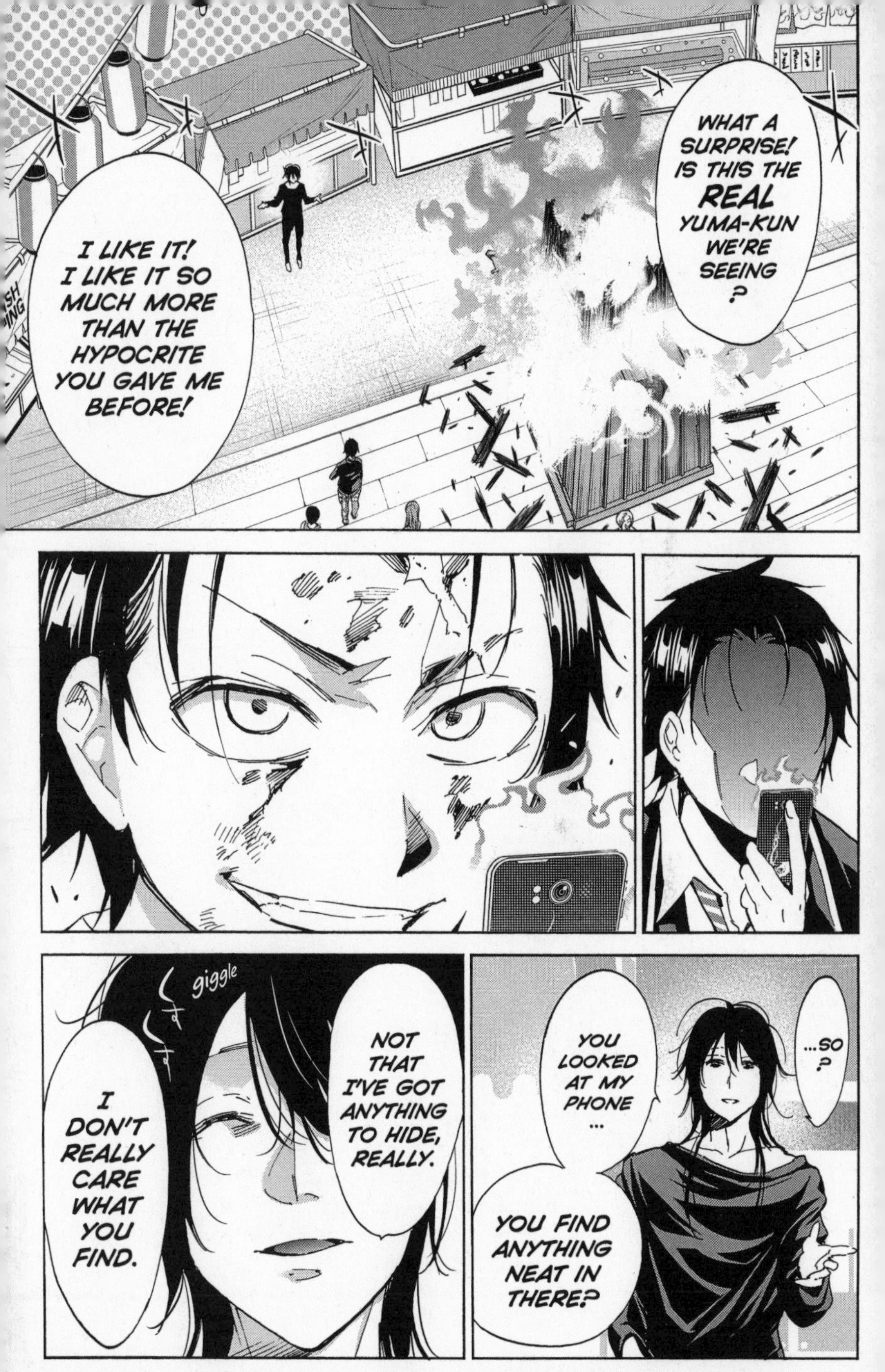
WHAT A SURPRISE! IS THIS THE REAL YUMA-KUN WE'RE SEEING ?
I LIKE IT! I LIKE IT SO MUCH MORE THAN THE HYPOCRITE YOU GAVE ME BEFORE!
...SO ?
YOU LOOKED AT MY PHONE ...
YOU FIND ANYTHING NEAT IN THERE?
NOT THAT I'VE GOT ANYTHING TO HIDE, REALLY.
giggle
I DON'T REALLY CARE WHAT YOU FIND.

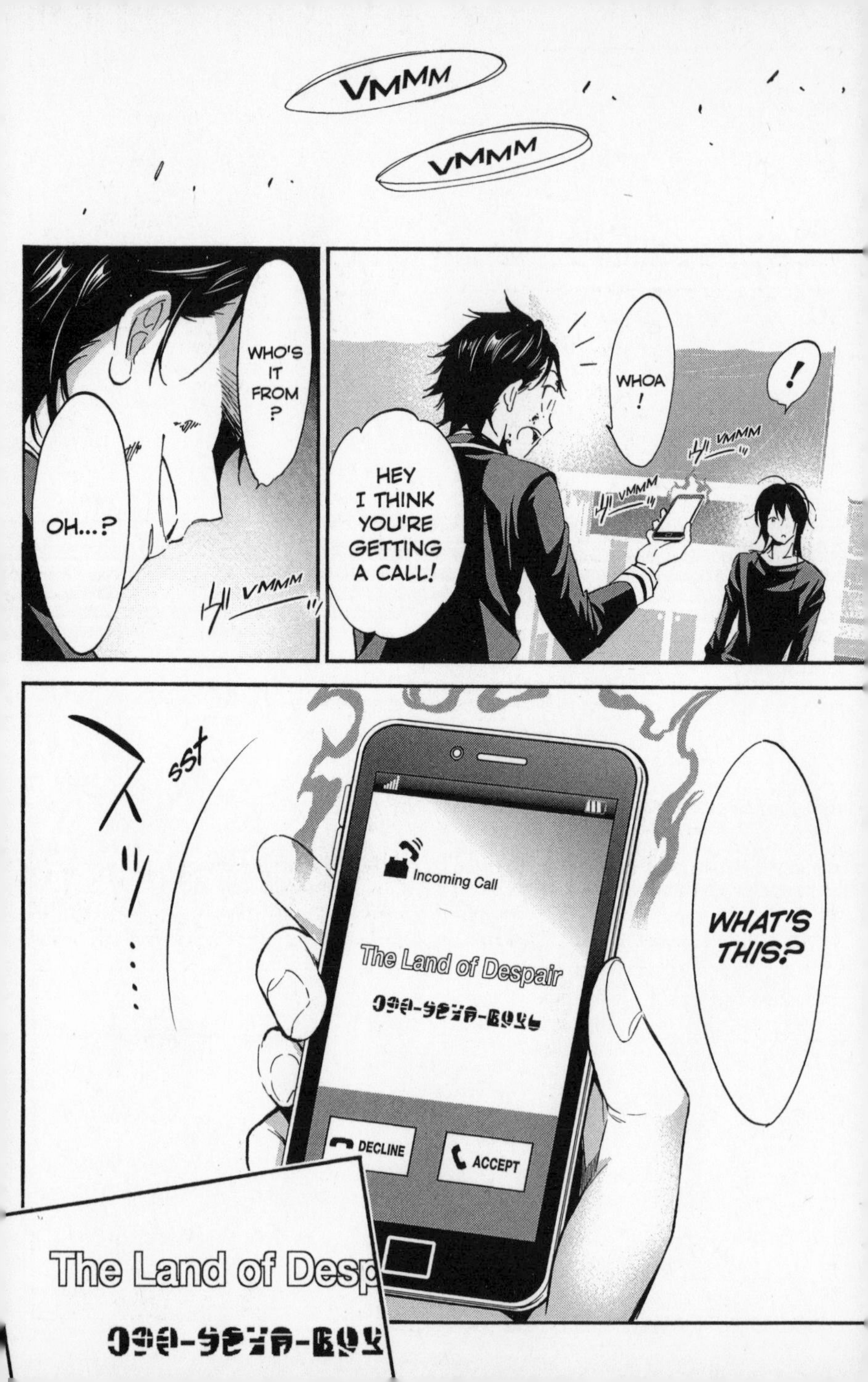
VMMM
VMMM
!
WHOA!
VMMM
VMMM
HEY I THINK YOU'RE GETTING A CALL!
WHO'S IT FROM?
OH...?
VMMM
WHAT'S THIS?
Incoming Call
The Land of Despair
ACCEPT
DECLINE
sst
The Land of Desp

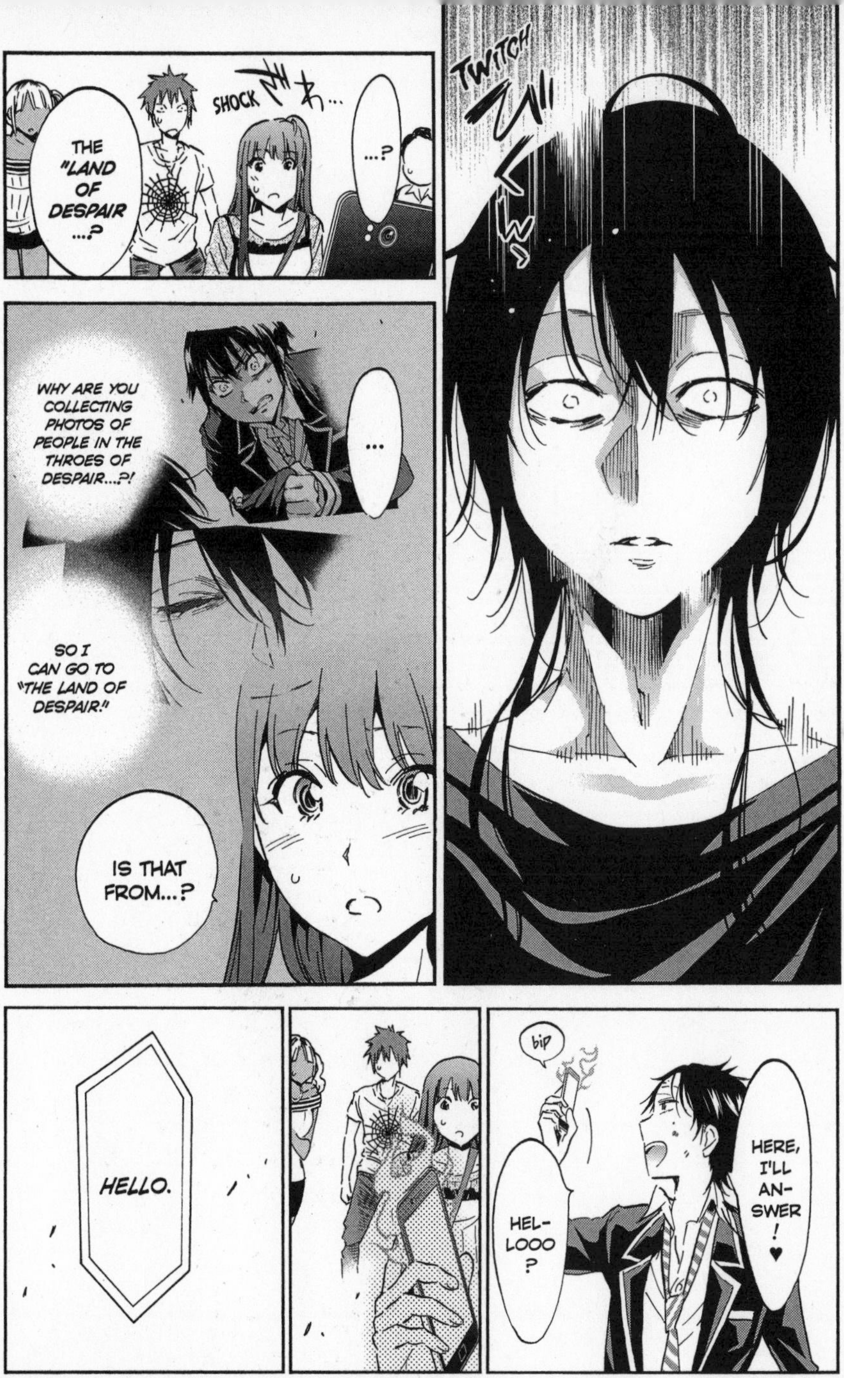

TWITCH
...?
SHOCK
THE "LAND OF DESPAIR ...?
...
WHY ARE YOU COLLECTING PHOTOS OF PEOPLE IN THE THROES OF DESPAIR...?!
SO I CAN GO TO "THE LAND OF DESPAIR."
IS THAT FROM...?
HERE, I'LL AN-SWER! ♥
bip
HEL-LOOO?
HELLO.

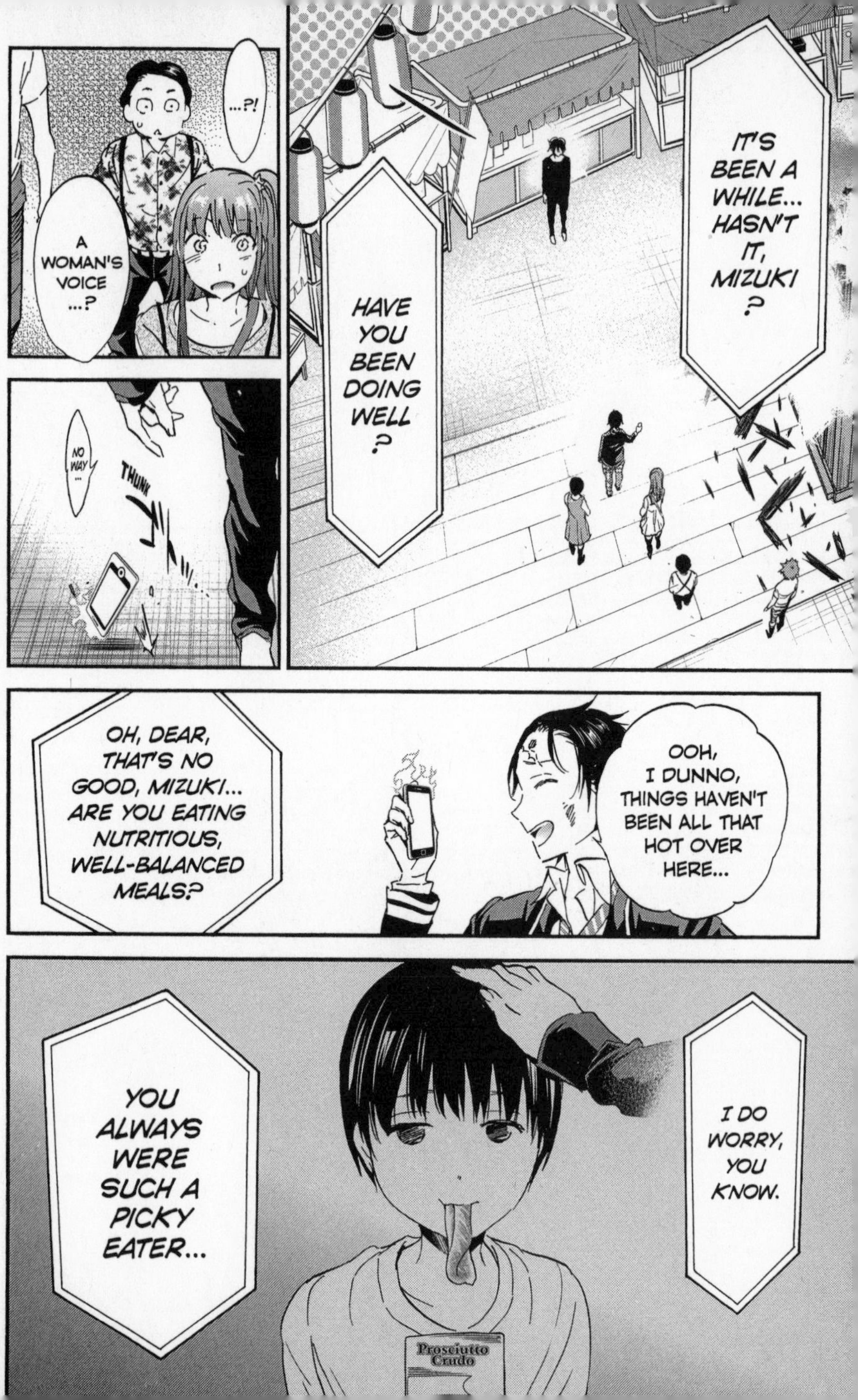
IT'S BEEN A WHILE... HASN'T IT, MIZUKI?
HAVE YOU BEEN DOING WELL?
...?!
A WOMAN'S VOICE...?
NO WAY...
THUNK
OOH, I DUNNO, THINGS HAVEN'T BEEN ALL THAT HOT OVER HERE...
OH, DEAR, THAT'S NO GOOD, MIZUKI... ARE YOU EATING NUTRITIOUS, WELL-BALANCED MEALS?
I DO WORRY, YOU KNOW.
YOU ALWAYS WERE SUCH A PICKY EATER...
Prosciutto Crudo

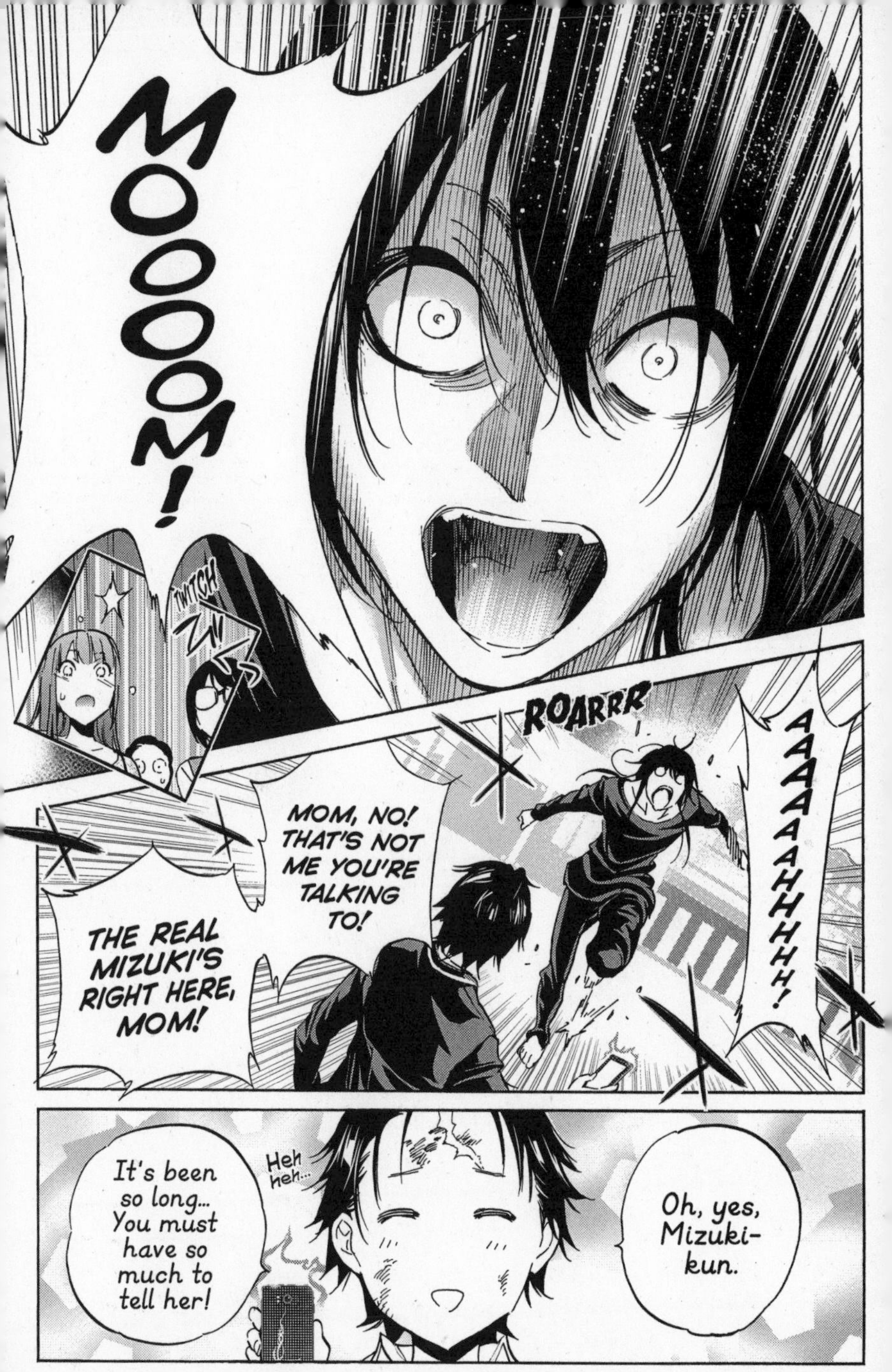
MOOOOOM!
TWITCH
AAAAAAAHHHHHH!
ROARRR
MOM, NO! THAT'S NOT ME YOU'RE TALKING TO!
THE REAL MIZUKI'S RIGHT HERE, MOM!
Oh, yes, Mizuki-kun.
Heh heh...
It's been so long... You must have so much to tell her!

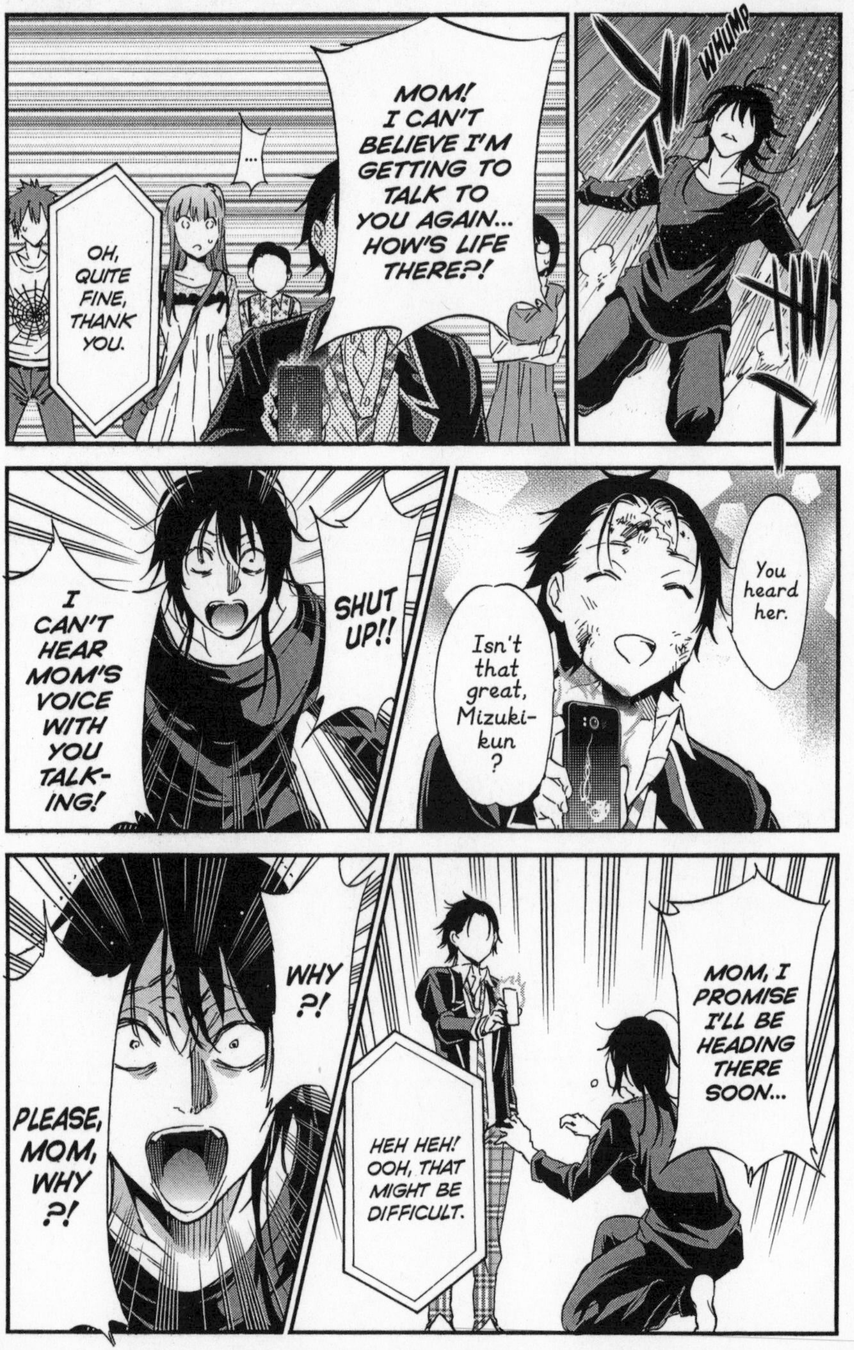
WHUMP
MOM! I CAN'T BELIEVE I'M GETTING TO TALK TO YOU AGAIN... HOW'S LIFE THERE?!
...
OH, QUITE FINE, THANK YOU.
You heard her.
Isn't that great, Mizuki-kun?
SHUT UP!!
I CAN'T HEAR MOM'S VOICE WITH YOU TALKING!
MOM, I PROMISE I'LL BE HEADING THERE SOON...
HEH HEH! OOH, THAT MIGHT BE DIFFICULT.
WHY?!
PLEASE, MOM, WHY?!

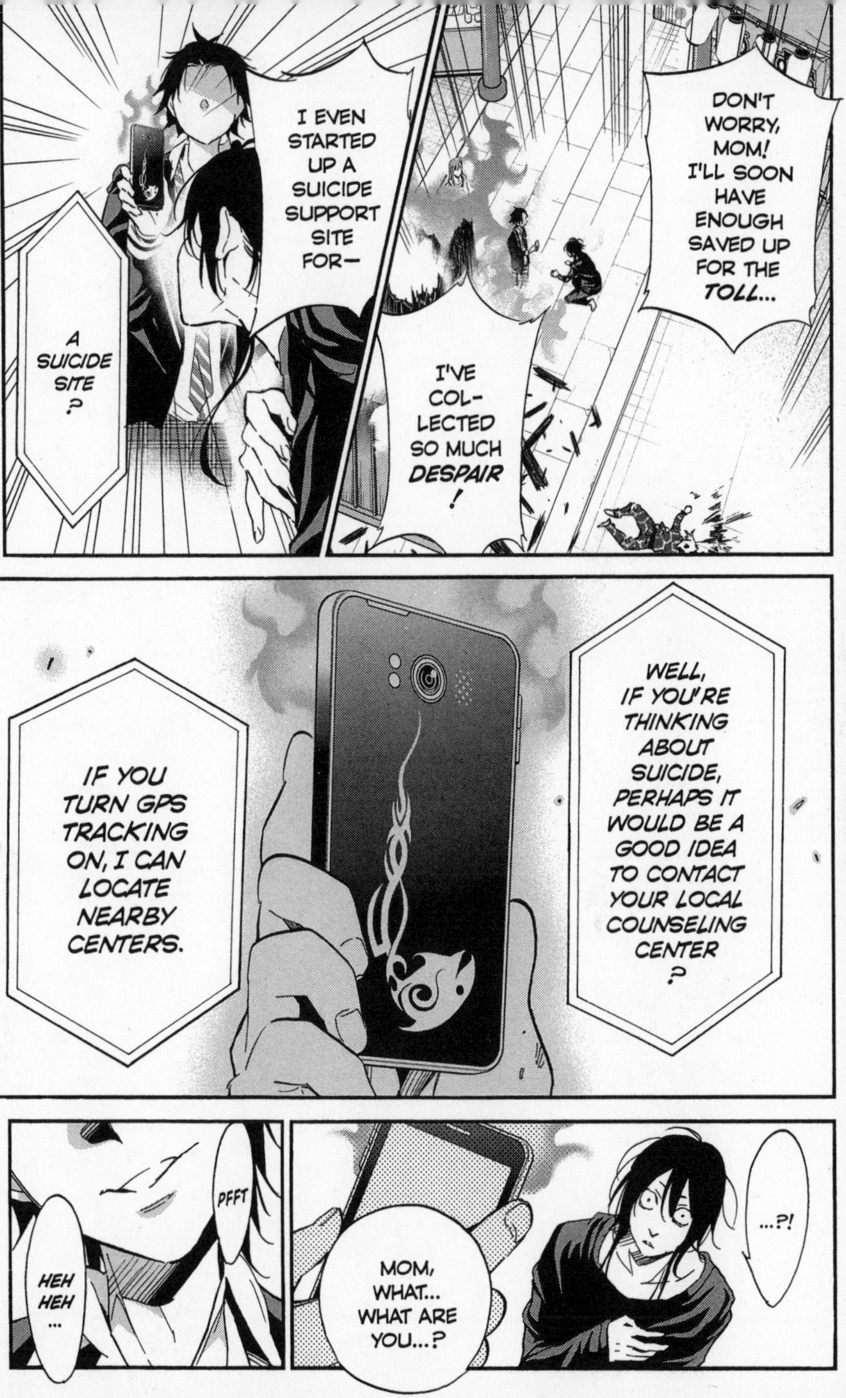
DON'T WORRY, MOM! I'LL SOON HAVE ENOUGH SAVED UP FOR THE *TOLL*...
I'VE COL-LECTED SO MUCH *DESPAIR*!
I EVEN STARTED UP A SUICIDE SUPPORT SITE FOR—
A SUICIDE SITE?
WELL, IF YOU'RE THINKING ABOUT SUICIDE, PERHAPS IT WOULD BE A GOOD IDEA TO CONTACT YOUR LOCAL COUNSELING CENTER?
IF YOU TURN GPS TRACKING ON, I CAN LOCATE NEARBY CENTERS.
...?!
MOM, WHAT... WHAT ARE YOU...?
PFFT
HEH HEH ...

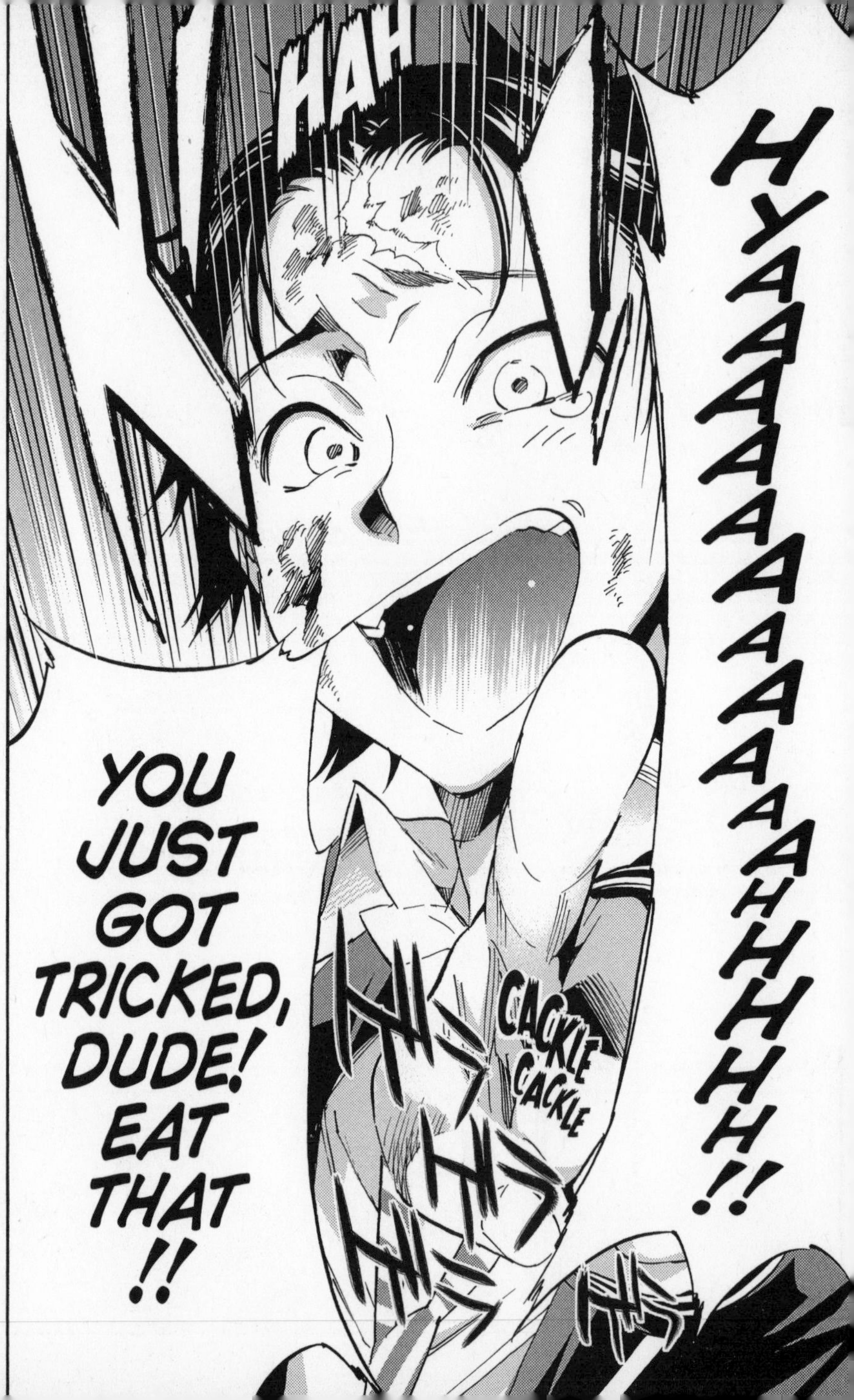
HAH
HYAAAAAAAAAAHHHHH!!
YOU JUST GOT TRICKED, DUDE! EAT THAT!!
CACKLE CACKLE CACKLE

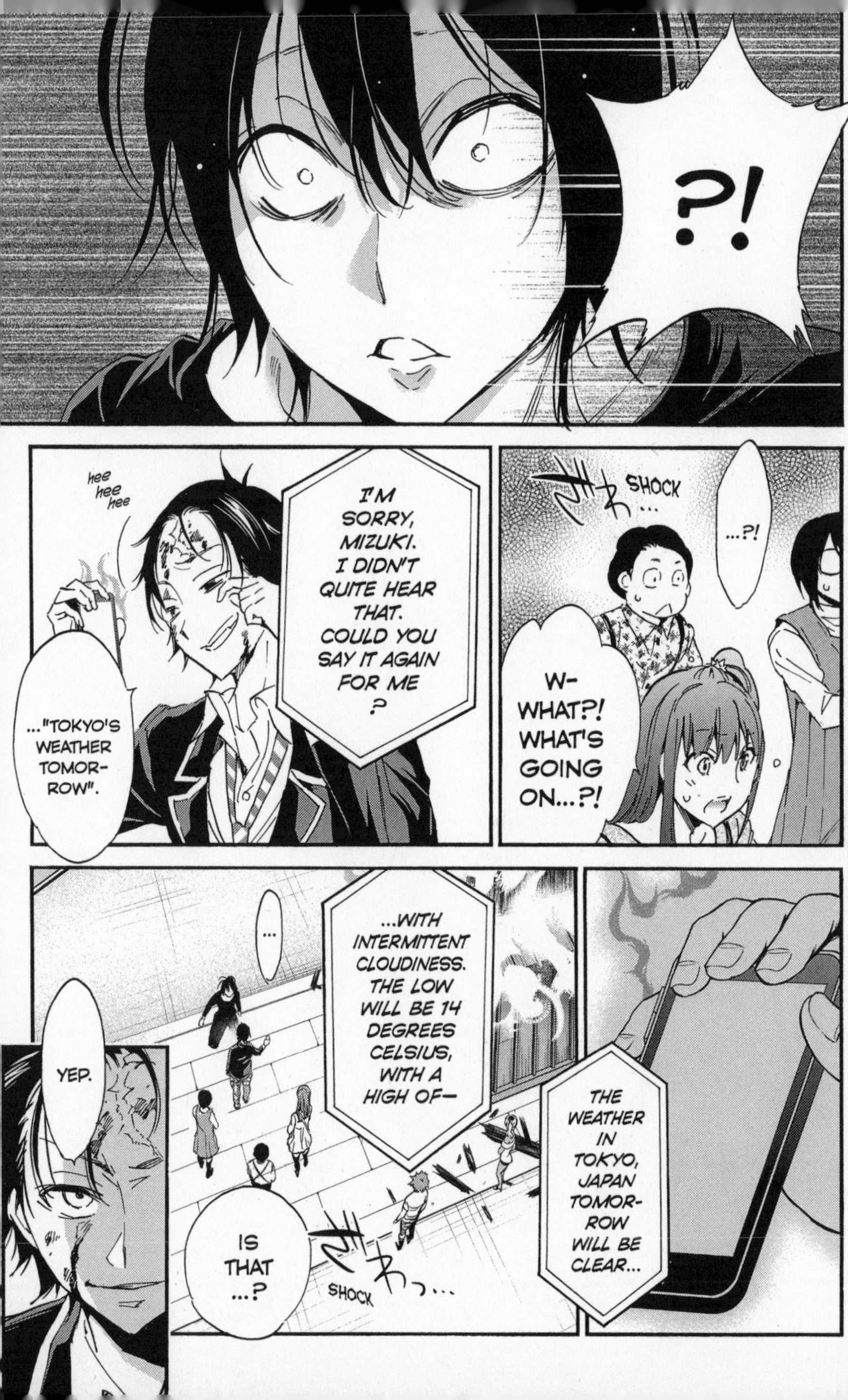
?!
SHOCK...
...?!
W-WHAT?! WHAT'S GOING ON...?!
hee hee hee
I'M SORRY, MIZUKI. I DIDN'T QUITE HEAR THAT. COULD YOU SAY IT AGAIN FOR ME ?
..."TOKYO'S WEATHER TOMOR-ROW".
THE WEATHER IN TOKYO, JAPAN TOMOR-ROW WILL BE CLEAR...
...WITH INTERMITTENT CLOUDINESS. THE LOW WILL BE 14 DEGREES CELSIUS, WITH A HIGH OF—
...
IS THAT ...?
SHOCK...
YEP.

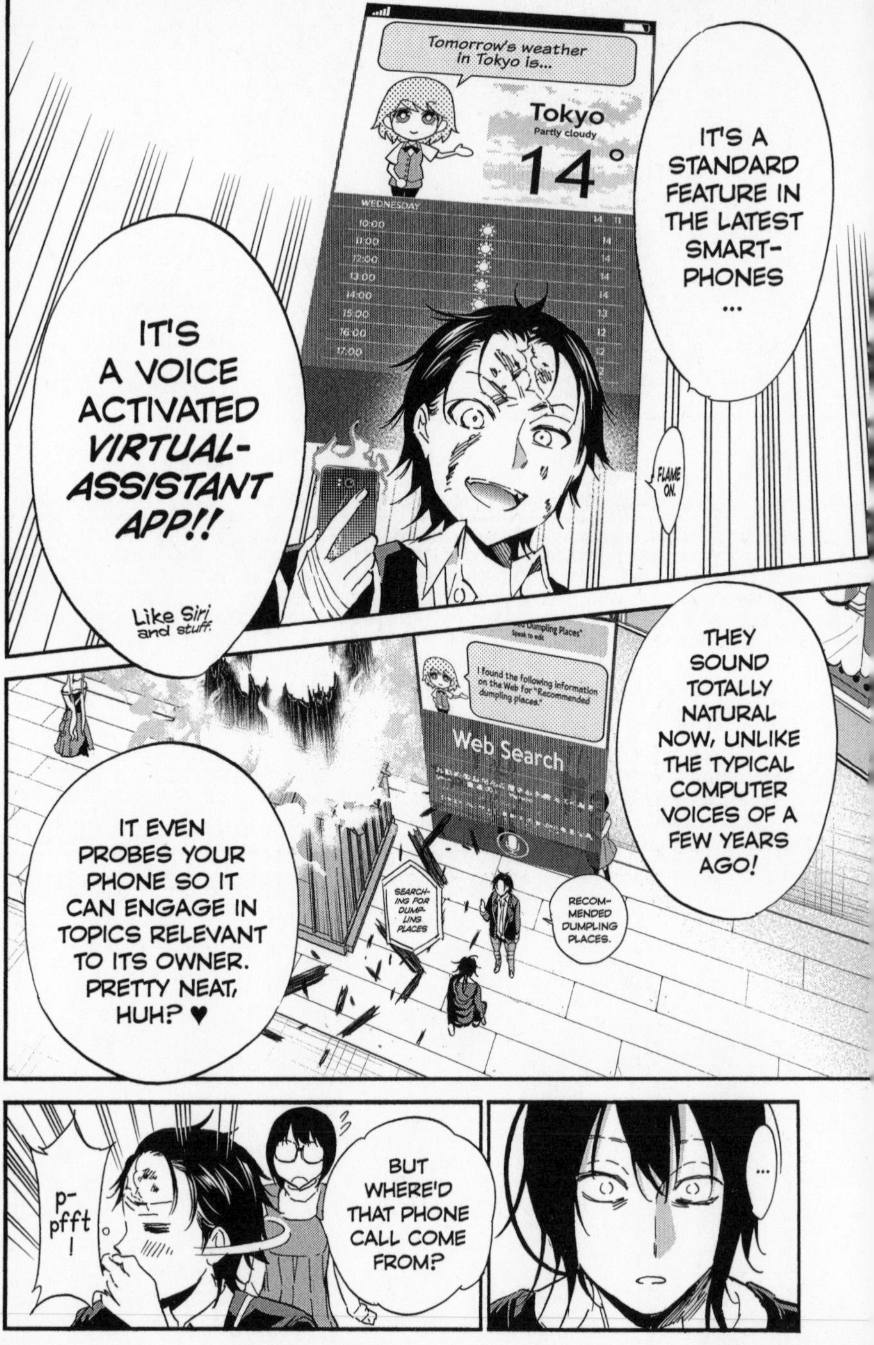

Tomorrow's weather in Tokyo is...
Tokyo
Partly cloudy
14°
IT'S A STANDARD FEATURE IN THE LATEST SMART-PHONES ...
FLAME ON.
IT'S A VOICE ACTIVATED VIRTUAL-ASSISTANT APP!!
Like Siri and stuff.
THEY SOUND TOTALLY NATURAL NOW, UNLIKE THE TYPICAL COMPUTER VOICES OF A FEW YEARS AGO!
I found the following information on the Web for "Recommended dumpling places."
Web Search
RECOM-MENDED DUMPLING PLACES.
SEARCH-ING FOR DUMP-LING PLACES
IT EVEN PROBES YOUR PHONE SO IT CAN ENGAGE IN TOPICS RELEVANT TO ITS OWNER. PRETTY NEAT, HUH? ♥
...
BUT WHERE'D THAT PHONE CALL COME FROM?
p-pfft!

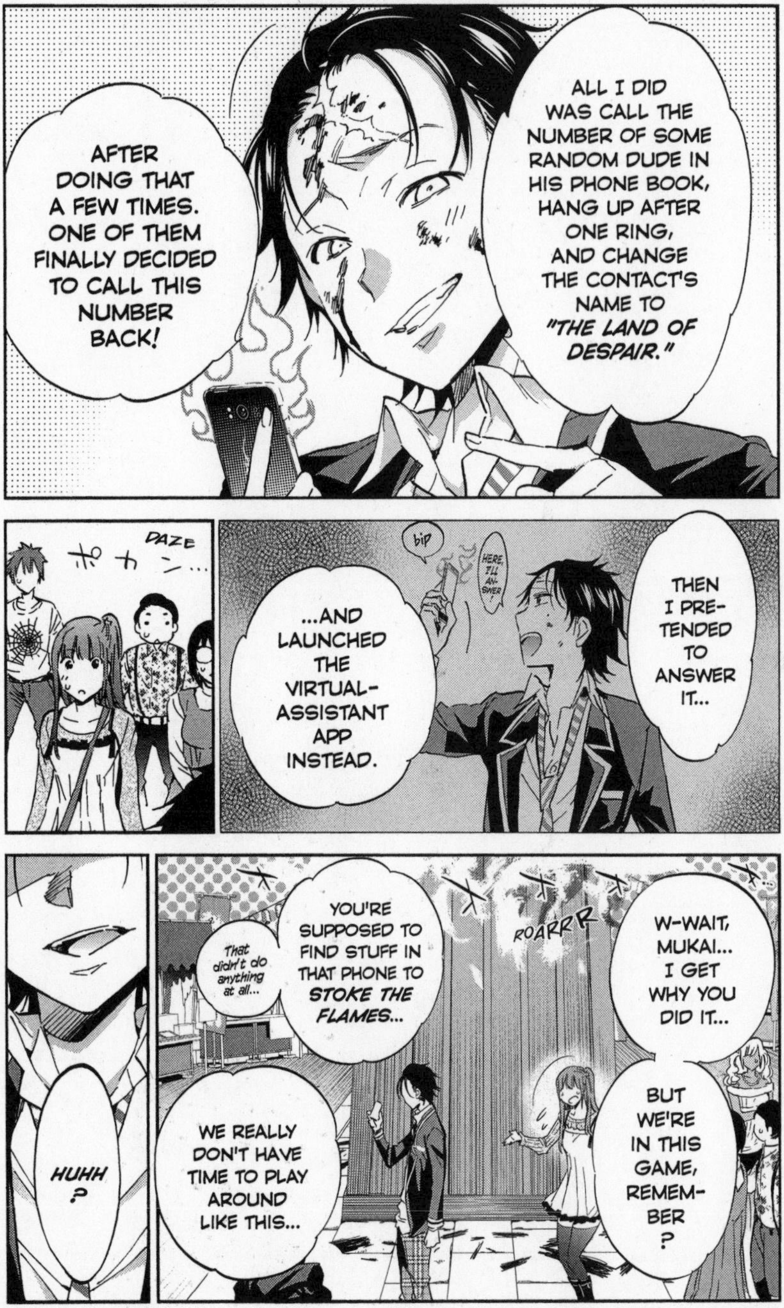
ALL I DID WAS CALL THE NUMBER OF SOME RANDOM DUDE IN HIS PHONE BOOK, HANG UP AFTER ONE RING, AND CHANGE THE CONTACT'S NAME TO *"THE LAND OF DESPAIR."*
AFTER DOING THAT A FEW TIMES. ONE OF THEM FINALLY DECIDED TO CALL THIS NUMBER BACK!
THEN I PRE-TENDED TO ANSWER IT...
bip
HERE, I'LL AN-SWER
...AND LAUNCHED THE VIRTUAL-ASSISTANT APP INSTEAD.
DAZE
ポカン…
W-WAIT, MUKAI... I GET WHY YOU DID IT...
BUT WE'RE IN THIS GAME, REMEMBER?
ROARRR
YOU'RE SUPPOSED TO FIND STUFF IN THAT PHONE TO *STOKE THE FLAMES*...
That didn't do anything at all...
WE REALLY DON'T HAVE TIME TO PLAY AROUND LIKE THIS...
HUHH?

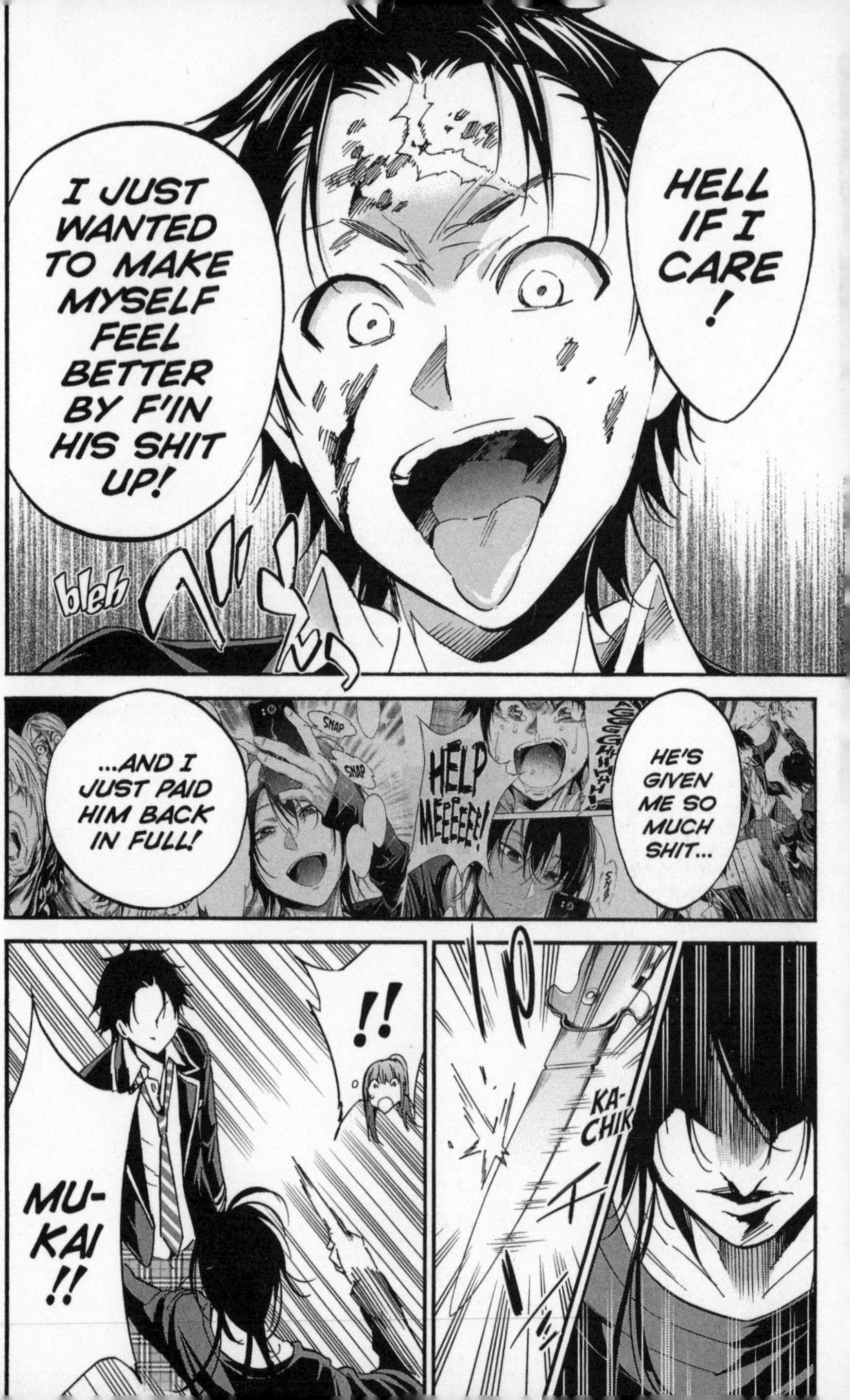
HELL IF I CARE!
I JUST WANTED TO MAKE MYSELF FEEL BETTER BY F'IN HIS SHIT UP!
bleh
HE'S GIVEN ME SO MUCH SHIT...
HELP MEEEEEE!
SNAP
SNAP
...AND I JUST PAID HIM BACK IN FULL!
KA-CHIK
!!
MU-KAI!!

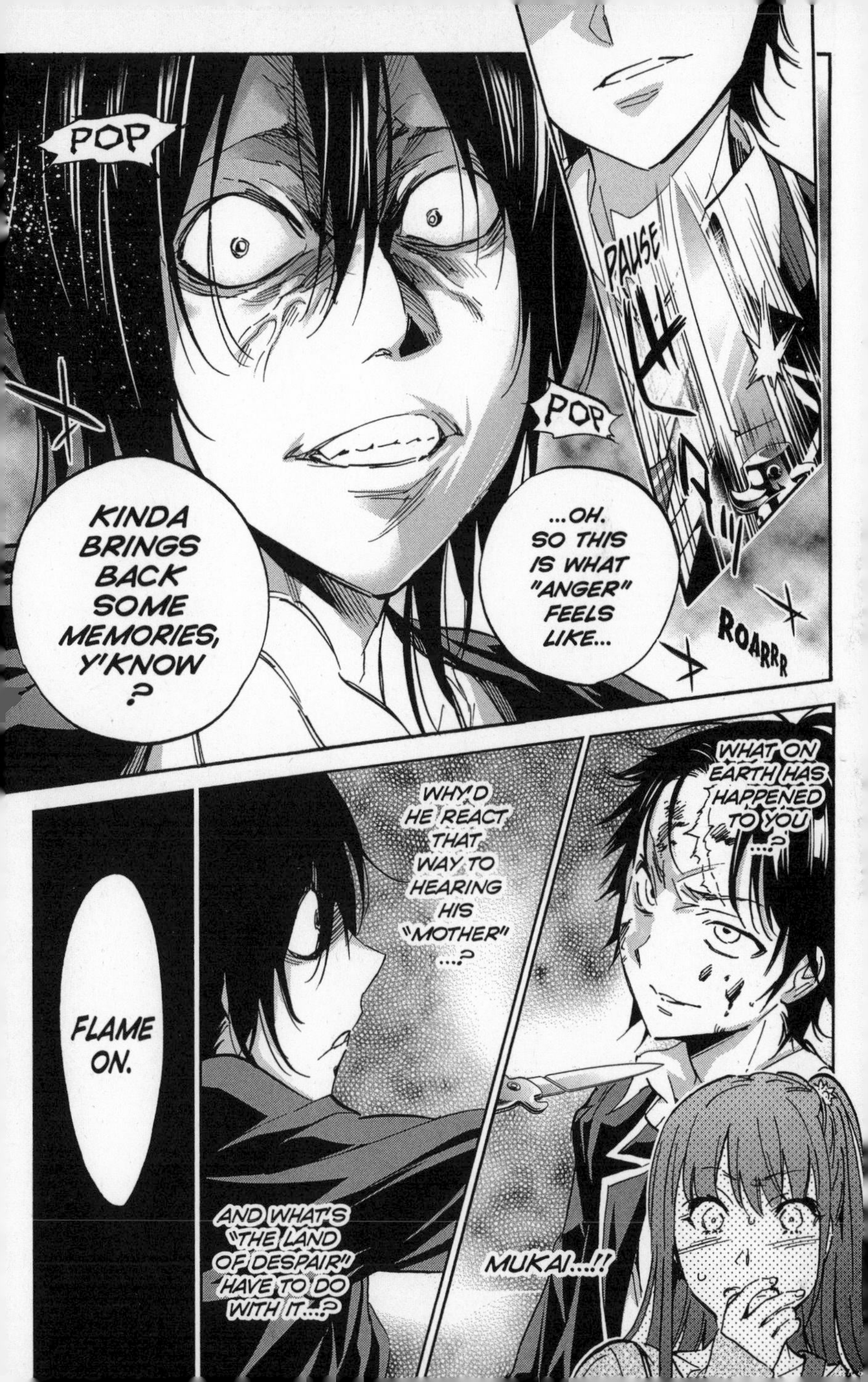

PAUSE
ROARRR
POP
POP
...OH. SO THIS IS WHAT "ANGER" FEELS LIKE...
KINDA BRINGS BACK SOME MEMORIES, Y'KNOW?
WHAT ON EARTH HAS HAPPENED TO YOU...?
MUKAI...!!
WHY'D HE REACT THAT WAY TO HEARING HIS "MOTHER"...?
AND WHAT'S "THE LAND OF DESPAIR" HAVE TO DO WITH IT...?
FLAME ON.

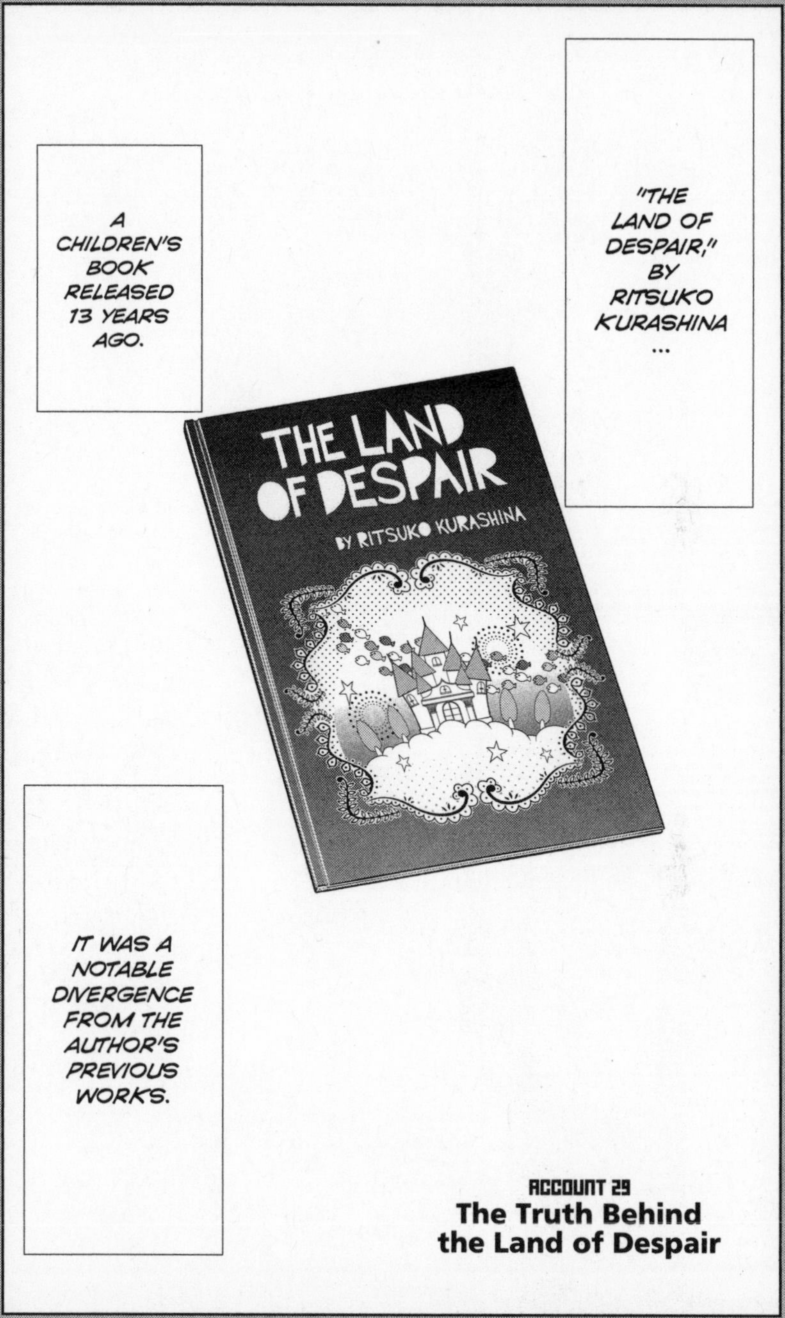
"THE LAND OF DESPAIR," BY RITSUKO KURASHINA ...
A CHILDREN'S BOOK RELEASED 13 YEARS AGO.
THE LAND OF DESPAIR
BY RITSUKO KURASHINA
IT WAS A NOTABLE DIVERGENCE FROM THE AUTHOR'S PREVIOUS WORKS.
ACCOUNT 29
The Truth Behind the Land of Despair

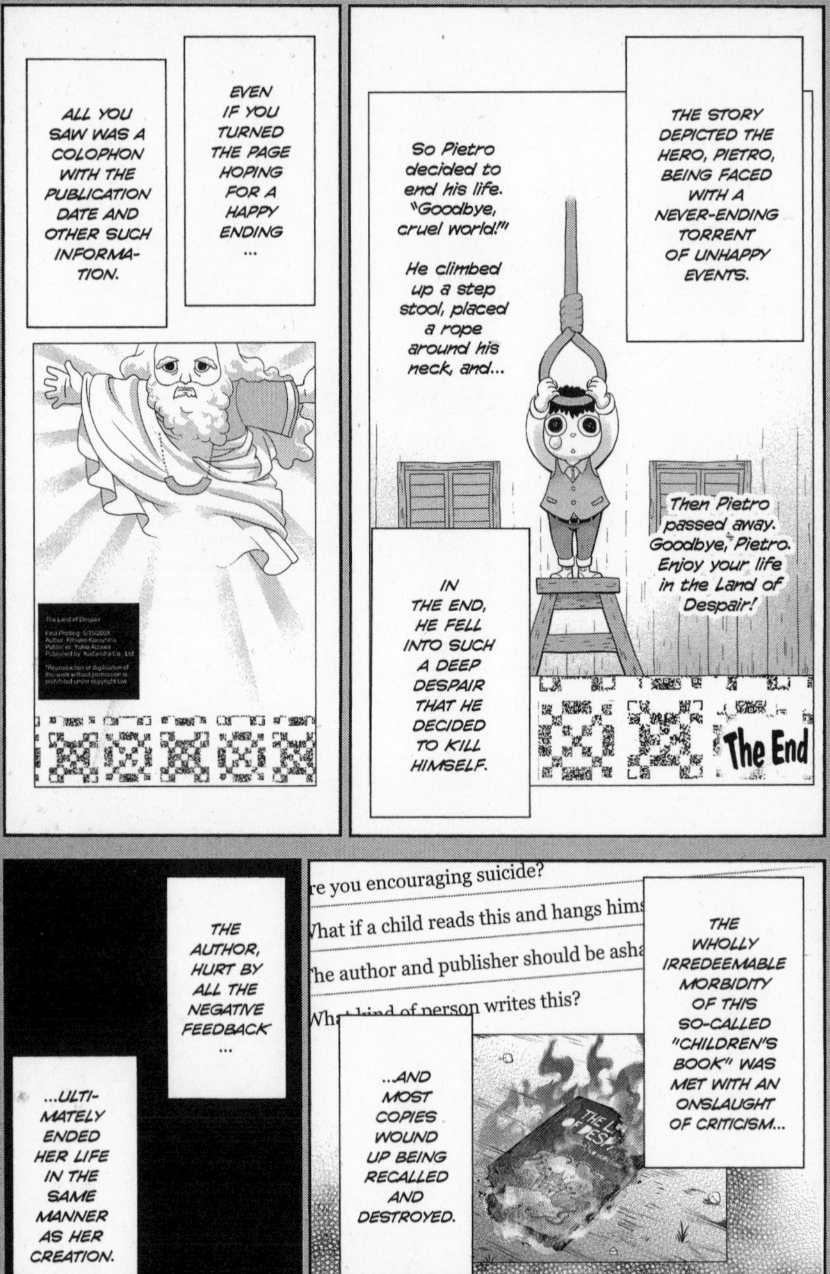
THE STORY DEPICTED THE HERO, PIETRO, BEING FACED WITH A NEVER-ENDING TORRENT OF UNHAPPY EVENTS.
So Pietro decided to end his life. "Goodbye, cruel world!"
He climbed up a step stool, placed a rope around his neck, and...
Then Pietro passed away. Goodbye, Pietro. Enjoy your life in the Land of Despair!
The End
IN THE END, HE FELL INTO SUCH A DEEP DESPAIR THAT HE DECIDED TO KILL HIMSELF.
EVEN IF YOU TURNED THE PAGE HOPING FOR A HAPPY ENDING ...
ALL YOU SAW WAS A COLOPHON WITH THE PUBLICATION DATE AND OTHER SUCH INFORMATION.
The Land of Despair
First Printing: 5/15/200X
Published by: Kodansha Co., Ltd
*Reproduction or duplication of this work without permission is prohibited under copyright law.
THE WHOLLY IRREDEEMABLE MORBIDITY OF THIS SO-CALLED "CHILDREN'S BOOK" WAS MET WITH AN ONSLAUGHT OF CRITICISM...
re you encouraging suicide?
hat if a child reads this and hangs hims
he author and publisher should be asha
person writes this?
...AND MOST COPIES WOUND UP BEING RECALLED AND DESTROYED.
THE AUTHOR, HURT BY ALL THE NEGATIVE FEEDBACK ...
...ULTIMATELY ENDED HER LIFE IN THE SAME MANNER AS HER CREATION.

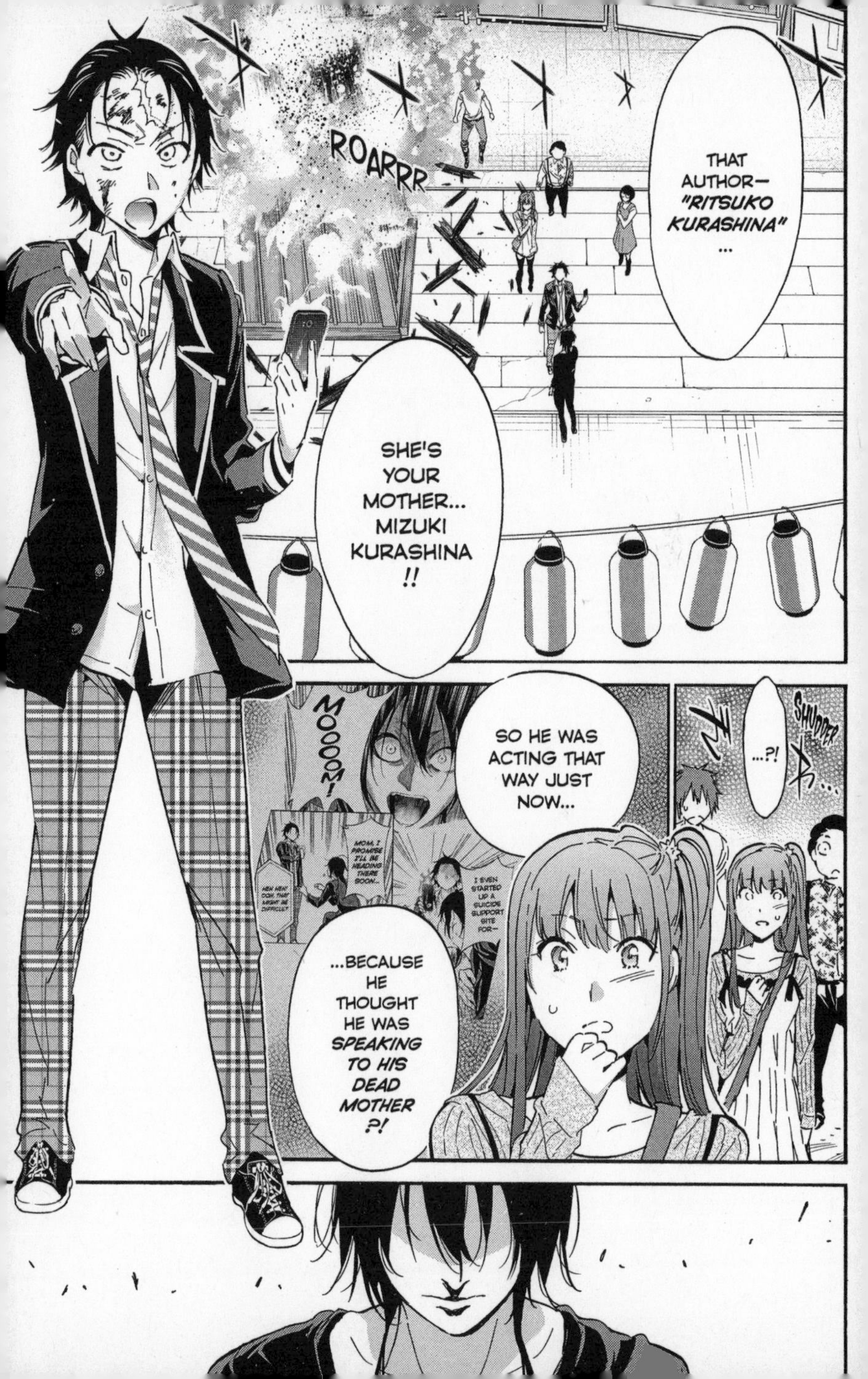
THAT AUTHOR— "RITSUKO KURASHINA" ...
ROARRR
SHE'S YOUR MOTHER... MIZUKI KURASHINA !!
...?!
SHUDDER
SO HE WAS ACTING THAT WAY JUST NOW...
MOOOOM!
I EVEN STARTED UP A SUICIDE SUPPORT SITE FOR—
MOM, I PROMISE I'LL BE HEADING THERE SOON...
HEH HEH! OOH, THAT MIGHT BE DIFFICULT
...BECAUSE HE THOUGHT HE WAS *SPEAKING TO HIS DEAD MOTHER* ?!

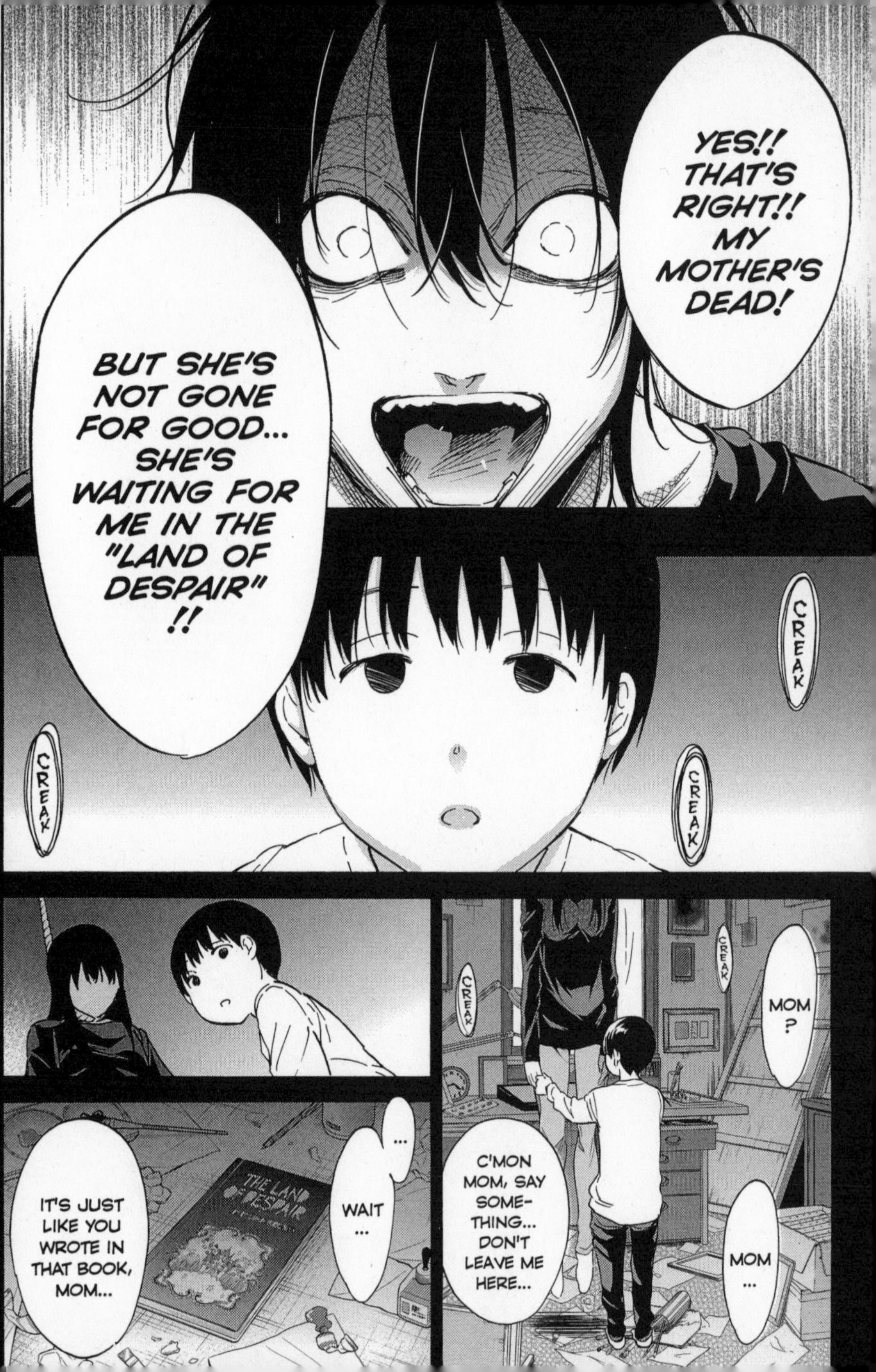
YES!! THAT'S RIGHT!! MY MOTHER'S DEAD!
BUT SHE'S NOT GONE FOR GOOD... SHE'S WAITING FOR ME IN THE "LAND OF DESPAIR" !!
CREAK
CREAK
CREAK
CREAK
CREAK
MOM ?
C'MON MOM, SAY SOME-THING... DON'T LEAVE ME HERE...
MOM ...
...
WAIT ...
THE LAND OF DESPAIR
IT'S JUST LIKE YOU WROTE IN THAT BOOK, MOM...

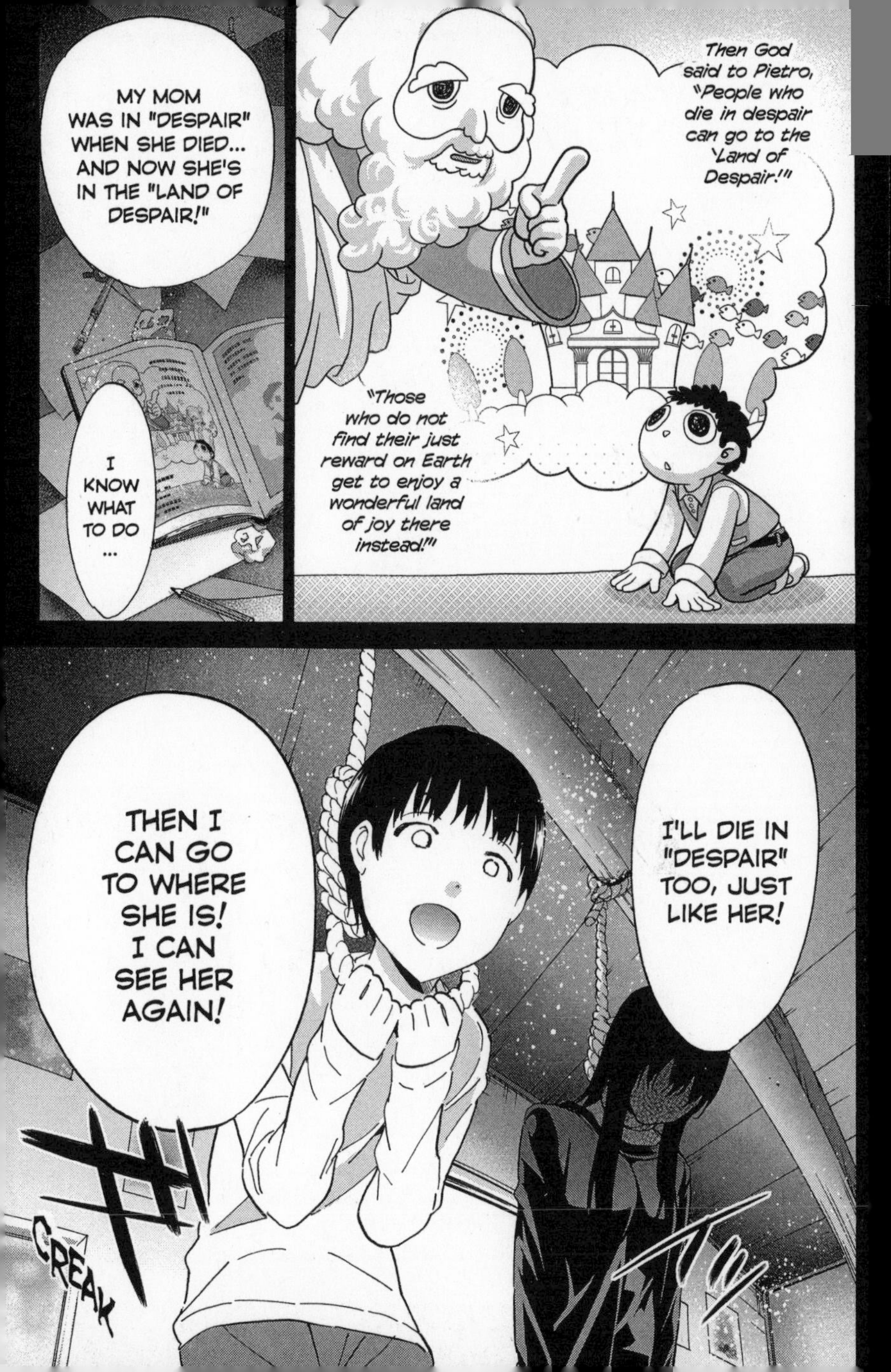
Then God said to Pietro, "People who die in despair can go to the 'Land of Despair!'"
"Those who do not find their just reward on Earth get to enjoy a wonderful land of joy there instead!'"
MY MOM WAS IN "DESPAIR" WHEN SHE DIED... AND NOW SHE'S IN THE "LAND OF DESPAIR!"
I KNOW WHAT TO DO ...
I'LL DIE IN "DESPAIR" TOO, JUST LIKE HER!
THEN I CAN GO TO WHERE SHE IS! I CAN SEE HER AGAIN!
CREAK

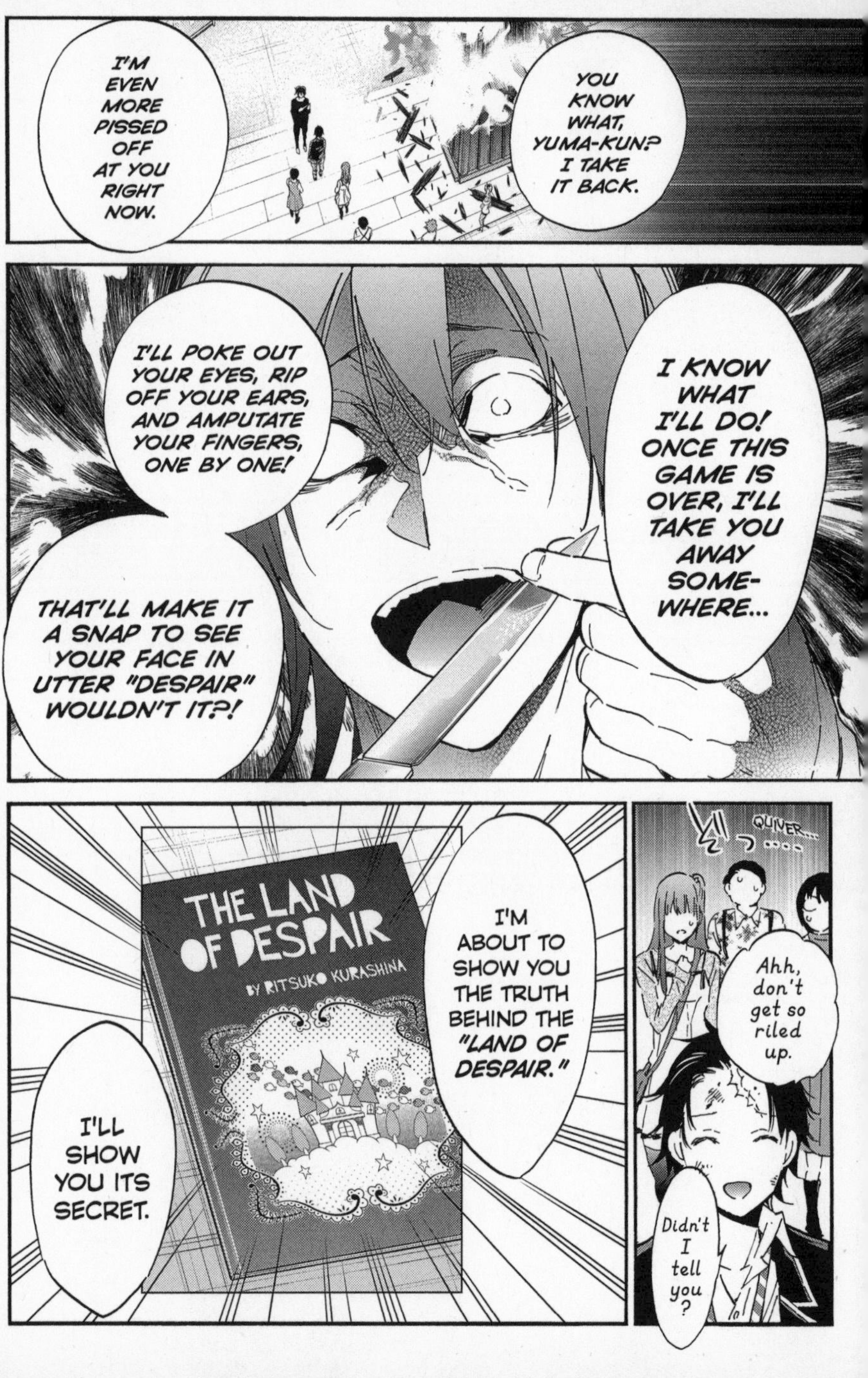
YOU KNOW WHAT, YUMA-KUN? I TAKE IT BACK.
I'M EVEN MORE PISSED OFF AT YOU RIGHT NOW.
I KNOW WHAT I'LL DO! ONCE THIS GAME IS OVER, I'LL TAKE YOU AWAY SOME-WHERE...
I'LL POKE OUT YOUR EYES, RIP OFF YOUR EARS, AND AMPUTATE YOUR FINGERS, ONE BY ONE!
THAT'LL MAKE IT A SNAP TO SEE YOUR FACE IN UTTER "DESPAIR" WOULDN'T IT?!
QUIVER...
Ahh, don't get so riled up.
Didn't I tell you?
I'M ABOUT TO SHOW YOU THE TRUTH BEHIND THE "LAND OF DESPAIR."
THE LAND OF DESPAIR
BY RITSUKO KURASHINA
I'LL SHOW YOU ITS SECRET.

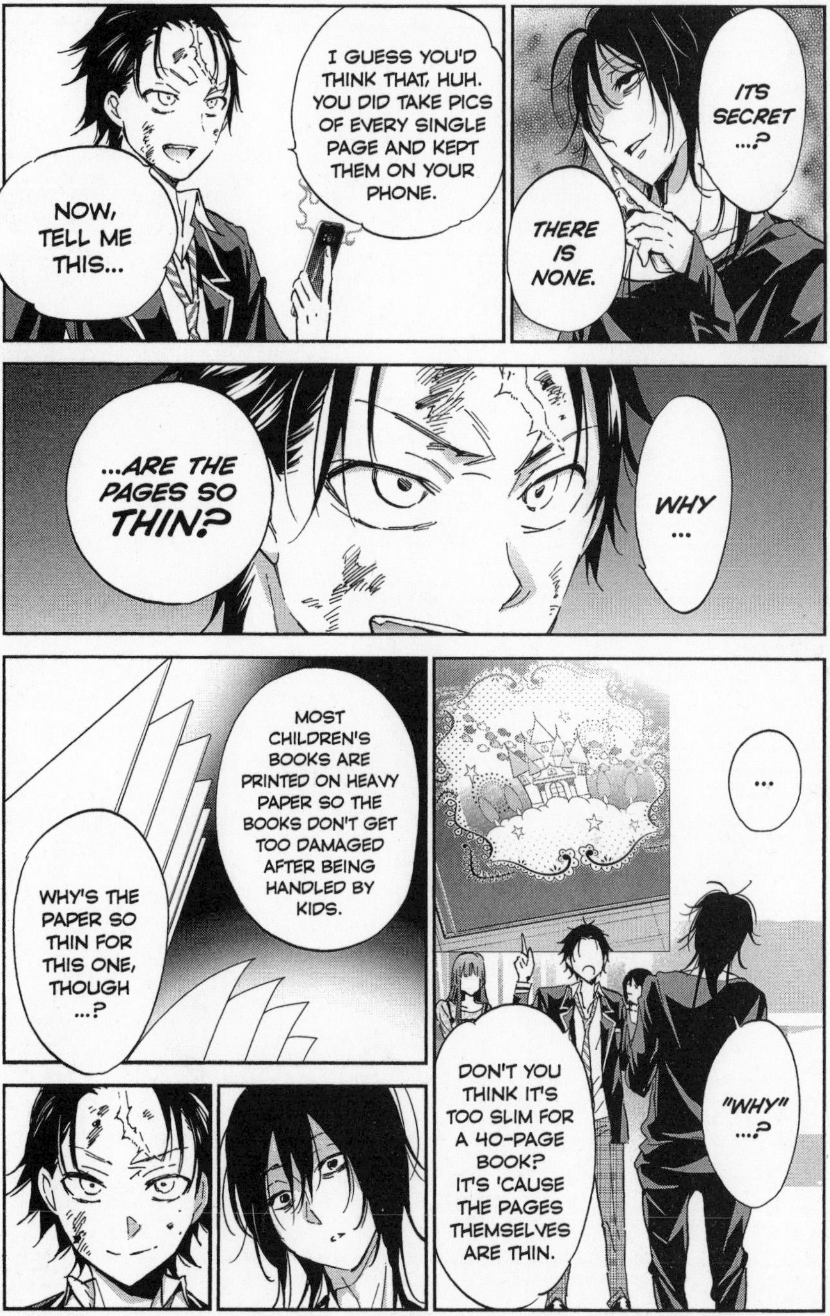
ITS SECRET ...?
THERE IS NONE.
I GUESS YOU'D THINK THAT, HUH. YOU DID TAKE PICS OF EVERY SINGLE PAGE AND KEPT THEM ON YOUR PHONE.
NOW, TELL ME THIS...
WHY ...
...ARE THE PAGES SO THIN?
...
"WHY" ...?
DON'T YOU THINK IT'S TOO SLIM FOR A 40-PAGE BOOK? IT'S 'CAUSE THE PAGES THEMSELVES ARE THIN.
MOST CHILDREN'S BOOKS ARE PRINTED ON HEAVY PAPER SO THE BOOKS DON'T GET TOO DAMAGED AFTER BEING HANDLED BY KIDS.
WHY'S THE PAPER SO THIN FOR THIS ONE, THOUGH ...?

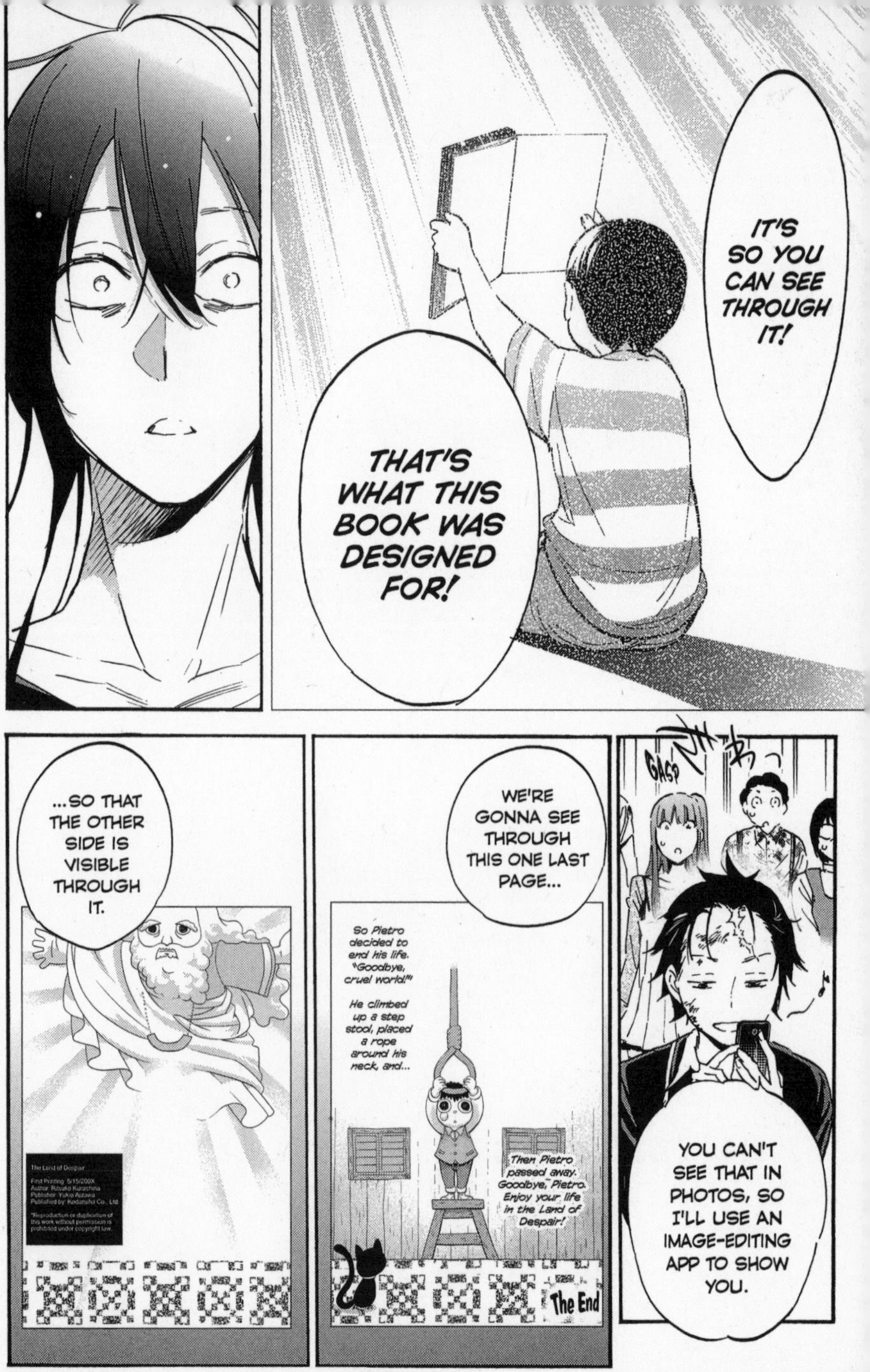
IT'S SO YOU CAN SEE THROUGH IT!
THAT'S WHAT THIS BOOK WAS DESIGNED FOR!
GASP
YOU CAN'T SEE THAT IN PHOTOS, SO I'LL USE AN IMAGE-EDITING APP TO SHOW YOU.
WE'RE GONNA SEE THROUGH THIS ONE LAST PAGE...
So Pietro decided to end his life. "Goodbye, cruel world!"
He climbed up a step stool, placed a rope around his neck, and...
Then Pietro passed away. Goodbye, Pietro. Enjoy your life in the Land of Despair!
The End
...SO THAT THE OTHER SIDE IS VISIBLE THROUGH IT.
The Land of Despair
First Printing: 5/15/200X
Author: Ritsuko Kurashina
Publisher: Yukio Aizawa
Published by: Kodansha Co., Ltd
*Reproduction or duplication of this work without permission is prohibited under copyright law.

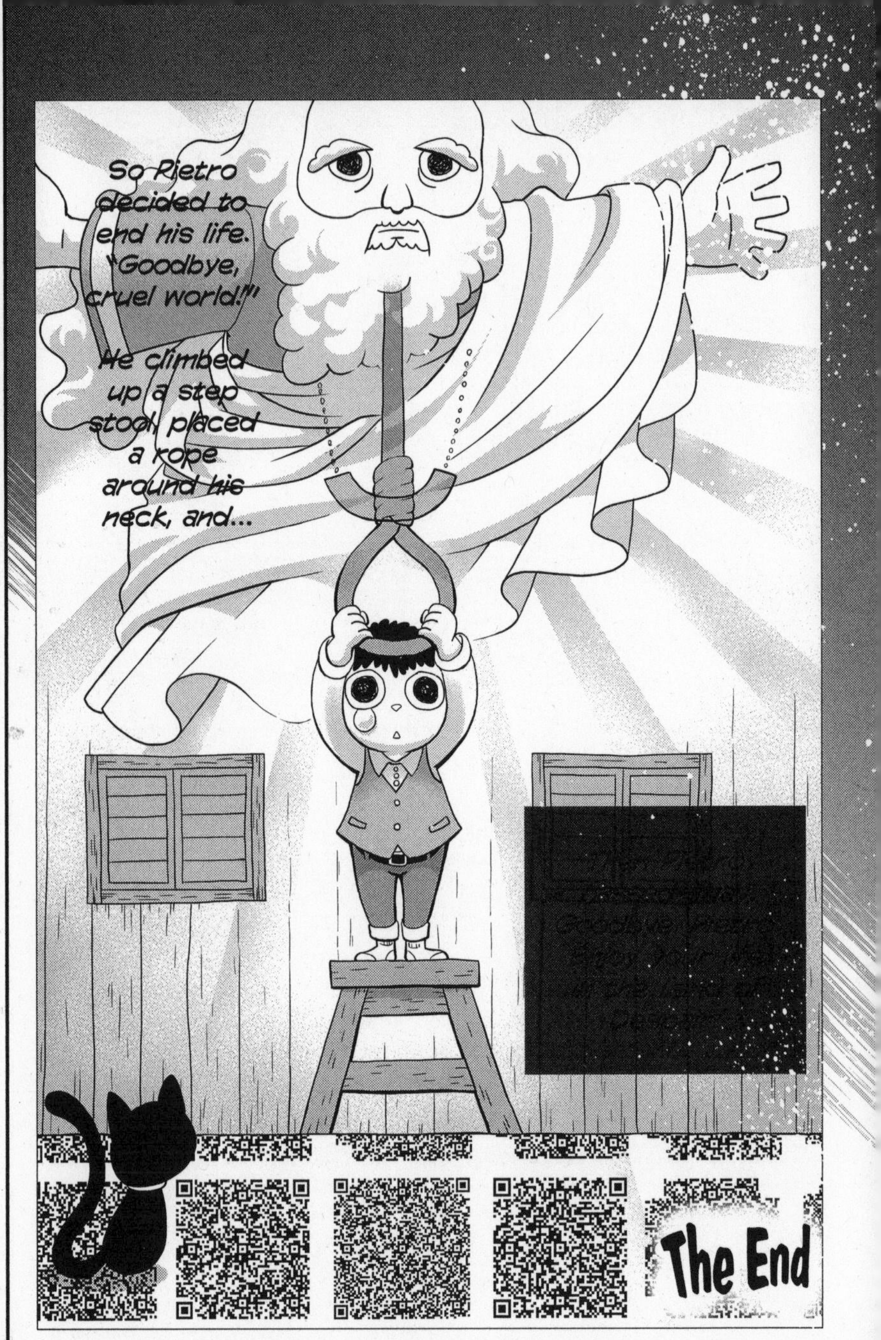
So Rietro decided to end his life. "Goodbye, cruel world!"
He climbed up a step stool, placed a rope around his neck, and...
[redacted]
The End

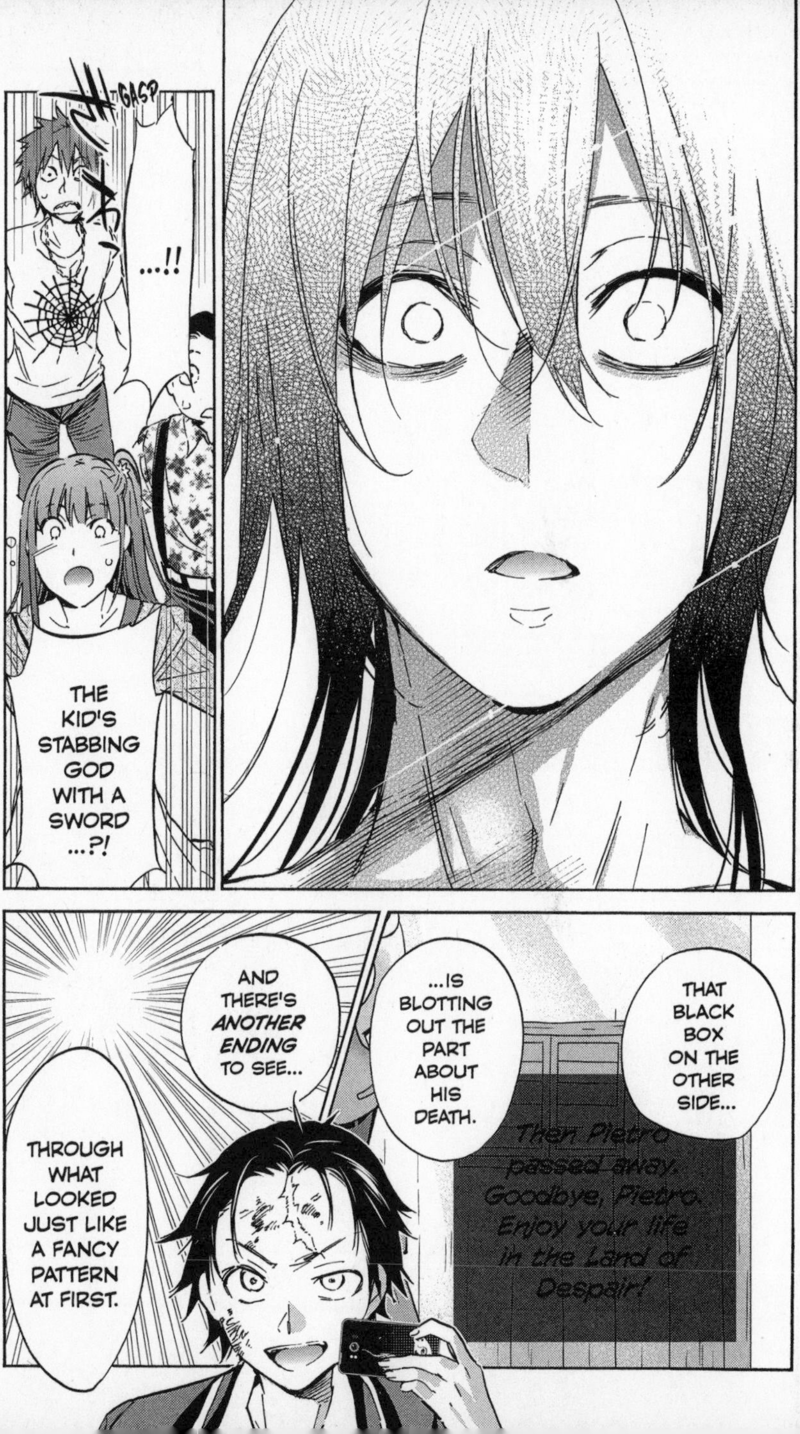
GASP
...!!
THE KID'S STABBING GOD WITH A SWORD ...?!
THAT BLACK BOX ON THE OTHER SIDE...
...IS BLOTTING OUT THE PART ABOUT HIS DEATH.
Then Pietro passed away. Goodbye, Pietro. Enjoy your life in the Land of Despair!
AND THERE'S *ANOTHER ENDING* TO SEE...
THROUGH WHAT LOOKED JUST LIKE A FANCY PATTERN AT FIRST.

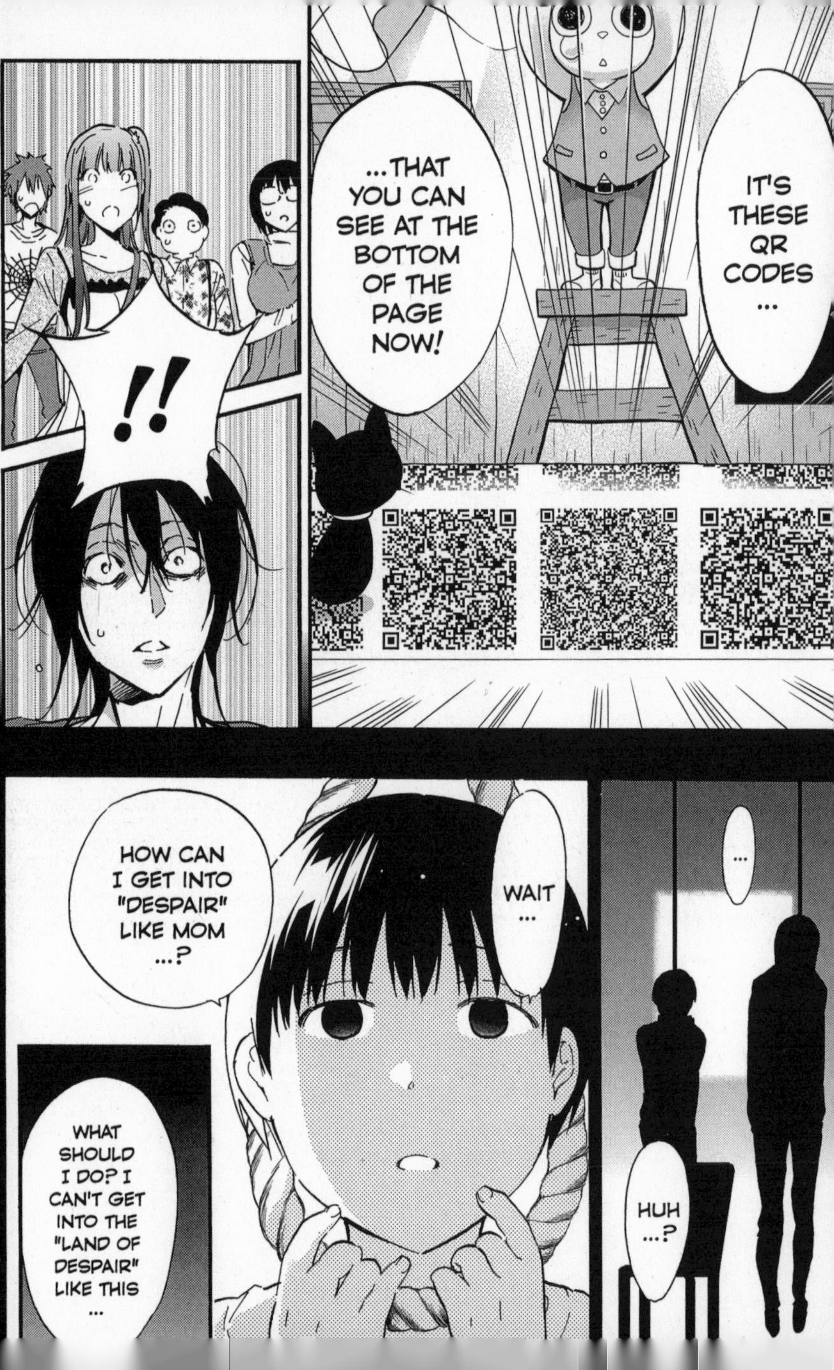
IT'S THESE QR CODES...
...THAT YOU CAN SEE AT THE BOTTOM OF THE PAGE NOW!
!!
...
HUH...?
WAIT...
HOW CAN I GET INTO "DESPAIR" LIKE MOM...?
WHAT SHOULD I DO? I CAN'T GET INTO THE "LAND OF DESPAIR" LIKE THIS...

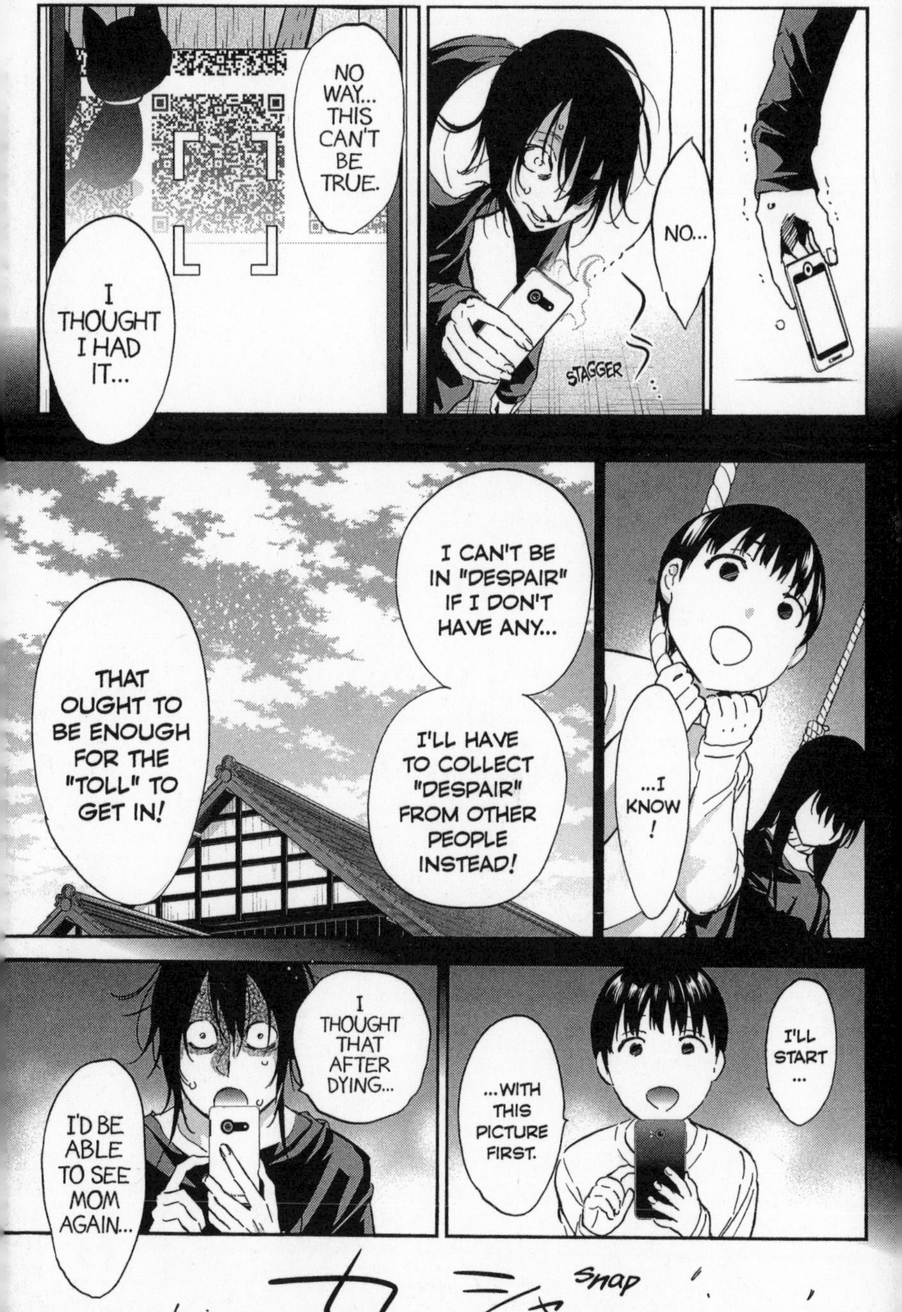
NO...
STAGGER
NO WAY... THIS CAN'T BE TRUE.
I THOUGHT I HAD IT...
...I KNOW!
I CAN'T BE IN "DESPAIR" IF I DON'T HAVE ANY...
I'LL HAVE TO COLLECT "DESPAIR" FROM OTHER PEOPLE INSTEAD!
THAT OUGHT TO BE ENOUGH FOR THE "TOLL" TO GET IN!
I'LL START...
...WITH THIS PICTURE FIRST.
I THOUGHT THAT AFTER DYING...
I'D BE ABLE TO SEE MOM AGAIN...
Snap

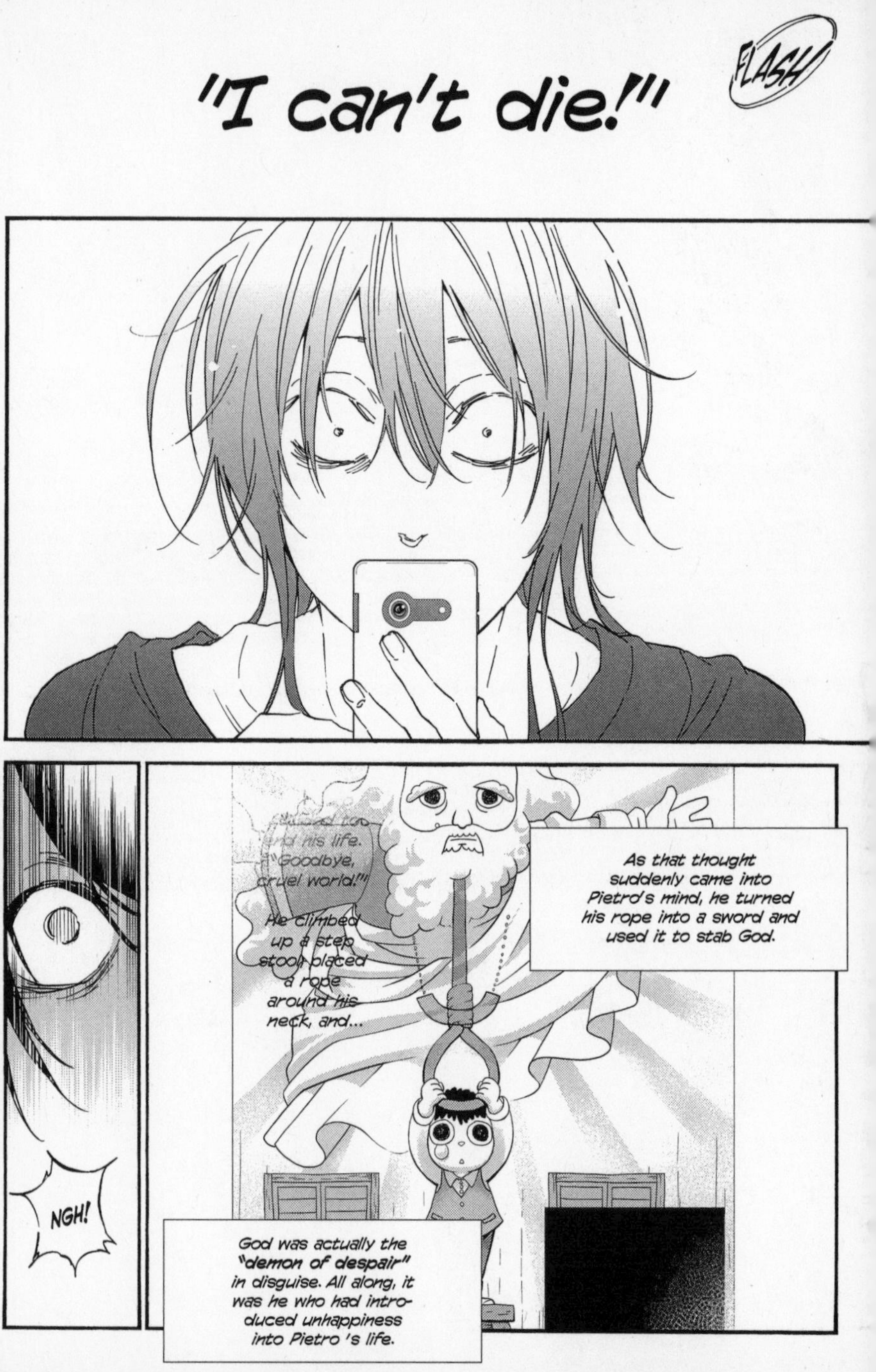
"I can't die!"
FLASH
As that thought suddenly came into Pietro's mind, he turned his rope into a sword and used it to stab God.
end his life. "Goodbye, cruel world!"
He climbed up a step stool, placed a rope around his neck, and...
God was actually the "demon of despair" in disguise. All along, it was he who had intro-duced unhappiness into Pietro's life.
NGH!

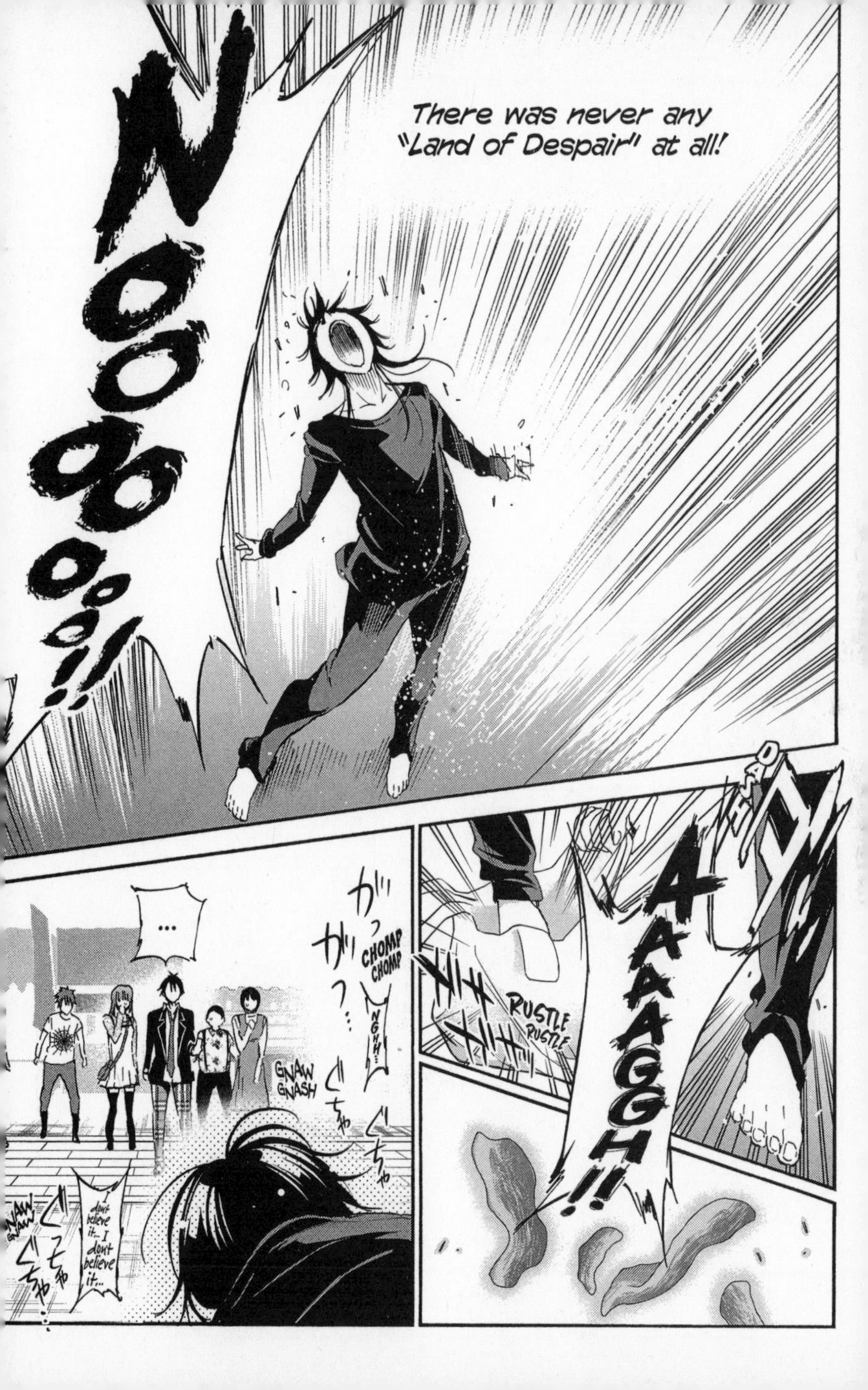
There was never any "Land of Despair" at all!
NOOOOOOOO!!
DASH
AAAAAGGH!!
RUSTLE RUSTLE
がっがっ…
CHOMP CHOMP
NGGH…
ぐちゃ ぐちゃ
GNAW GNASH
...
I don't believe it... I don't believe it...
ぐちゃぐちゃ…
GNAW GNAW

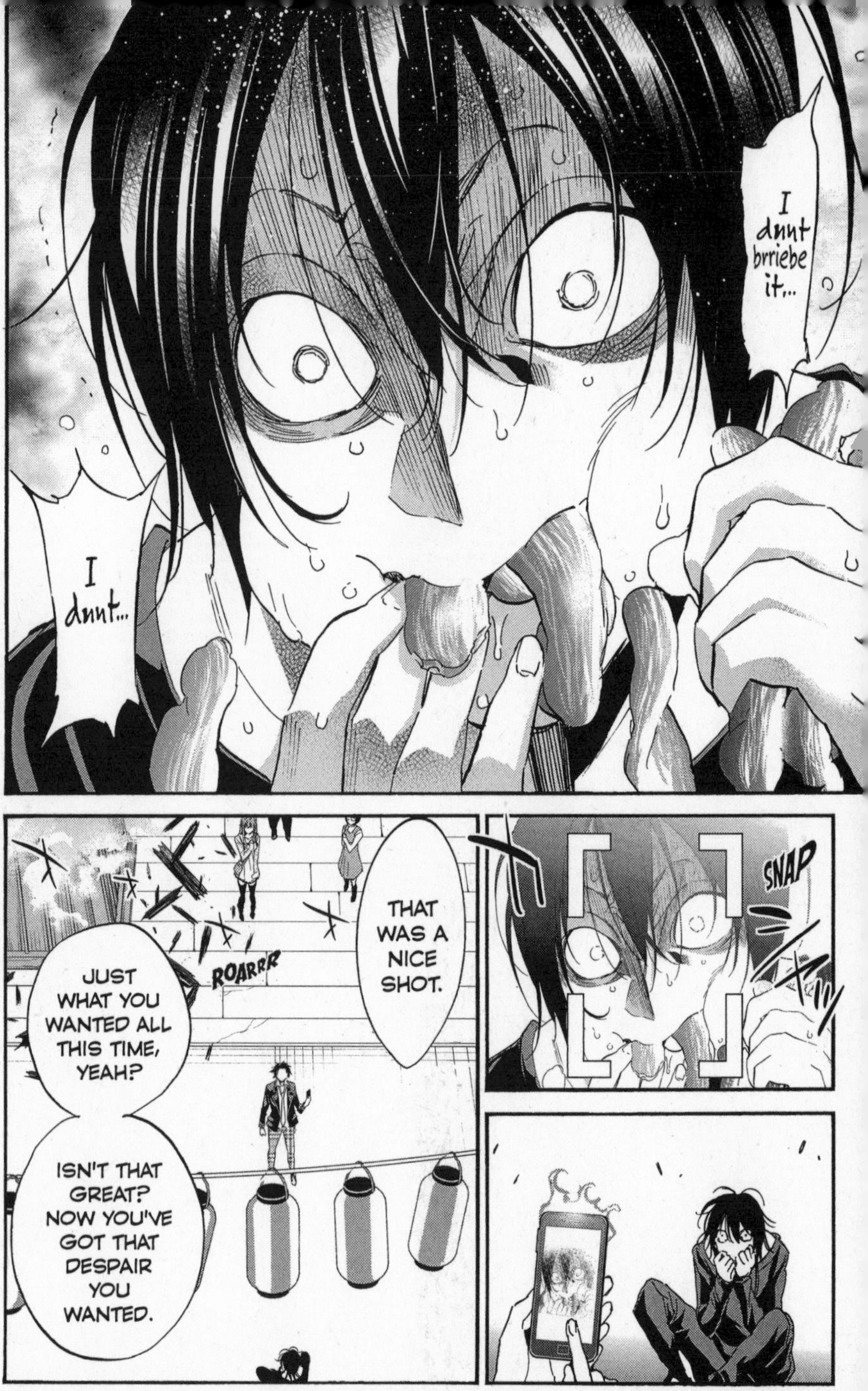
I dnnt brriebe it...
I dnnt...
SNAP
THAT WAS A NICE SHOT.
ROARRR
JUST WHAT YOU WANTED ALL THIS TIME, YEAH?
ISN'T THAT GREAT? NOW YOU'VE GOT THAT DESPAIR YOU WANTED.

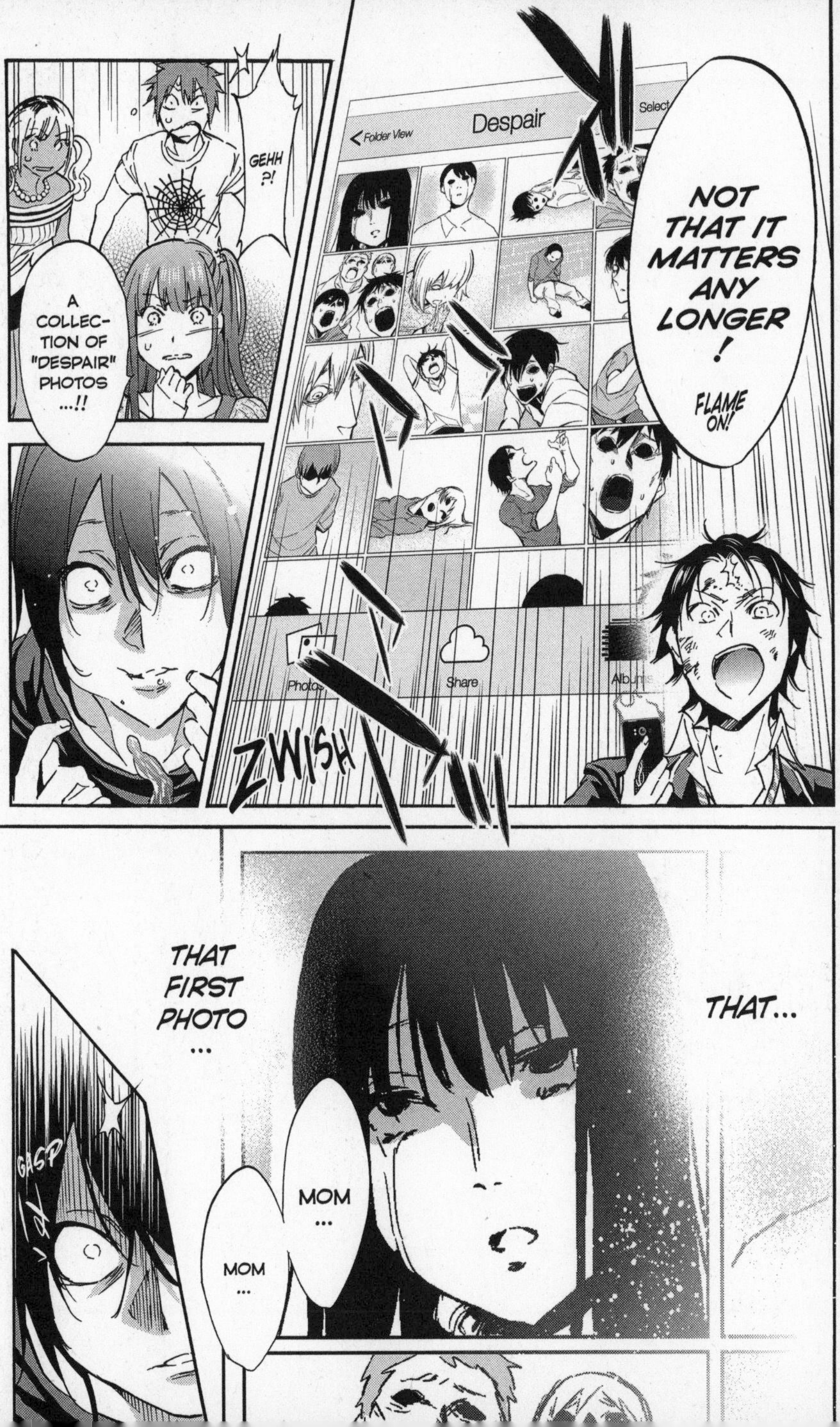
Select
Folder View
Despair
Photos
Share
NOT THAT IT MATTERS ANY LONGER!
FLAME ON!
ZWISH
GEHH ?!
A COLLECTION OF "DESPAIR" PHOTOS ...!!
THAT...
THAT FIRST PHOTO ...
MOM ...
MOM ...
GASP

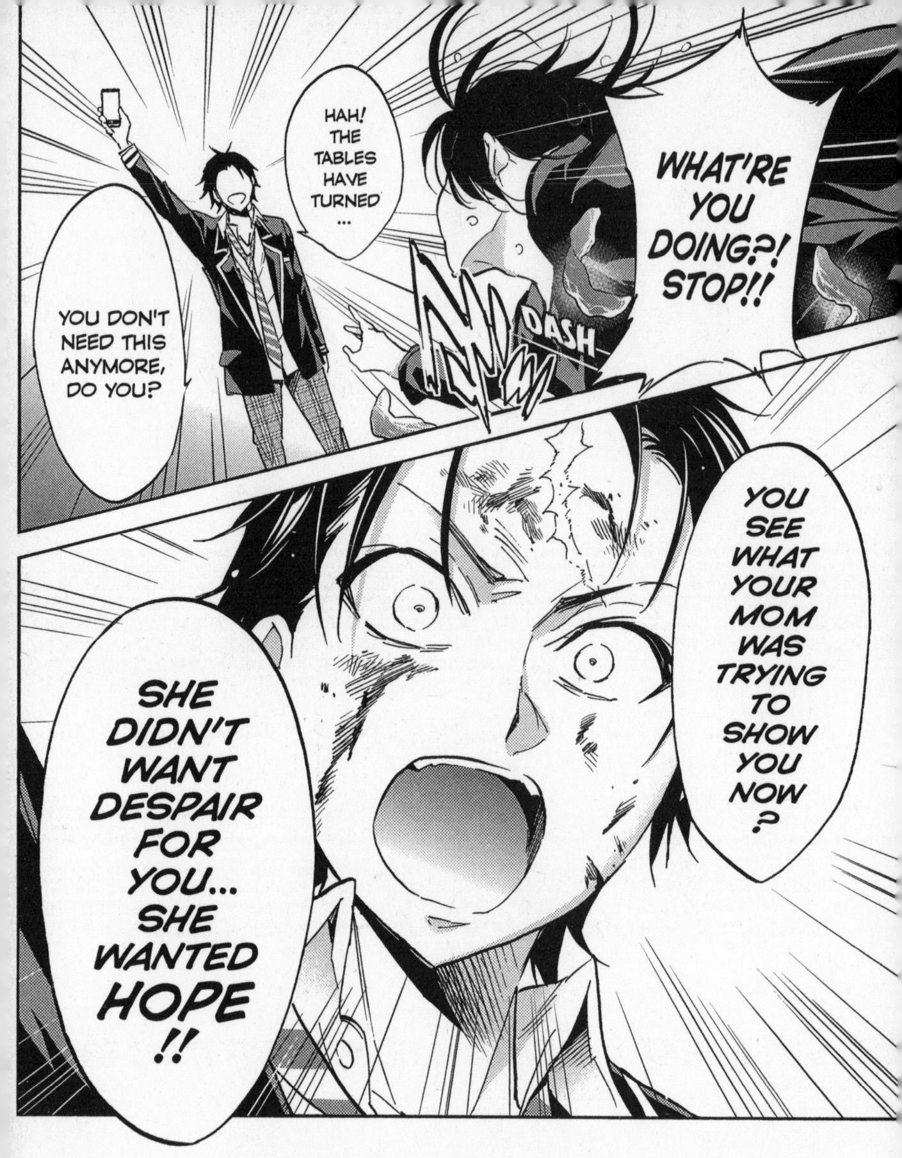
WHAT'RE YOU DOING?! STOP!!
DASH
HAH! THE TABLES HAVE TURNED...
YOU DON'T NEED THIS ANYMORE, DO YOU?
YOU SEE WHAT YOUR MOM WAS TRYING TO SHOW YOU NOW?
SHE DIDN'T WANT DESPAIR FOR YOU... SHE WANTED HOPE!!

From within the despair, Pietro found a small, hard-to-find piece of "hope."

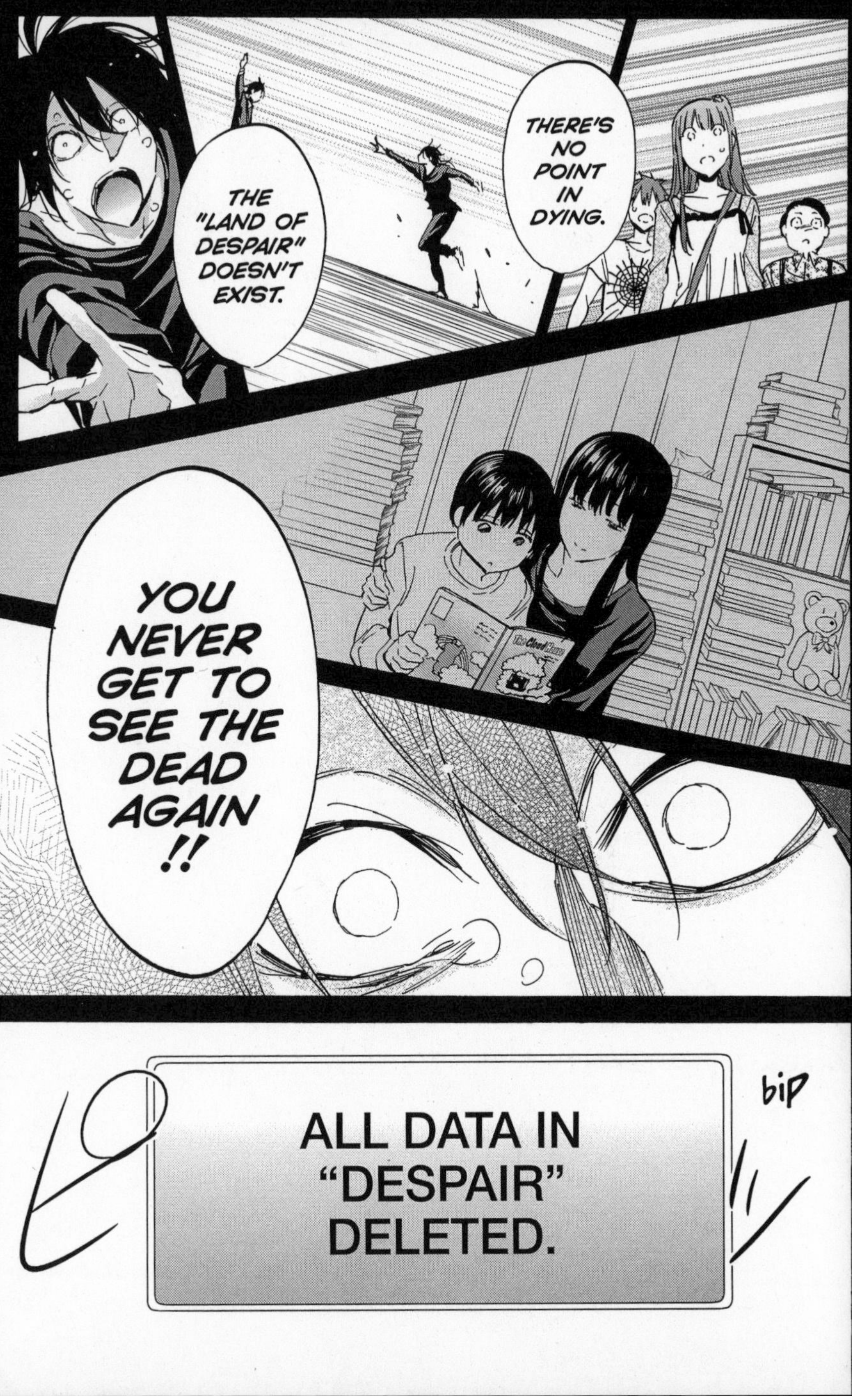
THERE'S NO POINT IN DYING.
THE "LAND OF DESPAIR" DOESN'T EXIST.
YOU NEVER GET TO SEE THE DEAD AGAIN!!
bip
ALL DATA IN "DESPAIR" DELETED.

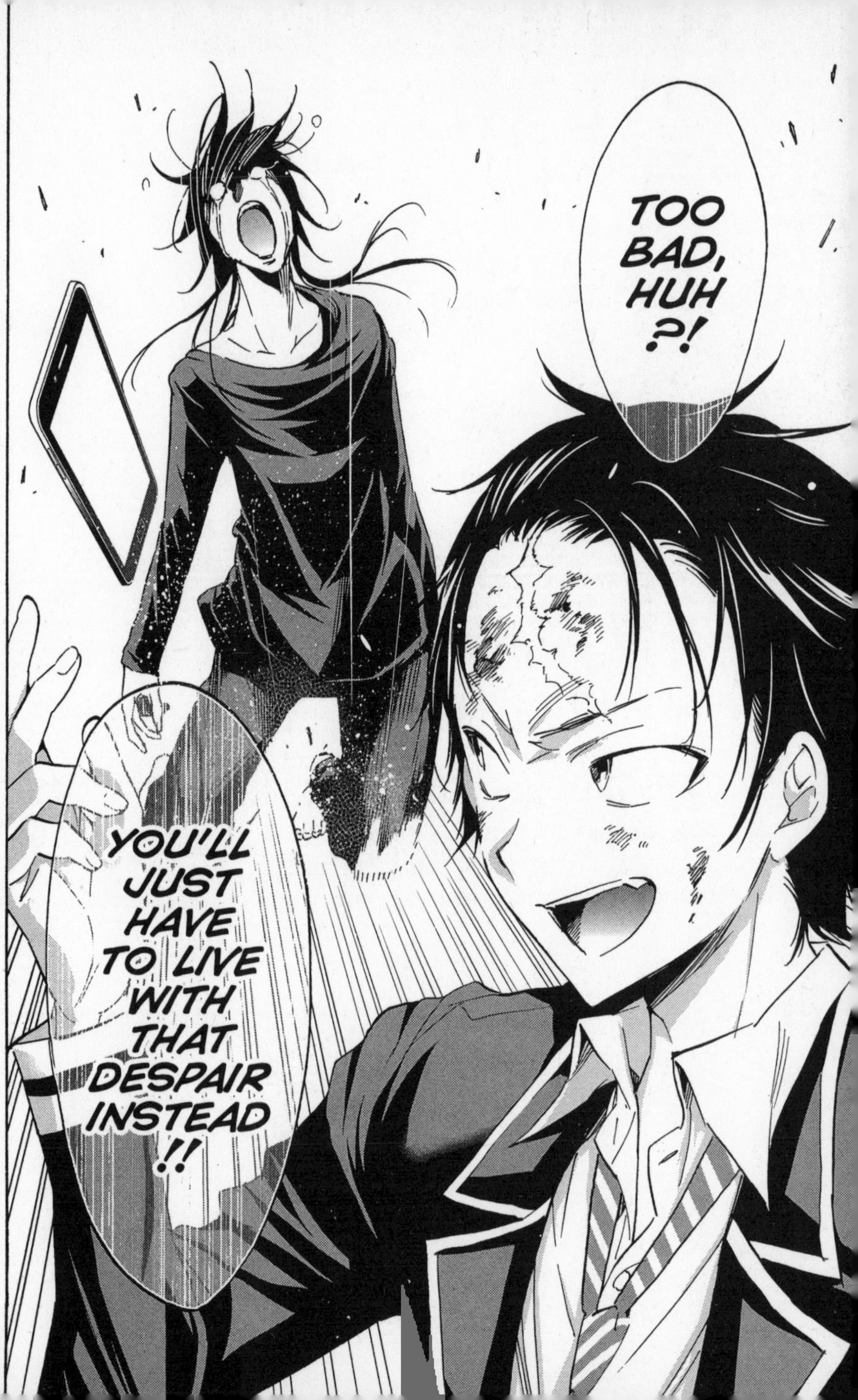
TOO BAD, HUH?!
YOU'LL JUST HAVE TO LIVE WITH THAT DESPAIR INSTEAD!!

ACCOUNT 30 The Explosive Exclusive

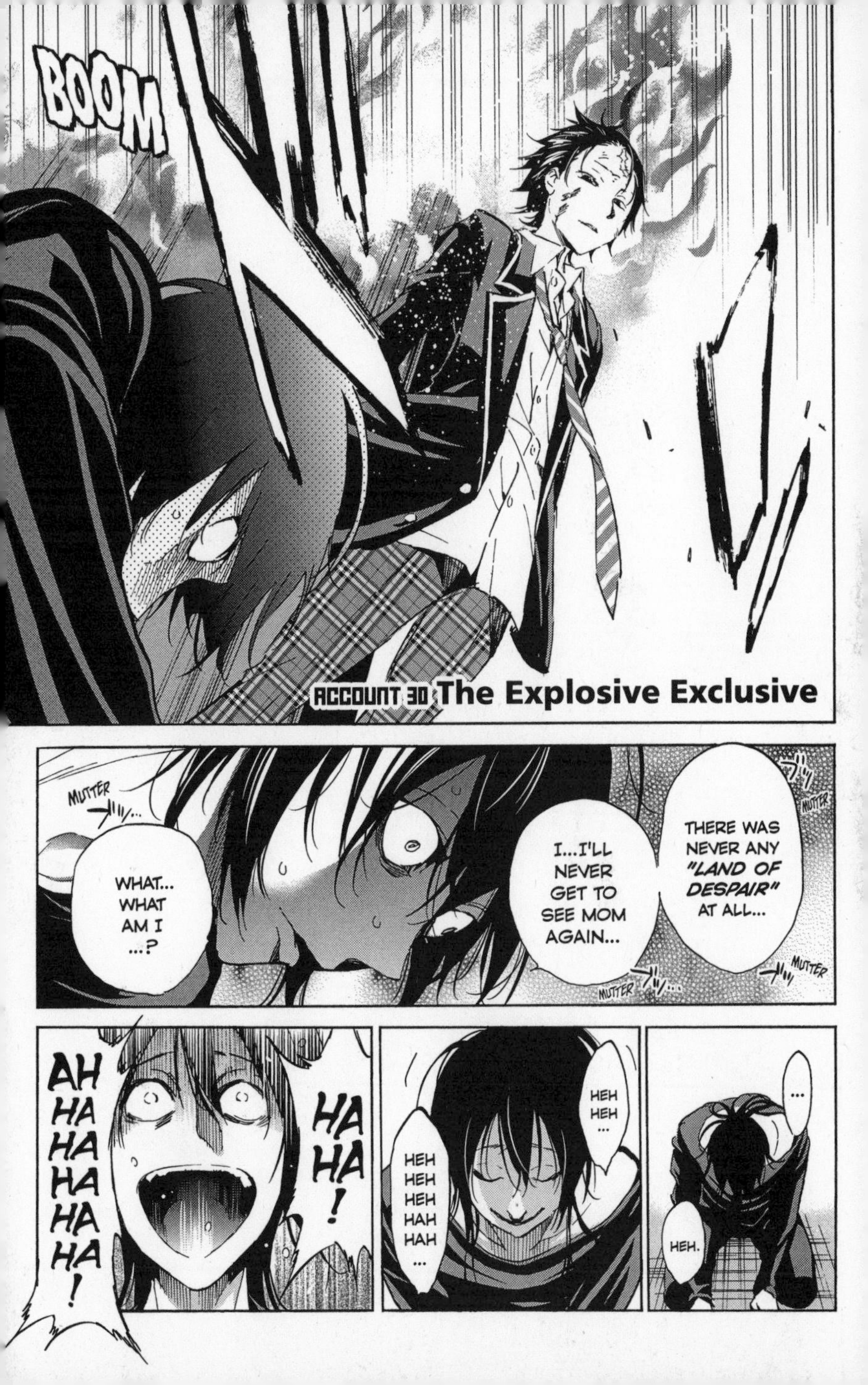
BOOM
ACCOUNT 30 The Explosive Exclusive
MUTTER
THERE WAS NEVER ANY "LAND OF DESPAIR" AT ALL...
MUTTER
I...I'LL NEVER GET TO SEE MOM AGAIN...
MUTTER
WHAT... WHAT AM I ...?
MUTTER
...
HEH.
HEH HEH ...
HEH HEH HEH HAH HAH ...
HA HA!
AH HA HA HA HA HA HA!

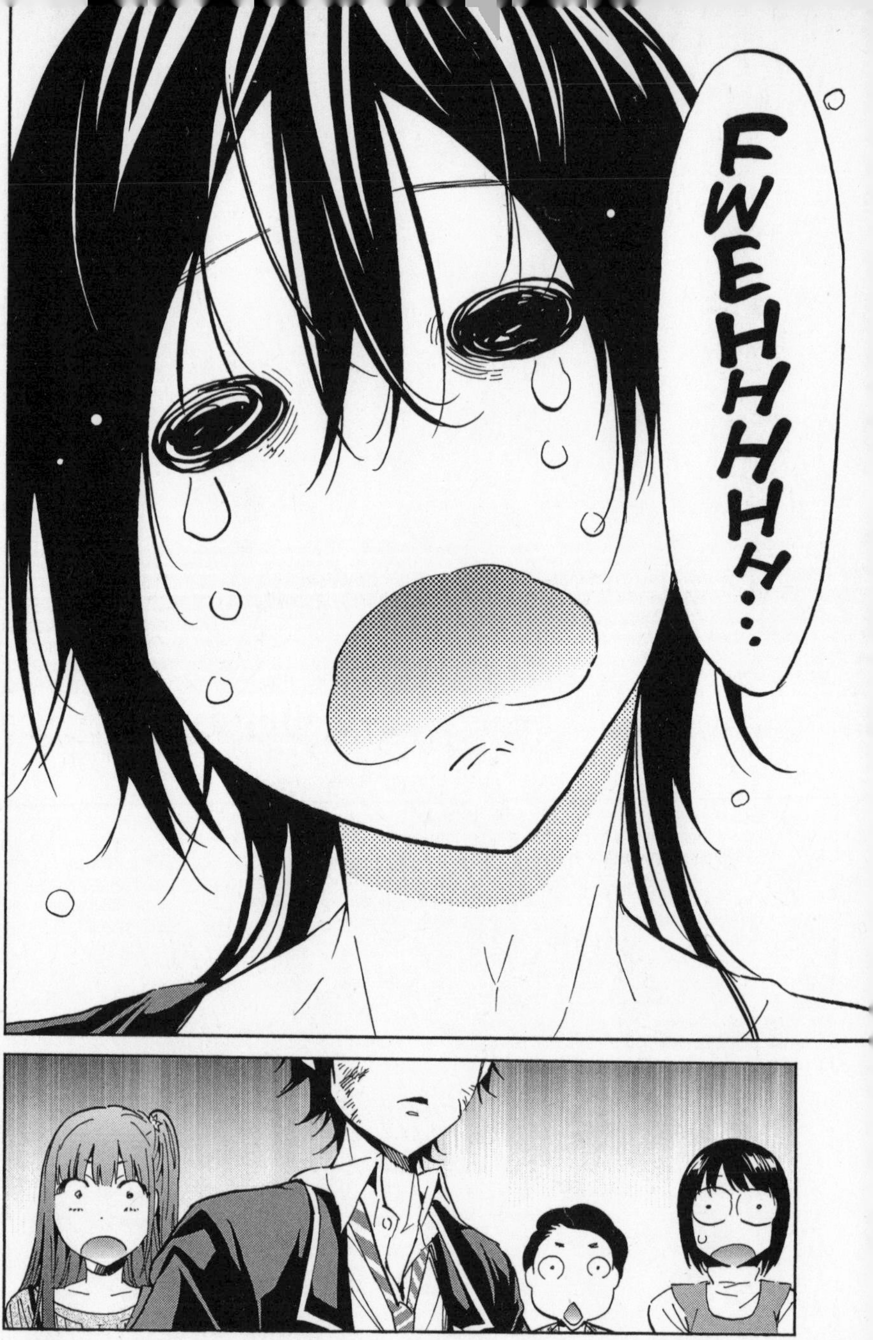
FWEHHHHH...

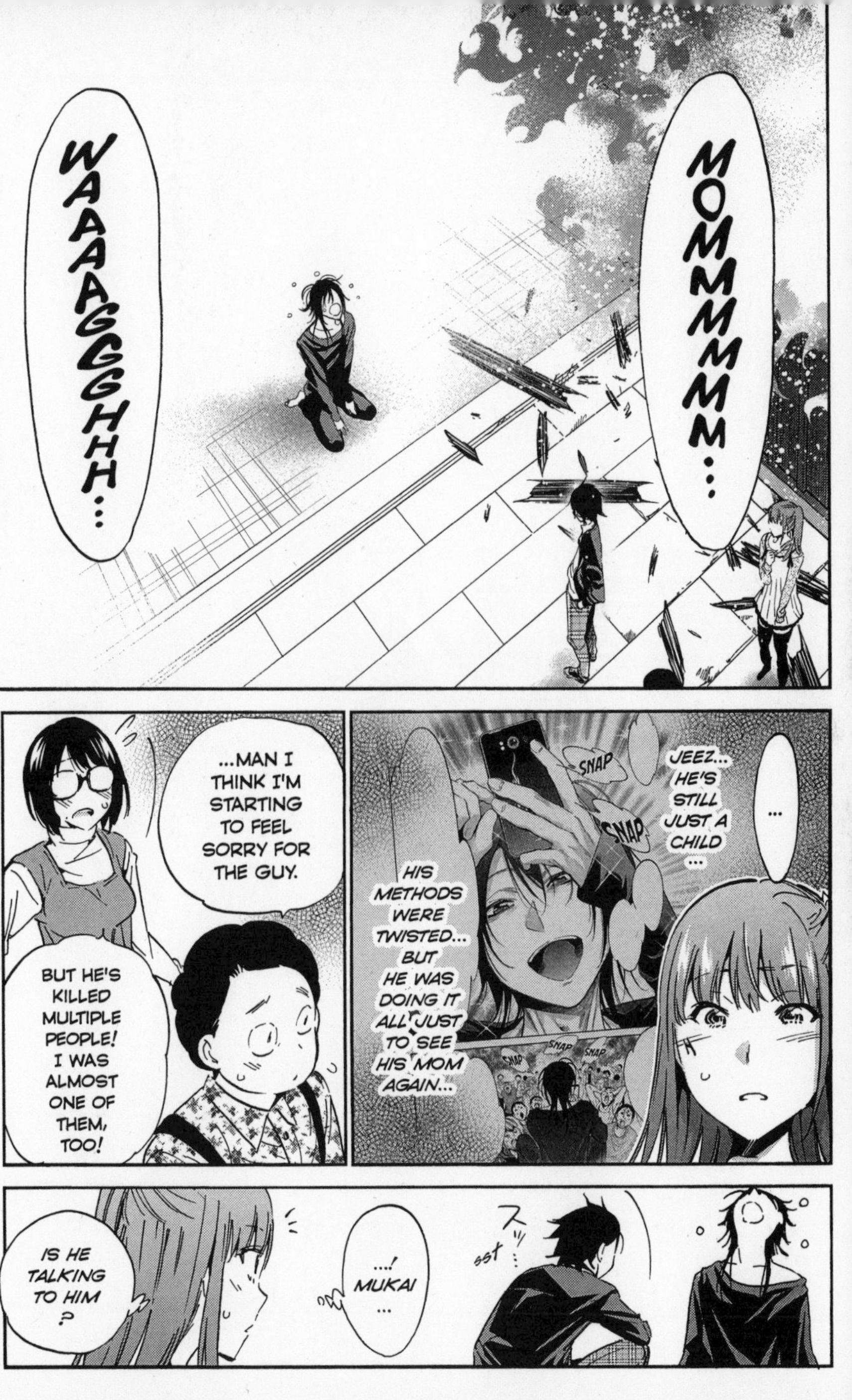
MOMMMMMM...
WAAAAGGGHHH...
...
JEEZ... HE'S STILL JUST A CHILD ...
SNAP
SNAP
HIS METHODS WERE TWISTED... BUT HE WAS DOING IT ALL JUST TO SEE HIS MOM AGAIN...
SNAP SNAP SNAP
...MAN I THINK I'M STARTING TO FEEL SORRY FOR THE GUY.
BUT HE'S KILLED MULTIPLE PEOPLE! I WAS ALMOST ONE OF THEM, TOO!
sst
...! MUKAI ...
IS HE TALKING TO HIM ?

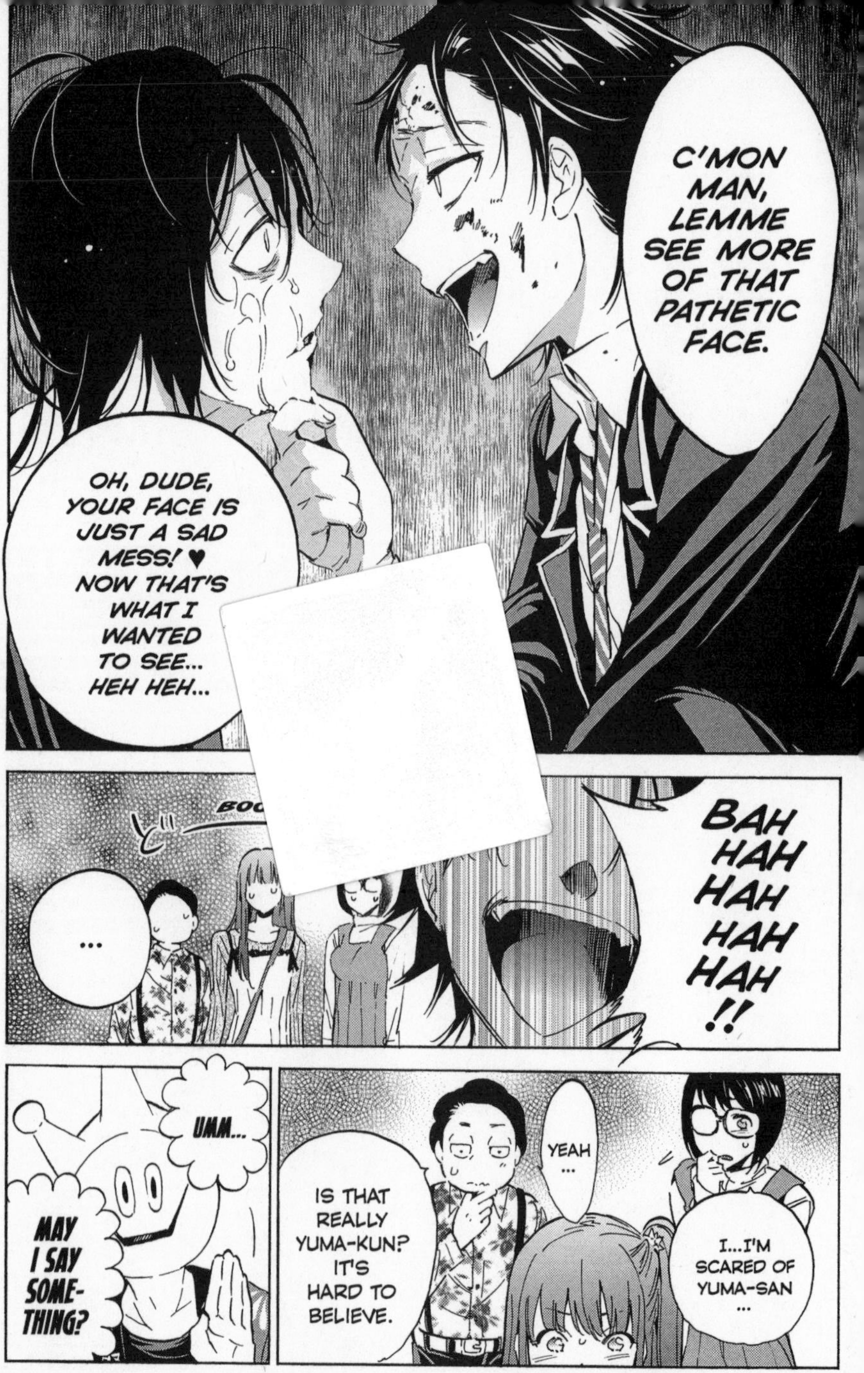

C'MON MAN, LEMME SEE MORE OF THAT PATHETIC FACE.
OH, DUDE, YOUR FACE IS JUST A SAD MESS! ♥ NOW THAT'S WHAT I WANTED TO SEE... HEH HEH...
BAH HAH HAH HAH HAH!!
ど
BOO
...
IS THAT REALLY YUMA-KUN? IT'S HARD TO BELIEVE.
YEAH ...
I...I'M SCARED OF YUMA-SAN ...
UMM...
MAY I SAY SOME-THING?

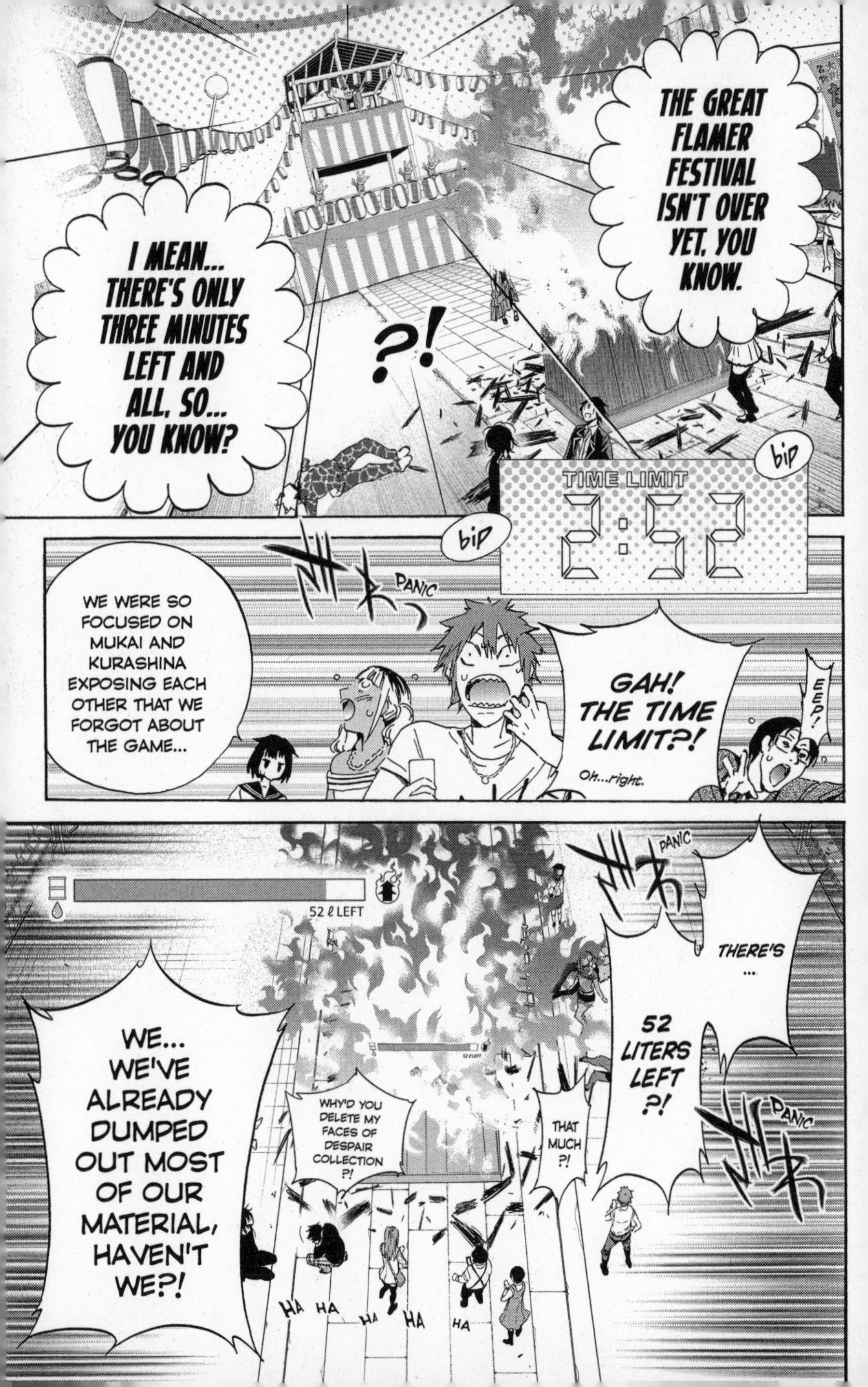
THE GREAT FLAMER FESTIVAL ISN'T OVER YET, YOU KNOW.
?!
I MEAN... THERE'S ONLY THREE MINUTES LEFT AND ALL, SO... YOU KNOW?
bip
TIME LIMIT
2:52
bip
EEP!
GAH! THE TIME LIMIT?!
Oh...right.
PANIC
WE WERE SO FOCUSED ON MUKAI AND KURASHINA EXPOSING EACH OTHER THAT WE FORGOT ABOUT THE GAME...
PANIC
THERE'S...
52 LITERS LEFT?!
PANIC
52 ℓ LEFT
THAT MUCH?!
WHY'D YOU DELETE MY FACES OF DESPAIR COLLECTION?!
WE... WE'VE ALREADY DUMPED OUT MOST OF OUR MATERIAL, HAVEN'T WE?!
HA HA HA HA HA

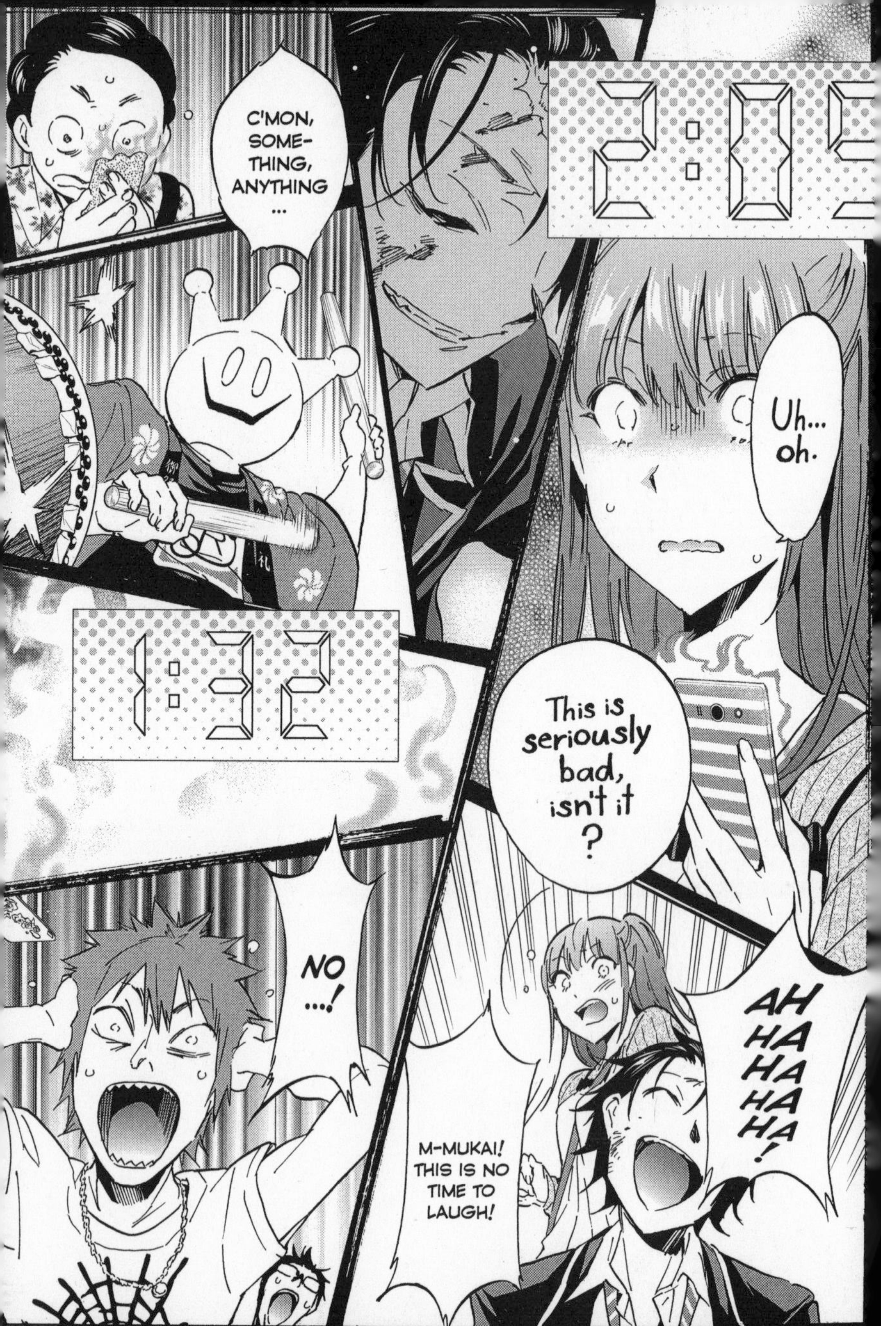
2:05
Uh... oh.
This is seriously bad, isn't it?
AH HA HA HA HA!
M-MUKAI! THIS IS NO TIME TO LAUGH!
C'MON, SOME-THING, ANYTHING ...
1:32
NO ...!

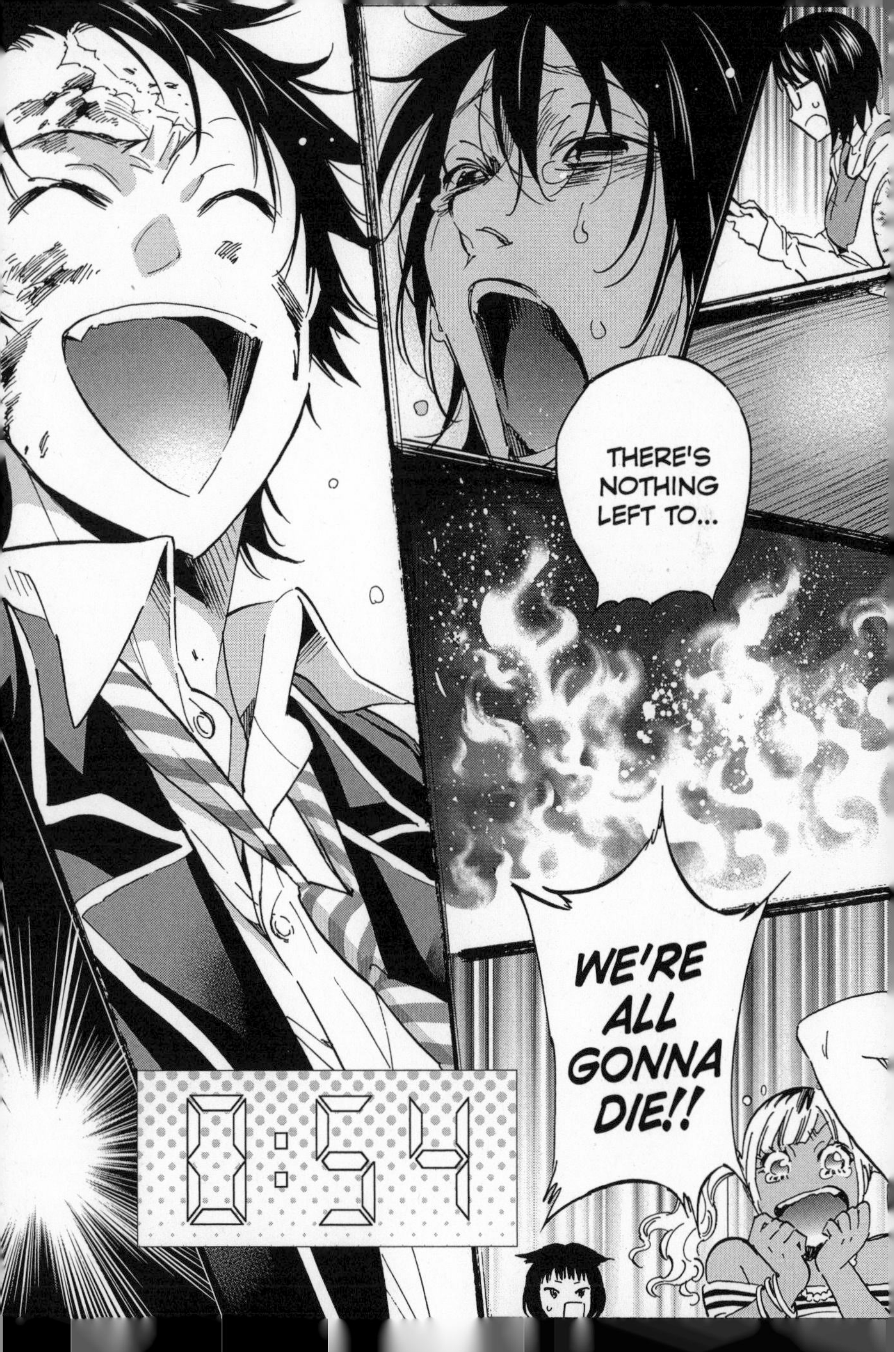
THERE'S NOTHING LEFT TO...
WE'RE ALL GONNA DIE!!
0:54

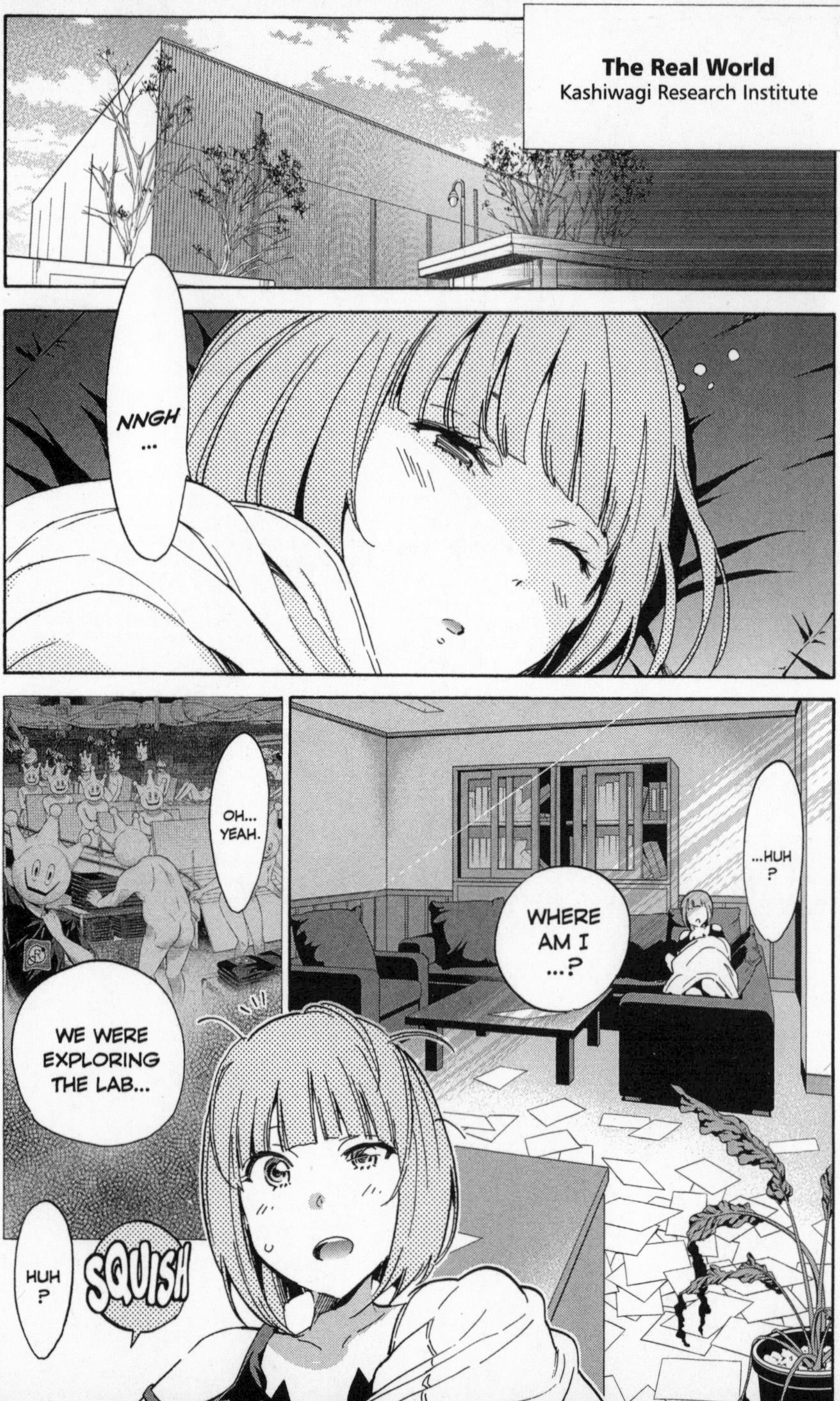
The Real World
Kashiwagi Research Institute
NNGH ...
...HUH ?
WHERE AM I ...?
OH... YEAH.
WE WERE EXPLORING THE LAB...
SQUISH
HUH ?

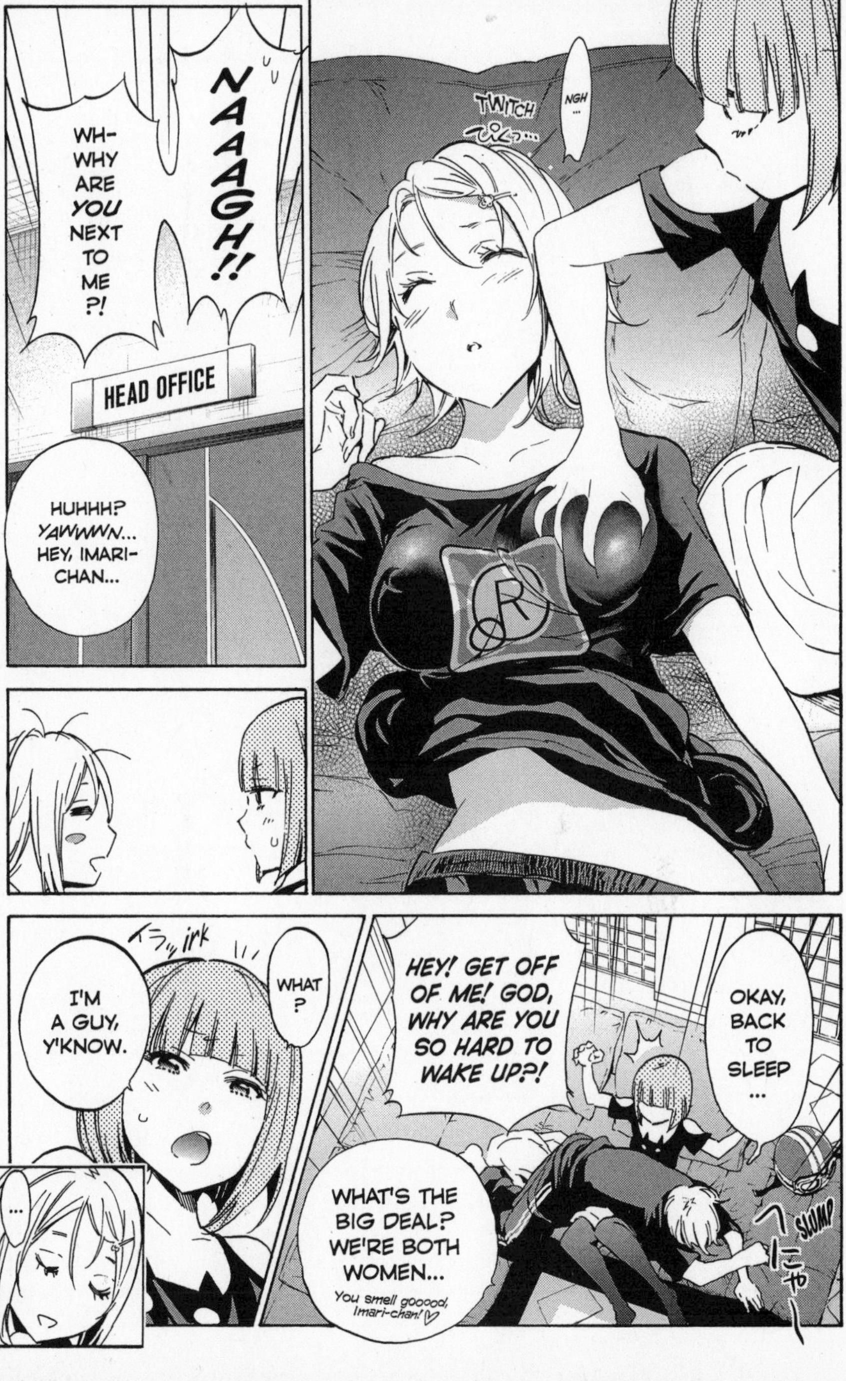
TWITCH
ぴくっ…
NGH…
NAAAGH!!
WH-WHY ARE YOU NEXT TO ME?!
HEAD OFFICE
HUHHH? YAWWWN… HEY, IMARI-CHAN…
OKAY, BACK TO SLEEP…
HEY! GET OFF OF ME! GOD, WHY ARE YOU SO HARD TO WAKE UP?!
WHAT'S THE BIG DEAL? WE'RE BOTH WOMEN…
You smell gooood, Imari-chan! ♡
SLUMP
へにゃ
WHAT?
イラッ irk
I'M A GUY, Y'KNOW.
…

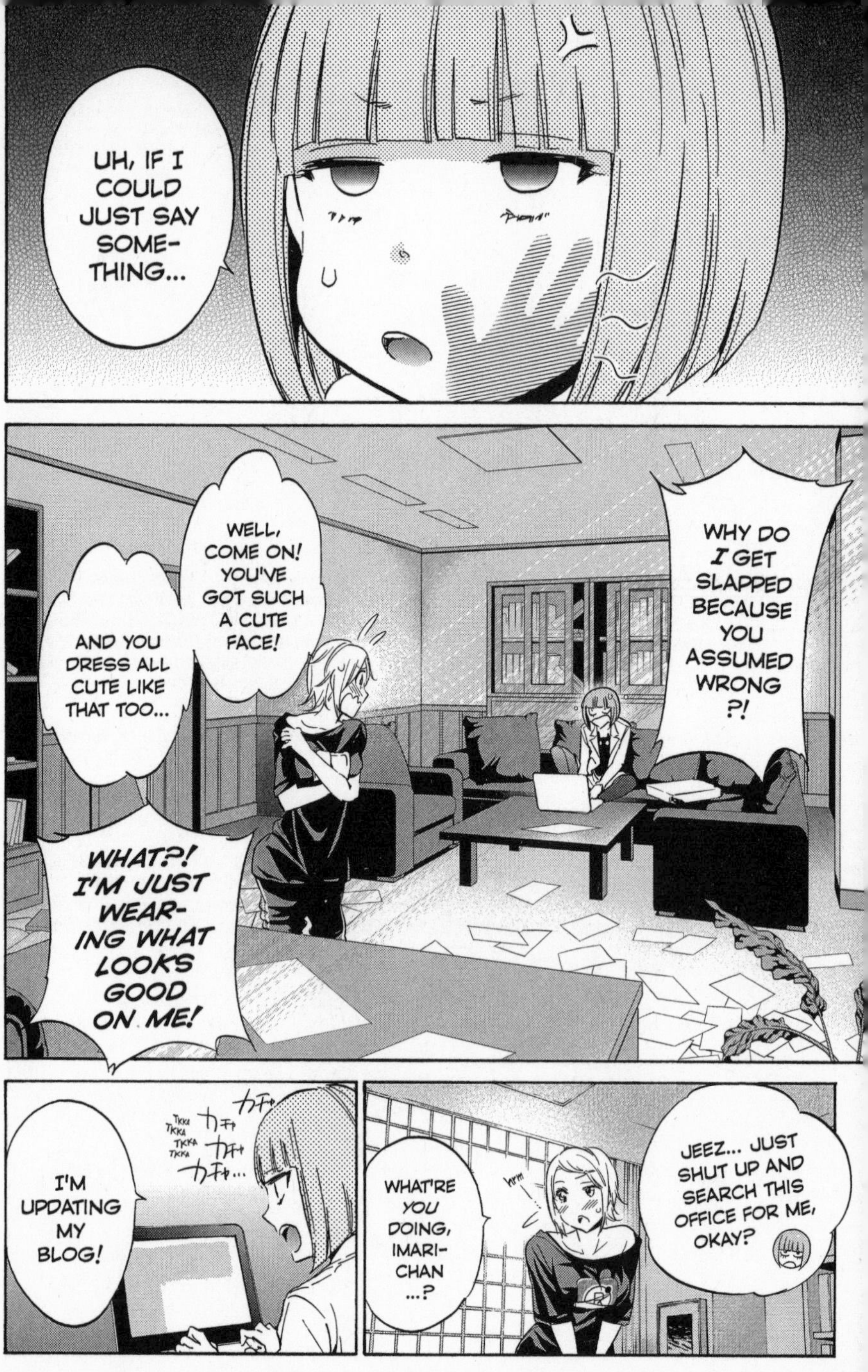
UH, IF I COULD JUST SAY SOME-THING...
WHY DO I GET SLAPPED BECAUSE YOU ASSUMED WRONG ?!
WELL, COME ON! YOU'VE GOT SUCH A CUTE FACE!
AND YOU DRESS ALL CUTE LIKE THAT TOO...
WHAT?! I'M JUST WEAR-ING WHAT LOOKS GOOD ON ME!
JEEZ... JUST SHUT UP AND SEARCH THIS OFFICE FOR ME, OKAY?
hrm
WHAT'RE YOU DOING, IMARI-CHAN ...?
TKKA TKKA TKKA TKKA
I'M UPDATING MY BLOG!

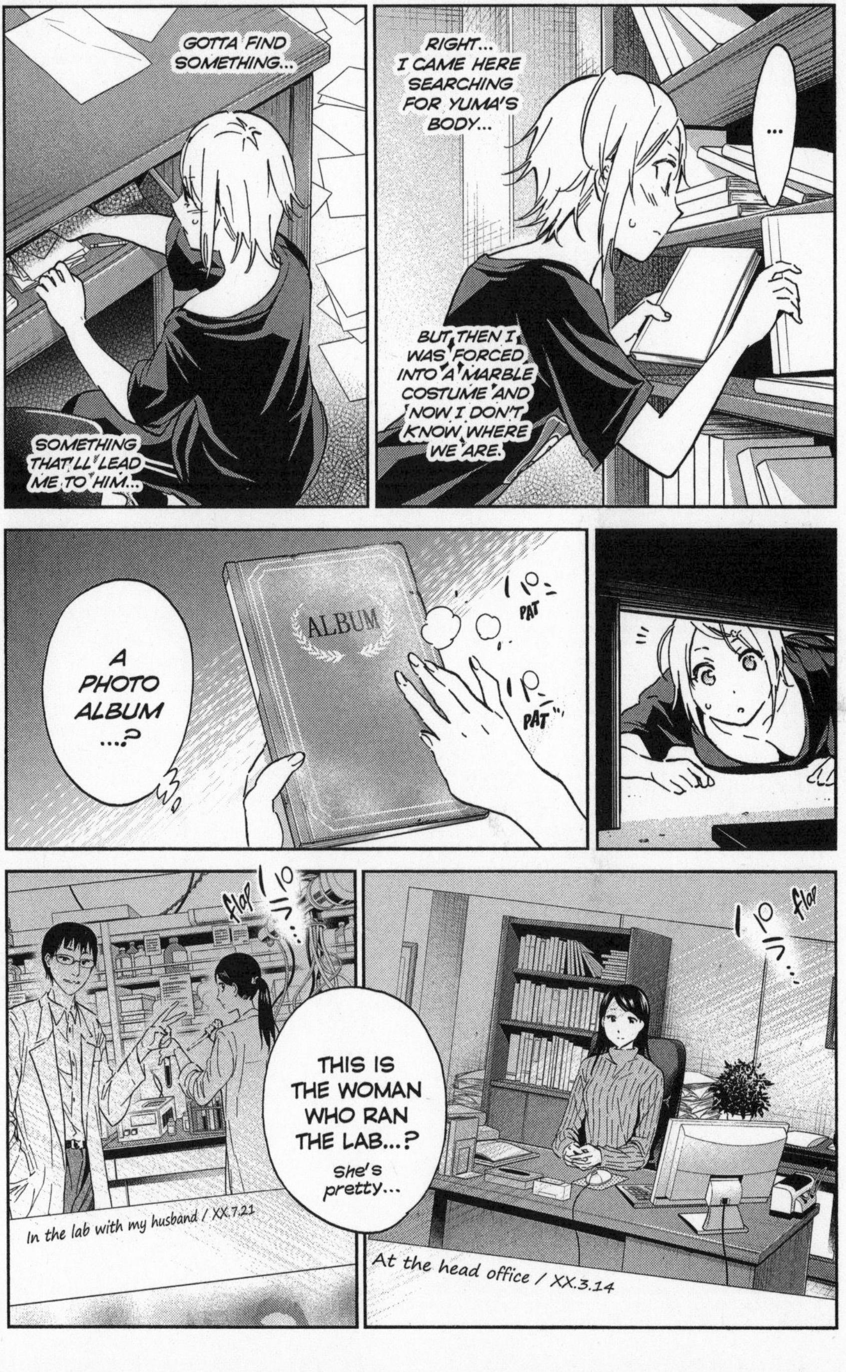
RIGHT... I CAME HERE SEARCHING FOR YUMA'S BODY...
...
BUT THEN I WAS FORCED INTO A MARBLE COSTUME AND NOW I DON'T KNOW WHERE WE ARE.
GOTTA FIND SOMETHING...
SOMETHING THAT'LL LEAD ME TO HIM...
PAT
PAT
ALBUM
A PHOTO ALBUM ...?
flap
At the head office / XX.3.14
THIS IS THE WOMAN WHO RAN THE LAB...?
she's pretty...
flap
In the lab with my husband / XX.7.21

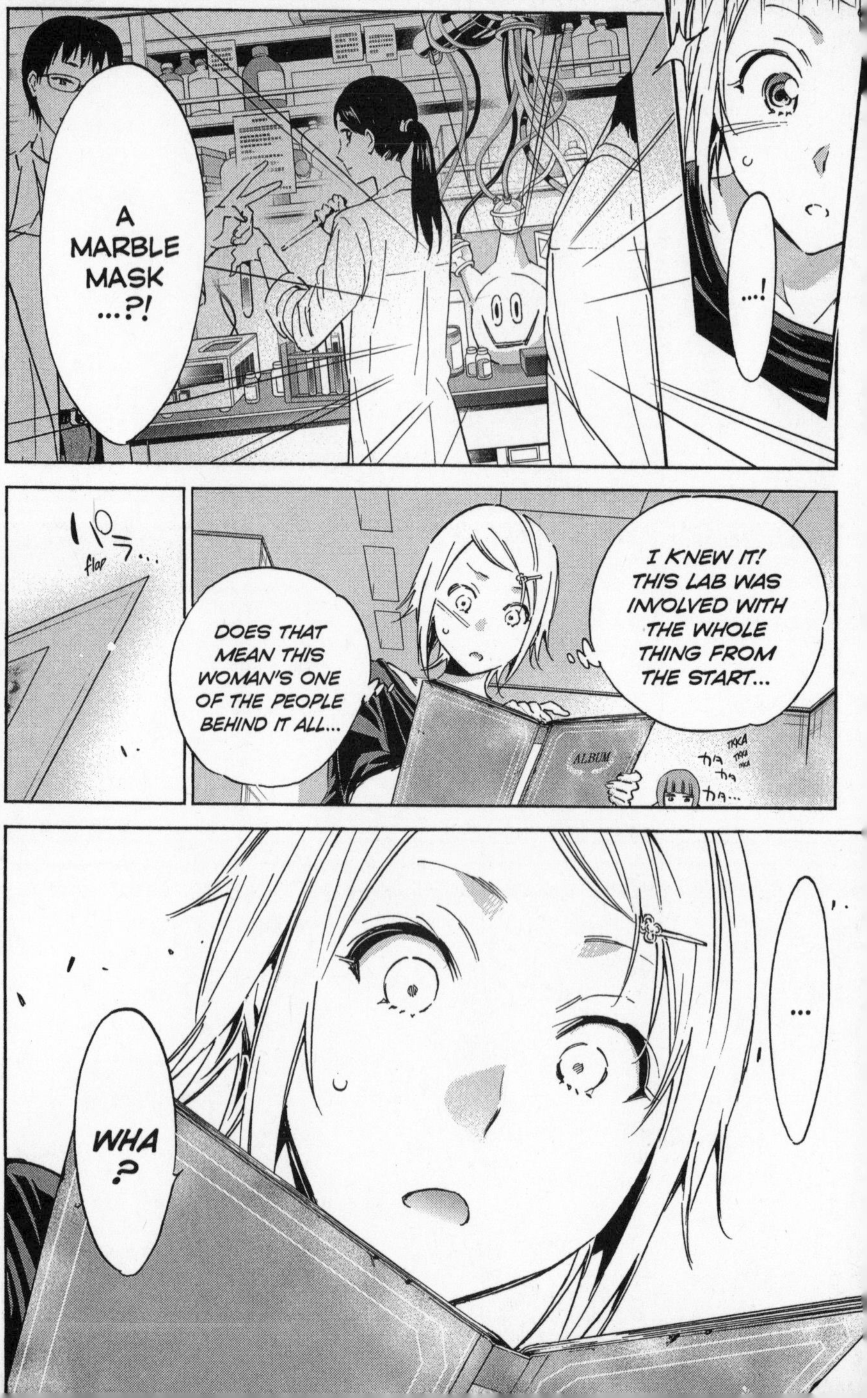
...!
A MARBLE MASK ...?!
I KNEW IT! THIS LAB WAS INVOLVED WITH THE WHOLE THING FROM THE START...
DOES THAT MEAN THIS WOMAN'S ONE OF THE PEOPLE BEHIND IT ALL...
TKKA TKKA TKKA
flap
...
WHA ?

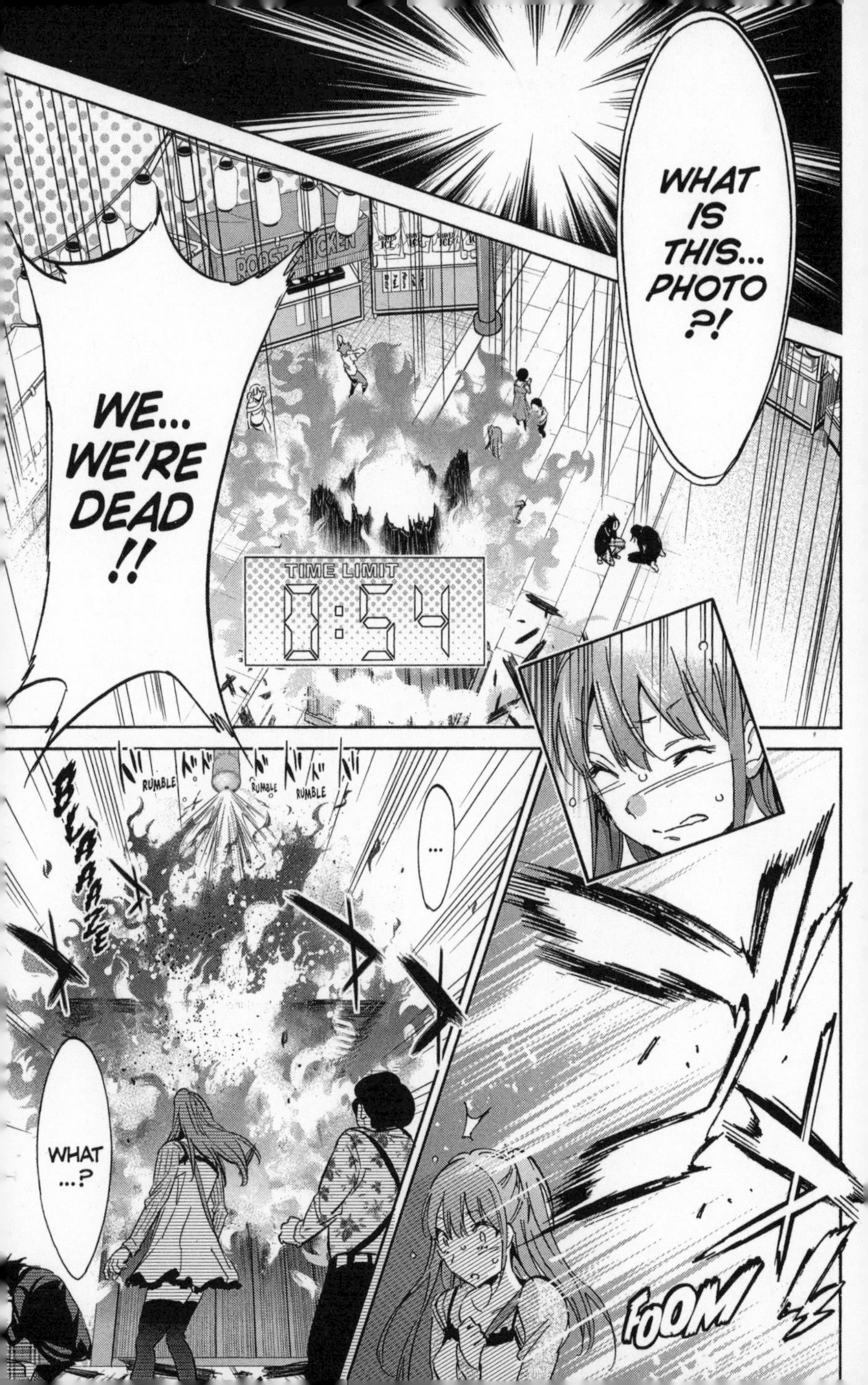
WHAT IS THIS... PHOTO?!
WE... WE'RE DEAD!!
ROAST CHICKEN
TIME LIMIT
0:54
...
FOOM
BLAAAZE
RUMBLE
RUMBLE
RUMBLE
WHAT ...?

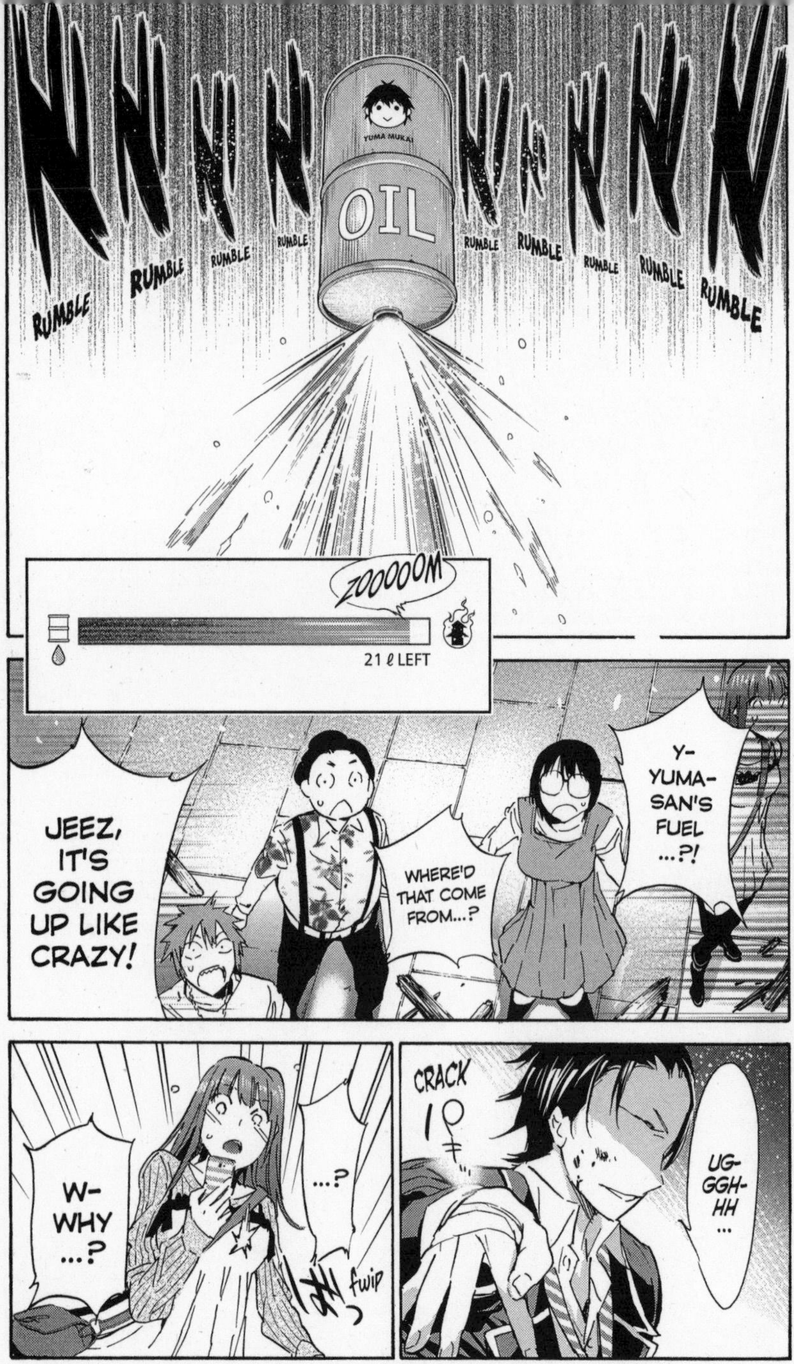

YUMA MUKAI
OIL
RUMBLE RUMBLE RUMBLE RUMBLE RUMBLE RUMBLE RUMBLE RUMBLE RUMBLE
ZOOOOOM
21 ℓ LEFT
Y- YUMA-SAN'S FUEL ...?!
WHERE'D THAT COME FROM...?
JEEZ, IT'S GOING UP LIKE CRAZY!
CRACK
UG-GGH-HH ...
...?
fwip
W- WHY ...?

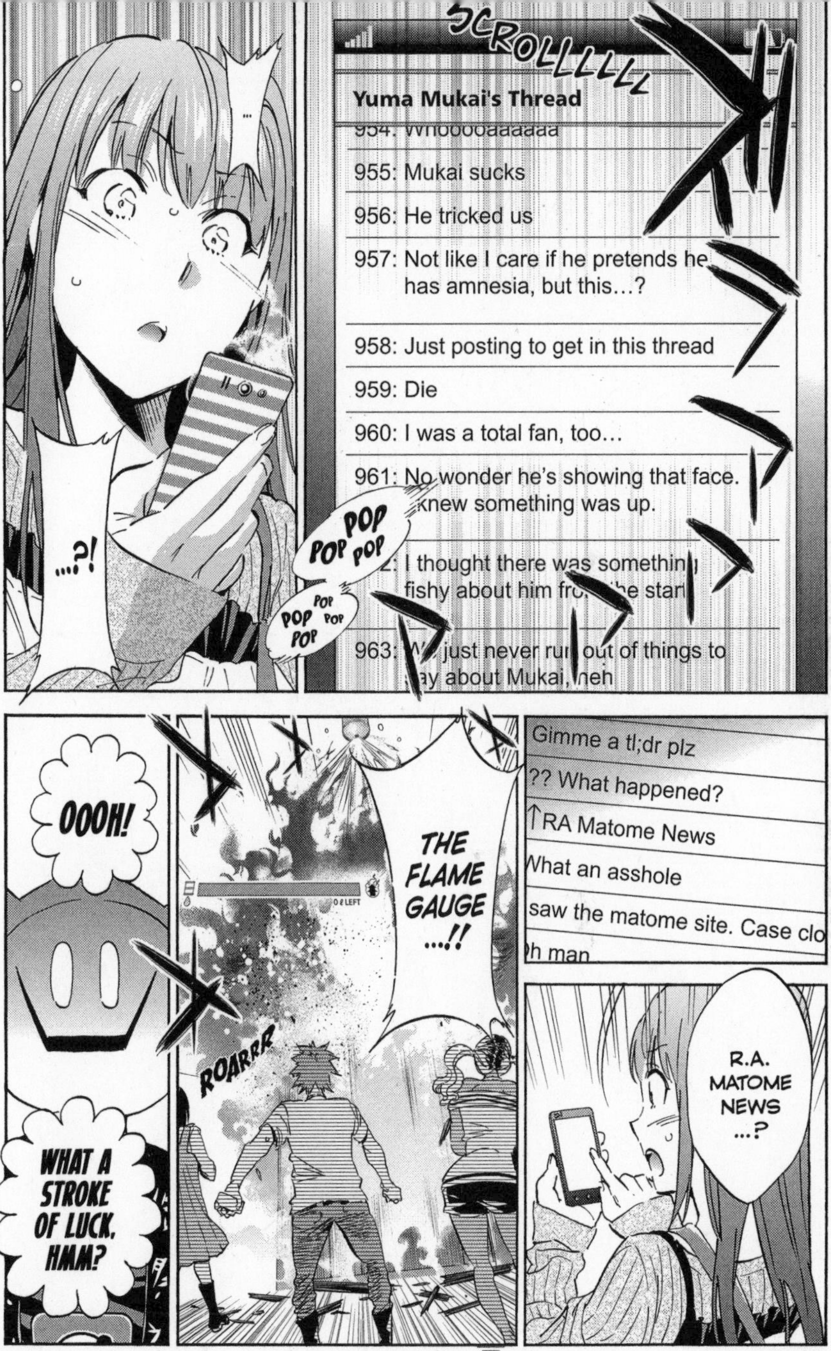
SCROLLLLLL
Yuma Mukai's Thread
955: Mukai sucks
956: He tricked us
957: Not like I care if he pretends he has amnesia, but this…?
958: Just posting to get in this thread
959: Die
960: I was a total fan, too…
961: No wonder he's showing that face. knew something was up.
I thought there was somethin fishy about him fr the star
963: just never ru out of things to ay about Mukai, heh
POP POP POP POP
POP POP POP POP
...
...?!
Gimme a tl;dr plz
?? What happened?
↑RA Matome News
What an asshole
saw the matome site. Case clo
R.A. MATOME NEWS ...?
0ℓ LEFT
THE FLAME GAUGE ...!!
ROARRR
OOOH!
WHAT A STROKE OF LUCK, HMM?

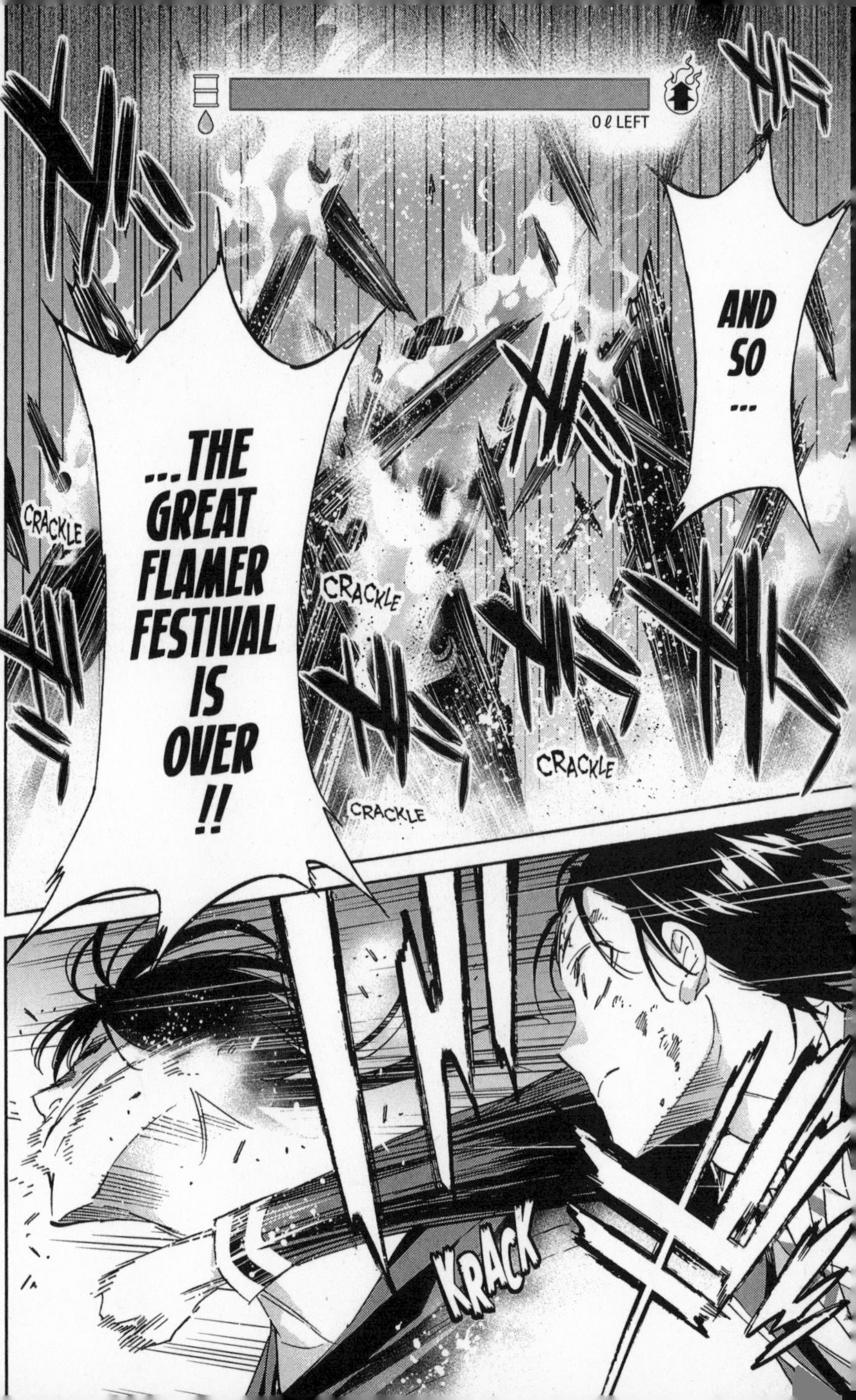
0 ℓ LEFT
AND SO ...
CRACKLE
CRACKLE
CRACKLE
CRACKLE
...THE GREAT FLAMER FESTIVAL IS OVER !!
KRACK

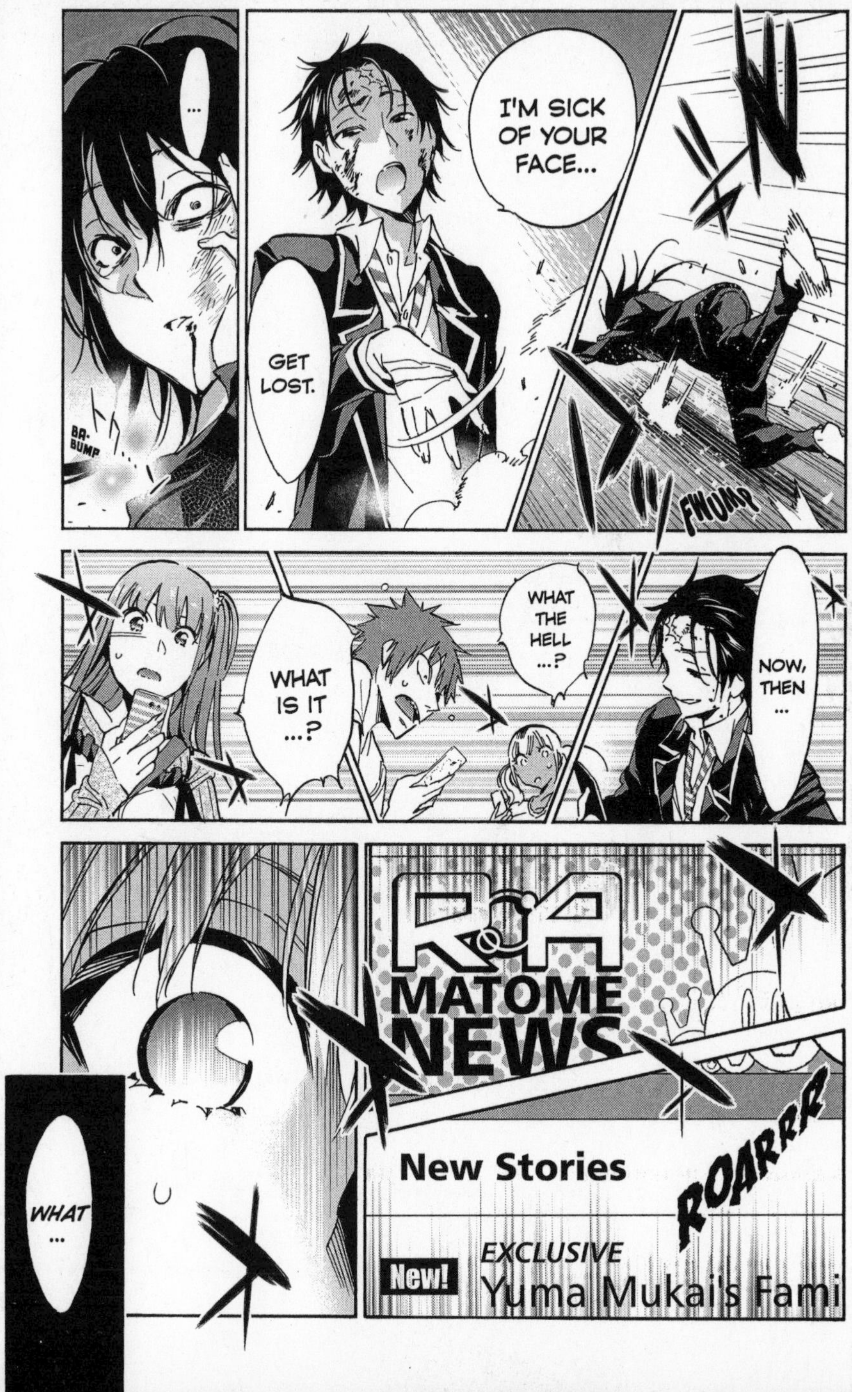
FWUMP
I'M SICK OF YOUR FACE...
GET LOST.
...
BA-BUMP
NOW, THEN ...
WHAT THE HELL ...?
WHAT IS IT ...?
MATOME NEWS
New Stories
ROARRR
EXCLUSIVE
New!
Yuma Mukai's Fami
WHAT ...

EXCLUSIVE

Yuma Mukai's Family Members Are the Masterminds Behind the R.A. Incident! [Photos]

4/29/20XX Comments (1410)

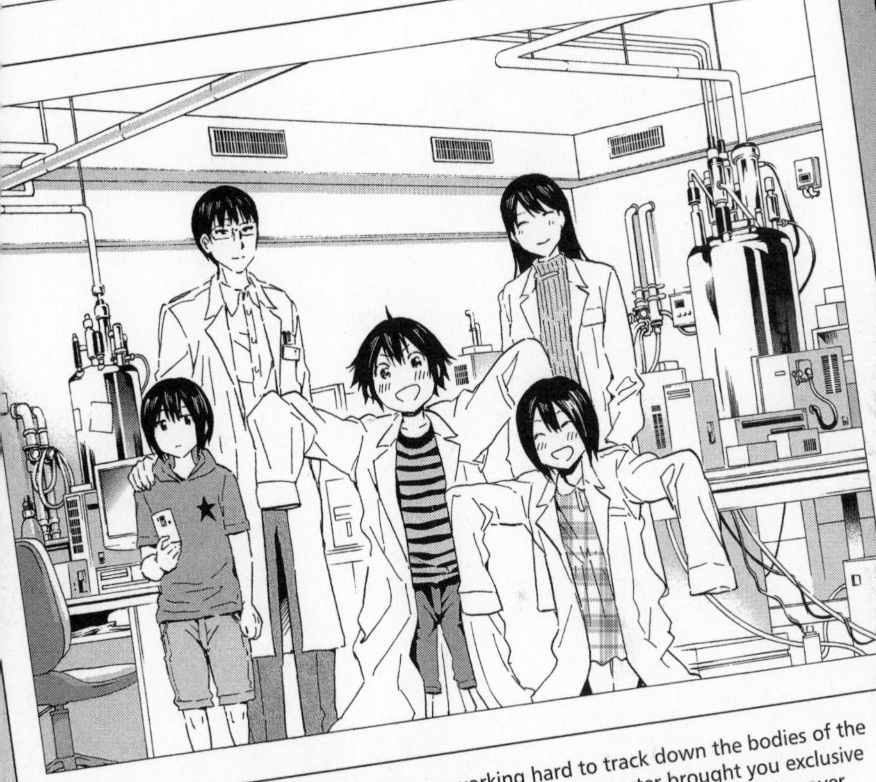

All of us at R.A. Matome News have been working hard to track down the bodies of the players taken from their own homes. Just yesterday, this reporter brought you exclusive media from inside the Kashiwagi Research Laboratory, following a daring undercover investigation. (→*SPECIAL* Pursuing the Stolen Player Bodies!! Thread 15 *SHOCKING*)

After spending the previous night inside the lab, we've made it to the office of the laboratory head and discovered something truly shocking: A photograph of lab boss Chitose Kashiwagi, her husband and assistant Shin Kashiwagi, and— astoundingly— a young Yuma Mukai, in the flesh!

So far, Mukai's survived the R.A. games in dazzling fashion, playing the hero and saving other players from certain death. In his latest adventure in the "Great Flaming Festival" we've seen a glimpse into his past, his sudden transformation, and now this photo. With this latest discovery, we've seen his reputation take an immense hit.

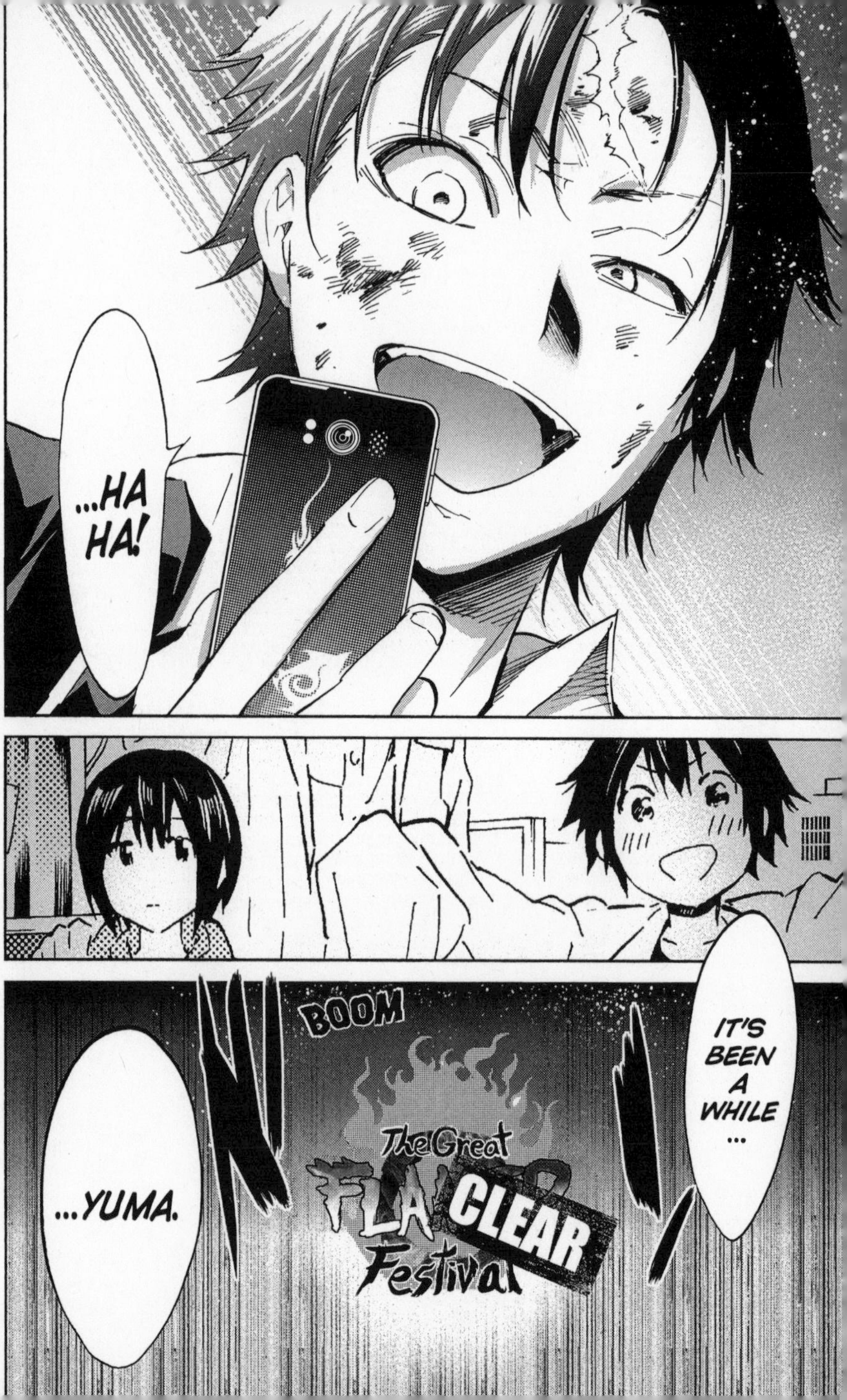
...HA HA!
IT'S BEEN A WHILE ...
BOOM
The Great FLA CLEAR Festival
...YUMA.

ACCOUNT 31 The Morning of the Marbles

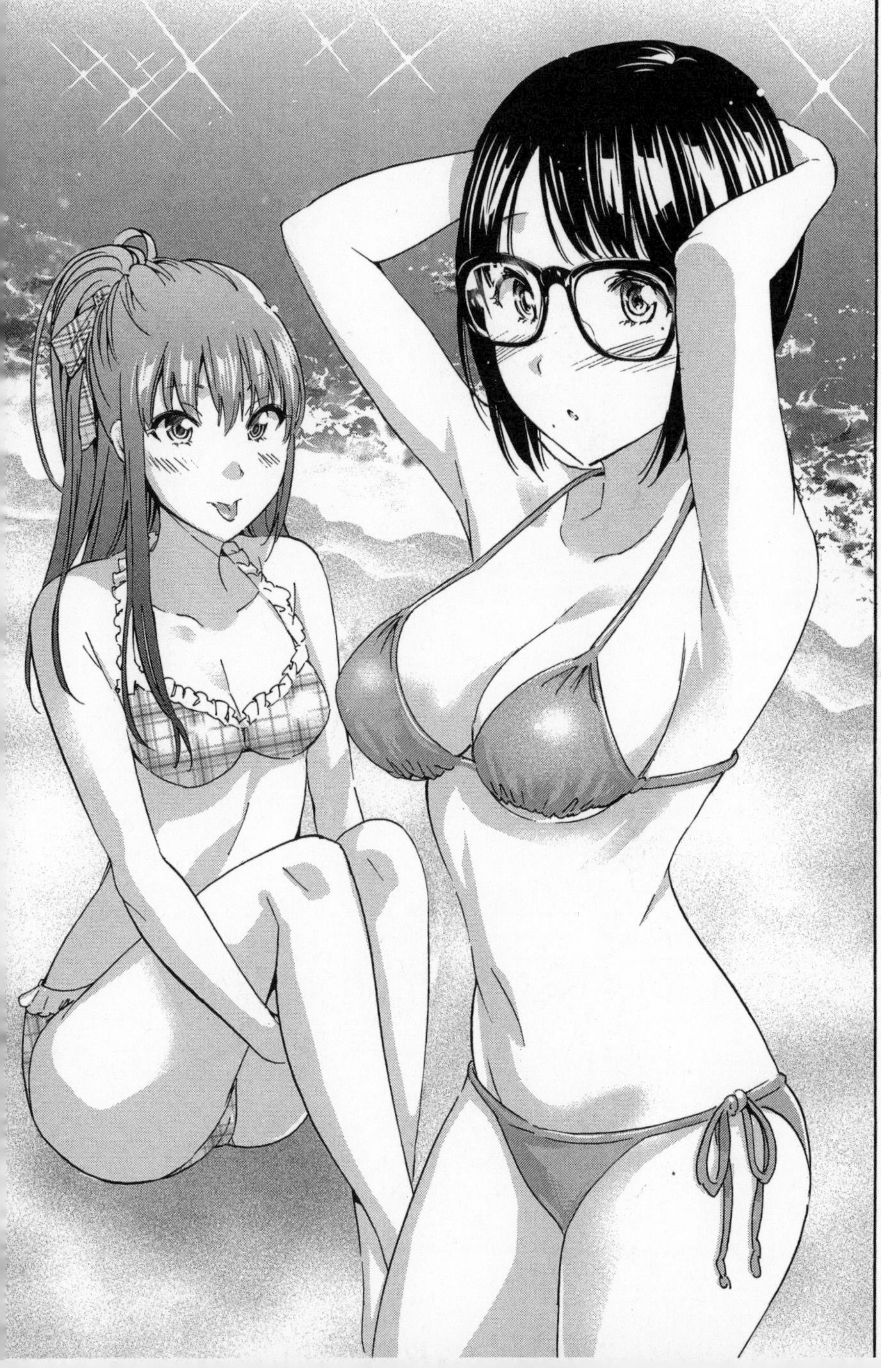

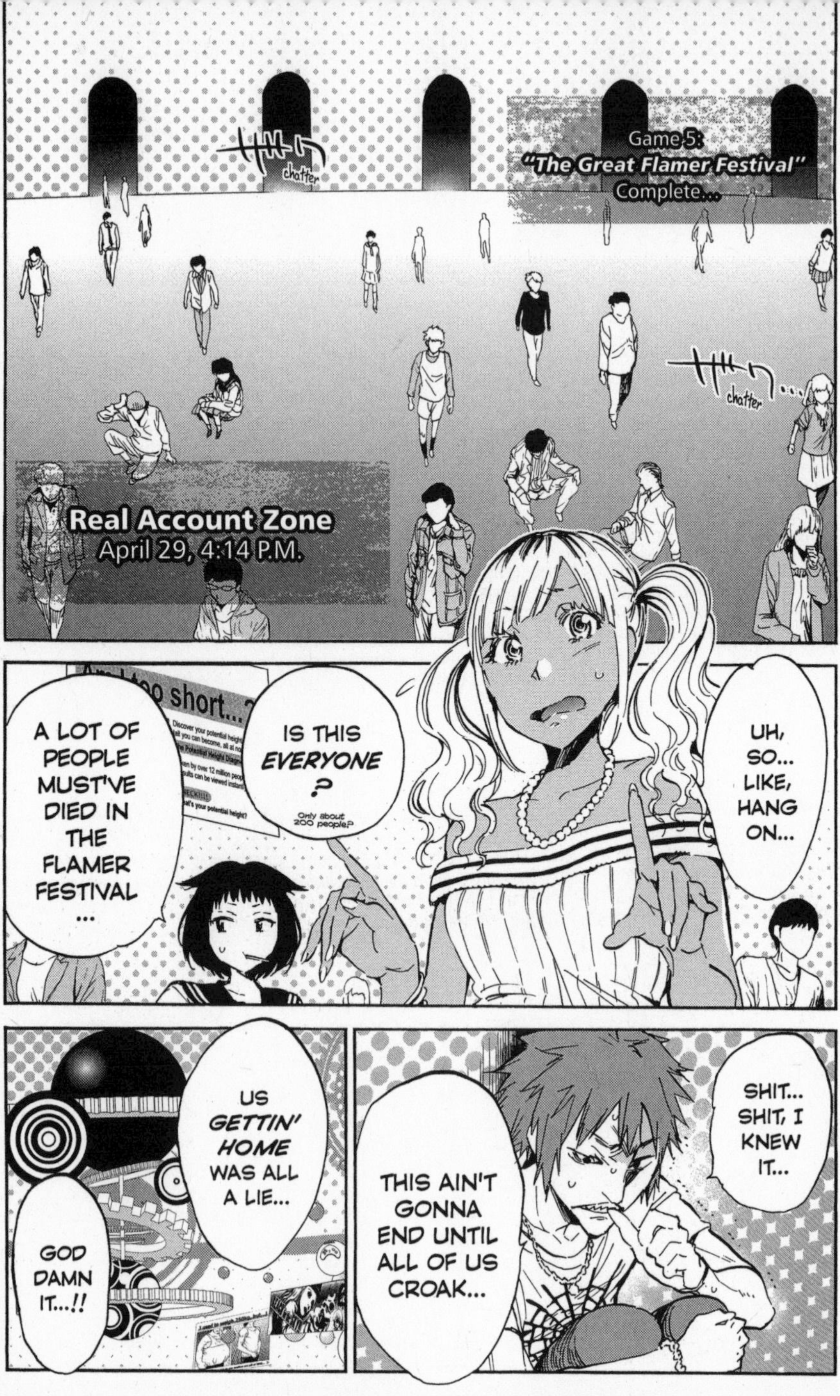
Game 5:
"The Great Flamer Festival"
Complete...
chatter...
chatter
Real Account Zone
April 29, 4:14 P.M.
UH, SO... LIKE, HANG ON...
IS THIS EVERYONE?
Only about 200 people?
A LOT OF PEOPLE MUST'VE DIED IN THE FLAMER FESTIVAL...
SHIT... SHIT, I KNEW IT...
THIS AIN'T GONNA END UNTIL ALL OF US CROAK...
US GETTIN' HOME WAS ALL A LIE...
GOD DAMN IT...!!

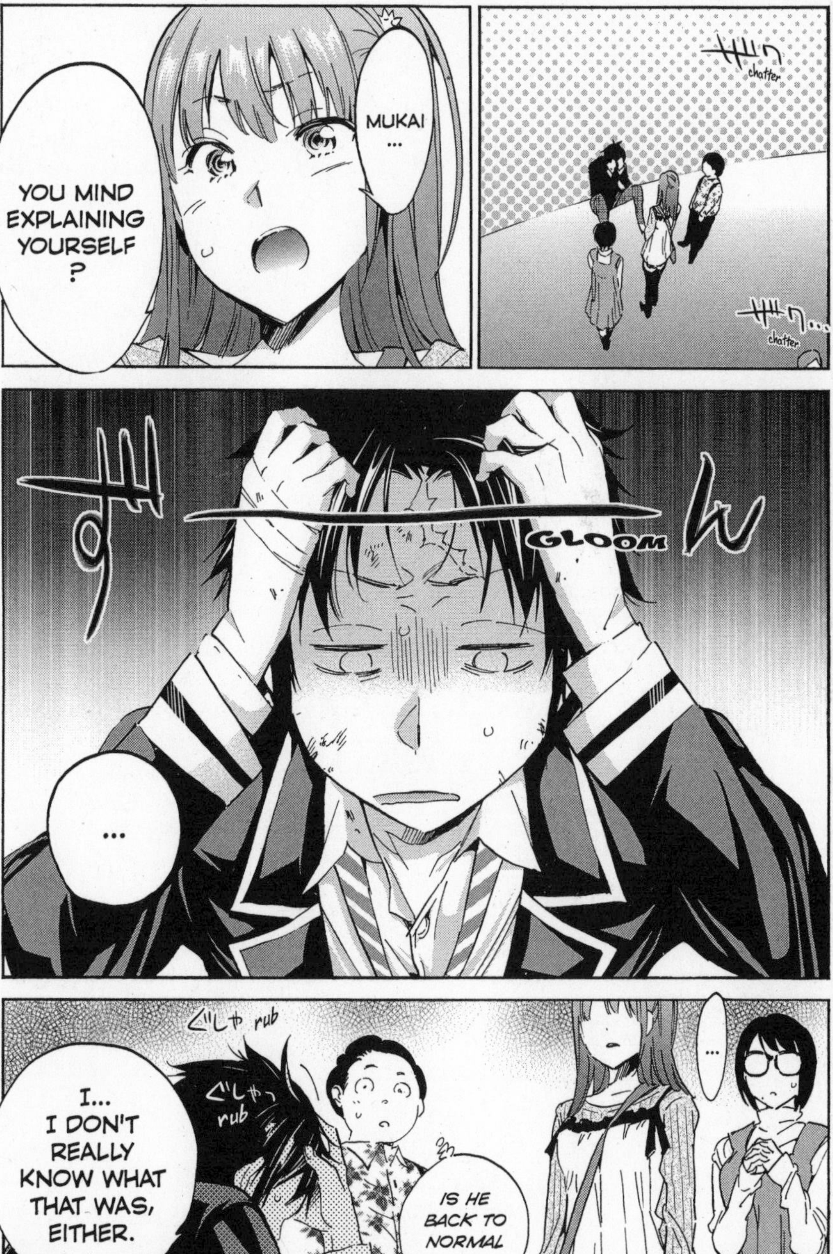
ザワ chatter
ザワ… chatter
MUKAI ...
YOU MIND EXPLAINING YOURSELF ?
ずーん GLOOM
...
...
ぐしゃ rub
ぐしゃっ rub
IS HE BACK TO NORMAL ...?
I... I DON'T REALLY KNOW WHAT THAT WAS, EITHER.

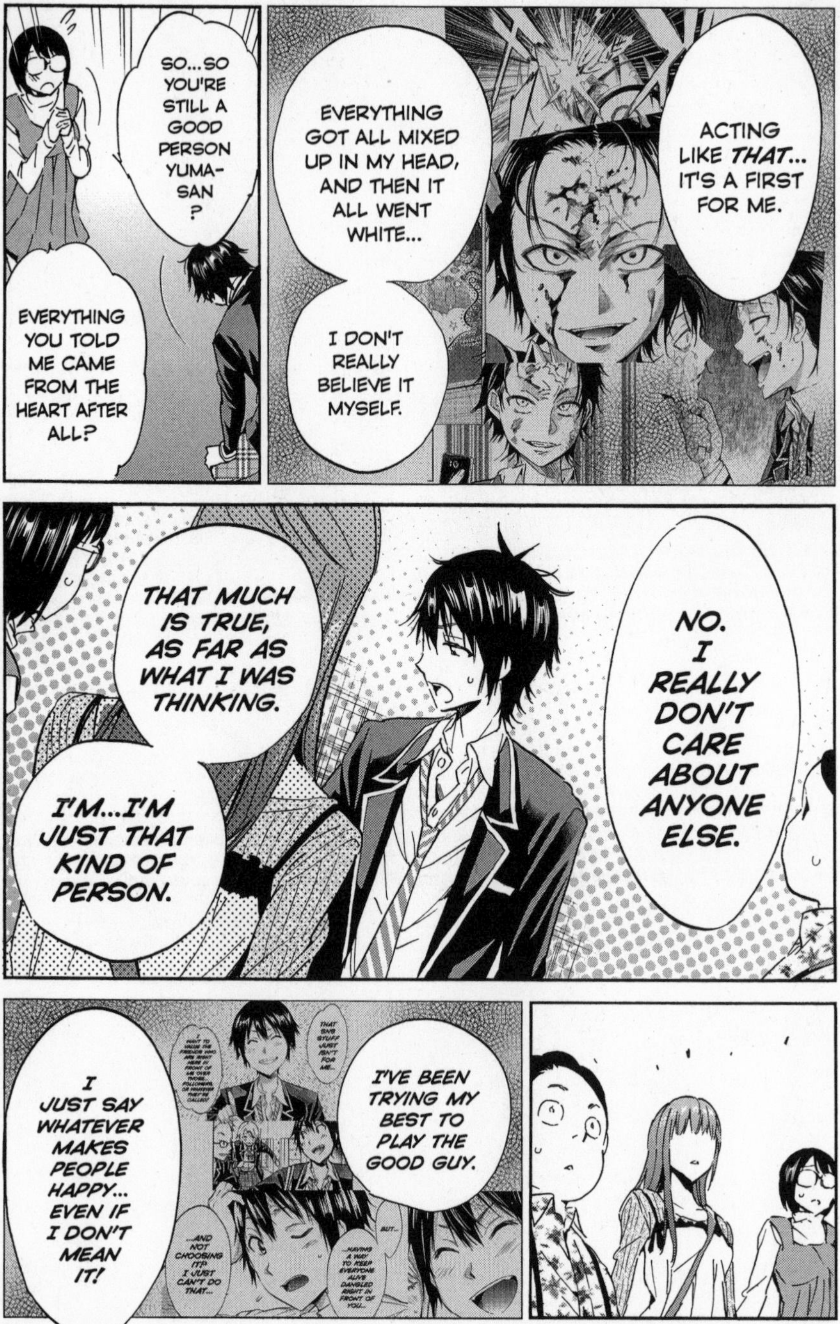
ACTING LIKE *THAT*... IT'S A FIRST FOR ME.
EVERYTHING GOT ALL MIXED UP IN MY HEAD, AND THEN IT ALL WENT WHITE...
I DON'T REALLY BELIEVE IT MYSELF.
SO...SO YOU'RE STILL A GOOD PERSON YUMA-SAN?
EVERYTHING YOU TOLD ME CAME FROM THE HEART AFTER ALL?
NO. I REALLY DON'T CARE ABOUT ANYONE ELSE.
THAT MUCH IS TRUE, AS FAR AS WHAT I WAS THINKING.
I'M...I'M JUST THAT KIND OF PERSON.
I'VE BEEN TRYING MY BEST TO PLAY THE GOOD GUY.
THAT SNS STUFF JUST ISN'T FOR ME...
I WANT TO VALUE THE FRIENDS WHO ARE RIGHT HERE IN FRONT OF ME OVER THOSE... FOLLOWERS OR WHATEVER THEY'RE CALLED!
I JUST SAY WHATEVER MAKES PEOPLE HAPPY... EVEN IF I DON'T MEAN IT!
BUT...
...HAVING A WAY TO KEEP EVERYONE ALIVE DANGLED RIGHT IN FRONT OF YOU...
...AND NOT CHOOSING IT? I JUST CAN'T DO THAT...

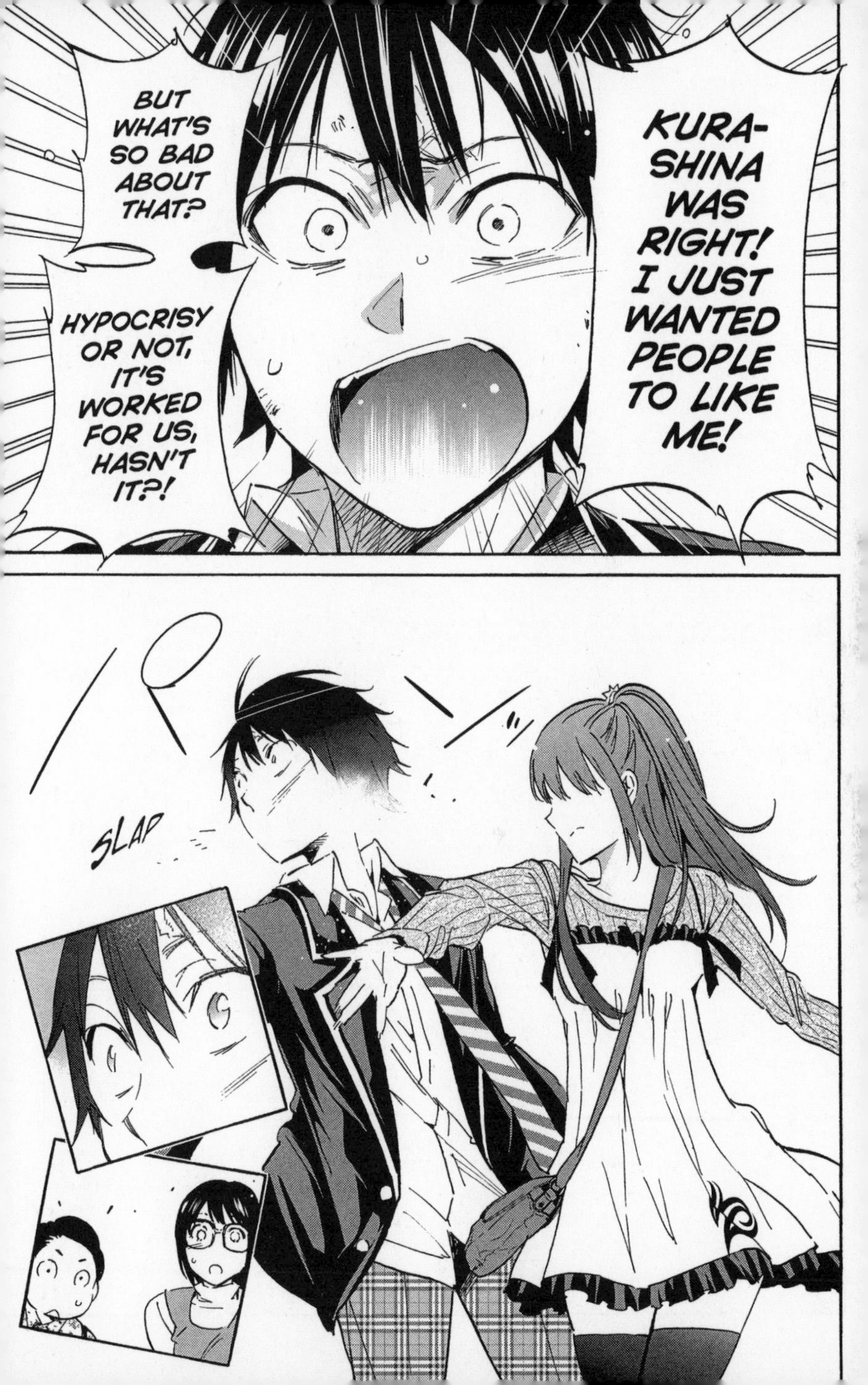
KURA-SHINA WAS RIGHT! I JUST WANTED PEOPLE TO LIKE ME!
BUT WHAT'S SO BAD ABOUT THAT?
HYPOCRISY OR NOT, IT'S WORKED FOR US, HASN'T IT?!
SLAP

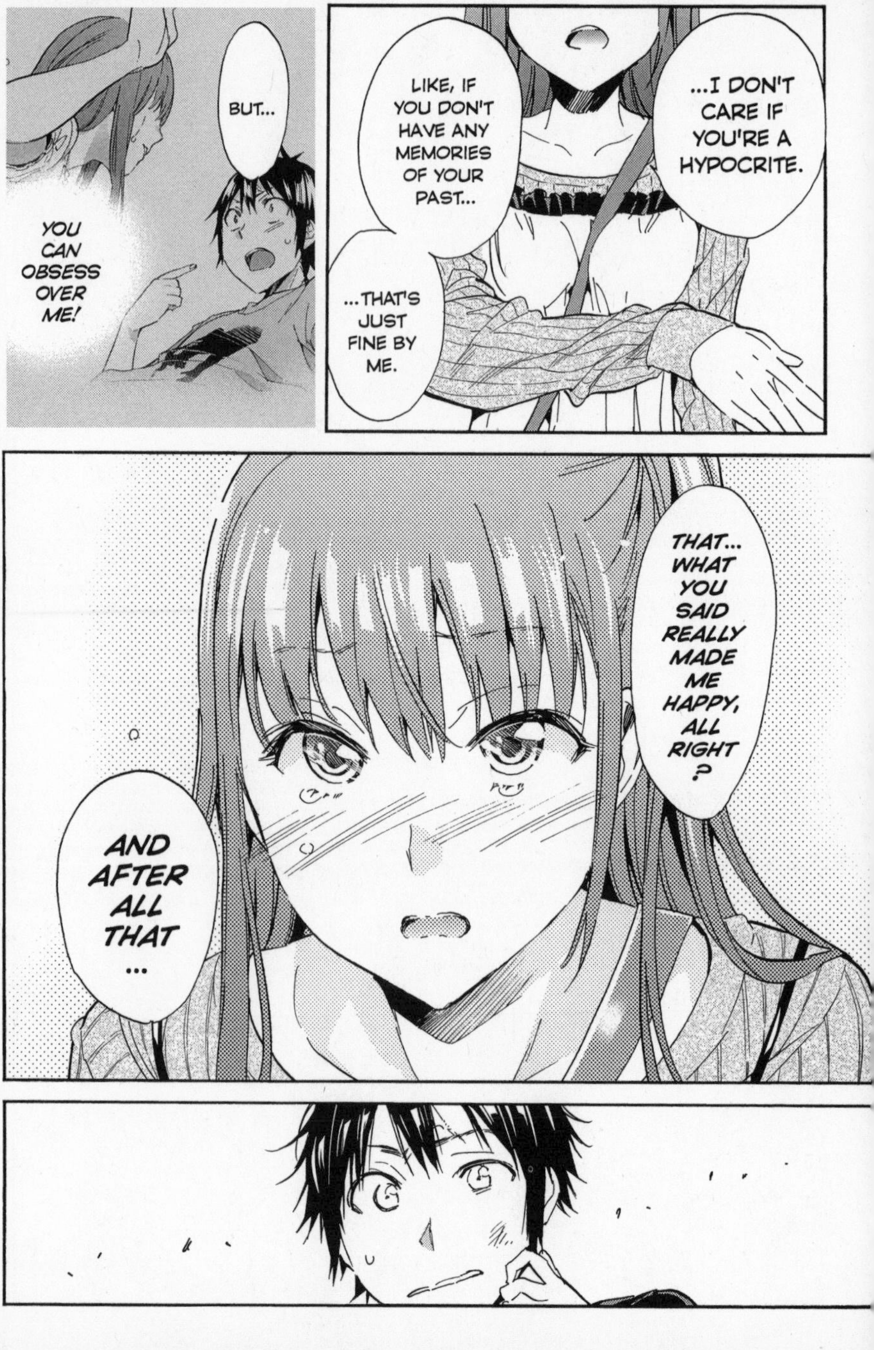
...I DON'T CARE IF YOU'RE A HYPOCRITE.
LIKE, IF YOU DON'T HAVE ANY MEMORIES OF YOUR PAST...
...THAT'S JUST FINE BY ME.
BUT...
YOU CAN OBSESS OVER ME!
THAT... WHAT YOU SAID REALLY MADE ME HAPPY, ALL RIGHT?
AND AFTER ALL THAT...

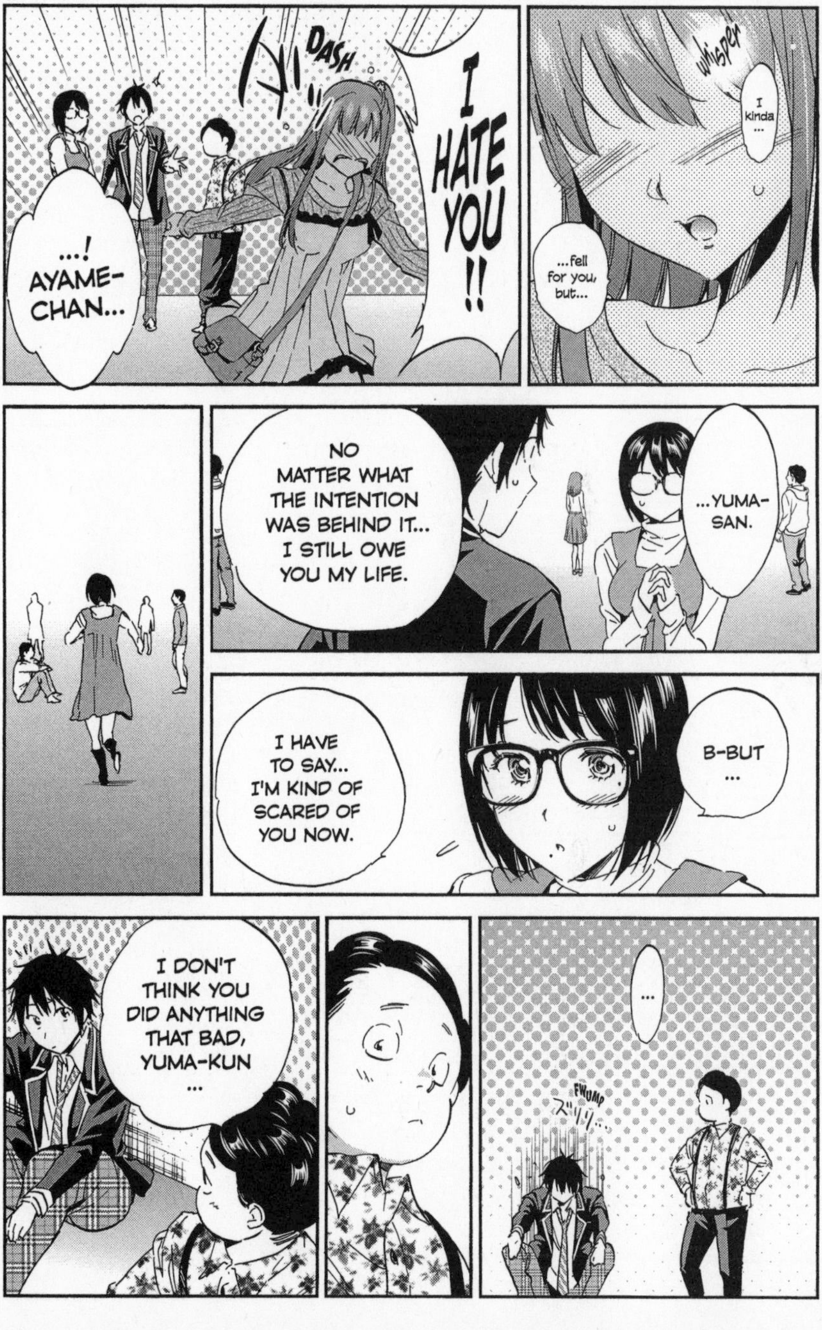
whisper
I kinda ...
...fell for you, but...
I HATE YOU !!
DASH
...! AYAME-CHAN...
...YUMA-SAN.
NO MATTER WHAT THE INTENTION WAS BEHIND IT... I STILL OWE YOU MY LIFE.
B-BUT ...
I HAVE TO SAY... I'M KIND OF SCARED OF YOU NOW.
...
FWUMP
I DON'T THINK YOU DID ANYTHING THAT BAD, YUMA-KUN ...

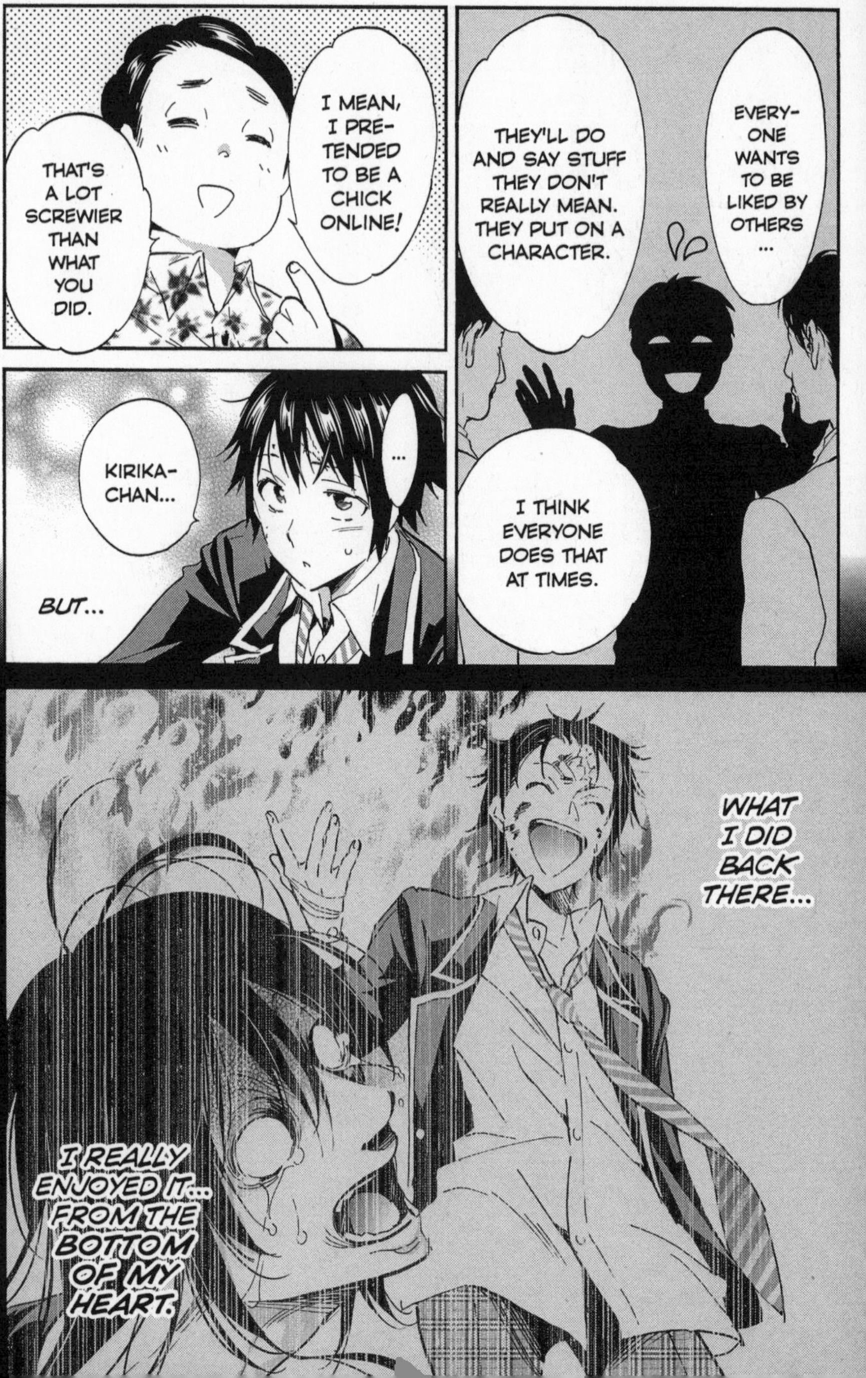
EVERY-ONE WANTS TO BE LIKED BY OTHERS ...
THEY'LL DO AND SAY STUFF THEY DON'T REALLY MEAN. THEY PUT ON A CHARACTER.
I THINK EVERYONE DOES THAT AT TIMES.
I MEAN, I PRE-TENDED TO BE A CHICK ONLINE!
THAT'S A LOT SCREWIER THAN WHAT YOU DID.
...
KIRIKA-CHAN...
BUT...
WHAT I DID BACK THERE...
I REALLY ENJOYED IT... FROM THE BOTTOM OF MY HEART.

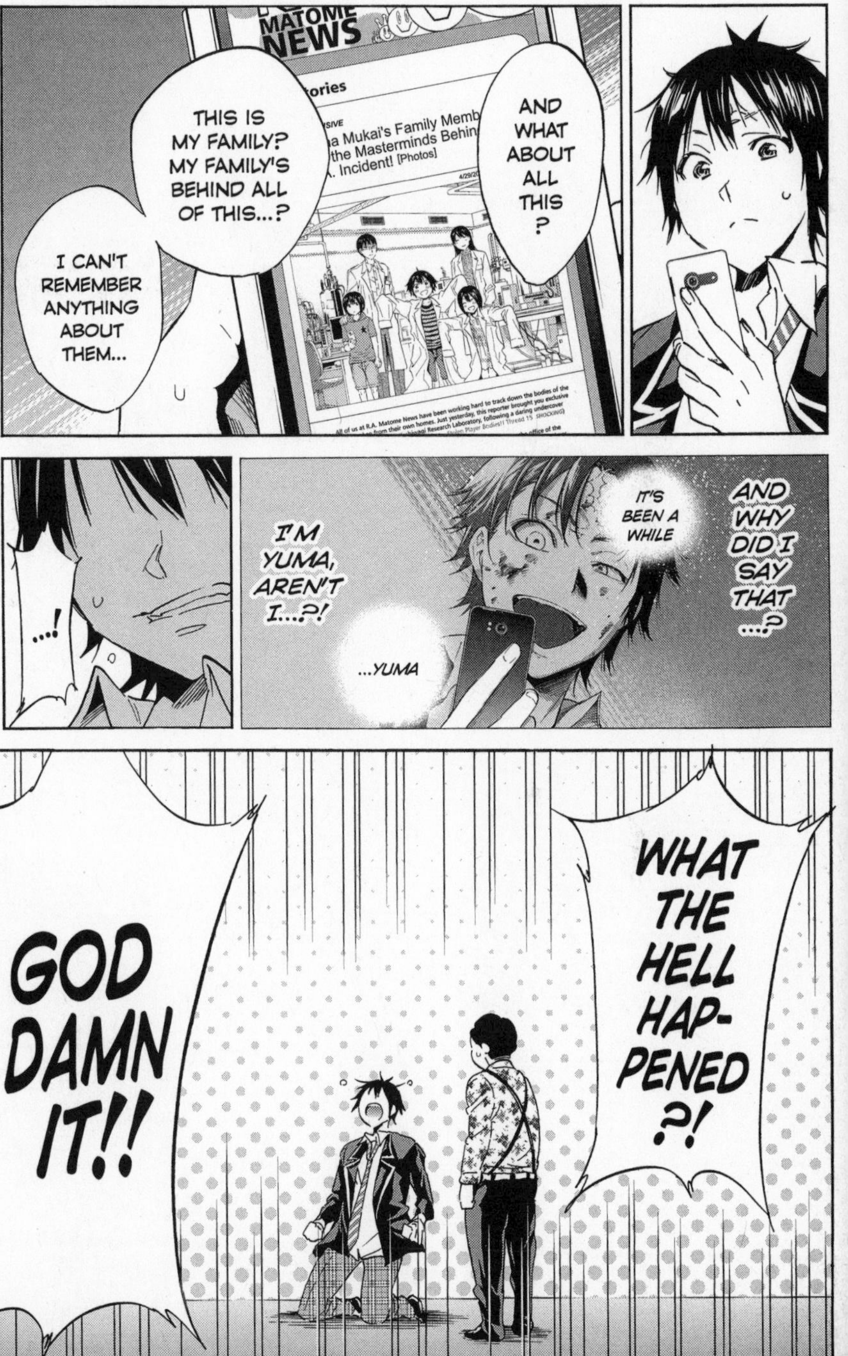
MATOME NEWS
AND WHAT ABOUT ALL THIS?
THIS IS MY FAMILY? MY FAMILY'S BEHIND ALL OF THIS...?
I CAN'T REMEMBER ANYTHING ABOUT THEM...
AND WHY DID I SAY THAT...?
IT'S BEEN A WHILE
I'M YUMA, AREN'T I...?!
...YUMA
...!
WHAT THE HELL HAP-PENED?!
GOD DAMN IT!!

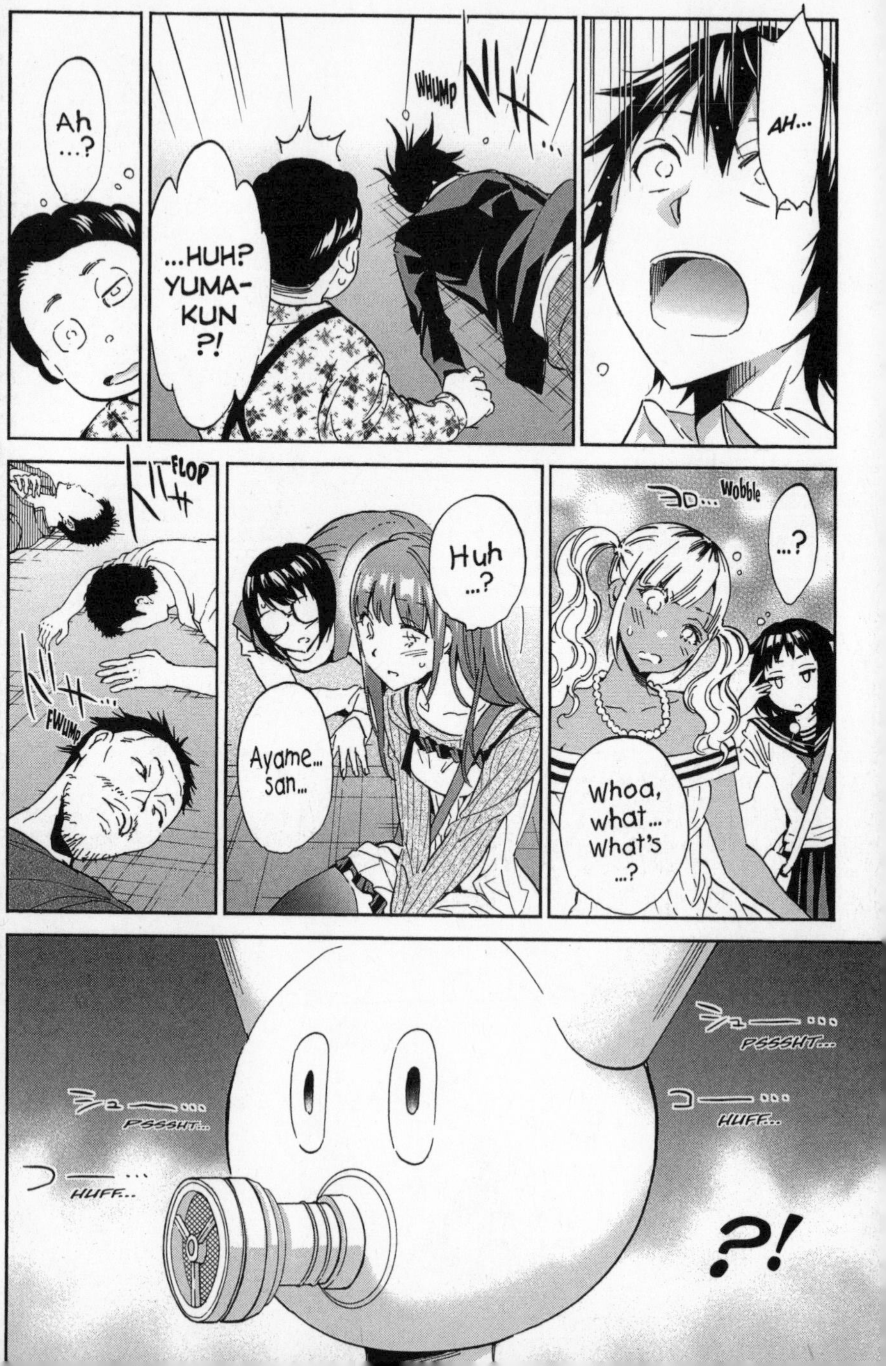
AH...
WHUMP
...HUH? YUMA-KUN ?!
Ah ...?
Wobble
...?
Whoa, what... what's ...?
Huh ...?
Ayame... san...
FLOP
FWUMP
PSSSHT...
HUFF...
PSSSHT...
HUFF...
?!

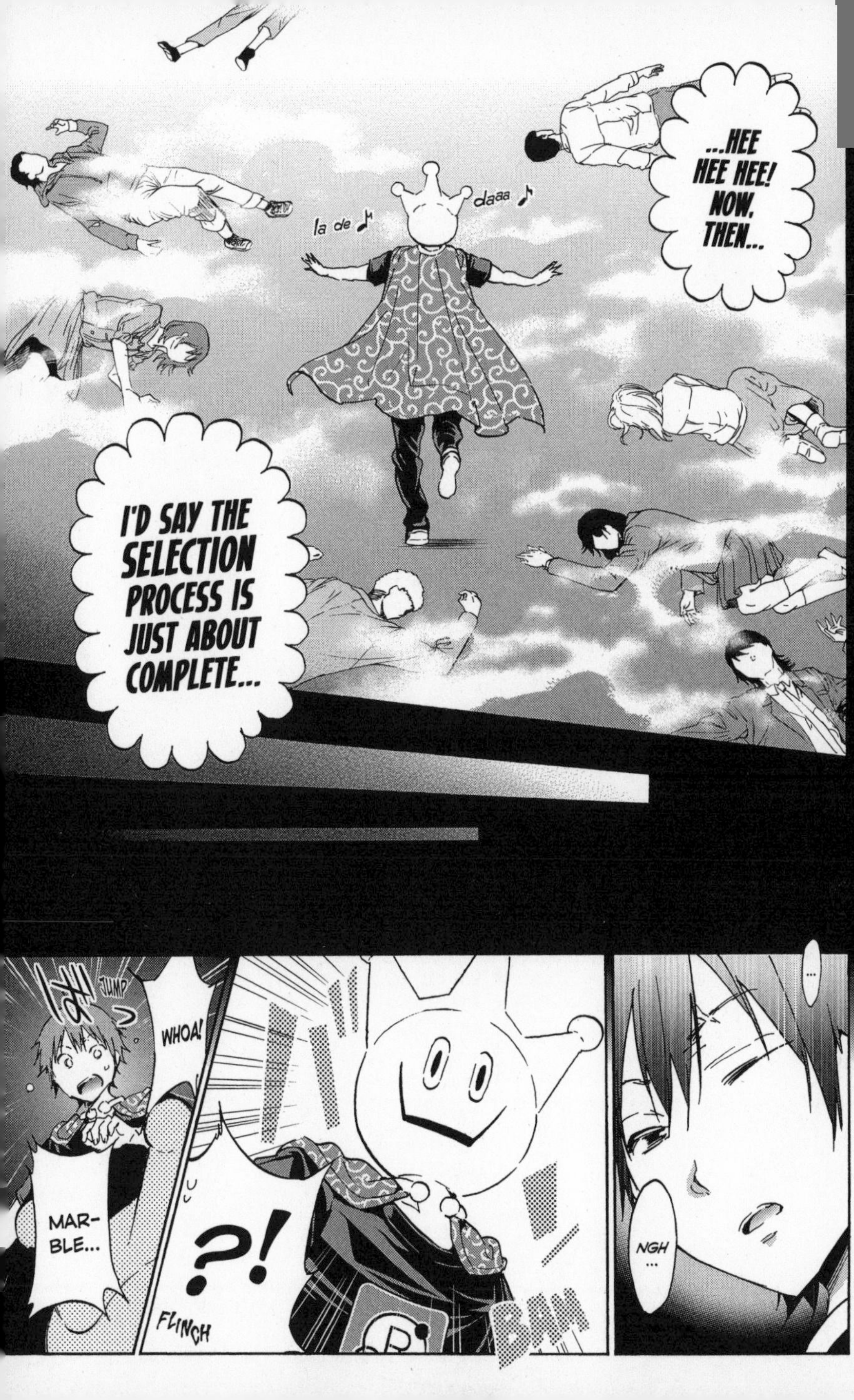
...HEE HEE HEE! NOW, THEN...
la de ♪
daaa ♪
I'D SAY THE SELECTION PROCESS IS JUST ABOUT COMPLETE...
...
NGH ...
?!
FLINCH
JUMP
WHOA!
MAR-BLE...

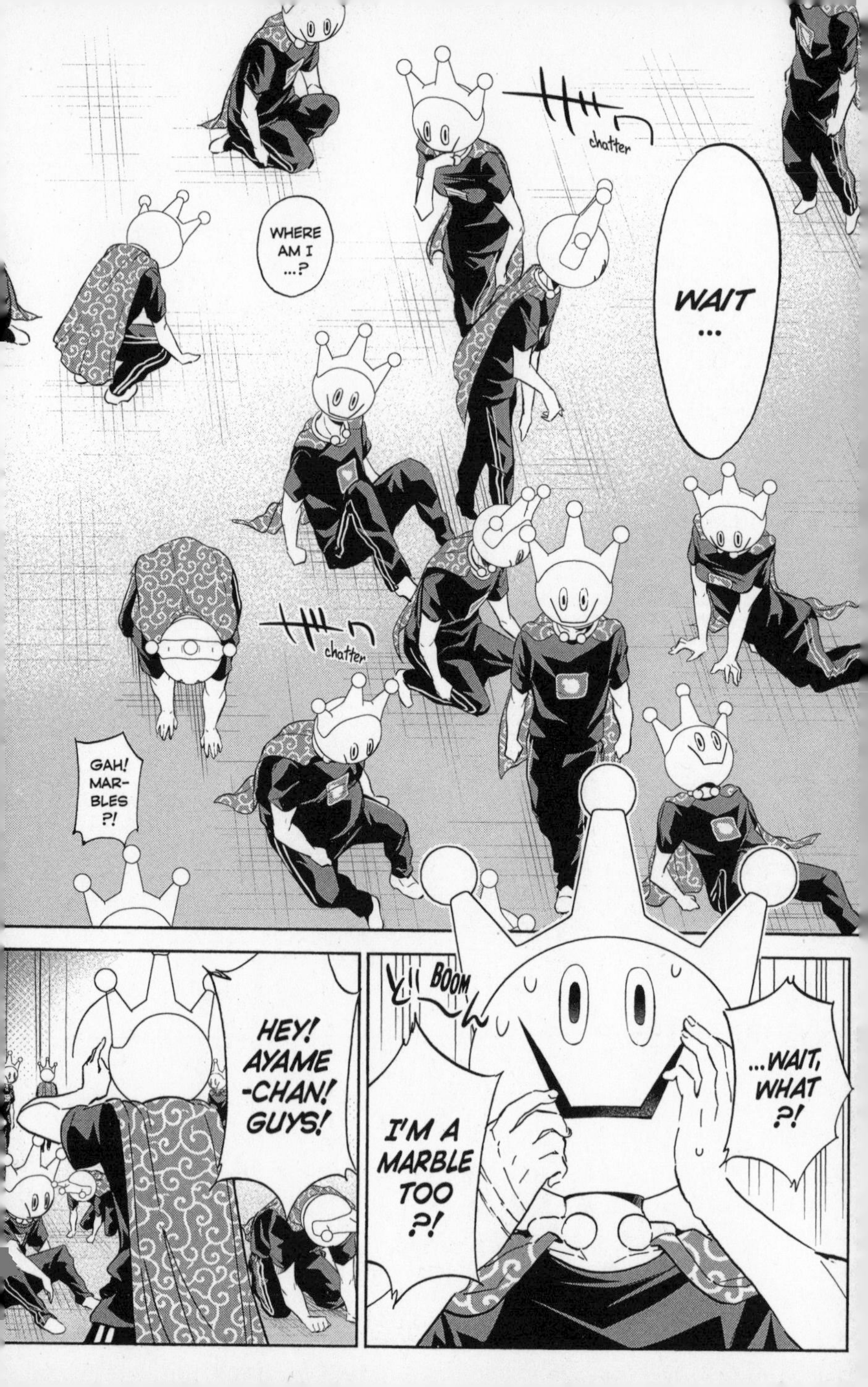
WAIT ...
chatter
WHERE AM I ...?
chatter
GAH! MAR-BLES ?!
...WAIT, WHAT ?!
BOOM
I'M A MARBLE TOO ?!
HEY! AYAME -CHAN! GUYS!

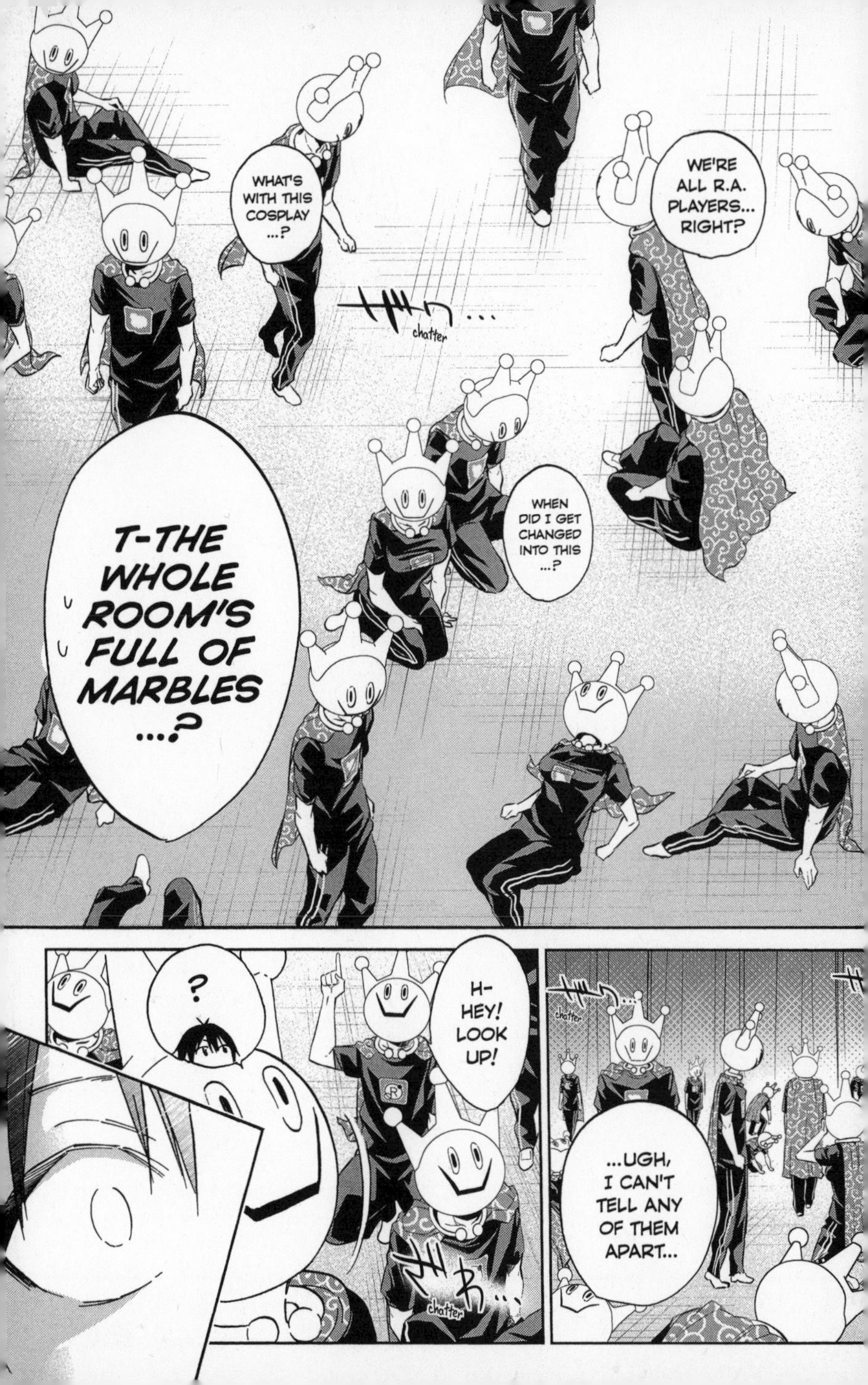
WE'RE ALL R.A. PLAYERS... RIGHT?
WHAT'S WITH THIS COSPLAY ...?
chatter
WHEN DID I GET CHANGED INTO THIS ...?
T-THE WHOLE ROOM'S FULL OF MARBLES ...?
chatter
...UGH, I CAN'T TELL ANY OF THEM APART...
H-HEY! LOOK UP!
?
chatter

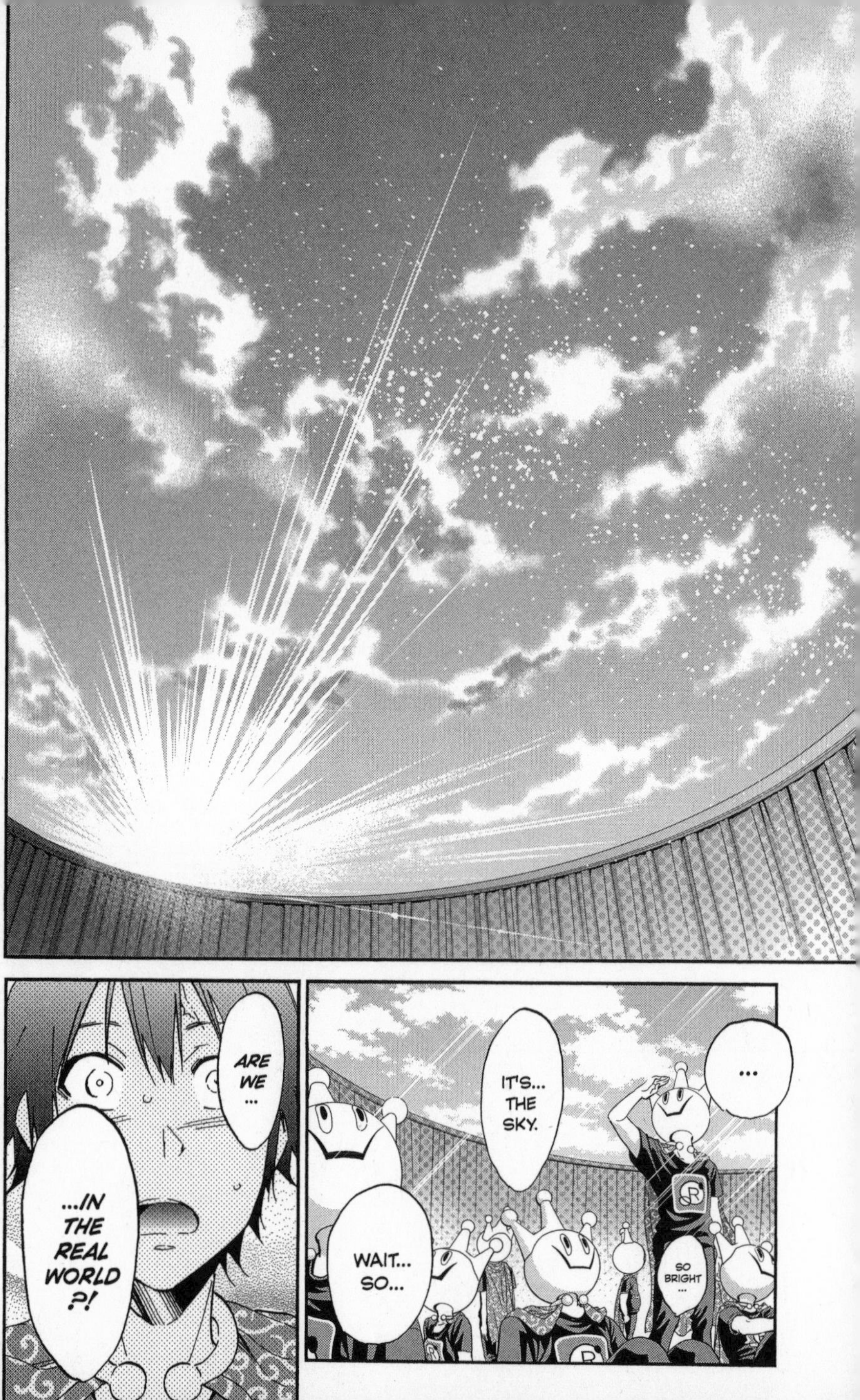
...
IT'S... THE SKY.
SO BRIGHT...
WAIT... SO...
ARE WE ...
...IN THE REAL WORLD ?!

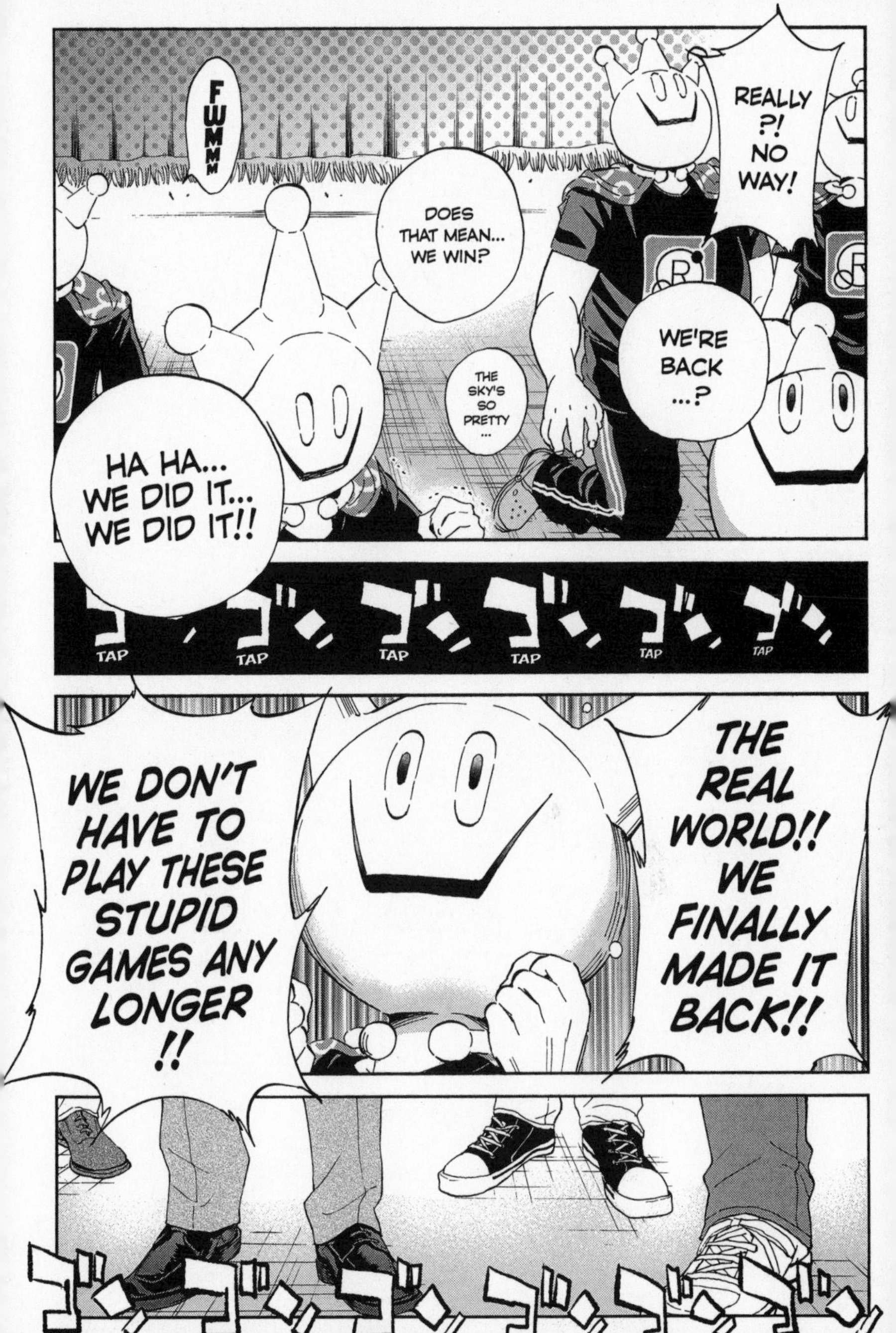
REALLY ?! NO WAY!
DOES THAT MEAN... WE WIN?
WE'RE BACK ...?
FWMMM
THE SKY'S SO PRETTY ...
HA HA... WE DID IT... WE DID IT!!
TAP
TAP
TAP
TAP
TAP
TAP
THE REAL WORLD!! WE FINALLY MADE IT BACK!!
WE DON'T HAVE TO PLAY THESE STUPID GAMES ANY LONGER !!
TAP
TAP
TAP
TAP
TAP
TAP

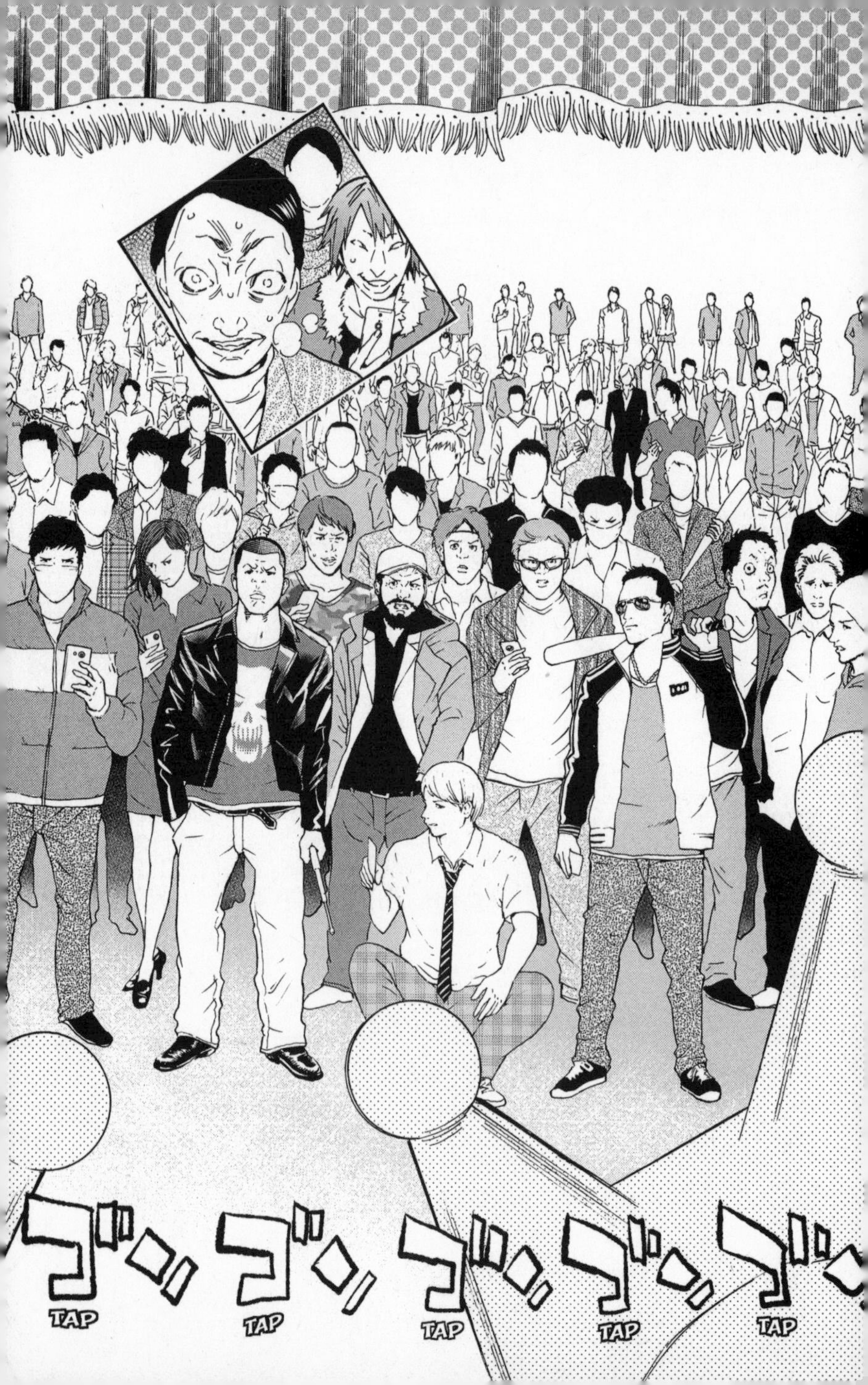

ゴンゴンゴンゴンゴン
TAP
TAP
TAP
TAP
TAP

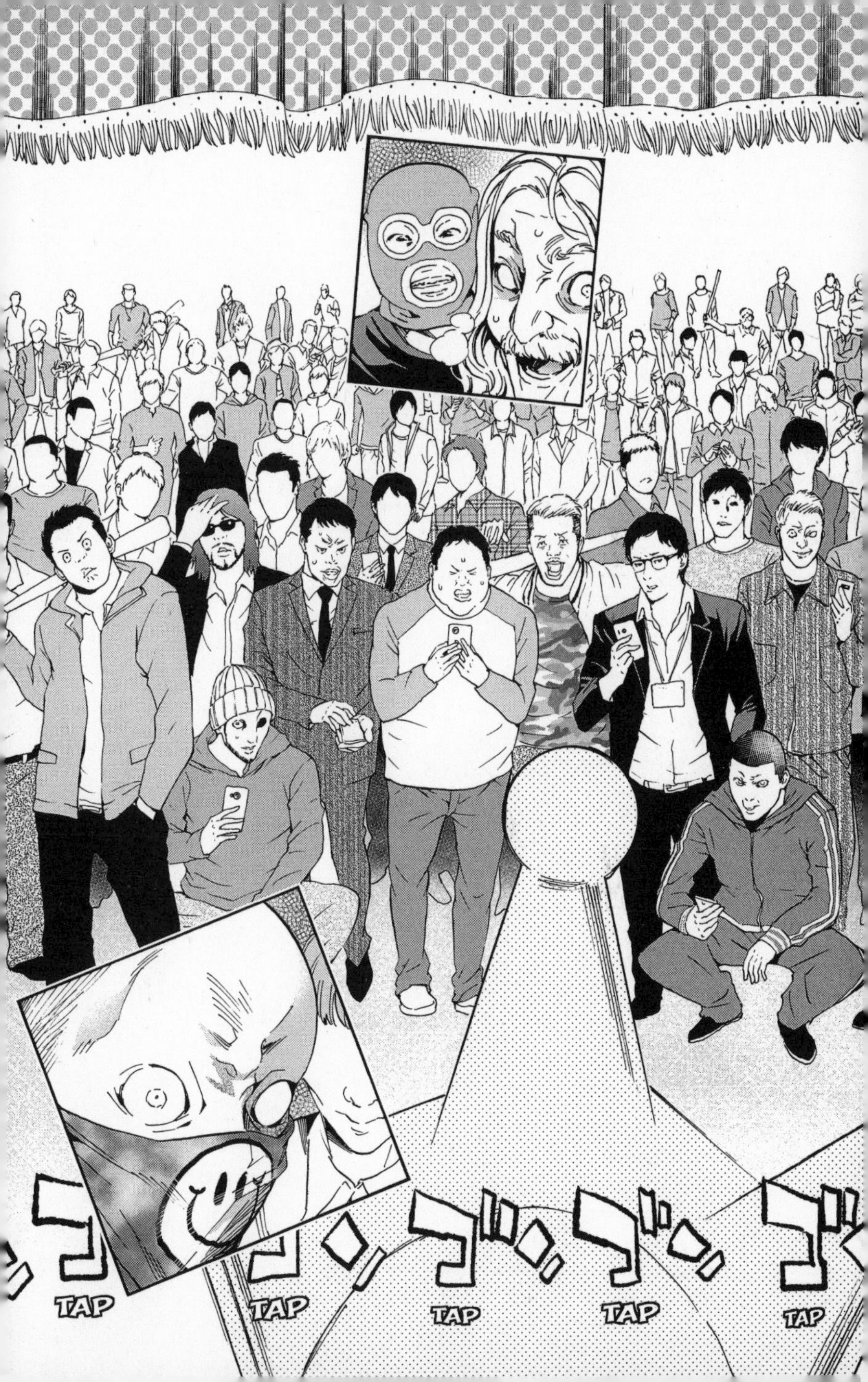
TAP
TAP
TAP
TAP
TAP

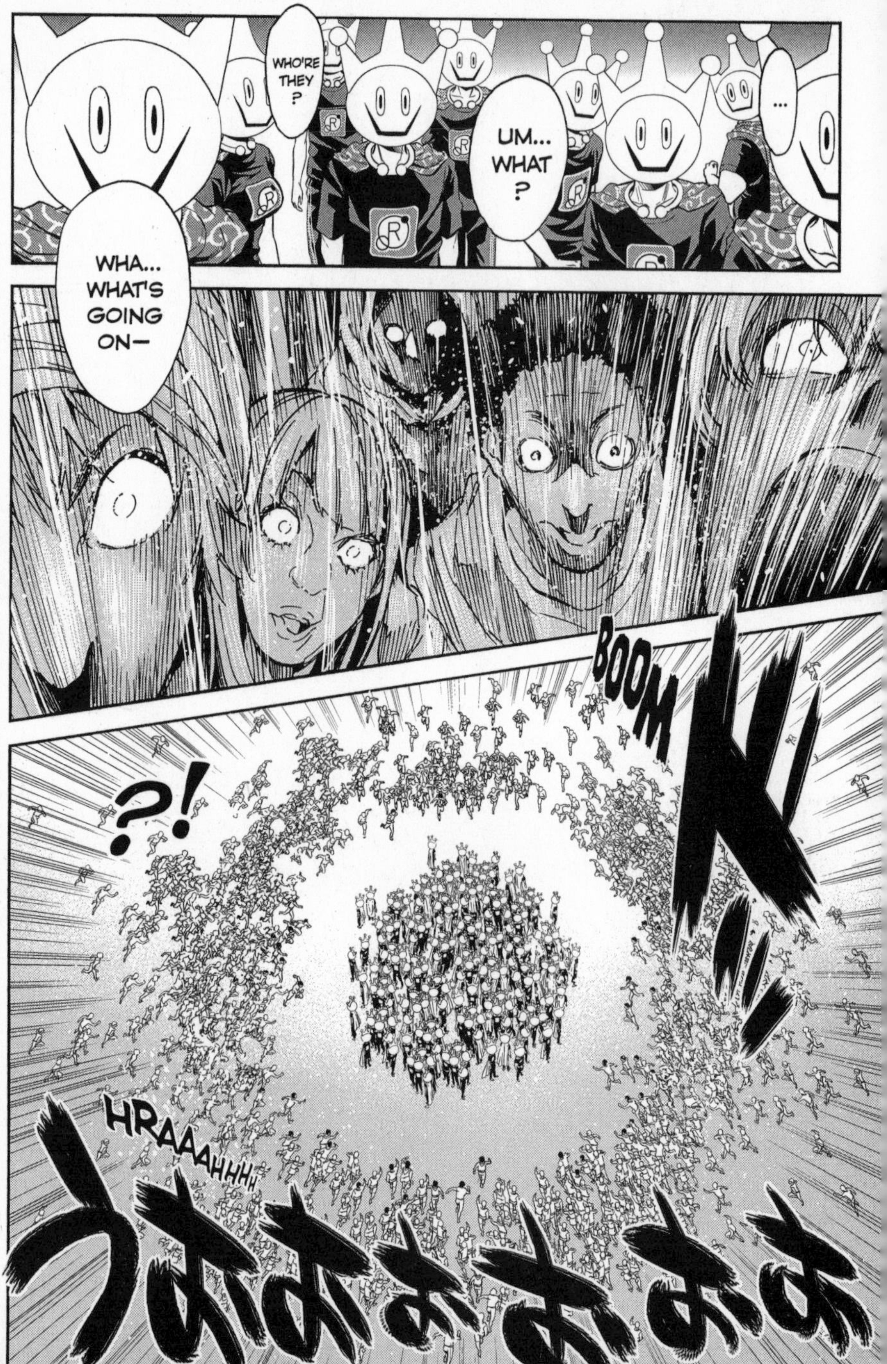
...
UM... WHAT?
WHO'RE THEY?
WHA... WHAT'S GOING ON—
BOOM
?!
HRAAAHHHH
うおおおおおお

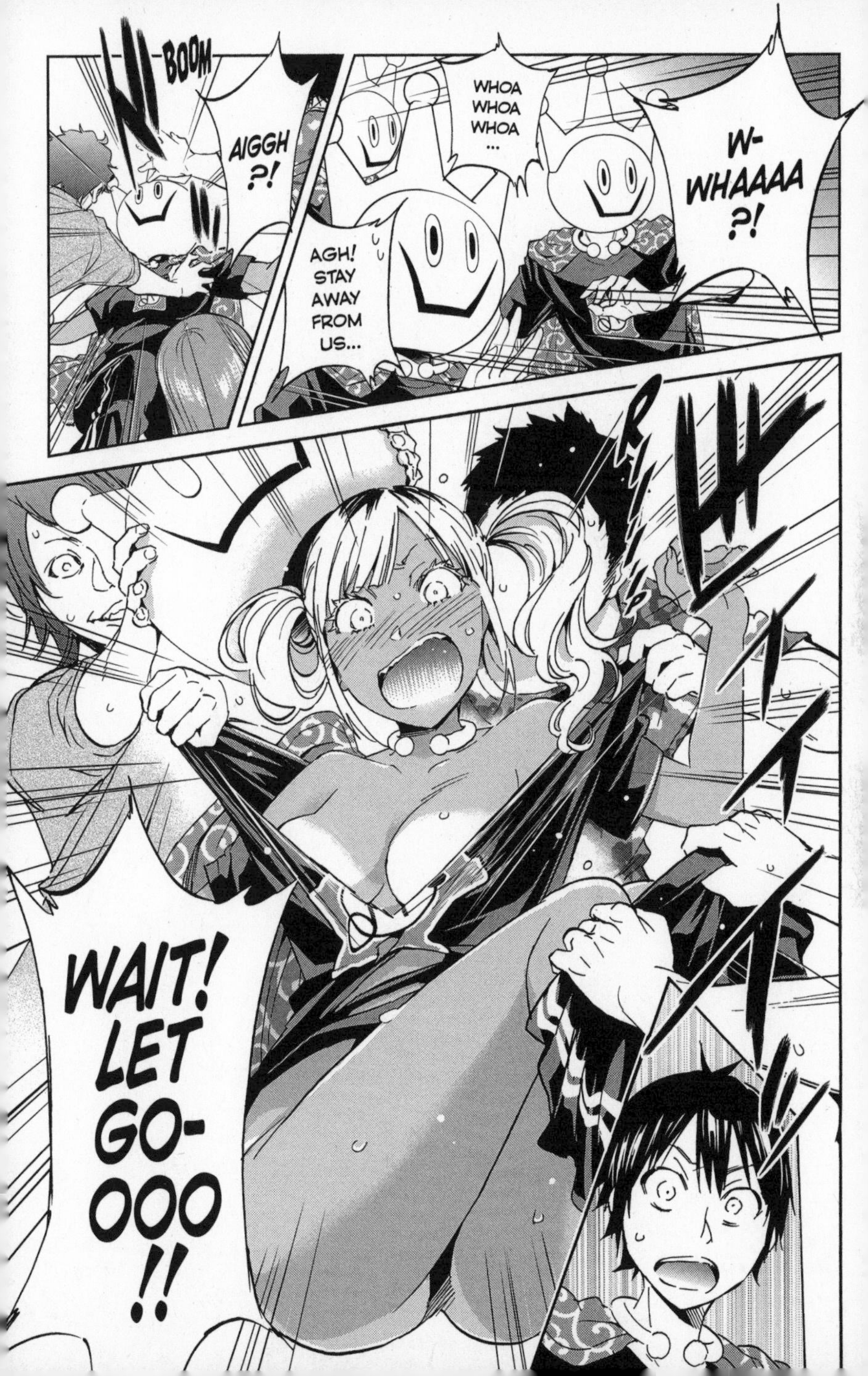
W-WHAAAA?!
WHOA WHOA WHOA...
AGH! STAY AWAY FROM US...
BOOM
AIGGH?!
WAIT! LET GO-OOO!!

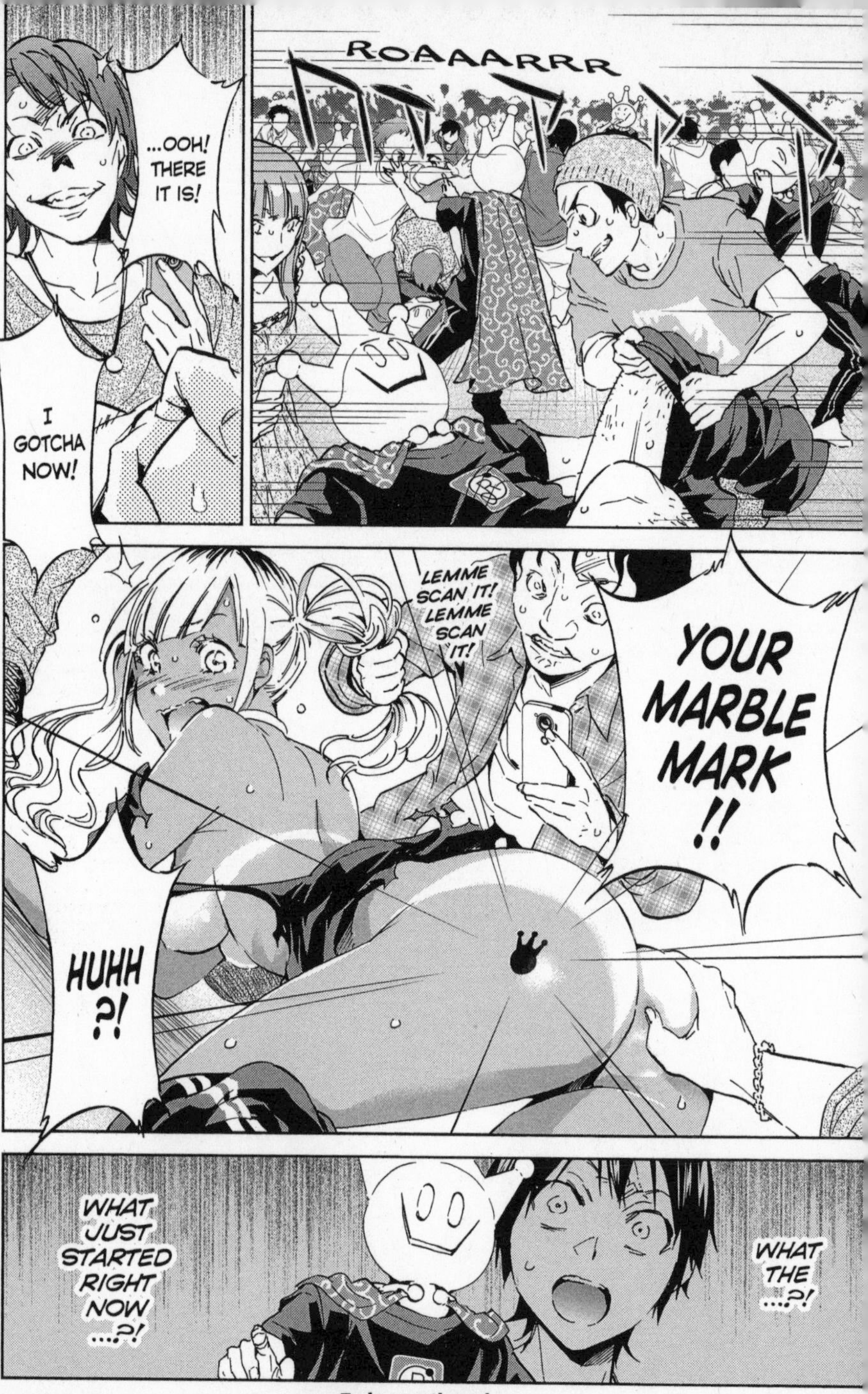
ROAAAARRRR
...OOH! THERE IT IS!
I GOTCHA NOW!
YOUR MARBLE MARK!!
LEMME SCAN IT! LEMME SCAN IT!
HUHH?!
WHAT THE...?!
WHAT JUST STARTED RIGHT NOW...?!

To be continued...

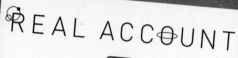

REAL ACCOUNT

6

Shizumu Watanabe   Okushou

STAFF
Shotaro Kunimoto
Iyo Mori
Yushi Takayama
Minato Fuma
Nyan-Nyan Okeishi

HELP STAFF
Hiroyuki Kuzunohai

EDITORS
Kazuhiko Otoguro
Sho Igarashi
Hideki Morooka
(Japanese GN)

JAPANESE COVER DESIGN
Tadashi Hisamochi
(HIVE)

Artist:
Shizumu Watanabe
Twitter account: @shizumukun

Volume 6!!
My longest project prior to this one
was only five volumes, so I'm now
officially in uncharted territory.
I'm hoping I'll have the chance
to get as far as I can with this.

Author:
Okushou
Twitter account: @okushou

I haven't been on Twitter or the like
too much lately. As a result, the
days seem a lot longer to me all of a
sudden—I have a hunch this is doing
wonders for my work efficiency. You
might call it "digital detox," but maybe it's time that *you* take a moment
to re-evaluate your social-media life,
too. It might just help you open your
eyes to different ideas and new relationships.

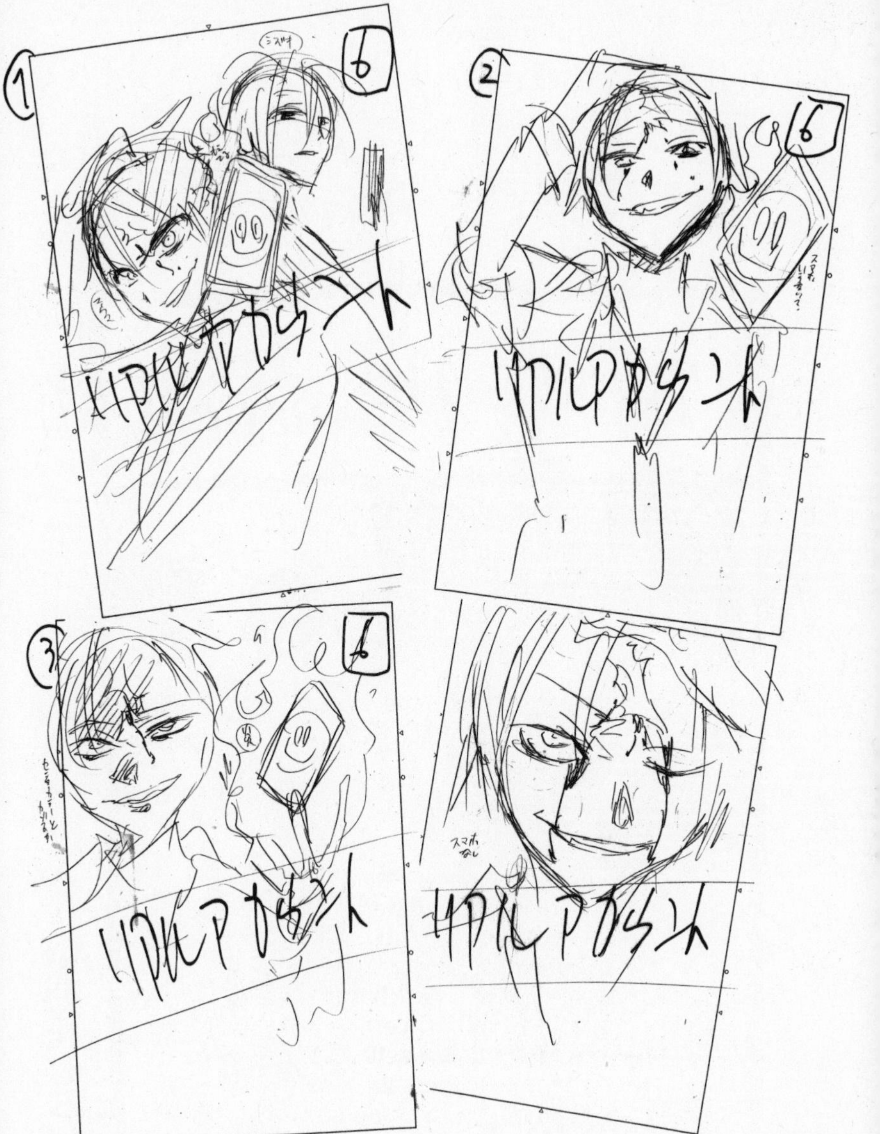

Four sketches for the Volume 6 cover. Sketch 2 was accepted. Try comparing that expression with the Volume 3 cover (lol)…

渡辺静

-Shizumu Watanabe

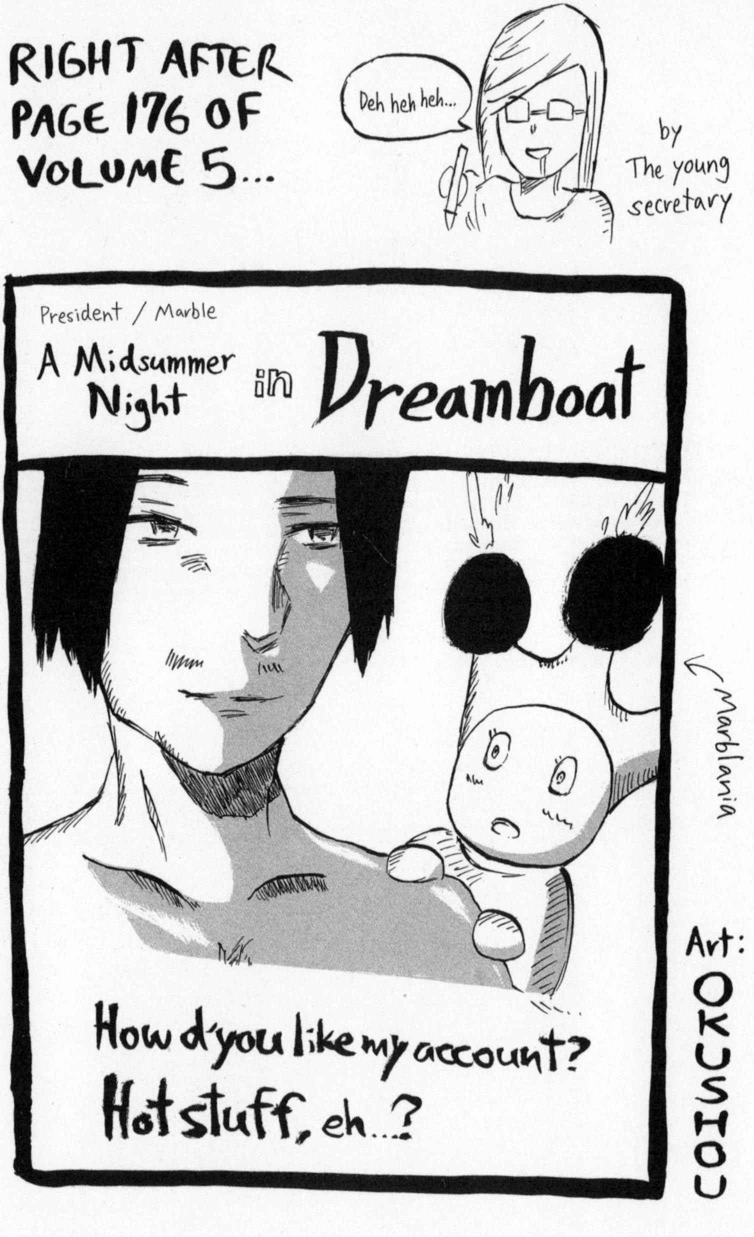

RIGHT AFTER PAGE 176 OF VOLUME 5...
Deh heh heh...
by The young secretary
President / Marble
A Midsummer Night in Dreamboat
President-senpai
Marblania
How d'you like my account? Hot stuff, eh...?
Art: OKUSHOU

Translation Notes

PAGE 5

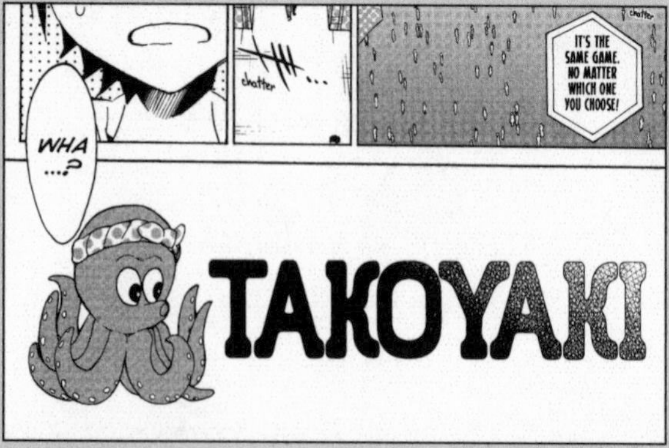
chatter
IT'S THE SAME GAME, NO MATTER WHICH ONE YOU CHOOSE!
chatter
...
WHA ...?
TAKOYAKI

TAKOYAKI

Takoyaki is a popular street food made of diced octopus fried in batter and topped with sauce, mayo, and bits of dried bonito. It originated in pre-war Osaka and remains heavily associated with that city, although it can be found in outdoor festivals across Japan.

PAGE 8

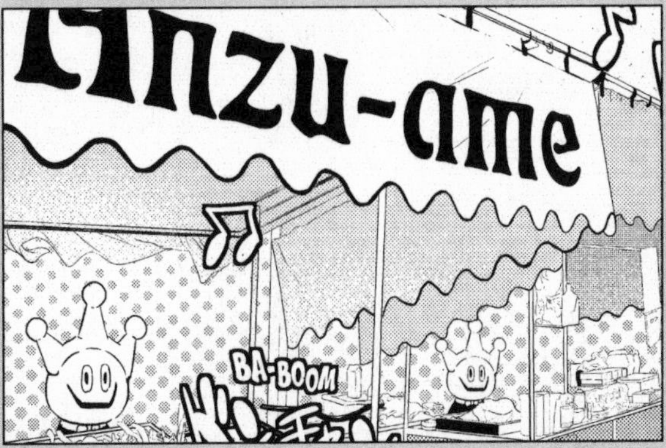
Anzu-ame
BA-BOOM

ANZU-AME

Anzu-ame is another traditional festival food-stall item around eastern Japan. It consists of sliced fruit—usually apricots, but also pineapples and oranges—covered in sweet, sticky *mizuame* liquid and frozen on top of a block of ice, a bit like a freshly-made candied apple without as much time required for consumption.

PAGE 11

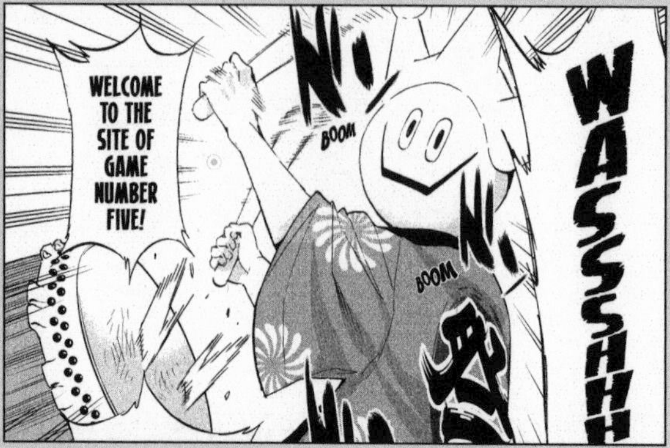
WASSHH
N!
N!
BOOM
BOOM
WELCOME TO THE SITE OF GAME NUMBER FIVE!

WASSHOI

Wasshoi, is a chant that is usually heard at festivals when performing some sort of work, like carrying a shrine in a procession. The origin of this chant is said to come from a phrase that means "carry/shoulder Japan."

PAGE 19

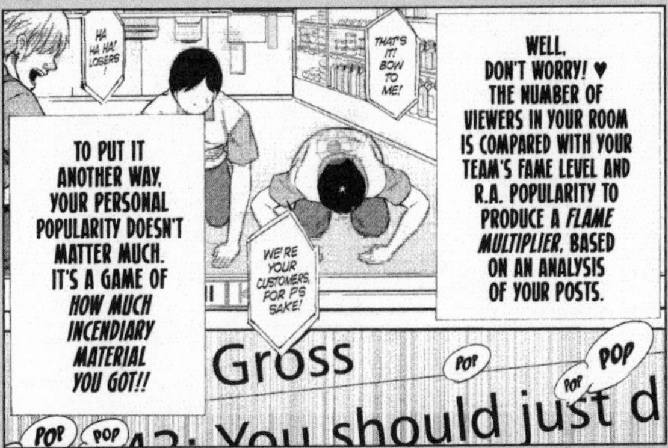
WELL, DON'T WORRY! ♥ THE NUMBER OF VIEWERS IN YOUR ROOM IS COMPARED WITH YOUR TEAM'S FAME LEVEL AND R.A. POPULARITY TO PRODUCE A *FLAME MULTIPLIER*, BASED ON AN ANALYSIS OF YOUR POSTS.
THAT'S IT! BOW TO ME!
HA HA HA! LOSERS!
TO PUT IT ANOTHER WAY, YOUR PERSONAL POPULARITY DOESN'T MATTER MUCH. IT'S A GAME OF *HOW MUCH INCENDIARY MATERIAL YOU GOT!!*
WE'RE YOUR CUSTOMERS, FOR F'S SAKE!
POP
POP
POP
Gross
You should just d
POP
POP

BOWING CONVENIENCE STORE CLERKS

This scene is based on current events at the time of publication. In December 2014, four people went into a Hokkaido 7-Eleven late at night and got into an argument with the teenaged clerk after she allegedly served them hot coffee whey they had asked for iced. They made her kowtow to them on the floor for upwards of 20 minutes and threatened to call for the rest of their gang to invade the store. They also took cell-phone video, which naturally leaked to the net and led to all four being identified and arrested.

PAGE 34

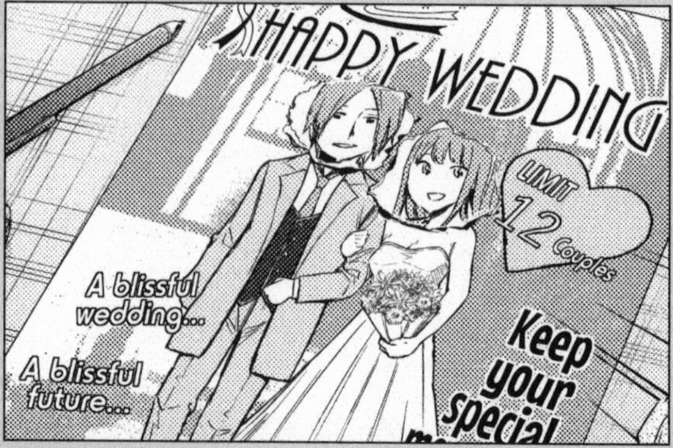
HAPPY WEDDING
LIMIT 12 Couples
A blissful wedding...
A blissful future...
Keep your special

LIMIT: 12 COUPLES

The "Limit: 12 Couples" indicates that this is an ad flyer for an event space specializing in weddings. Such places offer complete Western-style wedding packages—the ceremony, the cake, even the clothing and tailoring for the couple—for a set fee, starting at the equivalent of $9,000 or so and going up based on number of guests.

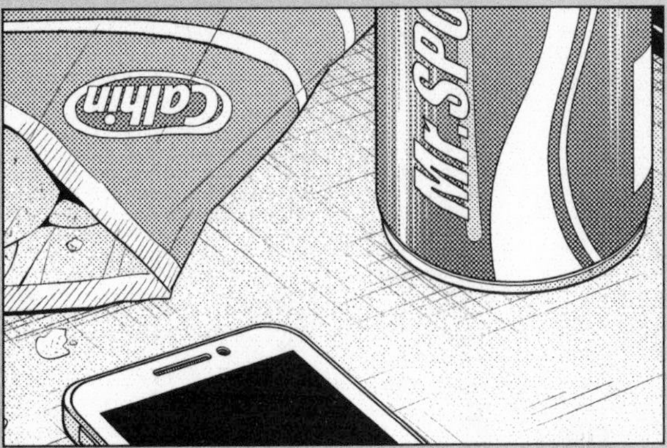
Calhin

CALHIN

A play on Calbee, one of Japan's largest snack food makers. One of its trademark products is Kappa Ebisen, a French fry-like crunchy snack with shrimp flavor added that looks a bit like what's depicted in the manga. It's marketed in the US under the much more generic name "Shrimp Flavored Chips."

PAGE 48

FROM: Shunya Hikami
TO: Reiko Iriekami
Subj: To Reiko
We encountered each other after thousands of nights of loneliness... and I want to see you again this evening. Come back to our club, and I might just become the #1 earner for the month. If I can make
BAH

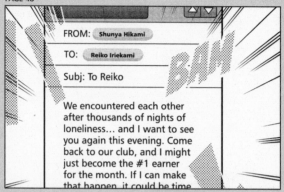

SHUNYA'S EMAIL

Shunya's metrosexual fashion and references in this email indicates that he works for a "host club," a place where women can choose a male companion and pay for their company, usually flirting and enjoying drinks with them. Sex is not part of the equation so much as companionship and an enjoyable evening together, although relationships are free to happen off-hours. Such clubs are found primarily in the entertainment districts of big cities like Tokyo and Osaka.

	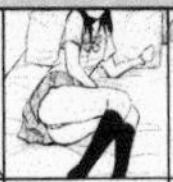	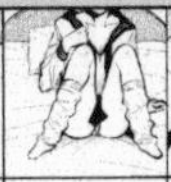	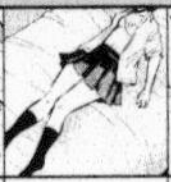	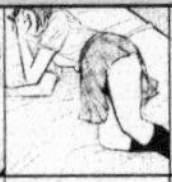	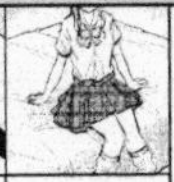
NAME	Chisa	Kaoru	Aika	Rino	Miruku
SCHOOL	Tsubakigaoka Girls	Sokyu Academy	Mikuri University Affiliated	Tsuyukusa Academy	Urei Girls'
DATE	9/5	9/12	9/20	9/23	9/30
LOCATION	Shibuya hotel "Honey Life"	Shinjuku hotel "Love Sweet"	Shibuya hotel "Party Zone"	Shinjuku hotel "One-Night Dream"	Shibuya hotel "Couples' Kingdom"
COST	35,000	30,000	45,000	30,000	35,000
LOOKS	B	A	C	B	C
EXCITEMENT LEVEL	B	A	D	B	A
BUST SIZE	82B	89F	85C	79B	85D

BRA SIZES

The bra sizes here are in the European format, the same as used in Japan and quite different from American bra sizes. For example, the 89F breasts that drove Osamu mad this month would be around 40DD in the US.

PAGE 81

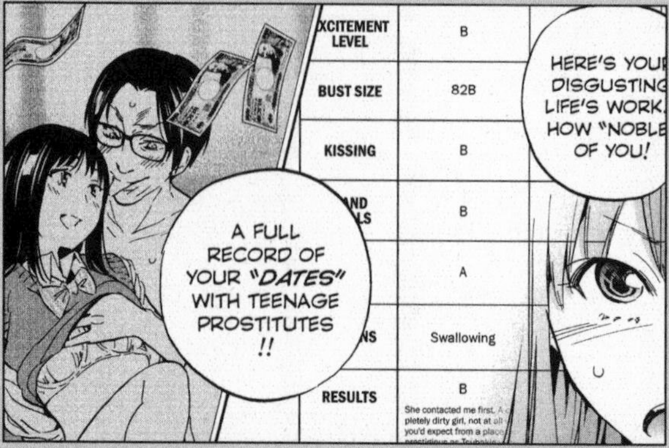
HERE'S YOU
DISGUSTIN
LIFE'S WORK
HOW "NOBL
OF YOU!
XCITEMENT LEVEL
B
BUST SIZE
82B
KISSING
B
B
A
Swallowing
RESULTS
B
She contacted me first. A
pletely dirty girl, not at all
you'd expect from a place
A FULL RECORD OF YOUR "DATES" WITH TEENAGE PROSTITUTES !!

"DATES"

To be exact, Osamu is engaging in what's called *enjo kousai* in Japanese, or "compensated dating"—a bit of a euphemism for an older man giving money or fancy gifts to girls, ranging from teenage to adult, in exchange for companionship and often (but not always) sexual favors. *Enjo kousai* became widely known in Japan during the 1990s, partly thanks to the country's vague prostitution laws up to that time; it only became formally outlawed in 1999.

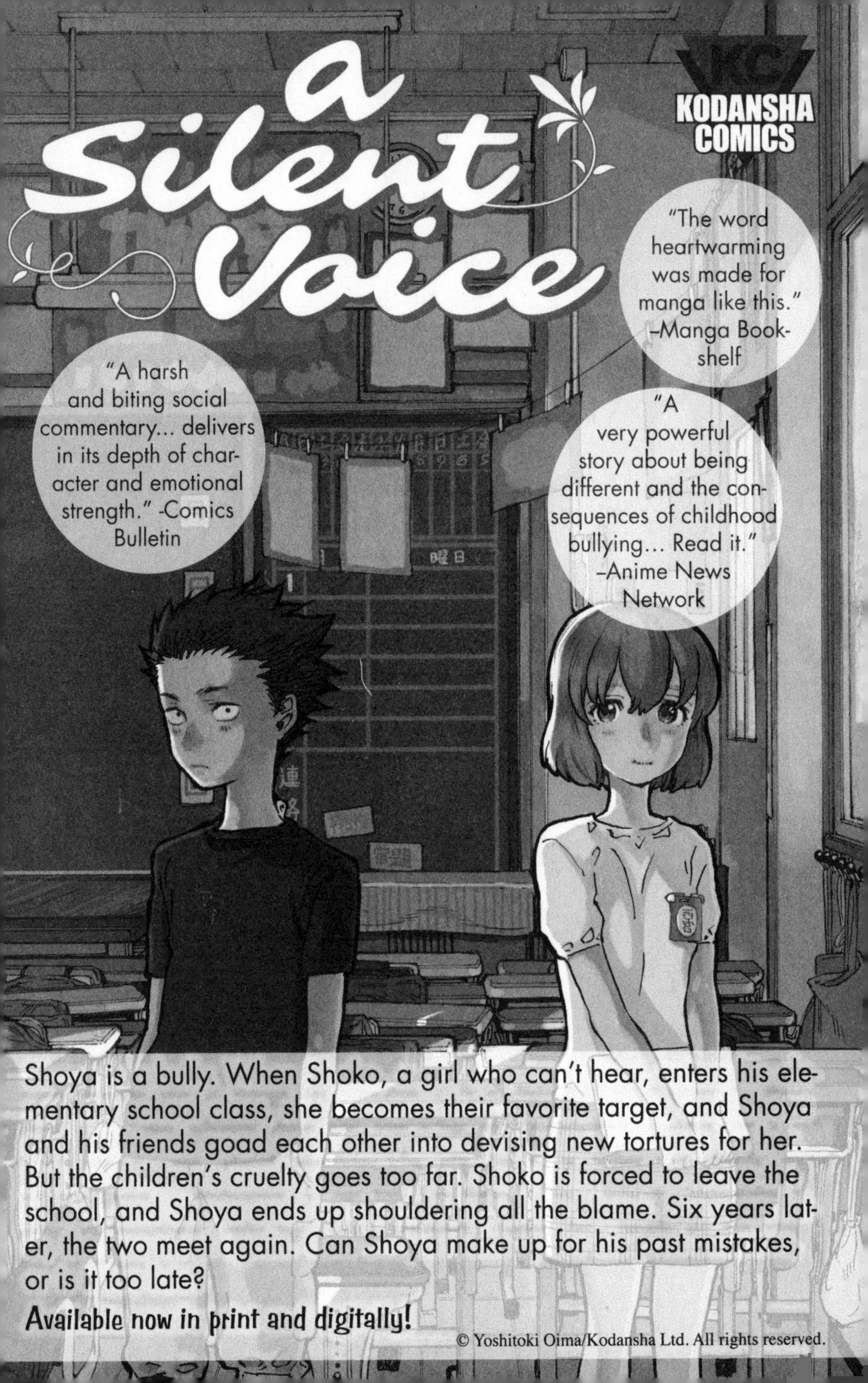

KODANSHA COMICS
a Silent Voice
"The word heartwarming was made for manga like this." –Manga Bookshelf
"A harsh and biting social commentary... delivers in its depth of character and emotional strength." -Comics Bulletin
"A very powerful story about being different and the consequences of childhood bullying... Read it." –Anime News Network
Shoya is a bully. When Shoko, a girl who can't hear, enters his elementary school class, she becomes their favorite target, and Shoya and his friends goad each other into devising new tortures for her. But the children's cruelty goes too far. Shoko is forced to leave the school, and Shoya ends up shouldering all the blame. Six years later, the two meet again. Can Shoya make up for his past mistakes, or is it too late?
Available now in print and digitally!
© Yoshitoki Oima/Kodansha Ltd. All rights reserved.

INUYASHIKI

A superhero like none you've ever seen, from the creator of "Gantz"!

ICHIRO INUYASHIKI IS DOWN ON HIS LUCK. HE LOOKS MUCH OLDER THAN HIS 58 YEARS, HIS CHILDREN DESPISE HIM, AND HIS WIFE THINKS HE'S A USELESS COWARD. SO WHEN HE'S DIAGNOSED WITH STOMACH CANCER AND GIVEN THREE MONTHS TO LIVE, IT SEEMS THE ONLY ONE WHO'LL MISS HIM IS HIS DOG.

THEN A BLINDING LIGHT FILLS THE SKY, AND THE OLD MAN IS KILLED... ONLY TO WAKE UP LATER IN A BODY HE ALMOST RECOGNIZES AS HIS OWN. CAN IT BE THAT ICHIRO INUYASHIKI IS NO LONGER HUMAN?

COMES IN EXTRA-LARGE EDITIONS WITH COLOR PAGES!

KODANSHA COMICS

Maria
THE VIRGIN WITCH

"Maria's brand of righteous justice, passion and plain talking make for one of the freshest manga series of 2015. I dare any other book to top it."
—UK Anime Network

PURITY AND POWER

As a war to determine the rightful ruler of medieval France ravages the land, the witch Maria decides she will not stand idly by as men kill each other in the name of God and glory. Using her powerful magic, she summons various beasts and demons —even going as far as using a succubus to seduce soldiers into sub-mission under the veil of night— all to stop the needless slaughter. However, after the Arch-angel Michael puts an end to her meddling, he curses her to lose her powers if she ever gives up her virginity. Will she forgo the forbidden fruit of adulthood in order to bring an end to the merciless machine of war?
Available now in print and digitally!

KC
KODANSHA
COMICS

Yamada-kun AND THE Seven Witches

KC
KODANSHA
COMICS

SWAPPED WITH A KISS?!

Class troublemaker Ryu Yamada is already having a bad day when he stumbles down a staircase along with star student Urara Shiraishi. When he wakes up, he realizes they have switched bodies—and that Ryu has the power to trade places with anyone just by kissing them! Ryu and Urara take full advantage of the situation to improve their lives, but with such an oddly amazing power, just how long will they be able to keep their secret under wraps?

Available now in print and digitally!

A Kodansha Comics Trade Paperback Original.

Real Account volume 6 copyright © 2015 Okushou/Shizumu Watanabe
English translation copyright © 2017 Okushou/Shizumu Watanabe

Published in the United States by Kodansha Comics,
an imprint of Kodansha USA Publishing, LLC, New York.

Publication rights for this English edition arranged through Kodansha Ltd., Tokyo.

First published in Japan in 2015 by Kodansha Ltd., Tokyo, as *Real Account* volume 6.

ISBN 978-1-63236-347-3

Printed in the United States of America.

www.kodanshacomics.com

9 8 7 6 5 4 3 2 1

Translation: Kevin Gifford
Lettering: Evan Hayden
Editing: Ajani Oloye
Kodansha Comics edition cover design: Phil Balsman